Deadlines and Diversity

Deadlines and Diversity

Journalism Ethics in a Changing World

edited by Valerie Alia,
Brian Brennan and Barry Hoffmaster

Fernwood Publishing

Editing: Douglas Beall
Design and production: Beverley Rach
Printed and bound in Canada by: Hignell Printing Limited

A publication of:
Fernwood Publishing
Box 9409, Station A
Halifax, Nova Scotia
B3K 5S3

Fernwood Publishing Company Limited gratefully acknowledges the financial support of The Ministry of Canadian Heritage, the Canada/Nova Scotia Cooperation Agreement on Cultural Development and the Canadian Studies and Youth Program.

Canadian Cataloguing in Publication Data
Main entry under title:
Deadlines and diversity

Includes bibliographical references.
ISBN 1-895686-54-7

1. Journalistic ethics -- Canada. I. Alia, Valerie
II. Brennan, Brian III. Hoffmaster, C. Barry

PN4756.D42 1996 174'.9097'0971 C95-9500333-1

Contents

Part Four: Journalistic Codes and Conflicts

Part Five: Ethical Issues in Contemporary Journalism

Preface

Arthur Kent

We work in a craft governed more by instinct than by rules. And few of the reporter's basic instincts are as keen as that dark, edgy pulse of cynicism stirred by any mention of the ethics or higher purposes of our profession. Suddenly a bright red mental signpost appears: "WARNING. Journalists Ahead Taking Themselves Much Too Seriously."

But who could argue that a review of our ethics and standards has ever been more urgently needed than right now. Our readers and viewers have never had more reason to question the value of the material offered up to them in the guise of news and analysis. Especially in the electronic media, the only frontiers being blazed these days are of bad taste, hyperbole and, occasionally, outright fraud. It doesn't take much digging to uncover the root cause—economics—the radical and frequently crude restructuring under financial pressure of practically all major media companies in recent years.

Owners and managers squeezed by increasing overheads and declining advertising revenues have reduced staff and coverage. Reporters see evidence in their newsrooms every day of fewer people working longer hours, with fewer resources to cover a far more complex world. Many agencies can afford less time for legwork, fact-checking and long-term investigative projects. And reporter-training schemes are high up on the budget slashers' hitlists. Sure, we're not alone as a business in all of this. But unlike other struggling industries, where the focus has shifted to improving products to increase sales in the 1990s, too many media companies are simply stretching, diluting or hyping their product to pull in a bigger audience or readership.

So we watch as "bottom line" meets "lowest common denominator" with depressing results. With smaller staffs and tighter budgets, management teams are tempted to report only those stories they think they can sell. Forget the casualty figures, the stats and percentages, they say, just tell us what will pull the biggest numbers, and do it. Ethical considerations play a predictable role in this atmosphere of hyper-commercialism: a bit part, with no dialogue if the number crunchers have their way.

The recent explosion in "tabloid" programming in U.S. television provides the clearest possible warning of how frail and ineffectual the news media's ethical bulwarks can be. The "reality-based" primetime shows of the three big commercial networks, ABC, CBS and NBC, are unabashedly shaped by numbers—the ratings, the minute-by-minute breakdowns of the nation's TV viewing habits. These exhaustive surveys are usually interpreted by show business executives in the networks' entertainment divisions, the electronic medium's unrivalled masters of sensationalism. This can't help but change the approach of the news executives working on these hybrid shows and so, in primetime news, "characters" are "cast" in "segments" or worse "booked"—in many cases, program producers negotiate fees and air dates with agents of supposed "newsmakers" who have books or stories to tell.

Tabloid programming has mushroomed, commanding as much as 70 percent of the big three news divisions' budgets and overshadowing hard-news coverage. Lurid tales such as the

O.J. Simpson, Menendez brothers and Tonya Harding sagas flood from our TV screens while much of the news that really matters is gathered by bureau teams operating with outdated equipment and smaller budgets. Put simply, many network managements have lost their sense of balance—the care that must be taken in juggling editorial and business imperatives; the restraint necessary to prevent hot, grabby stories from threatening the core of true commercial news broadcasting and publishing—where that essential commodity, news, should never be supplanted by a lower instinct for money-making or by a lower ethic.

But things aren't completely gloomy. As you'll discover in these pages, the study of ethics in journalism is something of a growth specialty in itself. Some of us who have challenged management on ethical grounds have won surprising victories and can now go on to run our own companies with the resources to commission, execute and distribute the kind of profitable journalistic product we cherish—good stories, well told and done for the love of clear, honest reporting. That product sells itself.

There's no question, though, that one of our objectives has to be the expansion of the written record of what, exactly, our craft and trade is all about. I remember walking into my lawyer's office just after we'd won a terrific settlement in our court battle with NBC television. Looking at the hundreds of fat, leather-bound law books lining the room, I sensed the gulf between our two professions. My lawyer's work is clearly defined by statutes, codes and regulations—by precedents, arguments and interpretations all spelled out in those bulging volumes that surround and embrace all practitioners of law every day of their careers. As for us, well, I remember when I first began studying journalism there just one book about the ethics of reporting within the laws of Canada, and my professor had written it.

"That's what made our case so tough," I told my lawyer. "We had to start from scratch, just to explain to a jury what journalism is supposed to be."

"But that wasn't tough," he said. "That was interesting."

He was right. Discovery is its own reward. So read on.

Introduction

Valerie Alia, Barry Hoffmaster and Brian Brennan

> Today's history is written the very moment it happens. It can be photographed, filmed, recorded. . . . It can be transmitted immediately through the press, radio, television. It can be interpreted, heatedly discussed. For this reason I like journalism. For this reason I fear journalism. What other profession allows you to write history at the very moment it happens and also to be its direct witness? Journalism is an extraordinary and terrible privilege (Fallaci 1976).

Many of us remember when journalists pounded away on loud typewriters, apprenticed their way into the field and slowly worked their way up from menial tasks to positions of responsibility. Journalism today, by comparison, is becoming more bureaucratic, academic and professional.

Most of the authors of this book know first-hand what it means to be a journalist in a changing world. Over the years, we have wrestled with ethical dilemmas wrought by changes in our jobs and made ethically problematic decisions; some of us have been both perpetrators and victims of unethical journalism. One of the editors (herself a journalist) turned to ethics after a personal tragedy; shocked by journalists' highly unethical treatment of her family, she first withdrew from, and then turned to ethical examination of, her profession. Others were pushed to consider the ethical implications of stories they produced in good faith. The experiences of some prompted them to challenge long-standing assumptions, and others have been struggling with ethical conflicts all along.

We come from different backgrounds and have taken different paths, but our shared goal in writing this book—and emphasizing the ethical dimensions of journalism—is to promote better journalism in a time of rapid and sweeping change.

To our knowledge, this is the first anthology of ethics in journalism that brings working journalists, philosophers and educators together. It is also the first anthology written by Canadians using Canadian (and international) material although some of us have also worked in the U.S. and Europe. We have deliberately not produced a book that is written in a uniform style or simply contains mutually echoing essays. Our intention is to recognize and celebrate diversity and to demonstrate the range of creative ethical thinking in Canada at this time. The authors come from different cultures and regions, and have diverse perspectives and experiences. They were chosen for the excellence of their work and the originality of their thinking. Most have spent their careers breaking new ground.

The desire to break new ground also directed the process used to create this anthology. Instead of assigning chapters and topics, we held a series of workshops in different parts of Canada (Quebec, Ontario and Alberta) so the authors could plan the book together. We grappled with both shared and idiosyncratic dilemmas, developed strategies and imagined a better future. We invited ethicist Deni Elliott to help focus the first workshop. We kept in touch with each other by phone, post and fax, and we told each other our stories, confessed our difficulties and sins and shared our problems. At the workshops, given a chance to break from work and take a swim, people instead grabbed tape recorders and interviewed each other. Given a free evening, small groups went off to work deep into the night.

We discussed objectivity and subjectivity in journalism, what it means to tell the truth and the constraints on truthtelling, multicultural representation and the bureaucratization of journalism. We talked about junkets, about the economic and political forces that shape journalism today and the problems certain groups have gaining access to the media. You will find the results of our conversations, disagreements and debates in many of the chapters; we cite and quote each other at times, having learned as much from the dialogue as from our separate experiences. Because we work on deadline and often in isolation, many of us have had scant opportunity over the years to dig into the issues which most concern us, and it was both instructive and therapeutic to share our triumphs and failures, solutions and dilemmas. The dialogue was important to us and now we would like to share it with the readers of this book.

It is a dialogue urgently needed, even though the call for a more open, critical and responsible practice of journalism is not always appreciated. We have noticed two strong responses to our work in journalistic ethics. The first response, expressed by colleagues from across Canada and elsewhere, is excitement and an enthusiastic commitment to participate. People have said, "How wonderful! We need to address these issues."

The second response has been resistance to uncovering journalism's "secrets." Some would prefer to leave the waters unstirred. Some journalists express discomfort, even anger, when doubts, imperfections and challenges are raised. Faced with an ethics course, some students are excited and keen to meet the challenge. Others are annoyed at "wasting" time instead of just "learning the ropes" (even though the ropes are wearing thin). Some educators share this attitude.

Many journalism programs have ethics courses, sometimes required, but isolate them from the "essential, practical curriculum" thus implying that ethics are not part of journalistic practice. To make a difference, ethics must be imbedded in the entire program and integrated in our professional lives and workdays. For example, there can be no teaching of "purely mechanical operations," such as television camerawork, without addressing the ethical implications of these operations, such as who is affected by the camera and how images can be manipulated.

Moreover, ethical practices must be inclusive practices. Even where ethics are valued, concerns about diversity and equality seldom have the prominence they need and deserve. The hidden assumption is that the producers and consumers of news belong to the "mainstream," dominant culture and, more often than not, are men. During the search for participants in our project, one person proposed what turned out to be a roster of all-white, all-male journalism ethics "experts." When challenged about the composition of this group, he said, "We don't disagree on the *principle* of diversity, it's just a matter of degree." Yet a full discussion of journalism ethics that included only white men would itself be unethical. Inclusivity and diversity are not mere "side issues," they belong at the core of ethical inquiry. A 1995 headline in the trade magazine *Editor & Publisher* read: "J-school faculties get F in diversity." Members of minorities hold less than 11 percent of newsroom jobs, not a figure to brag about. However, in journalism schools from which the future of journalism will spring, "only two percent of faculty members are people of color" (Hernandez 1995: 17).

Too much work in applied or practical ethics has been not only exclusive but reactive. From the start, we saw our project as participatory and proactive rather than as a panic-induced reaction to professionally embarrassing mistakes (such as the "Jimmy's World" piece that prompted a rash of U.S. texts on journalism ethics).[1] Our aim has been to discover and elaborate the goals, responsibilities and values of journalism and to use the resulting insights to develop approaches to doing journalism better. Critical self-awareness is needed to understand the manifold changes occurring within journalism and to respond to them in ways that preserve the integrity of the profession and those who practise it.

Deadlines and Diversity is written for practising journalists, teachers and students of journalism, ethicists, members of other professions who are exploring ethical questions and members of the public whose view of the world is created and informed by the work of journalism.

Different readers can use the book in different ways. One approach is to move through the chapters in order. The book has been organized to give coherence to such a sequential reading. Some chapters are grouped together and may be read as separate units, yet each chapter stands on its own and may be read independently. This suggests another approach in which the reader dips into the book at any point, selects what is most intriguing, relevant or provocative and explores at will, turning to material from the other sections as it becomes relevant.

For more than a decade, the literature on journalistic ethics has focused on relating journalistic pedagogy and practice to democratic theory and classical Western philosophy. The traditional approach to teaching journalism ethics employs the Socratic method, starting with theory and using cases to illustrate that theory. Although we have great respect for the literature and its practitioners, we find the theory-first approach too remote from the realities of everyday journalism. It tends to exclude or minimize the contextual realities that inform actual cases and to omit analyses of power and hierarchy and related questions of gender, class and race.

We offer an alternative approach which takes journalistic realities as the starting point. We include a rich array of cases to illustrate some of the themes and concerns of journalistic ethics and provide practical points of departure for discussion. Here is a real-life context in which to examine ethics.

We welcome you to join our conversations and hope you find them exciting, provocative and helpful.

Acknowledgements

The two-year process which led to the publication of this book was generously supported by a grant from the Social Sciences and Humanities Research Council and by assistance from the Westminster Institute for Ethics and Human Values. We express our gratitude for that invaluable support; without it, this would have been a collection of independent chapters written in isolation.

Deni Elliott helped get the project off to a productive start. For lively contributions to the ethics dialogue, we thank Max Allen, Patrick Boyer, Jim Butler, Stevie Cameron, Ramón Chávez, Clifford Christians, Raphael Cohen-Almagor, Don Curry, Willard Enteman, Helen Fallding, Pamela Freeman, Peter Hum, Cheris Kramarae, Thierry Le Brun, Bernie Lucht, Thelma McCormack, Craig McNaughton, Miles Morrisseau, Alison Moss, Howard Pawley, Tyler Resch, Gertrude Robinson, Laura Sky, Dan Smoke, Kate Taylor and Lee Wilkins. We also thank Stuart Adam, David Bell, Jean Dalgleish, David Flaherty, Susan Graber, David Restivo, Ivor Shapiro, Bob Steele, Gail Valaskakis, Jacqueline Wright, Michael Yeo, the Poynter Institute for Media Studies, the *Calgary Herald*, the Canadian Association of Journalists and the Canadian Federation for the Humanities.

Janet Baldock, Seanna-Lin Brodie-Keys, Sophia Harris, Christopher Irwin, Nancy Mucklow, Judy Noordermeer and Dan Restivo provided invaluable research and administrative assistance. The manuscript and other materials could not have been prepared without the aid of David Mills and the University of Western Ontario computer Help Desk; Heather York-Marshall assisted with database and bibliographic research. Douglas Beall is an energetic, considerate, thorough and good-humoured editor. We thank him and the other fine folks at Fernwood Publishing—Errol Sharpe, Beverley Rach, Brenda Conroy, Donna Davis, Lindsay Sharpe and Chauna James.

Part One

Moral Principles and Ethical Journalism

1. A Case Study: Eva the Evergreen Lady

Pierre Mignault

In January 1992, Montreal was hit by a cold spell as cold as they come. Minus thirty Celsius for more than a week. On one of those incredibly windy and cold nights, my friend Alain Picard, also a journalist, came to me and said, "It's so cold, you wouldn't leave a dog outside tonight. Why don't we go out and see what's happening with street people?" We each took along a television crew and patrolled the streets for awhile. We saw volunteers setting up makeshift kitchens on street corners and homeless people lining up for a bowl of hot soup. Then we made contact with a volunteer who worked the "hot air vent trail."

When it's that cold, some street people try to keep warm by staying close to buildings with hot air exhaust systems. Lydie Auger finds them, feeds them, leaves a blanket or two and then moves on. We had been following her around for about four hours and had sufficient material to do a routine piece on street people. Alain and I could team up and use each other's material so the story could be aired on both CBC and Radio-Canada newscasts at the same time.

It was midnight and we were just about to wrap up when Lydie pulled into a small parking lot in a busy section of town. The moon was full, the wind had died down, light snow was falling. Once again, she got out of her station wagon, pulled out a blanket and a bowl of stew. At first, we did not understand who it was for because there was no one in sight. All we saw was a deserted parking lot. There were no buildings, no air vents, just a row of evergreens bordering the street. Lydie went to the third evergreen and knelt down. There was a woman sleeping under the tree. Alain and I were shocked.

For the past two winters, a sixty-year-old woman had been living under an evergreen, right in the middle of the city, wrapped in a few blankets, three feet away from a busy sidewalk. She had relied on passersby and volunteers to feed her. With no air vent nearby, she had depended on her own body heat to keep warm. Because of the cold, she had not moved from under the tree for six days. She was surrounded by her own excrement; two rats lived with her.

It was Friday, January the seventeenth, a little after midnight. We called it quits. That weekend, Eva the evergreen lady did not leave our thoughts for a minute. We discussed the issue with everybody we met. Some of our friends said it was voyeurism, others said we had no right to invade her private life.

It was an extremely powerful setting for a television story on poverty and homeless people. It wasn't just another piece on an old drunk sleeping on a park bench on a hot summer day. It was a story about a sober old woman surviving at minus thirty Celsius with just a few branches as a roof over her head. It was a story that would not leave people indifferent.

We learned that the woman under the Christmas tree had become a symbol of human dignity. Municipal authorities knew she was there but did not intervene because no citizen had complained about her. Social services kept a watch on her but did nothing because she didn't ask for help. Community groups regarded her as a free human being, a symbol of the human dignity of street people. Here was Eva, an individual who had the right to choose where she wanted to live. Pressure groups that would normally have pressured the government for action hated us for investigating this story and making it public. We had landed right in the middle of a political fairy tale.

Eva's story left no one undisturbed. It had strong voyeuristic appeal and we knew that broadcasting it would have a significant impact on her privacy. In fact, her privacy was an obstacle without being one. Legally, the camera could point at her because she was in the public domain—her privacy had no legal grounds. But we were also aware that talking publicly about her private life would draw attention to her case and constituted an intrusion into her private life without her consent. It was not a legal issue but a moral one.

Our decision to do the story, despite Eva's right to a private life, was based on a judgment that our moral duty was to intervene and stay with her. This would not be just a winter snapshot. We would pressure our editorial desks to follow up on the story. As long as it was on the air, we could investigate. The more time we had to find facts that could shed some light on this sad case of human indifference, the more we hoped authorities would wake up and act. It was a case of a human being in distress, an emergency situation.

The authorities had based their inaction on Eva's right to choose where she wanted to live. They presumed she was fit to make her own decisions. I use the word "presumed" because whenever they asked Eva if she wanted anything, she answered, "Leave me alone." Over and over again: "Leave me alone." That's what she said to us as well. She did not want us to be around her, yet we stayed with the story.

Alain and I produced eight news reports, four in French and four in English, broadcast four days in a row on "Newswatch," CBC's Montreal supper-hour show, and its French equivalent, "Montréal Ce Soir." A week later, we broadcast a short documentary on "Newswatch" containing all the facts presented in the shorter news reports along with in-depth interviews. I will use material from this report to illustrate why, despite her right to privacy, Alain and I felt there was no ethical dilemma at stake. In our investigation, we traced Eva's life six years back. The facts we gathered convinced us that she truly needed help.

> Six years ago, I found a woman while patrolling the streets. She was sleeping on an air vent, she was hiding and very scared. As soon as I'd approach her she'd back off (Lydie Auger, volunteer).[1]

Rumours among people who knew the woman (social workers, volunteers and street people) indicated that she had come from Europe and had suffered through the Second World War. They were only rumours because no one really knows her. Eva's conversations are short, she never talks about herself, doesn't need anything and wants to be left alone. In fact, no one knows her real name but everyone calls her "Eva." So much for the mystery. What we found out during our research is that there were about fifty people in Montreal spending the winter in similar situations. The facts we gathered indicated that their right to choose where they wanted to live had been severely impaired over the years.

Six years ago, Eva did what most street people do when it gets too cold: she spent her nights curled up in a blanket on a hot air vent. In fact, until security guards chased her away, she had slept on the air vent behind the Hydro Quebec building in downtown Montreal, the building that houses the Quebec Premier's Montreal office. The story is the same for street people at most hot air vent sites. Eva got tired of being chased away and moved to the Atwater metro station in front of the Forum. We found file footage of her at the station, shot two years earlier. She just happened to be in the picture, sitting on the sidewalk with her back to the metro entrance. She had surrounded herself with green garbage bags filled with whatever people gave her—money, blankets, soda pop, cookies.

She no longer had a hot air vent but her makeshift house absorbed some heat from the metro wall. And once in a while she was able to seek warmth in the metro corridor. On May second, 1990, without notice, the city moved in and dumped her home—seventy green garbage bags—into a garbage truck. To them, it was garbage. To her, it was all she had. Montreal police reports revealed that twice the police had asked social services to do something, with no results. Eva never came back to the metro station. After a short stay in a psychiatric hospital, she ended up under the evergreen tree.

She crawled under the tree and made herself as inconspicuous as possible. During cold spells, in order to retain body heat, she did not leave her bed to go to the bathroom, thus the excrement around her. According to everyone in the "homeless network," Eva had exercised her right to choose where to live of her own free will.

> For the moment, the message that Eva is giving us is that this is what she wants. And we are respecting that, for better or for worse. She is a woman who knows what she doesn't want, that's for sure. What she does want we are not so sure. The people who are in contact with her, they are listening to what she's saying. For the moment she's not coming out and saying she wants to do this, this and that. People give her food, they give her some kind of assistance, but we don't know exactly where to go from there (Thomas McKewen, Quebec social services, intervention squad for the homeless).

> Reporter: "We are saying that basically she has a right to sleep outside and choose her lifestyle. Isn't that what society is saying?"
> Thomas McKewen: "I would say yes with certain reservations. If we were really certain this woman is hurting herself, we have an obligation to put her someplace where she can be warm."
> Reporter: "What do you mean by 'hurting'?"
> McKewen: "Well, if she is going to freeze to death."
> Reporter: "But right now, her body's full of blisters. Human waste is all around her. She's keeping warm just by her body heat, surrounded by rags and blankets. She's close to sixty years old. Isn't she hurting herself at minus thirty?"
> McKewen: (hesitation) "I would say yes."

End of story? Not quite.

The cold spell finally ended. No one did anything. Eva spent the rest of the winter there and lived. Suddenly, the following spring, city workers came to the evergreen and cut its bottom branches so they would no longer provide shelter. Once again, the garbage truck hauled away the garbage bags in which she kept her possessions. Once again, Eva was chased away.

In Alain Picard's follow-up report, a city official said they expelled her because "citizens complained." In other words, the officials who had not felt it necessary to intervene to help her at the height of winter had now decided she was a disturbance and it was time to act. By then, our confidence in the capacity of the system to think rather than follow rules was greatly diminished. We were also having doubts about the power of the press to increase social awareness.

And then it was winter again. A year had gone by when Alain suddenly got a call from a volunteer. Eva was in trouble. She had gangrene and did not want to go to the hospital. That night, we left our cameras behind, thinking this was no time for a public debate on human rights. We acted not as journalists but as private citizens. We helped Lydie Auger take her into the hospital. They examined her, gave her some pills and a bed. The next day she was gone. She had left the hospital before receiving treatment for her gangrenous foot. They said it was her right to refuse treatment and she had done so of her own free will. The hospital, too, was playing by the rules.

At that moment, I felt powerless. Despite the journalistic effort, nothing had been done to help her during the cold spell, and now, despite our efforts as citizens, nothing was being done to cure her disease. Everybody was playing by the book. Everything was nice and legal. This might have been the exception to the rule, the moral exception raised in the interview by the head of the intervention squad for the homeless: "If we are really certain that this woman is hurting herself, we have an obligation to help." It is my understanding that gangrene is fatal if not treated.

2. The Unbearable Lightness of Moral Principle: Moral Philosophy and Journalistic Ethics

Earl Winkler

Starting from Morality[1]

Historically, people have found many different ways to define and regulate morality. However, despite the diversity of people and perspectives, certain basic similarities are found among all moral codes. For example, all moral codes regulate violence and homicide, property exchanges, family structures and sexual practice, but they differ in the specific ways they address these common concerns. Moral standards are never static; they are socially constructed and change along with conditions, traditions and expectations. Different moral standards may be justified in different societies or in the same society at different times.

This chapter is grounded in ethical instrumentalism, a perspective which provides a compromise between universalism (in which one universal moral system governs all of moral life) and relativism (in which all moral perspectives are equal and above criticism and there are no universals). Cross-cultural criticism of moral values must be grounded in matters fundamental to human nature. The appropriate way to evaluate moral standards and judgments is not to consider whether they are "true" or "false," but whether they are "reasonable" or "unreasonable."

Michael Philips' (1993) version of instrumentalism goes farther. In his view, each of the domains of social life (family, economic institutions, education, science and professions such as law, medicine or journalism) is characterized by a set of socially recognized goals or values which support moral standards specific to that domain. For example, the family is supposed to provide intimacy, love and a nurturing environment for children; the system of civil and criminal justice is supposed to provide security and protect the rights of citizens. In this way, moral standards are justified for each domain.

Instrumentalism contrasts sharply with the "top down" approach of traditional theoretical ethics. Traditional theories begin with ethical principles, which are derived from basic goods and evils, and then attempt to apply these principles to specific cases. Following such a system requires the beliefs that its basic principles explain the whole of moral life and that the application is straightforward. Instrumentalism rejects these Olympian theoretical endeavours and proceeds from the "bottom up." In this system, one adopts the values associated with each domain unless those values are shown to be unreasonable.

In the past twenty-five years, work in applied ethics has led to a much deeper appreciation of the historically situated, domain-specific and socially contextualized nature of moral reasoning. Before the development of the field of applied ethics, philosophers did not address domain-specific moral standards or role-related virtues. Applied ethicists have challenged the traditional assumption that abstract moral theory can be made practical. They find traditional theory inadequate to explain variations in the weight of moral principles within different contexts. The "same principle" may have a different significance in different settings. For example, failing to help family members is considered worse than failing to help strangers; it is worse to kill your nephew for motives of greed than to kill the sadist who tortured and killed your nephew.

Context is extremely important. To understand the logic of moral judgments, we must first understand and explain variations in the weight of moral reasons in different domains and contexts. For example, if a drug dealer is shot, it is less bad for a former military paramedic to refuse to help him on the spot than for a doctor to refuse to treat the same patient in an emergency room. The explanation is domain-related: the doctor's professional responsibility determines his or her requirement to help.

An instrumental approach involves a continuing process of defending one's moral judgments against objections and rivals. It is a case-driven, inductive process carried out within a framework of cultural values and norms; professional functions, obligations and virtues; and legal precepts. Moral judgment is justified by appeal to shared moral beliefs which are not challenged by the particular issue in question.[2] Applied ethics offers important insights into the discussion of morality in journalism.

THE RISE OF APPLIED ETHICS

Interest in expanding our understanding of ethical issues concerning business, the environment and health care has grown remarkably since the 1970s. Biomedical ethics is the most mature and best defined of the sub-fields of applied ethics. Although influenced by the "liberation" movements of the 1960s and 1970s, it emerged principally in response to moral crises created by changing technology. In the years between the close of Second World War and the early 1970s, the power and potential of medical science expanded exponentially. New technologies confronted us with choices for which traditional moral values and principles of medicine seemed to give the *wrong* answers.

The Karen Ann Quinlan case offers a classic illustration. This famous case, which occurred in New Jersey in 1976, questioned whether Karen's father could decide on her behalf to have her artificial respirator removed. She was in an irreversible coma; her parents said her life was being artificially sustained and no longer had meaning for her.

Through the influence of Christianity, the ancient commitment of medicine to human well-being was linked to the sanctity of each individual life. For centuries, doctors were expected to make every effort to preserve the life of every patient. Ironically, this worked reasonably well so long as there were limits to what doctors could do to preserve patients' lives. The Quinlan case, and others like it, raised the difficult issue of the *quality* of the life being preserved as distinct from its mere biological extension.

Debate surrounding the Quinlan case led to a reinterpretation of the "sanctity of life" principle. Today, doctors are required to provide not every treatment to prolong life, but only those that serve a patient's best interests. Debate continues concerning how we should interpret "best interests" in different medical contexts and who should be responsible for proxy decision-making.

There are obvious and important differences among the established divisions of applied ethics. Biomedical ethics is focused within a particular institutional setting and concerns the practice of a closely associated set of professions. Business ethics is broader in scope because of the nature of the field. Environmental ethics has an even broader purview and includes the attitudes and behaviour of all people concerning resource use and consumption, and towards future generations, other animals and the natural world.

The differences notwithstanding, business, environmental and biomedical ethics have the same basic provenance. Modern industrial and technological processes, formerly seen as the engines of human progress, have led to global crisis. The *raison d'être* of environmental ethics is to make us more responsible to future generations and towards other living things. Just as biomedical ethics arose out of emerging tensions between traditional values and the realities of new medical possibilities, environmental ethics emerges from the ethos of western industrial civilization which was based on the moral supremacy of the human species and faith in a boundless opportunity for material progress through economic growth.

Traditional values and principles of western business practice are inadequate within the complex realities of the modern world. This is particularly obvious when it comes to responsibility for public health and safety, environmental risk and sustainability. Scandals on Wall Street may prompt endowments for ethics education in business schools but they do not explain the current level of interest in business ethics. A more likely explanation has to do with the desire to find principled ways to make business more socially responsible while preserving its essential nature as *business*. For example, realization is increasing that, in a globalized economy dominated by multinationals, the traditional corporate obligation to maximize profits for shareholders can lead to environmental exploitation and to tragedies such as the explosion of the Union Carbide factory at Bhopal. It is easier to criticize unethical practices than to frame a standard of corporate social responsibility which is both moral and profitable.

CONTEMPORARY CONCERN WITH JOURNALISTIC ETHICS

Along with the rise of applied ethics, interest in the ethics of journalism has grown. A primary question is what social forces and changing pressures have led to this concern. Jack Nelson of the *Los Angeles Times* appeared on a 1994 edition of the public television program "Washington Week in Review" and spoke about the case in which NBC "rigged up" video footage which illustrated charges that the gas tanks of some General Motors pickup trucks exploded on impact. He spoke of the competition for television advertising dollars which has encouraged a disturbing increase in "infotainment"—television programs that look like on-the-scene reporting but are actually dramatized productions edited for shock value which sometimes place interviewers in provocative roles. The trend towards "infotainment" is one factor contributing to the current interest in journalistic ethics.

To take a more provocative example from Pierre Mignault (see Chapter 13), what are we to think of the practice of "melt-down" reporting in television news? In a "melt-down," television journalists prepare a story to go with video images taken from several different, previously edited network sources. The sources may be distant and their images transmitted via satellite. The journalist creates the impression of being on the scene when in fact he or she was never there.

As Mignault says, the practice of "melt-down" news coverage clearly undermines the basis of public trust in the journalist, a trust based on the belief that the journalist was there and has first-hand knowledge of what happened. At the same time, competitive economic pressures incline or even compel journalists to use "melt-down" techniques. Increasingly, a small number of large news organizations monopolize the images from which international television news is assembled. If "melt-down" news is melding the news out of overheated and reactive material from hot spots where the journalist has never been, then this is "news" without much *personal* responsibility or credibility. If current economic forces are pushing us in this direction, then this is cause for serious concern.

We need to examine technological and economic forces and their effects on the business of journalism to understand what is driving current interest in journalistic ethics. We should not expect to discover a neat set of moral principles that will illuminate journalistic ethics and provide direct practical guidance. Instead, I propose a functional approach.

A FUNCTIONAL APPROACH TO JOURNALISTIC ETHICS

I believe the general moral principles or standards for any profession derive from ideas about the basic social functions of that profession.[3] The fundamental question is: What are the basic functions of journalism within a liberal, democratic society? As this question implies, ideas about the normative functions of "the press" (including print media, radio and television) in society depend heavily on political philosophy. That is, discussion of the functions of journalism, as of other professions, takes place against a background of shared understandings about the design of political and economic institutions and about people's basic rights and responsibilities as citizens. Here I outline the basic functions for journalism within a liberal, democratic society (Audi 1990) and provide brief discussions of illustrative cases within Canada.

THE POLITICAL, INFORMATIONAL FUNCTION

The press should supply people with information and ideas that are necessary and relevant to their roles as citizens. At a *structural* level, this gives rise to the familiar tension between the goals of corporate profit and the standards of journalistic responsibility. In a competitive journalistic world, there is always pressure to satisfy public taste in the delivery of news. If public funds are used to ensure adequate standards (for example, through national ownership of news networks), then this must be accomplished in a way that does not compromise the independence of the press.

At a *performative* level, the informational function requires a distinction between reporting and editorializing. In my view, the two aspects of the informational function differ only in degree, although this difference is important. Reporting is descriptive; editorializing is evaluative. However, all complex description involves interpretation, and all interpretation involves evaluation in some form.

However, responsible evaluation must rest on descriptive justification and appeal to facts; all interpretation is not equal. Reporting and commentary should be kept as distinct as possible. Recognizing that all journalistic information comes with some interpretive spin, reporting must strive for fairness and balance with respect to different points of view. A healthy and vigorous profession includes ideological, ethnic and dispositional variety among editors, commentators and reporters.

Objectivity and neutrality, truthfulness and accuracy inform journalistic practice. These values, in turn, are supported by moral and intellectual virtues which include honesty, perseverance, discernment, judiciousness, integrity and common courtesy. At the United Nations Earth Summit Conference in Rio de Janeiro, I repeatedly saw crews of newspeople rudely shove and knock people around in their frantic rush to position themselves for footage and interviews with political leaders and dignitaries. In one instance, two bystanders were nearly trampled by a semicircle of some fifty newspeople who, with cameras and equipment, were running backwards in front of Jane Fonda and Ted Turner.

Consider the 1994 British Columbia case of Gordon Wilson and Judy Tyabji—Canada's answer to the Gary Hart case in the U.S. It was learned that Wilson, the married leader of the Liberal opposition in British Columbia, was having an affair with Tyabji, the youngest member of the legislature. For weeks, the media relentlessly pursued these people. The case raises the problem of how to balance respect for the privacy of citizens and officials, and the public's need for information relevant to civil affairs. At the same time, it questioned possible misuse of power and Tyabji's qualifications for a position to which Wilson appointed her.

As this case illustrated, there is no clear line between which facts about officials' lives are, and are not, relevant to judging their fitness for office. The press must be judicious in such matters and must be guided by an item's importance to the public interest. A public appetite for the details of marital troubles, sexual liaisons and the like should not supplant the criterion determining legitimate public interest. It is interesting in this connection to note the increasing tendency of the legitimate press, in cases involving a questionable invasion of privacy, to let the tabloids run with a certain story first and then pick it up. In doing so, they exploit the excuse that any damaging information is already out.

The last point illustrates an important, general moral liability that runs throughout social life: the problem of moral cooperation. Most of the social goods that morality protects (for example, the right to privacy) depend upon general conformity with the norms and standards that protect them. When morality declines, conformity with norms and standards gradually erodes. Eventually a point comes where conformity only serves to damage the interests of the individual who continues to conform.

The current practice of disclosing information about the personal lives of political figures suggests an erosion of journalistic standards. There is an increasing tendency to publish such information without concern for whether such disclosure serves the political and informational function of the press. The reporter or news organization that tries to uphold the traditional standard is placed in a difficult position. This individual or organization must choose between honouring the standard—while losing revenues others gain by ignoring it—or succumbing to commercial interests and contributing to the moral decline. The tendency to resolve such dilemmas in the direction of self-interest is predictable; hence the fragility of this and other moral goods that directly depend on professional cooperation. "Melt-down" news illustrates this problematic pattern in a larger way. As competitive economic pressures increase and dependency upon electronic news-gathering dominates the smaller networks, traditional standards of individual reportorial responsibility are threatened. The nature and scale of the forces at work make them extremely difficult for the individual reporter to resist.

Consider another case involving the political, informational function of the press. A few years ago, the editor of a small-town British Columbia newspaper called me with the following problem: a distinguished doctor and pillar of the community was found dead of a heroin overdose in a bathroom at the hospital in which he worked. He had been preparing to go into the operating room. The hospital covered up the cause of death and the doctor's heroin addiction. Although some of the doctor's colleagues had known or suspected the drug problem for some time, nothing had been done.

Some time after the doctor's death, the newspaper editor learned the facts and telephoned the doctor's wife. She begged the editor not to publish the story because of her husband's reputation and record of community service and because their children were unaware of the circumstances and would be harmed by the publicity.

The editor decided to publish the story, as I had advised, based on the judgment that these were important issues, concerning public trust in the medical profession and the failure of medical professionals to act on their awareness of a colleague's addiction. He also believed that any effort to conceal the truth from the children would ultimately fail because too many people knew the facts.

THE HISTORICAL, EDUCATIONAL FUNCTION

A second function of journalism is to provide a range of perspectives on the life of the community, region and broader society and on the society's place in the world community. The media should help to preserve an historical consciousness by placing current events within their historical contexts. Sometimes journalism should remind us of the ideals that inform our traditions and ways of life. It should identify forces of social change and trace their implications for the development of values and modes of practice. This function of journalism is not only historical but sociological, philosophical and literary. Above all, the aim of journalism should be to help people see themselves in their world. This means providing *comparative* perspectives—historical, intracultural and intracommunity comparisons, and comparisons between our country and others. An important aspect of this function is the presentation of models of behaviour and character that reflect the gender, ethnic and cultural diversity of our communities and society.

We need to ask how successfully our news organizations reflect the cultural diversity of our communities. Especially at the middle and upper levels of management, news organizations continue to be staffed predominantly by white, middle-class males. In 1991 the Poynter Institute for Media Studies held a conference for print and broadcast journalists, educators and minority leaders on "Redefining the News: Reaching New Audiences Through Diversity." A central theme was that good reporting should be redefined to include cultural diversity. The conference addressed a wide range of practical strategies for change, including reshaping newsroom culture, new methods of developing story ideas, redesigning news beats and the cultivation of more varied sources (Poynter Institute 1991). Economic difficulties and other forces which contribute to social division, tension and hardship deepen the need to expand the range of news media perspectives.

Another issue related to journalism's historical and educational function is environmental coverage. As Noam Chomsky says,

> Modern industrial civilization has developed within a certain system of convenient myths. The driving force of modern industrial civilization has been individual material gain, which is accepted as legitimate, even praiseworthy, on the grounds that private vices yield public benefits, in the classic formulation. Now, it's long been understood—very well—that a society that is based on this principle will destroy itself in time. It can only persist, with whatever suffering and injustice it entails, as long as it's possible to pretend that the destructive forces that humans create are limited, that the world is an infinite resource, and that the world is an infinite garbage can.[4]

I disagree with Chomsky's statement that such things have been understood very well for a long time. For one thing, the crisis has worsened as the human population has increased, placing pressure on planetary resources and disposal functions. However, we should pay attention to the compelling and sophisticated arguments about biophysical limits to growth. Such arguments have important impacts on the continued "globalization" of the economy, or so-called "free trade," and the continuation of the system of work as we know it. In keeping with the historical and educational function of the press, I believe journalism has an obligation to convey, much more effectively, the profound nature of the environmental sustainability debate. Environmental problems are important and pressing. News organizations should assign reporters to the environmental beat and should make in-depth coverage of environmental issues as regular a part of local and national coverage as politics and the economy.

CLOSING THOUGHTS

I began by sketching a general conception of social morality, followed by an overview of journalistic ethics grounded in the primary social functions of journalism. Drawing on the recent history of applied ethics, I have argued that a theoretical overview of journalistic ethics cannot be expected to provide direct guidance for resolving concrete moral difficulties which arise from the practice of journalism. I have emphasized the importance of understanding the large-scale economic, social and institutional forces which affect journalistic practice in ways which cause ethical concern.

Theoretical models such as this one provide a general view of the social benefits, or "goods," which are supported and served by proper professional practice. In relation to these "goods," it is possible to formulate general ethical principles which govern the professional domain. In this connection, I spoke of principles of objectivity, balance, accuracy and truthfulness in journalistic practice. Principles such as these can help us organize and systematize our understanding of ethics in a field. However, our ability to use any set of principles to make practical moral decisions is limited by the very properties of abstraction and generality that make a theory comprehensive. Philosophy may help us map the moral landscape in instrumental terms, but we require interpretation and understanding of specific cases to navigate through that landscape.

I will close by illustrating the complexity of actual moral reasoning. Let us consider the familiar principle, easily derived from a functionalist account of journalistic ethics, that reporters should always tell the truth and accurately represent the news. Consider: on various grounds having to do with child protection, social workers regularly apprehend young children and remove them from their homes. While these activities rarely attract media attention, when they do, the cases tend to involve the misuse of power, typically in the form of a heavy bureaucratic hand snatching a child from the bosom of a poor but caring family.

If a reporter finds enough evidence to support a Dickensian tale, it makes the story interesting, that is, newsworthy. Such evidence usually comes from an aggrieved couple or from a single parent who is struggling. Their representations can be plausible and the people sympathetic. Fair enough. In the interest of balance, the reporter also interviews a representative of the department of social services, usually the social worker who took the child.

Typically, the social worker explains that the law protecting confidentiality prevents him or her from discussing the case. Instead, the social worker is willing to discuss general policy guidelines and other matters. Disturbingly often, the story is distorted: the reporter covers the parents' side of the issue and then says the social worker was contacted but "refused to comment on the case." Although this is literally true, this treatment conveys the impression that the social worker felt uncomfortable and reluctant when confronted and behaved as if there were something to hide.

It takes little reflection to realize that this kind of journalism is unfair and deceptive. It may not be quite as bad as deliberate deception by "manipulation of the facts" or outright lying, but it is still contrary to the principle that the news should be presented truthfully, accurately and fairly. So here we have a fairly easy moral judgment which falls under a familiar principle of journalistic ethics.

At the 1991 conference of the Poynter Institute for Media Studies mentioned above, the danger of misrepresenting photographic images through digital manipulation was a topic of major concern. It is possible to place a person in any context or background with whomever you choose. Recognizing the potential for abuse, many of the conference participants favoured an absolute rule prohibiting manipulations of photographic content on the grounds that it is misrepresentation and, in essence, lying. This issue provides a better opportunity to reflect on the relationship between ethical theory (principle) and moral practice (considered moral judgment) than the previous case.

Let us consider a rule that bans any manipulation of photographic content but nevertheless permits standard photographic techniques of burning, dodging or cropping. Those techniques are said to merely enhance images instead of altering their content—a distinction which is not altogether clear. Suppose you are doing a story on the relationships between the police and people in an inner-city neighbourhood and you take many photographs. When you enlarge a section of one photograph, you find an image of a burly policeman, seen three-quarters from the rear, with his arm raised; a woman watches him from the side, leaning away with a look of fear on her face. Here is what happened: the woman and the policeman were having a friendly conversation; the officer raised his right arm to wave to a passing motorist; and, at the same time, a factory whistle blew and the sound frightened the woman. In the full print, with both figures rather distant and small, you do not see the woman's expression and everything looks normal. If you crop and enlarge the photograph, the image implies that a woman is being intimidated by a policeman in a menacing pose.

It may be that the photographer remembers the scene, remembers that the people were talking, a loud whistle blew and so forth and realizes that this enlarged image is highly misleading. Even if the news story reveals poor relations between the police and the people in this neighbourhood, if the cropped enlargement is misleading, we should conclude that it is wrong to use it. Although only standard photographic techniques are used, the image still distorts and misrepresents. Generally, the rule allowing "standard" techniques will hold but this example shows its limitations.

By the same token, despite the potential for misuse, there are instances in which digital manipulation is justified. For example, a twelve-year-old boy photographed receiving an award had his fly unzipped. The newspaper, the *Orange County* (California) *Register*, used electronic techniques to zip up the fly before publishing the photograph. In this case the photograph was digitally altered to honour the boy without exposing him to ridicule. In this instance, the digital fly-closing produced an image which more accurately represented the truth of the occasion. However, even if "truth" was not better served, the newspaper could still be seen to have done the right thing.

We have focused on comparing different cases in relation to practical moral rules intended to guide journalistic practice. The principle is "Be truthful, accurate and fair." Regarding photographic imagery, the traditional rule has been that a photograph must have been taken at the scene and only standard enhancement techniques may be used. A newly proposed rule would ban any digital manipulation of photographic imagery. Both rules have exceptions. The practical moral truth requires us to appreciate the limits of the usefulness of principles and rules for navigating the quandaries of journalism.

Here are the beginnings of an interpretation of the journalistic principle of truthtelling and accuracy in relation to modern photographic technologies. Although the principle of truthfulness, accuracy and fairness has helped to frame our problem, it has not had much to do with solving it.

Today's journalists face many new challenges brought on by changing economics, technology and other forces. As journalists struggle to develop ethical principles for their profession, they must be prepared to engage in moral reasoning which adapts these principles to the requirements and realities of these changes.[5]

3. The Evolution of Journalistic Ethics in Quebec

Armande Saint-Jean

Journalistic ethics creates the values and defines the behaviours of an entire profession. Yet it is difficult to describe and analyze its guiding values, precisely because they refer to a living, human social practice. This difficulty accounts for the dearth of scientific inquiry and theory on the subject. However, recent work addresses both the foundations and the practical applications of journalistic ethics. The North American and European literature features three main approaches to journalistic ethics.

The first approach studies the legal and philosophical foundations of the moral principles which undergird journalistic ethics. In the United States, John C. Merrill uses Kant's categorical imperative to develop a philosophy of journalistic freedom. In France, Dominique Wolton, Marc Ferro, Alain Etchegoyen and others are inspired by Emmanuel Levinas and Hans Jonas to derive the moral obligations, individual and community responsibility which they consider to be the core of news ethics (Merrill 1974; Merrill and Barney 1975). In all of this work, journalism ethics is portrayed as a sum of abstract philosophical principles, removed from the realm of the social.

The second approach focuses on the practical applications of ethical principles. Starting with actual work situations, proponents of this view say bias and distortion are the media's primary moral problems. John L. Hulteng looks at ethical codes in his search for a workable theory of the social reponsibility of the press. Others favour legislative intervention to insure responsible reporting, or advocate a form of self-regulation, with local and regional media review agencies to safeguard and set standards.

The third approach has the largest following. It focuses on the ethical dilemmas in the everyday lives of journalists (Ferré 1989). Analyses frequently refer to existing codes and study interpretations of basic principles such as fairness or objectivity. Codes of ethics, or editorial policies of large media organizations, are examined for clues to how to understand basic principles by studying their applications.

There are flaws in all of these approaches. Most of the work on journalism ethics fails to define key terms and slips from the general to the particular without recognizing that the notion of *ethics* is itself ambiguous. Public interest is explained as part of a general search for moral orientation in the 1990s. The writing is often so general that it is virtually useless for understanding journalistic practices in a particular setting.

Defining and Situating Ethics

Our first task is to define journalism ethics and clearly locate its components. This will help us to study the evolution of journalism ethics in relation to the societal forces that influence them. Journalistic ethics does not evolve in a vacuum. It is deeply influenced by social, economic and political forces which prevail in the larger society in which journalistic activities take place. It relies on philosophical foundations, moral principles, legal obligations and professional rules of practice which are inherited through tradition. Its main components are located at the intersection of morality, legal codification and deontology (a set of moral principles applied to a specific activity).

Journalistic ethics involves duty, individual conscience, morality and law. Ethics brings a journalist to decide what is right and what is wrong in practice. In Merrill's words, ethics "is primarily individual or personal even when it relates to obligations and duties to others" (Merrill 1974; Merrill and Barney 1975). However, ethics is distinct from morality and from law: Ethics is primarily individual; law is primarily social" (Merrill 1974; Merrill and Barney 1975).

Journalistic ethics is based on three philosophical concepts: freedom, truth and responsibility. *Freedom* is the precondition for human choice and free will, the foundation of an ethical position. *Truth,* or rather the search for truth/s, defines the ultimate goal of a journalist's activity. In everyday reporting, there are rules to guarantee truthfulness, for example: avoid lies, distinguish between facts and opinion, transmit facts accurately. *Responsibility* involves the obligation, shared by individual journalists, media organizations and others involved in the newsmaking process, to abide by rules which guarantee people's right to receive accurate, honest and useful news and information "enabling them to make judgements on the issues of the time" (Hulteng 1981).

The philosophical components of journalistic ethics are distilled into a small number of agreed-upon principles. Among these are accuracy, fairness, impartiality, objectivity and truthfulness. All of these are found in the 1973 Code of Ethics of the Society of Professional Journalists, Sigma Delta Chi and most other codes. The rules for good journalism have a moral dimension: their interpretation corresponds to the prevailing moral principles of a given society and time.

Laws provide barriers and parameters for determining the territory in which journalistic activities take place. They codify fundamental rights and freedoms which are granted to individuals and groups (dignity, reputation, private life, etc.). In Canada, the principle of *freedom of the press* has had constitutional status since its inclusion in the 1981 Charter of Rights, Article 2b. However, the public's *right to know* is also recognized as a legal right, although codified only in Quebec's 1975 Charter of Human Rights and Freedoms. Laws concerning libel and defamation protect the individual's right to reputation, private life and dignity.

Aside from its legal supports, journalistic ethics is guided by a complex set of rules, regulations and norms which translate moral principles into practice. These deontological rules, which prescribe "proper" professional behaviour, emerge from a consensus within the professional community. They tell journalists to refuse "freebies," avoid conflicts of interest and refrain from lying or inventing facts.

This view of journalism ethics considers its individual and collective dimensions and brings together moral, philosophical, legal and practical considerations. The interpretation and application of underlying values and principles does not evolve in a closed circuit but is seen in the larger societal context. Moral principles are inherited from tradition, religion, philosophy and history; they evolve through time. While they provide guidance for dealing with individual journalistic dilemmas, it is left to the individual to interpret the type of responsiblity involved and the ways these principles should be applied. "Ethics . . . is personally determined and personally enforced—and should be" (Merrill 1974; Merrill and Barney 1975). The individual's ethical position is influenced by the professional setting and the social context. Obviously, there must be some agreement between the journalist's definition of moral principles, that of the media organization in which she or he works and that of the professional community to which she or he belongs. Otherwise, conflicts are frequent and work suffers.

THE SOCIAL-HISTORY APPROACH

Because journalistic ethics results from numerous interrelated social processes, its evolution is difficult to trace (Saint-Jean 1993). A socio-historical approach can help to unravel the relationship between socio-political context and development of ethical values which guide the profession. Our analysis is based on a case study of the evolution of journalistic ethics in Quebec from the 1960s to the present, more than three decades since the rise of the major political and social renewal known as the "Quiet Revolution."

Each aspect of the journalist's experience provides indices for interpreting and decoding ethical values and meta-ethical attitudes. These include the journalist's social role, status, conception of information, definition of the adversarial stance, level of autonomy, political and social commitments, and level of independence in conflict situations. The various dimensions of the journalistic profession do not evolve in a linear pattern but are profoundly influenced by the social, political, economic and cultural contexts in which its professionals are placed. In Quebec, as anywhere else, we must study the relationship between those professional characteristics and the concurrent events in society at large. In the following pages, we will explore the most important events which have shaped Quebec's history over the past three decades.

AUTONOMY

Independence and journalistic freedom have been the most persistent preoccupation of Quebec journalists for the more than thirty years. By autonomy, we mean the capacity to go about one's activities freely. This has considerable impact on impartiality and credibility. Journalists must constantly guard against invasion of their autonomy by other social agents. In the 1960s, journalists' strongest adversaries were press owners who had developed the habit of directly intervening in information production. Through strongly fought labor strikes, journalists finally gained legal protection in their collective agreements to keep press rooms autonomous. In the decade that followed, the threat shifted from authoritarian bosses to political and judicial authorities who used journalists as puppets. The result was the struggle for an information access law to curtail secrecy and grant journalists immunity in some judicial proceedings.

Ferocious attacks by federal members of Parliament against allegedly "separatist" journalists led to official distancing of the profession from all ideological options, including political parties and popular activist groups. In the 1980s, the threat shifted again. This time it came from advertisers, public relations professionals and marketing specialists who used subtle "infotainment" strategies to infiltrate the news with promotional discourses.

Ironically, despite journalists' struggles over the decades, they have failed to hold their own against media organizations. The press barons who were the adversaries in the 1960s invented all possible means to reaffirm their power over "their" media. This

Figure 1
Summary of various dimensions of the journalistic profession

Areas	1960–70*	1970–80	1980–90
independence (autonomy)	authoritative bosses as adversaries	political and judicial adversaries	marketing and advertising adversaries
conflicts of interest	end of patronage era	refusal of all ideological allegiance	threat from promotional offerings
adversarial stance (addressed to)	social conservatism	press concentration	influence of advertising and marketing
social and political commitment	promoting social change	labour union activism	neutrality and professionalism
journalists' status	part of intellectual elite	activist information workers	upper middle-class bureaucrats
journalists' role	agents of social change	critical witnesses	"good employees," public entertainers
function of information	democratic public service	forum for exchange and debates	product similar to any other commodity

* These periods correspond to three specific decades described in the original research and not simply to calendar dates.

included dismissing "uncooperative" editors. Among them were Gérard Pelletier, ousted by *La Presse* in 1965, and Michel Roy, who resigned from the same newspaper in 1988 to protest against the invasion of editorial autonomy. Press concentration was on the rise, making it impossible to introduce a co-management model (for example, at *Québec-Presse* or *Le Jour*) which would have allowed journalists to help define editorial policies.

In the 1970s, political and judicial powers became the adversaries. In 1970, the federal government invoked the War Measures Act to curtail the activities of FLQ "terrorists." This had a dramatic impact on the freedom of the press, both individually and institutionally. In the 1980s, the main threat to journalistic autonomy was from advertisers and public relations professionals who brought promotional discourse into news content. The marketing experts developed highly sophisticated methods that made it increasingly difficult for journalists to keep track of the transformation of information into promotion. As a result, the principle of journalistic independence is threatened. Great efforts are required to maintain press autonomy and protect journalistic freedom from political and economic assaults.

CONFLICTS OF INTEREST

The notion of conflicts of interest has evolved considerably since the 1960s. Much has been said of the era before the Quiet Revolution when a system of patronage dominated Quebec politics. It was largely associated with Maurice Duplessis' somewhat folkloric conception of power. Duplessis was the province's premier for three decades. Fortunately, this view of power disappeared with him in the early 1960s. During the Duplessis era, journalists customarily received envelopes with money inside and other gratuities in exchange for complacent coverage.

In the late 1950s and 1960s, unionization raised the level of journalists' earnings, thereby reducing the temptation to accept payouts in order to live. In the 1970s, the notion of conflict of interest was linked to ideological motives and partisan affiliation. Journalists were part of the activist social-reform movement that blew across the whole province at the beginning of the decade. They were therefore considered suspect and accused of using information for ideological purposes, to promote trade-union activism and support popular movements or even Marxist doctrine. To maintain autonomy and independence, avoid conflicts of interest and remain credible and neutral in the eyes of various organizations, movements and parties, journalists learned to abstain from any kind of partisan association.

In the 1980s, conflicts of interest were created by marketing and promotion which transformed journalists into involuntary salespeople. Quebec journalists had freed themselves from the strangleholds of authoritarian press owners, politicians, opposition and counter-power movements, only to find themselves prey to a new breed of "merchants of the temple," the public relations clan. Although the ethical principle of freedom is well established in matters of public and political debate, it still needs to be defended against the encroachment of economic interests.

ADVERSARIAL STANCE AND SOCIAL AND POLITICAL COMMITMENT

Traditionally, the press has taken an adversarial position in society. This oppositional function is labelled the Fourth Estate or the watchdog role. Theoretically, reporters are neutral witnesses who stand outside conflict and debate for the sake of objectivity. Recent history demonstrates that this pseudo-objectivity is an illusion, a myth brilliantly defended by the partisans of a conservative vision of the media.

It has been demonstrated that where Liberal doctrine prevails, instead of defending the opposition or those who are marginalized, the media end up defending and promoting the contemporary social order and dominant ideology. Journalists' participation in large social endeavours involves an ideological and moral commitment that is reflected in their reporting and their news production roles. Because these two dimensions—the press's adversarial or "watchdog" stance and the tradition of social and political involvement—are closely related, we will discuss them together.

The history of the press in Quebec clearly shows that journalists have always been in opposition to one type of political or economic power or another. Their adversarial position varies according to the circumstances, historical period and priorities established by the *confrérie*. Since 1960, this adversarial stance has changed, and its focus has differed in each period. At the beginning of the Quiet Revolution, journalists were on the side of the reformists, even the radical ones; they opposed social conservatives and promoters of the status quo. In the 1960s, their collective social commitment favoured social change which they promoted actively, favouring widespread agreement on values associated with evolution and democracy.

In the 1970s, journalists showed an activist enthusiasm in tune with the times. They focused on press concentration; their adversarial work was directed at questioning the activities of the press barons. They criticized the rise of sensationalism which they blamed on press concentration and competition with electronic media. Their social and political involvement included labour union activism, and they went so far as to abandon the sixties label of "intellectuals" and call themselves "workers" instead. Their ethical values leaned towards goals of social justice and equity.

In the 1980s, the adversary position focused on the growing influence of advertising, marketing and public relations. Nowadays, journalists say their profession is being invaded and distorted by a seemingly unstoppable wave of promotion. By the end of the 1980s, many former activists had become highly paid bureaucrats, protected by wall-to-wall collective agreements, who hid silently on the outskirts of the endless constitutional debate. The social commitment of the journalistic community has culminated in a new notion of professionalism whose aim is to protect what is left of editorial autonomy and independence and to otherwise maintain a benevolent neutrality. Today, journalism is committed not to ideas or ideologies but to the ideals of excellence and the production of quality information to defend against outside threats.

During the Quiet Revolution years, the focus of journalistic commitment was politics; during the years of social turmoil in the 1970s, the concern was the redefinition of social forces; in the 1980s, promotion invaded the very heart of journalism. In each decade, journalists were confronted with the need to define the new situation and establish the ethical position they should adopt. In each instance, they had to adapt their strategies to the prevailing political, economic and social contexts.

STATUS

In the same period, the status of journalists also evolved as the result of changes in the profession itself. The advent of television tranformed the old majority of scribes and writers into an heterogeneous group which now includes broadcasters, interviewers, hosts and showpersons of all sorts. Earlier divisions have disappeared; the public views *all* media people as journalists. A talk-show host is labelled a journalist, even if he or she is an actor, a former politician or a plain show-business artist. Who is a journalist and who is not? It seems almost impossible to draw a line because journalists themselves are reluctant to yield to any corporatist inclination and staunchly refuse to make their profession a distinct one.

In the 1960s, journalists were considered part of the intellectual social-reformist elite that was deeply involved in the Quiet Revolution, and they were virtually indistinguishable from other intellectual elites. In the 1970s, they became activist information workers who unionized their ranks and associated themselves with other groups of "exploited workers." Ironically, this egalitarian and socialist-leaning period coincided with the emergence of a new generation of stars—highly paid journalists whose names draw millions of readers and viewers. Although a small minority, this subcategory of news stars has a disturbing effect on the majority of ordinary journalists who become associated in the public's mind with the ambitions and fantasies of a few.

In the 1980s, the slow bureaucratization of the journalistic profession lowered its prestige and credibility in the public's eyes. Many complain that journalists are growing old, the inquisitive flame has faded and they look like other well-fed bureaucrats. Some embrace the Japanese corporate-style model of a "good employee" who is faithful to an organization which provides security and well-being in return (Demers 1989).

JOURNALISTS' SOCIAL ROLE AND THE FUNCTION OF INFORMATION

Along with the successive shifts in their social status, journalists redefined their roles in society as the definition of information and its functions changed. During the Quiet Revolution when Quebec was undergoing profound socio-economic restructuring, journalists saw themselves as agents of change. News and information were the tools for building a democratic and modern society. The notion of news-gathering as a public service was prevalent.

Later on, information was redefined and was seen as providing people with the opportunity to hold large and fundamental debates about the future orientation of society. In the 1970s, the media became forums for exchanging ideas. This period was dominated by social unrest, general strikes and the rise of the independentist Parti Québécois. News was viewed as a consciousness-raising tool whether the ideology was feminism or socialism, sovereignty or ecology. Located at the junction of many divergent currents, many journalists abandoned their activist stance and became critical witnesses, refusing to take sides in the many ongoing social debates. This attitude of reserve largely came about under the impact of the War Measures Act which Prime Minister Pierre Elliott Trudeau had used in 1970 against the population in general, and journalists in particular, to crush the separatist movement. That repressive measure brought about a form of self-censorship in the French Québécois press which some believe still dominates constitutional matters. In the mid-1970s, a number of federal cabinet members mounted a ferocious campaign against separatist journalists. The Parti Québécois was elected to power but the anti-journalism attacks continued. During the 1980 referendum campaign, journalists as a group were accused of promoting the destruction of Canada. These attacks cooled any political fervour journalists might have felt during those years of agitation and prevented them from playing a dynamic role in the political process.

In the 1980s, journalists joined the ranks of the upper-middle class. They began to be perceived as a group of greying bureaucrats, their role gradually reduced to that of the good employee. The minority who became media stars were assimilated into the world of performers and entertainers—thus the inevitable blurring of lines between show business and journalism. After a century of evolution in that direction, information has clearly become a commodity, news a volatile product and journalism a highly competitive industry with profit the one and ultimate goal.

In less than thirty years, the doctrine of social responsibility, which in the 1960s seemed to be galvanizing the profession, has yielded to a business mentality in which production constraints must be obeyed and wrongdoing is justified in the name of the public's right to know. In the 1990s, news has become a commodity, subject to the pressures of profit and the exigencies of the market, prey to every new trend. The trends include unedited direct reporting via satellite, fictional re-enactment of events and other techniques that provide viewers with (often inaccurate or manipulated) *images* of reality.

URGENT PROBLEMS

Those recent developments have led to displacement of responsibility. Ethical accountability is shifted from one level to the other, from the individual to the collectivity and ultimately to society at large, without actually being handled by anyone. This situation is undermining the profession. It has three major consequences: the recoil of press attention away from serious analysis of social problems; the profession's vulnerability to manipulation, disinformation and propaganda initiatives; and a failure to show intellectual leadership in the formation of public opinion.

Socio-economic changes are drastically restructuring most Western societies. Citizens need basic information to help them make informed decisions on environmental, economic and socio-structural issues. Such issues require in-depth research and analysis as well as the presentation of long dossiers in which the stakes are clearly outlined and contextualized. However, the industry considers that kind of reporting unprofitable. In recent years, superficial treatment of issues and simplistic coverage of spectacular events has been encouraged because this kind of news costs less to produce and is believed to be more profitable.

The kind of information the public needs in order to address serious and urgent issues cannot be produced through superficial, spectacular or simplistic coverage. For example, environmental problems are far too complex to be reduced to one- or two-day coverage of events such as the Chernobyl or *Exxon Valdez* accidents. The health and survival of our generation and future generations is at stake. To prepare an adequate environmental assessment, all pertinent data must be collected and weighed. Journalists must carefully evaluate the public relations campaigns of domestic and nuclear waste companies and go beyond a superficial presentation of bottom-line costs. Unfortunately, most media outlets are unwilling to tackle this kind of coverage and choose instead to supply the public with simplistic coverage of the most obvious events. It is no wonder newspaper readership is languishing and audiences prefer pictures to text.

The second major concern for the profession is the growing influence of advertisers, marketing experts and public relations professionals. This infiltration of public relations material into news content has led to an emphasis on events rather than issues, symptoms rather than causes. Debates are simplified to worst- or best-case scenarios (for example, in the treatment of constitutional issues). Powerful communication consultants hold press conferences and organize guided industrial tours which become the content of the news. They design electoral campaign strategies on which the media become totally dependent. Large and powerful structures such as the Pentagon or the United Nations control the coverage of the Gulf War or the Serbia/Croatia/Bosnia conflict.

On the commercial side, large companies bury reportorial initiative under piles of well-prepared material which subtly serves their own interests. It is becoming increasingly difficult for individual journalists to take knowledgeable critical positions vis-à-vis promotional overload. At the same time, press organizations are virtually incapable of resisting power centers' interpretations of events concerning themselves. Given the economic and production constraints the industry faces, it is likely that the media will succumb to the manipulative manoeuvres of the most efficient propagandists.

The third serious problem that confronts the journalistic community is its decreasing moral and intellectual leadership in contemporary societies. This loss is the result of two interrelated processes: economic stringencies on the production side and the perceptions of readers and viewers. In past decades, preoccupation with profit has blinded press organizations to the increasing diversity of audience interests. The increased use of opinion polls during election campaigns indicates a lack of sophistication in gauging the mood of the electorate. Instead, this understanding should come from in-depth reporting of what "real people" think.

Editorial writers and columnists have lost their influence which used to be built on shrewd observation of current events and on public trust. Affiliation with an increasingly shrill and irrelevant media organization tarnishes their editorial opinions and renders them indistinguishable from other interested parties. The public is frequently way ahead of journalists. We have seen many times that public opinion does not wait for editorialists' permission to challenge measures it considers unfair. On most social problems (for example, violence, poverty, health care, unemployment, government deficits, education) people usually have more articulate and qualified opinions than "good employee" journalists.

Increasingly, debate on critical issues is carried out in small and specialized circles with which journalists have little contact. As a result, the press is gradually losing its importance as an intellectual and moral beacon and is becoming closely associated with the realm of entertainment and spectacle. Recent polls on the credibility of and public respect for journalists relative to other professionals indicates that their prestige continues to fall.

CONCLUSION: A RENEWED CONSCIENCE

This rather dark view of the evolution of journalistic ethics is by no means limited to Quebec; the phenomena mentioned here occur beyond the boundaries of *La Belle Province*. Except for a few cultural particularities, the Quebec journalistic scene follows the same patterns and trends as in the rest of Canada and, for that matter, North America. Although these observations are based on my study of Quebec journalistic social history, the questions I have raised and my recommendations for change are addressed to the journalistic community as a whole.

Any change in the interpretation of ethical principles will have wide-ranging implications for the profession, and for the information product it creates. Because social conditions and professional practice are interrelated, solutions require a systemic, multilevel approach. The ethical dilemmas faced by journalists and media institutions cannot be solved with one-dimensional calls for a return to ethical responsibility. We must analyze the evolving interests of individual journalists, media organizations and the public, and articulate a new paradigm of the media's "public service" role. It is this author's opinion that such a redefinition will require the rehabilitation of the principles of responsibility, freedom and the search for truth/s.

4. Lies, Damned Lies and Journalism

Nicholas Russell

Journalism is all about truthtelling. The fundamental importance of truth in journalism is stressed by many newsroom policies. Yet what is truth? No journalist captures it all, not even one who totally immerses himself or herself in a story. At best, *most* of the truth is told. The journalist may be an eye-witness to history, but he or she can't possibly tell the whole truth and nothing but the truth, largely because it would be so boring. If, for example, the *New York Times* printed *all* the news that was fit to print, the press-run would take more than a week and readers would need more than a year to read the paper. So, journalists must rely on an edited version of truth, based on objectivity, accuracy and fairness—all of which are difficult to define and accomplish.[1]

Given the struggle to achieve good journalism,[2] the failure to define many of its elements and increasing pressures to "entertain" as well as inform, it is little wonder that the truth is sometimes bent, sources and audiences misled and direct lies told in the gathering or recounting of news. It can be argued that deceiving sources to gather news and telling lies to recount news may occasionally be defensible under rigidly controlled conditions.[3] How is the journalist to decide?

Sissela Bok (1978: 123–26) identifies three steps in ethical decision-making: self-examination, analysis of the options and consultation with the protagonists.[4] In the journalistic environment, the third step is largely impractical. While many of Bok's ideas are applicable to journalism, some other paradigm is needed here.

Three Useful Yardsticks

Three questions can be used to measure such activities. The first focuses on the nature of the journalist's motivation: *Is the journalist motivated primarily by a genuine desire to inform the audience?* Or is he or she driven by some other agenda, such as motives of self-aggrandizement—the newsroom bonus, promotion or a chance at a Pulitzer Prize?

The second question examines one result of this decision: *What does this decision do to the newsroom's credibility?* The integrity of the individual journalist is on trial, but the bad vibes generated by one newsperson can reverberate throughout the newsroom or even through the whole business. When Janet Cooke faked her story of a child heroin addict for the *Washington Post*, the entire news industry dropped another notch on the credibility scale.

The third question ties the first two together: *Can journalists comfortably confess their techniques to the audience?* If they feel they cannot, believing the audience will disapprove of their motives or techniques, then they should re-evaluate the situation and consult with senior editors.

April Fool!

The applicability of the three questions can be tested by referring to the long-standing newsroom tradition of April Fools' Day jokes. Although it might be thought of as a recent innovation, as newsrooms are urged to become more "entertaining," the tradition of April Fools' Day jokes goes back a long way. Horseplay has been sporadically present in the media for a century or more.[5] For instance, the *Guardian* of London has become famous for its April first jokes over the years.

Most April Fools' jokes are harmless and intended only to entertain. When CBC's Regina radio news reported (on April 1, 1992) that the provincial legislative building had been bought by a Texan for use as a casino, the audience was quickly told this was just a joke. Nobody was hurt or angered by the invention. But when the Durand, Michigan, weekly *Express* reported that the Nissan Motor Corporation would build a huge new plant in the town (which is near Flint, Michigan), thousands of unemployed autoworkers in the area were furious to learn it was only a joke. Readers of the Virginia City *Territorial Enterprise* have frequently been incensed over jokes in that paper (Sherefkin 1984; Stein 1986). It is clear that the jokesters were not primarily motivated by the desire to inform (Question 1), and it seems likely the newspapers' credibility would be seriously eroded by such pranks (Question 2).

Sometimes jokes get into the news package by accident. In the late 1960s, somebody inserted into a serious wire story on snakes in Australia a ribald reference to the "one-eyed trouser snake." Probably added as an inside joke to amuse colleagues, it slipped into at least one newspaper.[6] The joke failed the test of Question 1. Such jokes are widely discouraged in most newsrooms.[7]

TV: Special Problems?

The need to mix entertainment with news creates a variety of dilemmas for the journalist, especially in television. The transformation of the documentary into the docudrama may be driven more by ratings—or at least by the perceived need to preserve market share—than by the sincere desire to inform. As television becomes more and more pervasive and young viewers expect to be passively entertained (see Postman 1984), and as television consultants, hired as networks try to hold fragmenting audiences, urge more "infotainment" in news, so the need to entertain is seen as increasingly important.

Television, it is said, loves the person and hates the idea. Certainly the videocamera has an affinity to colour and action. So television news becomes theatre with handsome performers trying to make the news as palatable or even entertaining as possible. News expands into documentary, which in turn expands into mini-series. Should "The Valour and the Horror" or "The Boys of St. Vincent" be judged by the same criteria as mainstream news? Should words or scenes be re-created or even invented? The CBC was surprised by the negative reaction those shows provoked, but it might well have been anticipated after the breastbeating which followed the simulation by ABC news of U.S. diplomat Felix Block's alleged passing of secrets to a KGB operative ("ABC World News Tonight," July 21, 1989). Yet, a few people praised the concept of re-creations:

> Don't try to tell me that television viewers in today's U.S. cannot or will not tell the difference between the dramatization of a news event and the real thing if they are informed (docudrama writer Jesse Hill Ford, anonymous 1989).

> They [simulations] are a natural step in broadcast news. It is an idea whose time has come (NBC News producer Sid Feders, anonymous 1989).

Both sources have a vested interest in this debate. Many others quoted in the same article believed that viewers would *not* identify the difference between simulations and reality. And if simulations are a natural step, what will be the next?

Perhaps the next step has already been taken with NBC's "faking" of a truck explosion to "prove" some General Motors vehicles are susceptible to gas-tank fires ("Dateline NBC," November 1992). The furor which greeted that incident—and which included the firing of at least one executive and many NBC apologies—suggests such a step is unwelcome and regrettable. Once again, it is clear that if the newsroom had considered confessing how it made the video when it was shown—Question 3—it would have foreseen the audience's disapproval and would have shelved the project. That the program did not clearly reveal the manipulative nature of the re-creation suggests the makers expected a negative reaction.

Another TV news tool that borders on simulation is the double-ender in which an interviewer conducts his or her interview at long range from, say, a studio in New York, while the source sits in a studio in Regina or Rome. Does the audience know the interview is not live? Do viewers know if an anchor later re-asked the questions so it looked as if he or she did the interview although they never spoke to the source? And what is the motivation? Isn't this designed to mislead the audience into thinking that the anchor interviewed Ms. Politician whereas a humble researcher did the interview? When the audience learns this, doesn't it erode general media credibility? Certainly, Question 3 would provide interesting results: A message superimposed on the screen saying, "Researcher Joe Blow conducted this interview but anchor Jane Plain faked it later" would provoke howls of derision from viewers.

Recreations and simulations are such relatively recent phenomena that only a few codes of ethics, such as that of the National Association of Broadcasters (NAB), come close to addressing this issue:

> No programming shall be presented in a manner which through artifice or simulation would mislead the audience as to any material fact. Each broadcaster must exercise reasonable judgment to determine whether a particular method of presentation would constitute a material deception, or would be accepted by the audience as normal theatrical illusion (Radio Code, s.I, ss.9, Rivers and Mathews 1988: 258).

Because this appears in a "general" section of the NAB code rather than the "News" section, it is evidently not seen as a journalistic scenario. The *Journalistic Standards and Practices* issued to all news staff of the Canadian Broadcasting Corporation deals with the issue at length:

> 3. MIXTURE OF PRODUCTION FORMS.
> 3.1 RECONSTRUCTION AND SIMULATION.
>
> Any reconstruction or simulation must coincide as closely as possible with the event that it purports to portray. Reconstruction or simulation can be the most effective

means of conveying certain types of information, such as space exploration or the events surrounding an accident. If an event or portion of an event is reconstructed or simulated in the course of a program, that fact must be made clear to the audience by audio and visual means.

3.2 MIXTURE OF ACTUALITY AND DRAMATIZATION.
Journalistic programs must not as a general principle mix actuality (visual and audio of actual events and of real people) with a dramatized portrayal of people or events. The audience must be able to judge the nature of the information received. The mixture of forms renders such a judgment difficult because it may lend the appearance of reality to hypothesis. Should a situation arise in which such a mixture of forms is the only adequate method to convey the necessary information, the dramatized portion must be well identified" (CBC 1993: 77).

Print Is Not Immune

Some techniques seem to spill over from the creative non-fiction techniques used in the 1960s and 1970s by Hunter S. Thompson, Tom Wolfe, George Plimpton and others. Print is not immune to "massaging" the truth. Composite stories had some (short-lived) popularity until the Janet Cooke case, now held up as the awful example of this genre. The upheaval caused when the *Washington Post* surrendered its Pulitzer Prize for that story put a chill on composite writing for years. Another "creative" genre is the "You are there" historical feature. In the late 1960s, United Press International (UPI) ran a series of features on great moments in history; during Bicentennial celebrations, a number of American media re-created the making of the American Constitution. What differentiates these from, say, a TV double-ender is that they are clearly labelled re-creations. The newsroom can comfortably reveal the techniques because the motivation is simply a mix of entertainment and information.

Apart from tricks and accidents, misleading material can get into a news package as a result of faults at the stages of news-gathering or story construction.

News-Gathering

Ethically questionable techniques, such as eavesdropping, have probably been used since the beginning of journalism. Increasing ethical awareness has led to re-examination of methods of news-gathering. Yesterday's cub reporter who learnt to read upside down so he could get a good news "scoop" might well be castigated by today's ethicists. Witness the outcry generated when a television camera operator surreptitiously filmed material from a budget on a finance minister's desk (Schachter 1983). Under this heading might be placed sins of omission (neglecting to tell sources they are being tape-recorded) and sins of commission (stealing pictures from an accident victim; posing as a nurse to get an interview). Each is a form of lie.

The Pulitzer committee decided against giving a 1979 prize to the *Chicago Sun-Times* for a brilliant investigative series it ran for some months because the series was deemed "too deceptive." It focused on "The Mirage" bar which was run by two reporters. Through this deceptive device, they uncovered widespread abuses by local inspectors which led to scores of prosecutions.[8] The Pulitzer committee should have looked at the purpose of the series which was aimed at deceiving criminals not news consumers. It was designed to protect citizens, and the undercover method was probably the only way the story could have been effectively written. Would such activity affect the *Sun-Times*' credibility? It seems likely people would think more positively about the paper.

Even if the answer to Question 1 (What is the motivation?) is positive, the answer to the second question (What does it do to credibility?) may well be negative: journalists who practise such deceptions must expect criticism from their audience who frequently demand that journalists behave better than the people they investigate.[9]

In many newsrooms, guidelines forbid such practices. For instance, the CBC's *Journalistic Standards and Practices* (1993) has a section on "Clandestine Methods" and another on "Hidden Cameras and Microphones," including the following:

> As a general rule, journalism should be conducted in the open. The credibility and trust placed in the CBC's journalistic programming by the public depends largely on confidence in the ethical and professional standards of its practitioners. Covert methods . . . should only be employed with due regard to their legality, to considerations such as fairness and invasion of privacy and whether the information to be obtained is of such significance as to warrant being made public but is unavailable by other means (66–67).

The CBC handbook clearly forbids such activities:

> *Misrepresentation*: Deception must not be used to gain information. CBC employees, therefore, should not misrepresent themselves or their purposes to gain it. However, there may be occasions when it serves a legitimate program purpose for a journalist not to declare his or her profession but to seek information as an ordinary member of the public (65).

The principles are further spelled out under the "Hidden Cameras" heading, heavily revised in 1993:

> As a general rule, hidden cameras and microphones must not be used to gather information. Their use may entail criminal or civil liability or both. . . . Certainly, the use of hidden cameras or microphones raises some serious ethical questions, whether the recording is done by deliberately concealing the equipment or with equipment whose size or technology makes it inconspicuous or invisible to the person being recorded. . . . There may be occasions, however, when the use of such concealed recording devices will be in accordance with the law and where they may be regarded as being used in the public interest. Occasions of this sort, for example, could include a report on the selling of drugs on the street. Even when it is justified, covert recording risks damaging the public's trust in the CBC. . . . Authorization may be given only if the information gained serves an important purpose, is indispensable to that purpose and cannot be obtained by more open means. Moreover, it must concern illegal, anti-social or fraudulent activities or clear and significant abuses of public trust (66–67).

The principles are clearly enunciated but special exclusions permit the rules to be circumvented. Contrast, for instance, the much woollier statement in the British National Union of Journalists Code of Conduct:

> A journalist shall obtain information, photographs and illustration only by straightforward means. The use of other means can be justified only by over-riding considerations of the public interest (*Rule Book*, p. 54).

Such rules usually have such an escape clause. Compare, for instance, the Windsor, Ontario *Star*'s newsroom policy:

> There may be rare occasions when the assignment requires a staffer to go "under cover" or to use a specific ruse to gain certain information that would otherwise be unavailable, but such an action should be taken only as a last resort, and only with the proper approval of a senior, supervising editor. When information gained from such action is finally published, the extent of the ruse should be clearly communicated to the reader (Morgan, 1989: "General 6").

The latter paragraph effectively covers our Question 3: Can the reporter confess her techniques? Canada's largest daily, the *Toronto Star*, also forbids clandestine methods, yet as recently as August 1992 two reporters set up fake identities and wore body-pack tape-recorders for a sting operation (see Hammill 1993). Joanne Hammill, the Ryerson journalism student who reported the incident, quotes a *Star* editor: "'Deception is outlawed. Banned. Barred.' Having said that, he clarifies that there are always exceptions to the rule" (Hammill 1993: 22).

Clearly, exceptions must be possible: journalists need flexibility and occasionally must break the rules. However, they must recognize that, when they employ covert methods, their audiences may bracket them with the very people they seek to discredit. Although the public expects the *police* to use trickery to catch criminals, they are likely less forgiving of journalists because their motives are suspect. Too often, news consumers see the media as circulation-driven, motivated by the search for ratings, rather than as socially driven.[10] Many news codes (e.g., American Society of Newspaper Editors, National Association of Broadcasters, National Press Photographers Association, Society of Professional Journalists) fail to even mention misrepresentation or covert reporting.

Deception is difficult to define. Is it deception if a reporter dresses as a "bag lady" and takes to the streets for a few days to experience destitution and homelessness first-hand (see Palmer 1987)? Here there is no sense of operating in a criminal environment (as in "Connections" or "Mirage" scenarios). The reporter is not deceiving "bad guys," but some small lies to innocent citizens may be necessary to maintain her cover, and indeed the whole persona is a lie. Begging and vagrancy may contravene the law.

Journalists do not have special privileges or rights and must remind themselves that they are neither in the law enforcement business nor above the law. In the words of *Toronto Star* editor John Honderich, "The *Star* is not above the law, but nor are we investigators for the police" (Levy 1993: 16).

The journalist who is tempted to lie or secretly tape-record an interview to get a story should anticipate public condemnation for employing the tactics which, as an investigative reporter, he or she exposes (trickery and dishonesty). It may even be the journalist's *duty* to break the law. But fine journalism may not always be recognized by the audience as such. For example, John Sawatsky's revelations in the early 1970s about RCMP "dirty tricks" were greeted with outrage by many people who felt the Mounties were sacrosanct. And the Mirage incident demonstrates that a journalist of the highest probity who conducts important investigative journalism may be greeted by condemnation for using clandestine methods, even though the result enriches the community.

In Canada, discussion of the secret tape-recording of telephone conversations often bogs down in legalism.[11] But the point is not what *may* be taped, but what *should* be taped. If an interview is being tape-recorded merely to ensure accurate reporting, the reporter will have no difficulty telling readers or the source this, and the audience should respect the quest for accuracy. However, if there is some other motivation, use of the material should be challenged.[12] Theodore Glasser (1985: 20) says secrecy is not inimical to journalism and argues that secret tape-recording "is of little moral consequence—no more of an ethical dilemma than choosing between shorthand and verbatim note-taking." He conveniently ignores the audience's *perception* of such techniques. Taking notes is overt; secret tape-recording is a *covert* act, a lie of omission.

Clandestine methods are not limited to the investigative reporter. A range of journalists may be tempted to use furtive techniques, some of which may be justified. If a prominent restaurant reviewer booked a restaurant table in her own name, the maître d'hôtel would likely ensure she got the best service and food available with no expense spared—and no bill presented at the end. The reviewer would only be able to write about her experience as "royalty" rather than as a normal customer. Similarly, the travel writer who is identified by tourism officials as such will receive red-carpet treatment at hotels, restaurants and airports. Hence, the journalists are motivated to lie about their identity in the public interest. Yet if they use a false name to apply for a job as a tow-truck operator in order to expose dishonesty in the towing industry, they may be accused of entrapment and of using the same sleazy tricks as their subjects! Question 3 can help us to decide where the line is drawn. Journalists must describe in the stories the techniques they used—and let the audience decide whether the story justified the deceptions.

Few people would fault the media for the "deception" of preserving some people's privacy. For example, "Nancy B." was not the real name of the woman who, paralyzed from the neck down, won the right to have her life-support system turned off so she could die in dignity (in Montreal, February 1992). To refer to her by this pseudonym was neither true nor accurate, but the media took a high ethical road by adopting this fiction instead of publishing her real name.

PICTURE PICK-UPS

The media have long been obsessed with acquiring pictures to illustrate news stories. In the past, reporters were notorious for acquiring pictures at any price, even by lying about their purpose and identity (see, for instance, Sears 1988: 20, 35). Fortunately, the more shameful methods of "picture pick-ups" are now largely condemned. Peter Desbarats (1990: 175) remarks wryly that in his youth the theft of pictures from grieving families, or the telling of lies to obtain pictures, was "so common that the practice almost became part of the funeral ritual." He cites several incidents in his early days as a journalist in Montreal: "Deception was fine if it worked, and if you didn't get caught" (Desbarats 1990: 176).

Values appear to have changed too for the photographers themselves who in the past routinely posed pictures or re-created events (particularly if they arrived late). New technology allows print journalists to massage photographs beyond their wildest dreams. In the electronic darkroom, extraneous details can be removed, compositions changed and separate images blended together. This has led to considerable soul-searching (see Evans 1989; Rogers 1989; and Kenney 1991), but it is by no means a totally new concept.

Photographers have known for years that the camera can lie and have been perfectly comfortable with such image-altering techniques as "pushing" film, using telescopic lenses, "dodging" prints in the darkroom, retouching, masking and cropping.[13] Are such tricks a form of lying and cheating? If the photographer's motive is merely to enhance readers' understanding of the picture, then no harm is done. But if the purpose is to distort, then the media's credibility is seriously injured. Is the art editor comfortable with the thought that the audience might learn that the photograph was posed or electronically distorted?

A similar situation arises when reporters or editors alter quotations. The revision—with hesitations removed or bad grammar corrected—is in fact no longer accurate; it is a lie. But if the change is made only to enhance comprehension, then it may be acceptable. Question 3 applies here. Would the reporter be comfortable facing the source after changing the quote?

When reporters use trickery to obtain their story, it may remind the audience of old Hollywood movies in which reporters "never let the facts get in the way of a good story." The Ontario Press Council condemned a reporter for an Ontario daily, the *Guelph Mercury*, for getting information from a nursing-home official by implying that he wanted to have his mother admitted (*Editor & Publisher* 1993). The implication is that journalists should act ethically, especially if they wish to question other people's ethics. And the public may well dismiss reportage based on trickery. The reporter's motives may have been commendable (uncovering poor hospital practices), but such methods can lead to blanket contempt for all journalists who are seen as willing to stoop to any trickery to "sensationalize" and "sell newspapers."

However, as one researcher argues, dissembling is not usually necessary for good reporters:

> At times it's a tempting option, when you know you can obtain the material you want more quickly and easily by stretching the truth. But my response is that there are so many sources of information available in Canada to anyone that it hardly makes sense to create potential problems for yourself by lying. If one avenue closes to you, there are many more to choose from (Overbury 1985: xiii).[14]

PLAGIARISM

Common to all news media are the pitfalls of plagiarism. Plagiarism involves adopting significant chunks of other people's work and passing them off as one's own. Plagiarism is by nature a lie: it is driven by improper motives, it damages media credibility and it is not something the writer can comfortably confess to readers. It is not only an affront to the writer whose words have been stolen, it deliberately misleads the audience and hence threatens the foundation of trust on which the relationship between journalists and news consumers is built. Plagiarism would disappear if it were (1) clearly defined and banned by newsroom codes and (2) denounced loudly and heavily punished when it occurs.

The theft of other people's words is most likely to occur under three conditions: laziness, desperation or accident. None of these excuse plagiarism, although they may sometimes explain how it occurred.[15]

CONCLUSION

Does the end justify the means? Motives and techniques in news-gathering and reporting must be weighed against audience reaction and the recognition that the audience may not appreciate what is good for it. Nonetheless, good journalists must sometimes employ unconventional or "unethical" techniques when there is no other way to obtain information the public needs. However, it should be easier to identify where to draw the line if journalists first ask themselves *why* they're doing it, what *effect* this will have on their credibility and whether they are comfortable with the audience knowing *how* they did it.

Part Two

Objectivity and Subjectivity: A Useful Dichotomy?

5. An Exaggerated Death: Prefatory Comments on "Objectivity" in Journalism

Robert A. Hackett

The next two chapters, by Yuezhi Zhao and myself and by Rita Deverell, share two potentially controversial characteristics. They take as a problem what many journalists take for granted—the inherent desirability of pursuing objectivity—and suggest that the ethical principles of journalism can themselves raise new ethical problems.

The effort to remain detached and objective can be deceptive, biased, intrusive or otherwise self-defeating. We do not need to perfect our ability to put the existing ethic of objectivity into practice. We need to find new ways to think about and do journalism. To adapt Deverell's language, the next two chapters stand outside the circle of conventional approaches to journalism ethics.

We do not claim to "stand taller" than the many thoughtful journalists who do their best to inform the public under difficult, cynicism-generating circumstances, but we want to question assumptions and practices that are taken for granted in the daily grind of news work. Both chapters question the conventional distinction between "objective" and "advocacy" journalism. At some level, even the most objective journalism privileges some values and interests over others, even if it does not explicitly advocate them.

Both chapters assume that, as an ethical ideal, objectivity is still central to contemporary journalism. This prefatory essay will defend that assumption which, on first glance, looks as antiquated as linotype machines or battered Remingtons. Most journalists consider the term *objectivity* too ambitious and presumptuous and prefer to use terms such as fairness, balance and credibility.

The claim that "Objectivity is impossible because every human being has personal views and biases, but we do try to be fair and balanced" has the ring of a mandatory mantra (see, for example, Stewart 1980: 15). Journalists and scholars argue that objectivity has been discarded in favour of new (if not, in their view, improved) models. As Peter Desbarats (1990: 116) puts it: "Journalism has undergone a revolutionary process in recent decades that parallels . . . the effect of relativity on physics. As scientists abandoned the idea of absolute time, journalists lost faith in the value of objectivity, until then one of the constants of the craft." While Desbarats is less clear about what model has replaced objectivity, David Taras (1990a: 54) gives it a name, "critical journalism." Journalists are encouraged "to comment on as well as report news." Critical journalism has generated a newsroom "culture of disparagement," a pervasive cynicism towards politicians.

Journalism is not the only field in which faith in objective truth and separation of the observer from the observed is waning. We see the same trend in the social sciences and other fields (Anderson 1990). Nevertheless, journalistic objectivity is "a god that won't die": it still obliges reporters to follow its routines (Lind 1990: C, 18). Objectivity may be considered passé but an abundance of (sometimes bitter) arguments keeps it alive. "In defence of objectivity" is a title much-repeated in the recent literature (see Gauthier 1993: 497–506; Lichtenberg 1991: 216–31). Indeed, the ethos of objectivity, broadly conceived, continues to dominate North American journalism. Audiences and sources continue to expect their news to be free from the taint of personal bias. Terms such as "bias" and "objectivity" dominate public discourse. According to the 1980 Royal Commission on Newspapers, more than half the complaints submitted to the Ontario Press Council during its first eight years concerned "the honesty and objectivity of reporting" (Canada 1981: 149).

What about journalists themselves? Academic research based on participant observation, interviews and surveys demonstrates journalists' ongoing (if uneasy) commitment to the practices and criteria of objectivity. In the United States, a 1974 survey (Phillips 1977) found that 98 percent of reporters and editors "virtually defined journalism as adherence to the norm of objectivity"; journalists adopt "habits of mind, attitudes, and personal characteristics which depend on and are structured around the ideal of objective reporting." From her own and other studies, the author concluded that "the norm of objectivity forms the core of the defining logic and mission of news creation." Similarly, in a 1982 survey (Mills 1982), most of the 153 U.S. journalists polled equated ethics with "objective" coverage. The pattern continues into the 1990s: a recent survey (Donsbach and Klett 1993) found that most journalists in the U.S., Britain, Germany and Italy regard objectivity as an "important and indispensable professional value," although their specific definitions vary.

The most important study of news production ever undertaken in Canada confirms the importance of objectivity as a working ideology and a means of public legitimation. Through notions of objectivity, balance and fairness, journalists try "to be sensitive to the possible impact of their work" (Ericson, Baranek and Chan 1987: 104; also see Ericson, Baranek and Chan 1989). The ideal of objectivity continues to dominate journalism schools, ethics textbooks and written ethics codes. The code of ethics of the U.S. Society of Professional Journalists, Sigma Delta Chi, highlights objectivity as "the mark of an experienced professional," a "standard of performance toward which we strive." Subsequent points stress accuracy, the separation of news from opinion and advocacy, and nonpartisanship—all components of the ethic of objectivity.[1]

The Canadian Broadcasting Corporation's 136-page manual of journalistic policy (1982: 6–7) identifies accuracy, integrity, fairness and thoroughness as cornerstone principles which taken together "will achieve the optimum objectivity and balance which must characterize CBC's information programs." Although the statement of principles adopted in 1977 by the Canadian Daily Newspaper Publishers Association (now the CDNA) did not actually mention "objectivity," it did emphasize independence from any obligation "save that of fidelity to the public good," comprehensiveness, accuracy and (especially) "fairness" which includes "balanced presentation of relevant facts and substantial opinions, as well as clear distinction between news reports and expressions of opinion" (in Desbarats 1990: 231–32). The CDNA recently abandoned this code of ethics but not because it has dropped objectivity in favour of a public commitment to alternative ideals.

Does the word "fairness," currently in fashion, imply a fundamental departure from the ethics and practices of "objectivity"? It does allow greater recognition of subjectivity in news judgment—somebody has to decide what constitutes fair treatment and who deserves it. But on the whole, as American political scientist Lance Bennett (1988: 124–27) argues, "fairness" is simply old wine in new rhetorical bottles and has not led to new journalistic practices. The same can be said of the latest buzzword, "credibility"—surely, the credibility of news reports is grounded in accuracy, fairness and impartiality.

What about so-called "attack," "adversarial" or "critical" journalism? Has it supplanted objectivity as a dominant paradigm? In the years following the Vietnam War, the Watergate scandal and the ascendancy of television, journalists have been more likely to search for scandals and to criticize politicians, as compared with the 1950s, when "objectivity" led to uncritical reporting of Senator Joseph McCarthy's baseless accusations (Westell 1980).

However, it can be argued that post-Watergate adversarial journalism is ritualistic, superficial and highly personalized (Bennett 1988: 124–27). It victimizes politicians who do not play the game well, for example, former Prime Minister Joe Clark, who was saddled with a media-amplified "wimp" image in the 1970s. Rarely does adversarial journalism fundamentally challenge the image-making and agenda-setting power of political and business elites. Indeed, it could not take a consistently hostile and skeptical stance without undermining the credibility of its own news-gathering net which relies heavily on official and political sources (Tuchman 1978: 87). A "journalism of deference" characterizes news in North America (Dorman and Farhang 1987; see also Hertsgaard 1989). "Critical journalism" is less a contradictory alternative to objectivity than an aspect of it. The journalist is a "politically neutral adversary," an independent watchdog on whatever government is in power (Bennett 1988: 120).

To be fair, objectivity is not a single, unitary ethic. One research team (Donsbach and Klett 1993) identified four possible meanings (each with support among journalists): (1) negation of journalists' subjectivity, (2) fair representation of each side in a controversy, (3) balanced skepticism towards all sides in a dispute and (4) the search for "hard facts" with which to contextualize a dispute. Journalism has evolved considerably during the twentieth century, especially since the arrival of television and the upheavals of the 1960s. We see less naive positivism, less acceptance of the self-evident nature of facts, greater tolerance for a broader range of approaches to covering the news and more scope for the voices of reporters themselves. Journalism has become more explicitly interpretive. It is driven by commercial television's entertainment imperatives and audiences' demands for easy and understandable answers, instead of merely "balanced" presentations of "both sides," as they try to cope with a complex world. Promotional slogans for CTV National News and Vancouver's BCTV News promise to "make sense" of your world for you. During Canada's 1988 free-trade debate, viewers of CBC television news begged the network to provide, not a wealth of information objectively presented, but a definitive verdict: "Is free trade a good thing or not?"

And yet very few journalists would want to be accused of lacking objectivity. Media historian and sociologist Michael Schudson (1978: 193) sees "a hope for something new, a simmering disaffection with objective reporting," and yet "no new ideal in journalism to successfully challenge objectivity." The alternative models of advocacy and investigative journalism spawned in the 1960s and 1970s have not displaced it. With apparent disappointment, Robert Miraldi (1990: 14), a journalism professor and former reporter, describes objectivity as:

> the fuel that fires journalism's engine, an ideal and an ideology. It is the way a

> reporter approaches his [sic] sources, his material, and his public . . . the hidden frame of reference around which the American press organizes its existence . . . an unwritten guide book . . . passed on, unquestioningly, from one generation of journalists to another. To some it is a god and to others a devil.

But none can escape it because (as the next chapter affirms) the objectivity ethic meets deeply embedded social, economic and political needs.

Hackett and Zhao sketch some of the main criticisms of the objectivity ethos and argue that the current crisis of democracy further calls into question its adequacy as a framework for journalism. Whereas Hackett and Zhao write in broad strokes about objectivity, Deverell provides flesh and blood cases that demonstrate the inevitability—and value—of subjectivity. Deverell offers thought-provoking exercises for individual journalists; Hackett and Zhao sketch general directions for change. But readers should be forewarned: neither chapter is intended to provide a blueprint for journalism. Instead, the authors show how clinging to objectivity makes it hard to recognize the values and standpoints inherent in the apparently neutral practice of news reporting.

6. Are Ethics Enough?: "Objective" Journalism versus Sustainable Democracy[1]

Robert A. Hackett and Yuezhi Zhao

Journalism ethics is a hot topic these days. It is actively debated in a variety of venues: media watchdog institutes, professional conferences and seminars, journalism courses and the *Journal of Mass Media Ethics*. How are we to understand this vogue? One possibility is to see debates about journalism ethics as a movement, a platform for critiquing and reforming the practice of journalism. Although advocates of ethical reform are diverse, many would agree that:

- journalism does not serve the public interest as well as it could; as a vehicle for informing the public, it has significant failings;
- these shortcomings could be overcome if journalists would consistently and conscientiously apply sound ethical principles in their workaday decisions and practices; and
- whether as written codes or implicit criteria, ethical principles are understood and shared by journalists; the task of journalism is to live up to its own highest ideals.

The authors of this chapter are skeptical of the ability of journalism ethics, as conventionally defined, to bring about needed reform. We critically assess the above assumptions. We question the extent to which a reform movement based on existing ethical principles can revitalize public discourse and a sustainable democratic polity. We focus on objectivity, still a key aspect of contemporary journalism ethics. And we argue for the replacement of traditional ideals with a new paradigm, with new sensibilities and structures, ideals and institutions.

Assumptions of the Ethical Reform Movement

Critics point to many ways in which the news media system skews or filters out publicly relevant information. Among the structural causes of inadequate information are: concentration of media ownership; cutbacks in news-gathering resources resulting from recession and (in the United States) deregulation; reliance on official and institutional sources; the technological biases of television; and advertising priorities which lead to trivialized, sensationalized and entertainment-focused coverage.

There is a good deal of evidence suggesting that media often fail to inform the public about significant issues. During the 1991 Gulf War, one study found heavy TV viewers less informed about the background of the war than light or non-viewers. While it is not fair to accuse television of *causing* ignorance, at the very least it failed to give its viewers the "whole picture" (Morgan, Lewis and Jhally 1992). Another example: each year since 1976, Project Censored in the U.S. has identified important stories which were ignored by the major news media. The stories range from misspent tax dollars to issues of environment and health, stories whose dissemination is not in the interests of powerful institutions such as governments, the military, large corporations, media advertisers or news organizations themselves (Jensen 1993). Given their structural similarities with U.S. media (not to mention heavy reliance on U.S. news agencies), there is little reason to believe that Canadian media perform much better.[2]

To be sure, some would argue that the media system works because, through the logic of market competition, it "gives people what they want." After all, media audiences do not rise en masse from their sofas to demand radical reform. However, defence of the status quo has its blind spots. The economic logic of some media industries, such as newspapers, leads to monopoly rather than consumer choice through competition.

Media ownership is increasingly concentrated in the hands of multinational, multimedia conglomerates. Media content serves the interests of the affluent consumers whom advertisers most want to reach, leaving others relatively disenfranchised. In a culture which promotes privatized spectatorship and discourages political participation, media users seek gratifications other than relevant civic information and act more like consumers than citizens (Bagdikian 1992). The relative homogeneity of major media, their domination of the public agenda and their tendency to report their own shortcomings less vigorously than those of other institutions leave media audiences unaware of the need for alternatives.

The second assumption of the ethical reform movement—that it is up to journalists to improve their craft through more ethical practices—is more problematic. It lays the blame for journalism's shortcomings too directly at the feet of journalists. There is no reason to believe that journalists as individuals behave less ethically than do police, doctors or professors. One Canadian journalism educator contends that journalists' increased educational levels and "deepening interest in questions of professional conduct" have led to the demise of the "outrageous abuses" once common in mainstream North American journalism (Desbarats 1990). More important, this second assumption of the ethical reform movement implies that journalists themselves are the dominant force moulding the news product, but they ignore the structures which limit their autonomy and creativity. The "vocabulary of precedents" which journalists learn through newsroom practice may have more to do with the organizational imperatives of the corporations which employ them than with abstract ethical principles (Ericson, Baranek and Chan 1987). By focusing on journalists' behaviour, the rhetoric of ethical reform may divert attention from addressing important questions about the structure of news media (see, for example, Desbarats 1990: Chapter 8).

The biggest problem with the ethical reform movement is its third assumption, that existing ethical codes (written or implicit) offer the basis for improved journalism. Even if journalistic practice followed these codes, it would not necessarily be for the better. Much depends on which principles and assumptions journalism ethics endorses, and on what one believes about the ends towards which journalism ought to be aimed.

Part of the problem is that the observance of ethics may have unintended and undesirable consequences. For example: ethical journalism respects the privacy of law-abiding organizations and individuals who are not in public life, and actively pursues the "watchdog" function of scrutinizing potential abuses of power by government, an institution accountable to the public. Followed too vigorously, those ethical obligations may have contributed to the delegitimization of government and to the lack of critical scrutiny and public knowledge of the power wielded by private sector corporations.[3]

That example leads to the central argument of this chapter, that journalistic ethics, as they are currently understood, sometimes serve (however unwittingly) to reinforce undemocratic or destructive power relations in our society. To make this argument, we focus paradoxically on the ethic of objectivity, an ethic grounded in the independence of Canadian journalism from special interests.

WHAT IS THE ETHIC OF OBJECTIVITY?

Objectivity remains one of the central commandments of North American journalism, part of its defining ethos. It is actually a complex and wide-ranging ethic which can be broken down into components.

First, objectivity is most often thought of as a normative ideal, a set of desired goals towards which journalism should aim. These goals in turn can be broken down into several components, with implications for the stance and methods the journalist adopts in writing stories, as well as for the characteristics of the story itself. The first ideal of journalism is accuracy, factuality, completeness and relevance: a journalist should seek to tell the truth. Second, the journalist should take a stance of detachment, impartiality and independence, avoiding partisanship, the intrusion of personal biases or undue influence from outside interests. Third, an objective news account is fair, even-handed and balanced in presenting different sides of a contentious issue.

These ideals imply an epistemology, a theory of knowledge: it is possible to separate facts from values and the observer from the observed, so it is possible in principle to reflect and report the world as it is (on the meanings of objectivity, see, for example, McQuail 1992: 184–86, 196–204).

The ethic of objectivity also entails a set of news-gathering and presentation practices or "uniform technical criteria" (Ericson, Baranek and Chan 1987) which evolve and shift over time and differ between different media. Some of the contemporary practices considered to be hallmarks of objectivity can be summarized (Bennett 1988: 120; Hackett 1991: 81–84; also see Tuchman 1971/72):

- In selecting individuals to provide information and comments for a story, the journalist is expected to seek appropriate sources: those who have accredited knowledge, are recognized representatives of the relevant institutions and/or are personally directly involved in the story.
- The objective journalist avoids sensationalism, observes prevailing standards of decency and good taste and deploys "documentary reporting practices that permit reporters to give the public only what they can observe or support with physical evidence" and "only the facts that credible sources have confirmed" (Bennett 1988: 120).
- Objective journalism takes care to separate such observable facts from the opinions or evaluations of the journalist; these are confined to specialized genres such as columns, features and documentaries.

- As far as possible, straight news reports are descriptions of facts, or opinions, clearly attributed (often in point/counterpoint format) to relevant speakers and "authorized knowers." "Historical or explanatory frameworks which give an explicit interpretive basis (and bias) for construing truth" are often bracketed out (Ericson, Baranek and Chan 1989: 15).
- The journalist downplays his or her role as narrator of the news story, which is the standardized format for packaging the news (Ericson, Baranek and Chan 1987: 105).

The practices and ideals of journalistic objectivity (the argument goes) are nurtured within an institutional framework consisting of complex, specialized news organizations. Their roles and departments are compartmentalized (the marketing and advertising departments over there, the newsroom pristinely over here), they are staffed by professionals with appropriate skills and ethical commitments and they enjoy autonomy from the state (which in classical libertarian press theory is the main potential threat to freedom of the press).

That autonomy is reinforced by legal guarantees of freedom of the press, while the provision of revenue from advertisers and media audiences makes the commercial media more responsive to consumers and less vulnerable to pressure from the state.[4] (As a Crown corporation, the CBC is heavily dependent on state revenue but it has a legal mandate to operate at arm's length from the government.) Thus, it would seem that if journalists will only conscientiously observe the ethic of objectivity, the public will be able to make the informed political judgments essential to democratic self-government, based on a flow of relevant and impartial information and analysis.

It does not take a professional cynic to suggest that something is wrong with this picture. Over the years, the ethics and practices of objectivity have attracted an impressive array of critics both within and outside journalism. Their principle arguments against objectivity are summarized below.

OBJECTIVITY AS DECEPTION

Many critics say objectivity in journalism is a deception because it cannot live up to its (at least implicit) claim to provide truthful and comprehensive representations of the social and political world. As media theorist Denis McQuail puts it, objective news implies an "unwritten contract" which leads the news consumer to expect that "news can be believed, trusted, taken at face value, readily understood, without the need to 'read between the lines'" (McQuail 1992: 187). Sometimes the contract is explicit: CTV anchor Lloyd Robertson's sign-off phrase, "That's the kind of day it's been," is only somewhat less confident of its purported omniscience than Walter Cronkite's byword a generation ago: "And that's the way it is."

The claim that news simply reflects and reports "the way it is" can be challenged on several grounds. First, the ethic of objectivity does not rule uncontested over news discourse. Powerful external and internal pressures and limits applied to news production "are almost bound to deflect journalism from any ideal goal of recounting 'truth'" (McQuail 1992: 187). Audiences expect news to be entertaining and reassuring as well as true. Sources want the news to reflect their agendas. Journalists look to news as a source of income and social status. Advertisers regard news media as vehicles to reach potential consumers. Owners want the news to be profitable. Sometimes news organizations abandon the principle of impartiality and take up particular causes (Ericson, Baranek and Chan 1991: 174). News is produced—some would say manufactured—within organizations which must negotiate these and other pressures (Fishman 1980).

Even if such pressures and expectations could be made to serve the search for truth, we would still be left with the subjectivity inherent in the process of news selection. Whether or not a political or other agenda is at work, the dominant criteria of newsworthiness or "news values" have their own biases. For example, they favour single events over long-term processes, electoral politics over extra-parliamentary alternatives and drama, conflict and photogenic destruction over substantive significance (see Hartley 1980: 75–86; and Hackett 1991: 76–80).

The mere necessity of selecting from millions of potential sources and events means that news cannot possibly give an exhaustive or complete account of the social and political world. Of course, telling the news involves much more than mere selection, as if there were a pre-given menu of events, sources and issues from which to choose. A much more active process of providing frames of reference is required if the news is to make sense to its readers, listeners and viewers.

Usually implicit, such frames comprise "persistent patterns of cognition, interpretation, and presentation, of selection, emphasis, and exclusion, by which symbol-handlers routinely organize discourse" (Gitlin 1980: 7). The meanings of events are not inherent or self-evident; events are given meaning by being placed in "appropriate" contexts. These frames are most evident in headlines, in the juxtaposition of news stories under common themes, in the news angles and themes emphasized and the assumptions taken for granted within individual stories. Such framing devices are cues which invite the reader to accept the "preferred readings" embedded in news accounts. Most important, the frames are unavoidable in a storytelling format and they work to exclude or marginalize alternative ways of interpreting or contextualizing the same event.

The problem of implicit evaluation in news accounts is further compounded by a related problem: (usually unintentional) biases in the language used to label actions and actors. To their credit, many journalists are well aware of this kind of problem. Should they call certain protagonists "terrorists" or "freedom-fighters," "strikebreakers" or "replacement workers," "environmentalists" or "anti-loggers"? Are the picketers outside the abortion clinic "pro-life," "anti-choice" or "anti-abortion"? Is Belfast in Ulster or Northern Ireland? Should Canadian soldiers in the Persian Gulf be called "our" troops? Such choices can only be made on the basis of judgments about what exists, what is important, what is good or bad and what is related to what (Gerbner and Signorielli 1978: 192). Thus, reality judgements and normative values unavoidably intrude upon the selection of events, words and interpretive contexts. They undermine the claim—implicit in the objectivity creed—that news should simply "reflect" the world as it is and present "facts" rather than interpretations, values or ideology (Golding and Elliott 1979).[5] There are further epistemological problems concerning the ethic of objectivity. Journalists sometimes confront contradictory demands and one aspect of objectivity (e.g., accuracy, the non-distortion of reality) must be sacrificed to another (e.g., balance). In the 1980 federal election campaign, Liberal leader Pierre Trudeau made far fewer appearances than his two main rivals. "Balanced" television exposure of the candidates would have "distorted" the strategies and progress of the campaign (which is precisely what the

Liberals counted on the networks to do) (Gilsdorf and Bernier 1981: 64).

Some critics also see an incompatibility between balance and accuracy at a more theoretical level:

> A relativist, Mannheimian epistemology underlies the notion that bias is avoided by balancing between competing, incompatible worldviews, each with its own (limited and partial) validity. By contrast, the goal of avoiding distortion implies a positivistic, nonrelativist affirmation of the ultimate knowability of "the straight facts," whose visibility is temporarily obscured by the biased journalist (Hackett 1984: 233).

As it is often presented, the ethic of objectivity implies that the media can stand as detached observers, outside the events they report. "We don't make the news, we just report it," goes a standard defence. Journalists are increasingly (and sometimes uncomfortably) aware that such a defence is untenable: media are active participants in the social and political world. Many news reports are based on "pseudo-events" pre-planned or incited for the purpose of being reported (Boorstin 1980). Some observers say politics has become "an extension of media production" (Altheide and Snow 1979: 146). Media reports of "mugging" sensitized the public and authorities to this apparently new type of crime, generating an upsurge of "mugging" incidents in police statistics and a "moral panic" over the issue in British society (Hall et al. 1978).

Some social constructionist/deconstructionist critics take such doubts about the ability of news to reflect the world much further. They break radically with the very idea of objectivity, whether in journalism, science or any other field. In this view, there is no knowable, objective, pre-given reality to report and reflect; reality is a social product and it can only be apprehended (constructed?) through language, through interpretive and cognitive frameworks which engender their own criteria of truth and relevance. We have no independent, objective way of judging whether one framework is more adequate to the real than another. We are left with a relativist cognitive universe of endlessly shifting and competing texts, narratives and sign-systems. In this universe, there is no way to judge whether survivors of the Holocaust or neo-Nazis who deny its occurrence provide a more accurate account of what actually happened. In the words of one (otherwise quite useful) communications textbook, reality is simply "the sense or product of discourse" (O'Sullivan et al. 1983: 194).

We do not take this relativist position, currently fashionable in post-modernist academia. That argument overprivileges the status of language, collapsing the world into the word. It is logically self-contradictory: in claiming to offer a valid account of how language-in-the-world works, it surreptitiously depends upon the possibility of objective knowledge at the very moment that it denies it.

We accept, in principle, the possibility of valid (though never infallible) knowledge of the social world. However, language and the media, help actively to construct our perceptions of the world; they do not and cannot function as transparent reflections of reality.[6] We recognize that the process of news selection and construction is inherently value-laden; the practices labelled "objective journalism" do not yield news "from nobody's point of view," as a former president of CBS News Richard S. Salant once claimed (Epstein 1973). In that sense, the ethic of objectivity can indeed be described as deceptive.

OBJECTIVITY AS CONSERVATIVE

The other dominant critique of objectivity is linked to an analysis of journalism as (sometimes unwittingly) reinforcing dominant social relations, hegemonic worldviews and/or established power holders. The ethic of objectivity is attacked either because it disguises this arguably repressive role of journalism or because it is an active part of it.

How can Canadian journalism, which proclaims its impartiality and independence from the state, be implicated in legitimizing established power? We have already noted that the process of constructing news accounts is inescapably selective. Events to report, sources to quote, language to describe and frames to interpret are all selected (consciously or otherwise) from a potential infinity of alternatives. Critical analysts argue that, in practice, a narrow range of values, interests and reality-judgments structure and inform those choices, and such choices tend to reinforce existing arrangements of power.

For instance, the content of commercial media disproportionately massages the relatively conservative sensibilities of affluent consumers, the people advertisers are most keen to reach (Bagdikian 1992, Chapter 6). Such class bias helps to explain why upper-middle-income "tax revolts" get much more media play than the ongoing hardship of the genuinely poor. However, this is not necessarily the result of conscious editorial decisions to appeal to affluent consumers. Rather, in major media, it is reinforced by the social milieu of journalists themselves. When the Vancouver press crusaded against (and helped to reverse) a 1993 attempt by B.C.'s NDP government to increase property taxes on the tiny minority of houses worth over $400,000, a study by journalism students revealed that many of the *Vancouver Sun*'s top managers and columnists themselves owned such homes (Roberts 1993: 30).

Through their everyday routines, news media construct a hierarchy of access: the leaders of dominant political parties and the officials of established institutions are privileged as sources to the point where they become the "primary definers" of public issues (Hall et al. 1978, Chapter 3). And in selecting events to transform into news stories (or even defining what counts as an "event" in the first place), news organizations are routinely oriented towards the "phase structures" of other bureaucratic organizations. Thus crime, for example, is covered as a set of individual cases structured by the police and judicial bureaucracies, each beginning with a reported crime and an arrest, and ending with a trial verdict—to the exclusion of, for instance, the treatment of prisoners in their cells or the patterns of social violence and deprivation which generate crime (Fishman 1980).

To be sure, the operations of objective journalism sometimes embarass or even help to overthrow individual politicians and lead to hostile coverage of particular government policies. But—and this is crucial—the news values which guide the selection of events also amplify a presumed consensus around basic social values: possessive individualism, representative liberal democracy, welfare-state capitalism (with a growing emphasis on capitalism and a diminishing emphasis on the welfare state) and the national myth of Canada as a tolerant, caring society at home and a peacekeeper abroad. What counts as news are events which dramatically confirm, violate or threaten those values (Hartley 1980).

One of the consequences of this assumption of consensus is that oppositional social actors who want to challenge the nature of this consensus publicly find themselves marginalized and denigrated. They are pressured to moderate their stance, abandon radical, systemic critiques and package their grievances as minor reforms which can be managed by the existing political and economic system (Gitlin 1980: 290–91; Robinson 1993: 64).

The dominant values of free enterprise and liberal democracy are the touchstone for dividing news stories into the three categories or "spheres" of consensus, legitimate controversy and deviance (Hallin 1986: 116–18). The narrative conventions of objectivity (careful attribution of quotes to sources, the counterbalancing of spokespersons for "both" sides) are applicable to the sphere of controversy. But in covering events and social actors assumed to represent values shared by the entire community, journalists have more latitude to set the scene sympathetically and in their own words, to indulge in supportive narrative embellishment (Hackett 1991: 250). Coverage of Rick Hansen's round-the-world wheelchair odyssey exemplifies a consensual story. The key point is that the borderlines separating the three spheres are politically and ideologically charged and contested; and they are established by those with the greatest power to make their definitions of political and social reality stick. It makes a great deal of difference whether Paul Watson's "direct action" environmentalism is narrated as a form of "terrorism" (i.e., placing it within the sphere of deviance) or as a legitimate form of protest. In general, the institutions of liberal democracy and the principles of the marketplace are assumed to be consensual values, so opponents of these values are cast into the realm of deviance. Through that process, news tends to equate liberal democracy and capitalism and to "naturalize" both, representing them as above and beyond history, as the natural state of affairs to which all rational people would conform if they had the choice. The hubris of this assumption was fairly evident in North American media coverage of the collapse of the Soviet bloc (Hackett 1991: 283–95).

The media's definition of politics has a "conservatizing" bias. Anglo-Canadian journalism is oriented towards political events and things and, for two centuries, Parliament has been its most important topic (Adam 1976). Indeed, *politics* is virtually defined in the news as Parliamentary politics and electoral competition, a definition which is consistent with other news values (conflict, personalities, elites and drama) and with the classical liberal assumption that power resides in the state's formal institutions of political representation, institutions that are separated from the economy, domestic life and so on (Hackett 1991: 79–80).

This liberal equation of power, democracy and representative electoral politics has two critical ideological consequences. First, groups "which may exert power but which do not make news disappear, by definition, from view, and with them the visibility of power itself. Prominent among the absentees are the owners of property and their corporate representatives" (Golding and Elliott 1979: 210). Second, the conflation of democracy with electoral politics implies that the non-electoral forms of politics undertaken by oppositional social movements are merely theatrical, irrelevant or even irrational and illegitimate (Schlesinger 1978: 168).

In all these ways, news representations tend to reinforce dominant values and interests. Other critics go further, to attack not only representations in the news but also the social relations reinforced by "objective" journalism. As a culturally important form of storytelling, news implicitly addresses or positions its audiences in certain ways.

Typically, mass-market journalism invites its audiences to think of themselves as consumers. This invitation is most evident in the advertisements and in the pseudo-editorial material designed to service advertisers (such as the travel, automotive or real estate sections of a typical North American daily newspaper). But it is also evident in assumptions embedded in straight news accounts—for example, that the most newsworthy aspect of industrial disputes is the disruption of consumer goods and services (Hackett 1983).

Television news (and perhaps the mass press) also positions its audiences as political spectators, not protagonists, who are "done to" by politicians and special interest groups. News achieves this ideological positioning not by violating the norms of objectivity but precisely through them, by presenting itself as a neutral, impartial observer and/or interlocutor of the powerful on behalf of the people (Connell 1980). Such positioning of media audiences is also conservatizing because it displaces alternative ways of thinking about ourselves (as workers, as political beings) that could facilitate popular political mobilization (McQuail 1992: 188; Lichtenberg 1991: 228).

Political mobilization is further inhibited by the rhetoric and practices of news "balance" and impartiality which implicitly devalue strong political commitment (as well as engaged journalism). If the journalist truly balances between contending views (the argument goes), the news consumer may have no rational way to decide between them, and thus balance ends up promoting political cynicism, skepticism and apathy.

Other critics suggest that the (apparently) equal, balanced presentation of "both sides" of an issue has other conservatizing effects: it favours familiar, conventional views over those which are less familiar to audiences, it often reduces complex issues to a simplistic for/against format and it allows elite voices (e.g., government and opposition party leaders) to define the limits of debate (Bennett 1988: 119; Hackett, Gilsdorf and Savage 1992: 28; Cook and Ruggles 1992: 37–59).

The above-mentioned conservatizing effects certainly do not result from a conspiracy or even from conscious intentions. Nor do they result from violations of the ethic of objectivity. To the contrary, they are often a by-product of that ethic, as it is conventionally understood and practised. Journalists collectively construct a hierarchy of access in the news by conscientiously following the requirement to use "appropriate" sources for their stories. It just so happens that the sources who are most available, articulate, convenient and apparently authoritative are usually spokespersons or decision-makers in powerful institutions (Gans 1980).

The critiques of objectivity as deception and as conservative legitimation are thus linked. "Objective" journalism systematically produces partial and ideological representations of the world while disguising or "hiding" that ideological role from its audiences and even its practitioners.

The appearance of objectivity helps to gain the trust of media audiences, and thereby wins their consent to the "preferred readings" which are unavoidably embedded in the news. The claim to be offering objective news also helps media owners to justify their oligopolistic domination of the public sphere and thereby pre-empt government regulation, meaningful public accountability and effective competition from radically "alternative" media.

Given its limitations, why does the ethic of objectivity retain such dominance over the ways news is produced by journalists and understood by audiences? In part, the answer lies in the attractiveness of "objective journalism" by comparison with the flagrantly partisan press of the last century and the authoritarian control of the media in many countries today. More specifically, objectivity, however unevenly and unequally, meets some deeply entrenched political, economic and social needs for various constituencies in the news system. Historically, the triumph of "objective journalism" over the partisan papers of the nineteenth century was associated with the commercialization of the press and its pursuit of mass audiences to deliver to advertisers.

"Objective journalism" serves the interests of media owners and advertisers by rendering the media acceptable to broad audiences. For journalists, as for other middle-class occupational groups (doctors, lawyers, academics), objectivity enhances the claim to professional status and provides a set of "strategic rituals" to protect them from the hazards of their trade, such as missed deadlines, libel suits and the wrath of sources and superiors (Tuchman 1971/72: 660–79).

The routines of objectivity sometimes provide openings for interest groups and social movements to make self-interested interventions in public discourse (Hackett 1991: 279). Those routines also help to define and manage the symbiotic relationship between news media and the state: politicians acquire access to the media's mass audiences, journalists acquire access to political sources and media organizations are granted a stable legal and political environment (Hallin 1986: 68–70).

Media audiences buy into the objectivity paradigm. Although audience members may express skepticism about individual stories or news outlets, there is also a deep-seated need to believe in the truth and authenticity of news (Bennett 1988: 186–87). To acknowledge that news may be systematically limited or distorted is psychologically discomfiting. It would require one to renounce a convenient and accessible map to a confusing world, reserve judgement, admit ignorance and reject the taken-for-granted pool of knowledge shared with neighbours and co-workers. It would mean recognizing that understanding requires intellectual labour more demanding than the consumption of pre-packaged images and narratives.

The ethic of objectivity was not always so closely wedded to prevailing interests; it once had a quite forward-looking, progressive function. In both the U.S. (from the 1820s and 1830s) and in Canada (later in the nineteenth century), the origins of the objectivity ethic can be traced to the democratic Enlightenment discourse of the emerging labour press, with its demands that both the state and the press should represent the universal interests of all citizens. While that discourse had its own limitations and was eventually taken over and domesticated by the popular commercial dailies of the late 1800s, the labour press helped to bring about a "paradigm shift" from below. Its demands for representation of the popular interest in both press and politics eroded the authoritarian toryism of Canada's political culture and the elite partisan press system of the time (Repo 1986; Schiller 1981). We argue that contemporary North American journalism needs a similar paradigm shift from below if it is to contribute positively to viable democracy in the twenty-first century.

Journalism and the Dual Crisis of Democracy

Journalism is not and cannot be value-free. In the Western world, it has been linked historically to the eighteenth-century emergence of a middle-class public in Europe and North America, and to the achievement (and containment) of democracy within an industrial capitalist social order. Underlying its apparent cynicism and apoliticism, North American media reportage of the political world continues to be informed by "enduring values" which include (in U.S. sociologist Herbert Gans' (1980) analysis) ethnocentrism, altruistic democracy, responsible capitalism, individualism, moderatism, social order and national leadership—the values of nation-state-centred liberal-democratic capitalism.

Can the creed of objectivity contribute positively to the prospects for viable, sustainable democracy in the twenty-first century or does journalism need a new model? Because North American journalism is deeply embedded in the values and sensibilities of liberal-democratic capitalism, the question must be answered in the context of stresses on and contradictions within that social order, stresses which add up to a crisis of global proportions.

The ideological biases of North America's objective news media were thrown into sharp relief by the way they covered the end of the Cold War and the collapse of the Soviet empire. The media celebrated and naturalized capitalism ("free market economies") and representative liberal democracy (equated with "democracy" per se) as the only possible positive future for humanity (Hackett 1991: 283–95; Hallin 1992: 68–70). In that celebration, the media fell into binary reasoning: if communism doesn't work, then capitalism does—the product of not only Cold War logic but centuries of Manicheanism and dualism in Western philosophical thought.

But it doesn't follow. The media's celebration of the inevitable spread of liberal democracy, bringing about the end of history (in the words of a celebrated article by Francis Fukuyama), is premature to say the least. Capitalism can co-exist with authoritarian regimes, and it should be abundantly clear by now that there is no necessary relationship between market economies and political democracy. Equally important, that celebration turns a blind eye to serious flaws and contradictions in liberal-democratic capitalism, flaws which may not be resolvable within the limits of the system. Long-standing criticisms of liberal capitalism by both its traditional conservative and its socialist opponents have increased urgency in an era of "globalization" and "rationalization."

To be sure, the old conservatives were defending hierarchy and privilege, deference and difference; but they rightly sensed that liberalism assumes the universal applicability of market relations which corrode more "traditional" human values of family, community, place, ethics and mutual obligation outside the framework of financial gain. In subordinating all aspects of human life to the logic of market relations, commodity exchange and capital accumulation, in making continual and ever-quickening technological progress compulsory, in establishing liberalism as virtually an official ideology (by making acceptance of its assumptions a precondition for admission to the public forum), in homogenizing cultures and colonizing the imagination around the world, liberalism has even been identified by some of its critics as a new form of totalitarianism (Portis 1988). Unlike the old, inefficient totalitarianism, with its secret police and torture chambers, the new totalitarianism achieves the subordination of all aspects of human society to a single principle by capturing consent.

The brutality and bankruptcy of Stalinism does not invalidate the socialist critique of liberalism's virtual equation of freedom with ownership of property. Acquisitive and possessive individualism is the ideological by-product of a system which structurally (and increasingly on a global scale) produces massive poverty as the counterpart of extreme concentration of wealth. Capitalism has few frontiers left to conquer. Transnational corporations operate globally; some of them command resources greater than the GDP of most countries. Yet billions of people live in conditions of desperate emiseration. The socialist vision of citizenship as including access to basic human necessities remains as relevant as ever.

Citizenship based on nation-states is not enough. The nation-state is increasingly incapable of carrying the burdens of citizenship and political obligation or of effectively addressing the central dilemmas of contemporary life. Like most other political ideologies, liberalism assumes the nation-state is the repository of political virtue, the guarantor of rights and security, the container of political life (for example, see Walker 1988).

The nation-state faces dissolution from above, brought about by the process of "globalization" and the associated growth and power of unaccountable, hierarchical supranational organizations and arrangements which represent elite interests (IMF, NAFTA, the proverbial Trilateral Commission, etc.), and disintegration from below, brought about by the growing chaos in many third world countries, by the growing millions of effectively stateless refugees and "guest" workers and by the upsurge of racism, ethnicism and micronationalism in many countries, including Europe and North America.

Ecology identifies a third crucial blind spot of liberalism: it has no notion of the limits to growth. It assumes the limitless expansion of human wants and the continual acquisition of property and consumer goods. We live in an economy predicated upon perpetual expansion, and liberalism is its ideological grease. Yet we are also witnessing a continuing crisis of the overconsumption and degradation of global resources and environment, a crisis built into the logic of capitalism, technological progress and dominant models of "development" in the third world.

Another blind spot is suggested by feminist theory. Neither the notion of elected, representative institutions as the embodiment of the public sphere nor the definitions of individual rights in the private sphere addresses the political economy of the domestic household, the exploitation of women's labour and, for many decades after the triumph of liberal democracy, the exclusion of women from the body politic (through denial of suffrage and full legal rights).

A further critique sees liberal democracy as insufficiently democratic—partly because of the discrepancy, oft noted by socialists, between formal legal and political equality, on the one hand, and substantive inequalities of social class, on the other. A related critique argues that the political institutions of contemporary liberal democracies (parties, elections, parliaments) sharply curtail the opportunities for genuine political participation; they have become simply mechanisms by which citizens can at best select candidates and parties from a narrow range of alternatives.

Once in power, those parties are in turn so strongly influenced by the society's most powerful unelected elites (e.g., the corporate elite) and structural forces (e.g., the debt crisis of the capitalist state) that they can no longer function as popular representatives (see Miliband 1973; Wallace and Miliband 1975). North America's recent populist revolts, notably those of Ross Perot in the U.S. and the Reform Party in Canada, are partly products of a political malaise, of a perceived gap between the system's democratic legitimation and its actual performance.

No list of crises would be complete without noting the diffusion and deepening of militarism in many parts of the world, and the spread of intrastate conflict in the ex-Soviet bloc and elsewhere. While such conflict cannot be blamed entirely on Western capitalism, it is exacerbated by the search by Western arms merchants for new export markets, now that the Soviet empire no longer provides a rationale for military spending; and it indicates the unpreparedness of international security organizations (chiefly NATO and the U.N.) to deal with ethnic and regional conflict in a post–Cold War world.

These crises are expanding and deepening along with the process of globalization and the triumph of market relations over alternative social and cultural logics throughout the world. Globalization may be undermining people's sense of place in the world and sense of control over their communities and destinies. It helps to produce crises of meaning, identity, values and community—and backlashes of micronationalism, racism and fundamentalist religion which claim to reassert traditional identities.

Such backward-looking and destructive forms of reaction to globalization remind us not to throw out the liberal-democratic baby with the multinational-corporate bathwater. Liberal democracy contains principles (such as the rule of law, equality before the law, respect for individual human dignity and rights, representative democracy as the accountability of government to the governed, and the right to participate in choosing those who rule us) which are significant achievements of human civilization. Liberalism, like any effective ideology, does contain a utopian kernel, a vision of human emancipation: freedom, equality and fraternity (Jameson 1981). Not only is liberal democracy unlikely to achieve its own historically professed ideals, it is not even likely to survive unless the global system's fundamental crises are addressed far more vigorously than at present. Meaningful human survival requires sustainable economies within a new global civic society, which cannot be realized without a complex popular project of reinvigorating the best of liberal democracy while transcending its limitations.

What does this have to do with journalistic ethics? After all, the news media (and still less their ethic of objectivity) neither created these crises nor can they solve them alone. Yet the media are relevant. On the one hand, we have profound global crises; on the other, the necessity for public awareness and the critical re-examination of dominant institutions, as a basis for profound social and cultural change. In between, one of the variables is a media system driven by commercial imperatives and clinging to outdated notions of objectivity which are inadequate and in some respects impediments to communication for sustainable democracy, for several reasons.

First, by insisting that news simply reflects the world and/or balances impartially between the major viewpoints *within* the liberal-democratic ideology, the ethos of objectivity works to disguise the values necessarily embedded in news judgment and thus works to short-circuit debate about what values journalism should reflect if it is to contribute to sustainable democracy. Similarly, the myth of objectivity serves as too convenient an excuse for the media's failure to adequately recognize and report on themselves as part of the North American power structure. While North American journalism is changing in this respect, it is still weak in analyzing its own role in social and political life.

Second, journalism's pursuit of objectivity has too often resulted in a rather passive dependence on politicians and other elite sources, interrupted by spasms of scandal-mongering and personalized criticism. Neither reflex is very helpful in a political era characterized by personalized image-making and by the increasingly perceived fragmentation, homogenization and irrelevance of political parties.

Finally, even at its professional best, objective journalism means journalists are speaking on behalf of others. Even with the best of intentions, that function can lead to distortion of messages and alienation of the excluded.

TOWARDS JOURNALISM FOR SUSTAINABLE DEMOCRACY

If one accepts the preceding analysis of domestic and global crises and the role of journalism in this dual crisis, then a question arises immediately: what do we do next? Rather than offering a blueprint for a new paradigm, this section simply aims at a minimalist goal of hinting at general directions and agents of change and, above all, arguing that working journalists should think about these problems and come up with their own answers. Here we set out some of ours.

As a first step, media should institutionalize the practice of self-reflexivity, encouraging journalists and others to analyze and engage in dialogue about the fundamental biases and impact of news discourse. In particular, there should be more media commentary from "outside the paradigm" and more open acknowledgement of the intrinsic value- and interest-ladenness of journalism, as a precondition for debate about the values and interests journalism should serve.

Although we have focused on the limitations of the ethos of objectivity, it is important to emphasize that we are not arguing that journalists should return to the era of the partisan press, stumbling from unexamined assumptions to predetermined conclusions. We recognize that conventional "quality" journalism does have a useful role in a democratic society: there is a place for the kind of journalism in which journalists constantly strive to put aside personal prejudices and act as an honest conduit for a wide range of relevant perspectives in public discourses.

Indeed, journalism could play a more active role in reinvigorating democratic politics by doing more of what it already does at its best: focusing public attention and accessing a range of voices on substantive issues. To be sure, a revitalized public sphere may require a greater diversity of public voices. Dan Hallin (1992) argues that if the usual political sources (parties and their leaders) are not saying anything very interesting, then journalists should act as active interlocutors, seeking credible people who are (Hallin 1992).

We have argued that journalism's processes of selection and interpretation necessarily embed certain interests and values: the liberal ideals of open, accountable government and free speech, for example, as well as (less admirably) consumerism and bias towards the more affluent. Sustainable, civilized democracy in the coming century almost certainly requires rethinking some of these commitments, and once the ethic of objectivity has been publicly demystified, journalism's role in relation to these requirements can be discussed more openly and without apology.

The "watchdog" role that journalism has traditionally (and very unevenly) adopted towards government needs to be extended towards the global mega-corporations and transnational financial institutions, such as the IMF and the World Bank, that have become virtually private, unaccountable and unscrutinized governments. Journalism's biases in favour of free speech and economic prosperity should be expanded to include ecological survival and the peaceful resolution of political disputes.

Conversely, on a shrinking planet, the media's promotion of consumerism and consumption-oriented "lifestyles" needs to be abandoned, even reversed. And we can debate whether the exclusions necessary to maintaining the conditions of civilized discourse can be openly acknowledged, and even celebrated: do racists, for example, deserve equal time with their victims?

Nor are we arguing for the replacement of objectivity-as-usual by a single, monolithic model. Different types of journalism are needed for different purposes and constituencies (Curran 1981). Sometimes people need to speak in their own voices. There should be greater opportunities within the media system for the expression of "honest bias," and for direct access for advocacy groups to reach their own and broader constituencies. Community radio offers one model for such access but currently it stands on the margins of the system.

Journalism for sustainable democracy involves not only a rethinking of traditional ethics, but also profound structural and financial reforms to reduce the dominance of commercial logic and corporate power within the media system without simply introducing heavy-handed state control (see, for example, Bagdikian 1992, Chapter 13).

These reforms, including genuinely international (rather than centralized "globalized") media, should allow greater diversity of voices. Such reforms could include not only breaking up the oligopolistic conglomerates which dominate the media and providing greater state support for public broadcasting (financed by a tax on advertising), but also improving access for non-commercial, non-state community and alternative media to distribution systems. A detailed discussion of structural reforms, however is beyond the scope of this chapter. Rather, the point is that the discussion of journalism ethics needs to be expanded to include an examination of the institutional and ideological paradigms of journalism within which particular ethical dilemmas arise.

There is no single agent of change. If a journalism adequate to confronting the current crises of democracy is to emerge at all, it will principally come from below, not from media organizations or governments. As Herbert Schiller put it in a 1991 talk in Vancouver, a government tackling the power of corporate media would need a "Jesus Christ complex": it would have to *want* to be crucified. Change will come from increasingly media-literate audiences; social movements mobilizing to improve the perilous state of our species and planet and the alternative media often associated with these movements; and from journalists themselves, especially younger ones who have less of a stake (or future) in the dominant corporate media and their regime of objectivity.

The first step is simply to engage in further reflection and debate about the ethical imperatives for journalism within that broader context of democratic crisis. To think and talk about the world differently is to begin to change it.

7. On Subjectivity: What You Can See Depends on Where You Stand and How "Short" You Are

Rita Shelton Deverell

My journalistic work, and the work of those I supervise, benefits, I believe, from rigorously assessing and revealing subjectivity. Journalists in repeated waves have tackled the objectivity debate. One side of the argument is that total objectivity is not possible but worth reaching for and highly desirable. The other side revels in there being no such thing as objectivity. The non-objectivity side extols personal journalism such as Norman Mailer's, floods its work with "I's" and throws caution to the wind.

This chapter is about the greater information, insight and accuracy that can come from being honest about our subjectivity as we encounter subjects (people) and objects (issues) in our daily work. In this way we can make our individual and collective subjectivities into working tools.

Robert Hackett and Yuezhi Zhao's chapter develops a theory of journalism beyond objectivity, a journalism for "sustainable democracy." What follows here are guidelines for the rigorous practice of the craft of subjective journalism. In Hackett and Zhao's terms, one either exposes the mainstream liberal-democratic bias or vigorously pursues and allows another range of sources to speak. This chapter is not about "anything goes" journalism. It is about information gathering and sharing from a greater diversity of sources, including oneself and the agendas of one's groups of identity.

At Vision TV the world's first multifaith television network, where I am senior producer/anchor, we specialize in point-of-view television. Our mandate is to explore anything related to the spiritual, to ethics, to values. Of necessity, we frequently ask ethical, personal and subjective questions about events. We ask who else has a stake in this story and is not being included. This approach frequently points out that events have several sides, not just two sides. At Vision we deal with actions and perceptions that come out of people's deepest convictions and subjectivity and the effect on reality. The skill of analyzing subjectivity, therefore, is crucial to my work. And, I believe, it is also crucial to all journalistic work that goes beyond the headlines.

Vision TV, by its very nature brings a wide diversity of voices to the table, on and off the screen. More than liberal democracy is represented. Our staff is composed of people of different faiths, cultures, ethnicities, classes, gender and sexual orientations. I am a black woman educated in theatre arts, philosophy and the history of religions who grew up in the segregated southern United States. As network anchor, I symbolize the diversity of voices that is Vision TV.

The serious difficulties of the two-sided objectivity/subjectivity debate became evident to me in recent journalistic writings about the suicide of poet Sylvia Plath. Suicide is a visible, factual event that apparently puts an end to one person's story. Yet when we examine the reporting of suicide, the difficulties of seeking a stance above the story become stark.

The act of suicide, and I would assert all human activity, is interpreted through the infinitely subjective filters of our own lives. What we can see depends on where we stand and whether our height is similiar, less or greater than the victim's. I use the term *height* here to refer to experience, cultural heritage and those circumstances in which we have power or are powerless.

One journalist's fascination with suicide as a metaphor for the problem of objectivity was contained in a sixty-five-page article in the August 23, 1993 issue of the *New Yorker*. In "The Silent Woman" Janet Malcolm examines the biographies written about Plath after her suicide in 1963. What the biographers were able to make of the poetry and the death is seen to be determined by where they stand subjectively in relation to objective events.

Says Malcolm: "The writer, like the murderer, needs a motive. . . . If it had been truly impossible for X to take a side, her book would not have been written; it would not have been worth taking the trouble to write. Writing cannot be done in a state of desirelessness. The pose of fair-mindedness, the charade of even-handedness, the striking of an attitude of detachment can never be more than rhetorical ruses; if they were genuine, if the writer actually didn't care one way or the other how things came out, he would not bestir himself to represent them."

Malcolm's long article on where Plath's biographers stood then became a subject of insight for Stan Persky in the *Globe and Mail* on September 4, 1993. Persky states that Malcolm's account of the multiplicity of biographers tells you a great deal about the central subject, Sylvia Plath. We receive more information, insight and accuracy from the diversity of biographers, each with their different agendas.

Malcolm took on the job of investigating the subjectivity of the biographers seriously. My contention is that being objective, standing above reality as if we were not involved in it, is not the central challenge of reporting. Accurately revealing and assessing our subjectivity and the subjectivity of others, knowing where "we" stand in relation to "them," is for me the central challenge of reporting.

I contend that when we hide our subjectivity from the public, the next step is to hide it from ourselves and to deny its right to exist. A well-publicized example was the case of Dale Goldhawk, journalist, versus the CBC. During the very public free-trade debate, Goldhawk was president of ACTRA (Alliance of Canadian Radio, Television and Cinema Artists), his professional union, which took a strong anti-free trade position. He was also the host of the network radio show "Cross Country Check-up" on which free trade was frequently discussed. Goldhawk was asked to step down as president of the union because fronting the anti-free trade position was deemed by the CBC to be inappropriate for an unbiased host.

Goldhawk's position, however, was totally accessible to the audience. It was not hidden. An anti-free trade stance could be seen to be the only one the journalist's union could take. Goldhawk's position, in my view, did the audience less harm by being visible than by being run underground. His revealed subjectivity as a person affected by political events was indeed an important part of the story. It was part of the information needed by the audience to make informed decisions.

Three examples from work I have recently supervised at Vision TV illustrate how the use of subjectivity is a key factor in the information and insight we generate.

Example 1: The Subjectivity of Power— When the Mainstream flows by the Margins

The assigned story was traditional aboriginal medicine as practiced in Toronto. Key to the story was interviewing people, Native and not Native, who were participating in a weekly healing circle. If at all possible, part of the ceremony was to be videotaped.

The reporter had received permission from the leader to be there with a camera at one of the weekly meetings. Over the telephone he had convinced the leader of the worth of our televising this healing circle. The year before, Vision TV had shot a story with the leader's family. We had followed the ground rules the two of us had agreed upon and given ourselves time to find another subject if the leader's family decided they were unable to be interviewed. Therefore, Vision TV had a positive history with the source which we wanted to maintain.

When I arrived, all of the aboriginal participants were standing outside on the sidewalk and were unwilling to go inside the building where the circle took place.

The leader was going around speaking inaudibly to each person, seemingly telling them not to go away. The reporter was giving instructions in a very audible voice to the crew to set up in the middle of the non-existent circle. The leader was leaning against the outside wall. I quietly asked if we were going to be able to tape.

He said to me, "No, your boy will not follow our lead to gain people's confidence. He misinterprets silence for consent." As supervisor my next action was to pull the plug, removing the reporter and the crew from the scene. This was followed by a long chat with the reporter in my office in which it was obvious that he had no sense of the difference between where he stood and where the leader of the healing circle stood. And without being able to perceive and bridge that distance he had no story.

When the reporter realized he had a serious problem, there were at least two ways he might have negotiated entry. Both would involve backing off the aggressive "I-must-get-the-story" position he had taken. One way would be to keep the camera outside and negotiate ground rules with the leader and the group that would allow the camera in. The second way would be to decide that this is not the evening to tape, stay and become part of the process and then talk about taping.

The reporter was a mid-twenties Anglo-Saxon, tall male with a deep voice who assumed that his need to make a television story about traditional aboriginal healing was shared by the folk in the healing circle. Their priorities and way of decision-making were different than his. The reporter was actually unable to "report on" the circle because, in both the literal and figurative sense, he could not see it. A possible explanation for the reporter's lack of success was his lack of experience. Perhaps after ten years of working he would not get himself into the same position where he could not deliver.

Greater understanding about negotiating entry is unlikely for reporters, however, if they work in media outlets where they and their editors assume a thesis, particularly about communities other than their own, and set out to prove it. Most likely this reporter will work in media outlets where diverse communities are not on the inside. He will work where the mainstream is defined as male, Protestant, middle class and trained in the school of each story having two sides. This reporter's ability to negotiate entry will not improve until he notices the difference between matters of public accountability and private concern. In a democracy, public figures have to speak to the press. When ordinary citizens are our subjects, a unique relationship has to be built that gives each person a reason to speak. Those unique relationships develop between two subjectivities.

Recently I heard one veteran reporter (a white woman) ask another veteran reporter (an aboriginal man) why the people of Davis Inlet were so unwilling to speak to her about their epidemic of teen suicides. She stated that her motives were good and she only wanted to call national attention to a serious situation. The aboriginal reporter said, "I cannot give you lessons in how to make stubborn Indians talk."

What is being discussed here are techniques to release the subjectivity of others who are the "objects" of our journalistic work, so we gain a more accurate picture of reality. We need lessons on how our subjectivities interact. We are learning how to make the stubborn speak with a view to greater understanding, compassion and accuracy. The young reporter who tried to do a story on aboriginal medicine had indeed been outside it. Had he been able to perceive where he subjectively stood and measure the distance to the subjectivity of those in the circle, he would have been able to negotiate entry. He also would have created a story where the viewer could judge the influence of both subjectivities.

EXAMPLE 2: THE SUBJECTIVITY OF HERITAGE— THE VIEW FROM THE LOSING SIDE

One of my colleagues told me he wanted to do a documentary on the Anglo-Indian community. He had been born a part of this tiny community that had resulted from intersexualizing during the British occupation of India and had sided with the British during the Indian movement for independence. The beautifully crafted half-hour show that emerged from his idea was a result of a subjective interest. The reporter's personal search determined the shape of the report. It seemed best to be intellectually and aesthetically honest about why we were doing this documentary. The subjective approach turned out to be the richest approach.

The Anglo-Indian community as a subject matter most likely would not have occured to anyone not part of the community. There is very little literature and no audio-visual material on this group. My colleague had access to information because he was an insider. He also knew what the questions were and the history that was usually withheld from the young. Central to Anglo-Indian history as experienced by my colleague was a cloud around the community's status and therefore his personal status. Was the community's past something to be proud of, ashamed of or both? Was this community in favour in present-day India, in disfavour or both?

The final documentary had as much audience appeal as other current affairs subjects. After all, most of us have parts of our backgrounds that are mysterious. We are interested in uncovering the mysteries of heritage. A striking side effect of the project was releasing and identifying the subjectivity of my colleague so he could release, name and see the subjectivity of others. Prior to the making of this documentary, my colleague did not know clearly where he stood. It is a reporter's job to tell us where others are standing. That is difficult if you do not know where *you* are.

Example 3: The Subjectivity of Age and Experience— The View with More Hindsight than Foresight

In the fall of 1993, I worked on a half-hour program called "The 25 Year Itch." It was about the breakup of long-term relationships. There is some evidence that the breakup of relationships that have lasted longer than twenty-five years is a 1980s and 1990s epidemic, although the greatest number of divorces still take place in the first five years of marriage. It used to be if you stayed married as long as twenty-five years, you stayed married.

Noticing this as a subject is most likely a result of my age, length of marriage and the breakup of several marriages around me. It was difficult to not become subjectively involved. This subject surfaced for me right after our twenty-fifth anniversary party in 1992 for family and long-time friends. The party, held in the home of a couple who had been married more than thirty years, incorporated some of the elements of our 1967 wedding and reception: the original singer and songs, hot dogs and soft drinks for refreshments and two people who were in our wedding party as masters of ceremonies. A joyful addition was the rock band of our seventeen-year-old son. A painful addition was the news that our host felt that his thirty-plus years with his wife had contained a lot of suppressed rage. These friends split shortly thereafter, making my world and the world of their adult children less secure. Research turned up more than enough similiar stories to make a show.

Age is a subjective factor that influences our worldview and what we are able to see as subject matter. Unless we recognize the effect of age on our perceptions, we may simply define our chronological view as mainstream. In a recent referendum on the Canadian constitution I voted "yes." The other three people in my production unit, all under thirty, voted "no." They are the new mainstream and they are needed to broaden the subjectivities, the understanding and the information of our media outlet.

The three examples cited here—aboriginal medicine, the Anglo-Indian community and long-term relationship breakups are, like most stories, in a state of flux. Unlike a suicide story, we do not know the ending and there are many characters in each story. I would assert that the most effective and honest way to report on those characters, events and facts is subjectively. The reporter needs to know where she stands in relationship to others—how much power she has, what her heritage is, how much experience she has—in order to report on others. A reporter is not flying objectively above events. Instead, she needs to know exactly where she is standing beside or inside the events for the most informative reporting to take place.

Rich reporting requires time to find out how many stories are within the story. In these examples, we have to be inside the story enough to know that it is a story, to be able to see it. Putting ourselves inside gives us greater, not less, access to information. It gives us a vantage point from which we can see many sides. Then we give others an opportunity to see with us and we increase the amount of information, accuracy and truth in the world.

Example 4: The Subjectivity of Political Events— What Did You Do in the Gulf War, Mommy?

The dangers of not knowing where we stand become perhaps most physically and psychologically destructive when the issues are national or international. Our subjectivity in cases of war and violence becomes an unconscious group subjectivity, group personality and group stance.

The unrecognized group identity prevents asking the widest range of probing and useful questions.

We place ourselves and our audiences in danger of grave misinformation, inacccuracy and dishonesty when we do not recognize the subjectivity of political events. The example here is the war that broke out in the Persian Gulf in January 1991. A scant three years after this war, we in Canada see it as possibly not our war. We had the information, the citizens and alternative stories to tell at the time the war broke out. Our agenda, however, was set by the American government and the American news media.

Everybody's lapel did not sport a yellow ribbon, symbolizing good luck to Canadian soldiers, during the 1991 United Nations action. We are about to meet three of those Canadians in their work settings: an elementary school teacher, a national radio journalist and me in my capacity as senior producer at Vision TV. We all had questions, points of view about the war, and experiences with fellow Canadians that made the ribbons an impossibility.

THE "TEACHER"

In Mrs. A's classroom the twelve- and thirteen-year-old children are disturbed. For the first time in their parents' lives and their lives, Canada is at war.

Mrs. A. is a staunch supporter of the media literacy program in the schools. Activities to make students aware of and able to assess the impact of television, film, advertising and radio on them are a part of the Ontario schools' curriculum and Mrs. A. contributes curricular ideas to the National Association for Media Literacy.

Mrs. A. is a respected teacher with more than twenty years of experience in a big-city English Canadian school board. She serves on several board and school committees, has two children in the system herself and has always felt that she has to actively participate in the community to make it the best possible place.

As a concerned teacher, Mrs. A. decides that something has to be done about the children's sense of fear. She also wants them to know more about how media shapes the war, including our responses to it. Mrs. A. decides the class should have a discussion about how the Gulf War might be ended. What are possible strategies for peace? The children are given this question as their assignment, along with watching as much news as possible. They are not assigned a news source and are free to take what is available to them.

Mrs. A.'s parents immigrated from Lebanon and she has lived her more than forty years in Canada. Her Lebanese heritage, until this day, has been a source of spiritual and folk wisdom and provided a sense of belongingness. Something indefinable has told Mrs. A. that her heritage is not appropriate staff room talk right now. During her class's media literacy discussion, she comes to see herself as a member of an invisible and unacceptable minority group.

Mrs. A. related this to us:

> When the war broke out it was a prime time—I thought—to get my students in media literacy involved in how media cover what I call tragic events. . . . One of the things they were supposed to do was to watch as many different programs as possible where the war was being discussed. And then we were going to break into groups and discuss how this information was being presented and what they learned. . . . I was in the hall doing hall duty and there were about three or four boys off to one side who

> were into a discussion. . . . One boy was telling the other boy that he knew exactly how to solve the situation in the Middle East. . . . He says it's simple: You just kill all the Arabs in the world and then you'll have no more wars.
>
> I got everybody into the classroom. . . . And I said, "O.K., what we're going to discuss is the possible solutions to what's going on in the Middle East." I happened to hear a discussion in the hall . . . and the entire discussion seemed to centre around this solution. I just wonder if I could repeat it to you. In order to solve the problems . . . you just kill all the Arabs in the world. They just sat there and looked at me expectantly and I said, "Which one would like to kill me?"
>
> There was dead silence. They looked at me and said, "But Mrs. A., you're not one of them!" And I said, "Darlings, my parents are Lebanese, so I'm of Arabic descent. Would it really solve your problem in the Middle East if you were to kill Mrs. A.?" And needless to say, we wound up in one of the most powerful discussions we've ever had.

It was a good discussion, but the sense of being "the other" has not left Mrs. A. Maybe that is who she had been all the time. She experienced having an invisible background that was not welcome in Canadian society.

The "Journalist"

Powerful discussion about the war, it appears, can happen in the classroom but not in the newsroom. In the Journalist's national newsroom the competition is so great that you don't take time to go to the bathroom. It is best to watch your seat if you want to stay ahead of the other newshounds.

The Journalist is a writer. In her radio newsroom she takes available sources, makes phone calls and writes copy for the newscasters. She reports to a senior editor. In these exchanges it becomes obvious that the range of sources is narrow and American-government controlled. It also becomes obvious that a broader range of sources is not being sought, welcomed or imagined.

The Journalist had wanted nothing more than to make it in the field. She had studied for it, worked for it and was very glad to have been hired. The Journalist was born in a Muslim country and had come to Canada as a young child. She viewed her Canadian upbringing and education as a way of joining the mainstream. Journalism as a career flouted some of her cultural traditions: she would be independent, not sustained by men, self-supporting.

But it was not until the Gulf War that it became evident that her subjectivity was not being added to mainstream considerations. It could only be absorbed. In the newsroom the Gulf War story was not, and seemingly could not be viewed, as multifaceted. The Journalist could not ask colleagues to stand, even for a moment, where she was standing, to pose the questions from where she was. In a very real sense the dominant working "culture" of the newsroom was not the Journalist's and she could not influence that approach or the points of view considered.

As the Gulf War went on, it became obvious to the newsroom that it was very difficult to get information. The Americans were keeping tight control. The Canadian sources of information were CNN, NBC, ABC and CBS. Canada was in the war and no one seriously questioned how we got there or whether we should stay; and no one in the newsroom suggested that that was part of the story.

There were no observations about the language of the war, says the Journalist. Although later we asked ourselves about smart bombs, surgical strikes and desert storms, there were no questions about a war that apparently had no human victims. Suddenly it seemed to the Journalist—who had been trained like the others to always question the source, to be curious, to ask about vested interests—that colleagues in the newsroom weren't asking any questions. That practiced aggression of the news trade that made one guy try to find out more than the next had dried up, and the official line from the official sources was all there was.

Noam Chomsky is quoted by the Journalist to describe her experiences; the media, she says, took their cues from the government and helped create the idea of "worthy" and "unworthy" victims. Fellow journalists should have asked how Canadians, by using American rhetoric, created victims in Canada.

Further, observes the Journalist, the Gulf War really put multiculturalism to the test. Their war experiences suggested to Arab and Muslim Canadians that they, unlike other groups, were not allowed to dissent without having their loyalty to Canada questioned. Once again, Canada treated immigrants badly in wartime. Muslims and Arabs became expendable in the public's mind, as had Canadian Japanese during the Second World War. Surely journalists are best placed to pose questions about our attitudes and go after the answers; but not in the Journalist's newsroom nor any of the others she could see.

Then the Journalist started to get calls from her mother who, hearing the news reports, could do nothing but cry. Mother was not crying because friends or relatives were in danger, but because the war was being reported as without victims. There was little coverage from the point of view of Canadians whose friends and relatives were being killed and whose ancient cities were being destroyed.

The question is not whether media were pro-Saddam or anti-Saddam. There is ample analysis of how words and pictures "demonized" a political figure. What is less evident is the demonizing of a culture, faith and civilization, and by implication all persons who participate in those groups wherever they may be found. Arab becomes "terrorist". Muslim becomes "fundamentalist" or "fanatical". And for the Journalist the two-sided conflict culture of the newsroom condemned a whole civilization as "the other side".

The Journalist was forced to come to the conclusion that the questions in her mind were not being asked by anyone in the newsroom. For once it was better to hide one's questions. Her background, rather than being useful in analysis and in finding contacts, was an unwelcome one. She needed to hide who she was. The Journalist experienced a profound feeling of alienation from her training, from the place she had always wanted to work.

Finally, it seemed to her, the work would have to be done elsewhere, a place where there was more than one point of view, where you could be questioning all things. The Journalist, like the Teacher, was suddenly afraid and outside of the society she thought was hers. As the Producer finds out in the next case, giving people air time who had other than a pro-war point of view was indeed a challenge.

THE "PRODUCER"

Showing support for what was obviously going to be an unpopular venture, my executive producer telephoned to say he was backing the Gulf War special we were putting together at

Vision TV "regardless"—regardless of the fact that the regular commercial sponsors had pulled their commercials out of the three-hour, primetime block where the special was placed. What had alarmed the sponsors was that "The Gulf: Crisis Revisited" planned to acquaint us with the anti-war movement in the United States, the peace movement in Canada, analyze the media coverage and tell about some of the incidents of discrimination that Arab and Muslim Canadians were experiencing.

Vision TV specializes in point-of-view television. Its mandate is to reflect the spiritual. We bill ourselves as "alternative." Religions and cultures in Canada are diverse—liberal, conservative and orthodox. Our network had over the past war-torn months carried the view of a number of conservative Christians that the American cause in the Middle East was supported by God.

The "peace special" included a wide range of material that was broadcast on Vision as the war heated up: interviews with peace activists, teachers who taught peace, a monk who worked through non-violent resistance. It also included community television broadcasts that received little play in the States. "Paper Tiger Television" chronicled the peace movement and the opposition to the war. There was footage of peace marches and demonstrations, rap videos created for the "paper tiger network" and stories about communities organizing to evade the draft.

Vision's commercial sponsors were alarmed at the mere mention of alternative voices on the Gulf War. And even though the program stated at the outset that it was not balanced, that it took the peace point of view, members of the audience were alarmed as well.

> Letter to Vision TV
> cc: Office of the Secretary General, CRTC
>
> On Friday, March 1, 1991, at 10:00 p.m., Vision TV ran an hour-long collection of material which had nothing to do with religion; nothing to do with ethics and nothing to do with morality. (That it had nothing to do with entertainment is a given.)
>
> The hour aired amateurish propaganda of an insidious kind. It was largely staged material presented as though it were real. It degraded the values of our society to no constructive or productive purpose. I would appreciate your reviewing this propaganda piece in order to determine if the airwaves of Canada are well-served by material which I could not characterize without resort to impolite language.
>
> I'd also be interested in knowing how this material relates to Vision TV's broadcast license.

> Letter to Vision's President
>
> I recognized very early on that the network that you operate has a very clear left-wing bias in the programming that it produces and I have accepted that. Most of the shows that Vision TV produces involve nothing more than a bunch of smug and sanctimonious over-weening left-wing academics and clerics pouting and whining and arguing moot points back and forth. That is fine with me and it pretty much explains why your ratings rank below those of old Beachcombers reruns.

> Last evening's program, "The Gulf: Crisis Revisited," went too far, however. I am sorry to say that several times while watching it I flew into a furious rage. How can you justify such patently and unapologetically unbalanced and pro-Iraqi programming on your network? It was an absolute outrage. I could count on one hand the number of times that I heard the word "Kuwait" uttered. No one mentioned, even in passing, the incredible, horrific atrocities that the Iraqi military commited in Kuwait against a peaceful civilian population. . . .
>
> I can respect (although I do not agree with) the pacifist sentiments of your network. But what I do not respect or even understand is why you have chosen to align yourself with Saddam Hussein and ignore completely the plight of the Kuwaiti people.
>
> The only thing that makes me more angry than your radical politics is the fact that I am not able to stop financially supporting your network without cancelling my cable TV subscription, thereby losing CNN, a source of truly objective news reporting and dissemination. And the only thing that pleases me about your network is that it reflects such a tiny minority of opinion.

The CRTC ruled that, indeed, Vision had shown enough pro-war programs not to unbalance the system with a three-hour peace program. Many viewers were delighted with "The Gulf: Crisis Revisited." They stated that the points of view expressed in this one special were not seen at any other point in any of the war coverage on any other media outlet.

During the Gulf War, Mrs. A. experienced being the unacceptable "other" in the country where she was born. The Journalist discovered there was no objectivity about the war in the newsroom; it had only one side. And at Vision TV we found out that even on a point-of-view network the right of the peace point of view to exist was not allowed during a war. We experienced the rewards and consequences of holding up a third side of a two-sided argument. This is indeed a scary place to be because it changes not only the content but the form of our work. It takes us to the place in reporting where, like art, we are discovering a different language for every job we do.

Our information, accuracy and understanding have been increased, however, by gaining access to our subjectivity and to the subjectivity of others. We find out more when we can work with heritage, power, age/experience and politics. The stories themselves and the many sides of the stories we were able to see were the result of serious examination and used individual and group subjectivity. Here are some techniques for doing that, for measuring our personal cultural distance from the subjectivity of others:

Exercises in the Art of Subjectivity for Journalists and Journalism Students: How to Know Where We Stand and How "Short" We Are

1. *Know thyself, even the effect you produce.*
2. *Give each other feedback on how we will appear when entering a variety of ethnic, social, gender and cultural group situations.* The reporter doing the aboriginal medicine story was too tall, too loud and too dictatorial. He needed to be attuned to a variety of physical and verbal cues. We can, of course, modify our effect. That is what this lesson is about. And we can never listen enough.

3. *Practise negotiating entry*. How many groups different from our own can we actually get into and gain trust? Keep track of the techniques. These groups are good places to begin research for subsequent stories. We have to be trustworthy to gain trust. Make a chart of the ways we are the same and different from the groups we are entering or individuals we are talking to (differences in power, heritage, age/experience, politics, at least). This is a measurement of cultural distance.
4. *Answer the questions for yourself.* When stories are about deep feelings, personal material and deep convictions, let's ask what has happened to us that is similiar or exactly the same and be honest about what we have experienced and not experienced. We should not ask others questions that we are not willing to ask and answer ourselves.
5. *Practise listing how many sides can we see to the story*. Never be satisfied until we have at least three. Can the story be told from the perspective of people who are not obvious at all?
6. *Go to those whose side does not catch our sympathy*. Why is this person this way? Learn to see the stories of all human beings as having a beginning, middle and end that makes sense in their terms. Their terms may not be right or rational, but we need to get inside their point of view.

Part Three

The Politics and Ethics of Inclusion

8. Cultural and Racial Diversity in Canadian Broadcast Journalism

Lorna Roth

Here I take a critical look at Canadian broadcast journalism. First, I provide a detailed overview of the policy and legislative frameworks through which diversity may be expressed on broadcast channels. Second, I examine several issues of representation in employment and portrayal. After equity issues are identified and elaborated upon, I turn to basic problems of depicting multicultural/multiracial communities and raise ethical concerns which emerge from mainstream and specialty services. Finally, I identify the key components of an inclusive broadcasting system. These include fair employment and self-representational practices for multicultural and multiracial communities; recognition that "white is a colour too"; acknowledgement that multiple cultural/racial images and accented voices are legitimate sources of (off- and on-air) information; awareness that different peoples operate within distinct cultural, spatial and temporal codes that must be known and respected by mainstream journalists; and the knowledge that, with few exceptions, journalists would benefit from cross-cultural orientations and anti-racist training before they cover an event or issue outside the cultural communities with which they are familiar.

The chapter ends with a series of appendices. Appendix I inventories existing broadcast media outlets supported by "ethnic"[1], Northern and community broadcasting policies. Appendix II presents preliminary guidelines and considerations for inclusive journalistic practices. Appendix III contains an interview with Rita Shelton Deverell describing her 1983–84 grievance with the CBC when she was refused the right to audition for a part because she is black (included as an example of a broader cross-cultural issue that may arise in journalistic practice); and Appendices IV and V contain letters from Joan Beatty (CBC Television, Regina) and Conway Jocks (community radio station manager at Kahnawake during the 1990 Mohawk/government confrontation),[2] addressing ethical issues which arose in the course of their work.

A Constituency-based Broadcasting System

Through a set of progressive policies that promote positive self-definition of group differences, Canadian broadcasting practices are beginning to represent significant evidence of cultural and racial diversity. These policies contrast with those that see assimilation as the way to transcend group differences. According to Iris Marion Young, an egalitarian politics of difference

> involves a reconception of the meaning of equality. The assimilationist ideal assumes that equal social status for all persons requires treating everyone according to the same principles, rules, and standards. A politics of difference argues, on the other hand, that equality as the participation and inclusion of all groups, sometimes

> requires different treatment for oppressed or disadvantaged groups. To promote social justice . . . social policy should sometimes accord special treatment to groups (Young 1990: 158).

Canadian broadcasting policy has shifted from a "right-to-receive services" approach based exclusively on the extension of services to all parts of the Canadian territory (including remote regions) to one which legally enshrines the broadcasting rights of three minority constituency groups: women, first peoples and multicultural and multiracial communities ("visible minorities"). In the present Broadcasting Act (1991), each of these groups is allocated a special status. Each has the right to be fairly portrayed on the airwaves and equitably represented on staffs throughout all broadcasting services—public, private and community (Canada 1991a: S.3(d) (iii)).

Up to and including the 1968 Broadcasting Act and its 1976 modification,[3] legislation specified that all Canadians were entitled to broadcasting services in English and French as public funds become available (Canada 1968: s.z(e)) and national broadcasting service should "be extended to all parts of Canada as public funds become available (s.z(g)(ii))." Once centrally controlled services had been provided geographically throughout most of the country, by the late 1970s Canadians (particularly members of minorities) began to look at other ways to extend broadcasting policies and practices.

Canada has a long-standing alternative tradition of constituency-based services. According to Liora Salter (1980), who first used the term to refer to a reformulation of the notion of community, "constituency" refers to "people sharing multiple overlapping relationships in a system of power." Constituency groups share a common relationship to powerful institutions and to those who hold power within a given society.

Between 1968 and the passing of the new Broadcasting Act on June 4, 1991, Canadian policy-makers and regulators participated in public and private consultations with the goal of modifying the 1968 Act and its 1976 version. The objective was to streamline it technologically and make it more reflective of constituency rights already enshrined within other Canadian legislation, namely Section 15 on Equality Rights in the Charter of Rights and Freedoms (1982), the Multiculturalism Act (1988), the Human Rights Act (1976–77) and the Employment Equity Act (1986).

During this period, three constituency groups were outstanding in their relentless demands to make the principles of the Broadcasting Act more culturally, racially and gender-inclusive. The three groups consisted of Canada's first peoples, its ethnic populations (those whose ancestral homelands are outside of Canada but whose ethnic backgrounds are of neither British nor French origin) and women. They demanded more accurate portrayals (both positive and negative) and equitable employment opportunities in what remain white, male-dominated mainstream broadcasting venues.

As a result of their concerted lobbying, broadcasting services within Canada have changed considerably for those groups and also for community and disabled groups. We now have the following constituency-based services: eight ethnic radio stations, four ethnic television stations, thirteen regional Native communications societies in the North,[4] 117 first peoples community radio stations across the country, fifty-seven community radio stations in various non-aboriginal local communities, twenty-six campus-based radio stations and a dedicated Northern satellite transponder service called Television Northern Canada which provides native-language and English programming to ninety-four communities in the Arctic, about one-third of Canada's territory (Personal correspondence, August 20, 1993).[5] Although there is not yet a specialty service for disabled people, CBC Newsworld (a national all-news network) has two time slots for programming produced by the Disability Network group and all hearing-impaired people have the option of closed-captioning service on Canadian channels.

Until 1991, evaluations of women's integration into mainstream institutions showed continuing disparities in salaries and project funds. Although women held about one-third of the available jobs in broadcasting, their job categories remained linked to traditional roles: "wardrobe, hairstylist, makeup artists, secretaries, and assistants" (Saint-Jean 1991: 118). Furthermore, many women's jobs are temporary or part-time. Nonetheless, by 1991, after the debates around the need for new legislation had already been circulating for at least a decade, there were important breakthroughs in opportunities for senior management and creative positions for women (Saint-Jean 1991: 119, 122).

Although women's integration into the broadcasting sector has been slow, it too has gained momentum by the enshrinement of the constituency group principle within the Broadcasting Act of 1991 at Section 3(1):

> (d) the Canadian broadcasting system should: . . . (iii) through its programming and the employment opportunities arising out of its operation, serve the needs and interests, and reflect the circumstances and asipirations of Canadian men, women and children, including equal rights, the linguistic duality and multicultural and multiracial nature of Canadian society and the special place of aboriginal peoples within that society.

Three supporting policies regulate Section 3's legislative requirements for constituency recognition: A Broadcasting Policy Reflecting Canada's Linguistic and Cultural Diversity, the Northern Broadcasting Policy (called the Native Broadcasting Policy since 1990) and the Policies for Community and Campus Radio.

ETHNIC BROADCASTING

For the last three decades, Canada's multicultural/multiracial populations have lobbied the CRTC and federal and provincial departments of communications to enshrine the right to receive and transmit ethnically balanced depictions of society on public and private broadcasting channels. Ethnic minority groups have identified common objectives for the production of local, regional and sometimes traditionally oriented cultural programming. They have demanded cultural and artistic justice, redistribution of broadcasting powers, fairer transmitter access and cognitive equity in all forms of visible and audible portrayals.

Canada's multicultural/multiracial communities argue for improved representation on mainstream and specialized national and regional broadcasting services at all levels—technical, administrative, cultural and policy-making. Some say that ethnicity should not be defined as a content characteristic at all, that all persons should have equal access to a wider variety of roles in broadcasting and cultural industries (Canadian Multiculturalism Council 1988: 53–58).

The federal government's response to these arguments is called "A Broadcasting Policy

Reflecting Canada's Linguistic and Cultural Diversity." More commonly referred to as the "Ethnic Broadcasting Policy," it was an international "first" when it was established in 1985. Since then, it has facilitated the development of local and regional, though not national, undertakings in Canada. In the past, most ethnic broadcasting undertakings were urban-based, privately funded, commercially oriented and multilingual. The reason was that the scarcity of available frequencies made cross-cultural and multilinguistic collaborative networks necessary. In the future, as technological advances such as signal compression open a multiplicity of frequencies at reasonable costs, we can expect to see an increase in single-community ethnic broadcasters in the media arena.

As for integration of multicultural/multiracial communities into mainstream institutions, until the passing of the new Act, only broadcasting networks with one hundred or more employees had begun employment-equity programs. Budget cutbacks continue to restrain these efforts.

NORTHERN BROADCASTING: FIRST PEOPLES COMMUNICATIONS

The Northern Broadcasting Policy was the result of a concerted pressure group strategy by Northern first peoples communities and their supporters. Until the early 1980s, a variety of experimental domestic satellite-access projects demonstrated first peoples' skills in organization, management, design and administration of training programs and maintainance of complex broadcasting undertakings. By 1983 the federal government had issued broadcasting licenses to thirteen regional Native communication societies in the North. The Northern Broadcasting Policy, announced on March 10, 1983, identifies five principles which have governed the subsequent development of Northern broadcasting:

1. Northern residents should be offered access to an increasing range of programming choices through the exploitation of technological opportunities.
2. Northern native people should have the opportunity to participate actively in the determination by the CRTCof the character, quantity, and priority of programming broadcast in predominantly native communities.
3. Northern native people should have fair access to Northern broadcasting distribution systems to maintain and develop their cultures and languages.
4. Programming relevant to native concerns, including content originated by native people, should be produced for distribution on Northern broadcasting services wherever native people form a significant proportion of the population in the service area.
5. Northern native representatives should be consulted regularly by government agencies engaged in establishing broadcasting policies which would affect their cultures (CRTC 1983: 2).

The federally funded Northern Native Broadcast Access Program (NNBAP), made public at the same time, is an implementation vehicle. It was originally provided with $40.3 million to be distributed over a four-year period to the thirteen regional groups to produce twenty hours of radio and five hours of television programming each week. The goal was to establish alternative, culturally relevant and linguistically reinforcing radio and television venues in the North to complement the Southern, urban-oriented live broadcasting that had been parachuted into the North since 1973. The NNBAP has been extraordinarily successful, despite systematic federal funding cutbacks.

First peoples broadcasting policy has been in existence for more than a decade. Policies subsequent to the Northern Broadcasting Policy have clarified its principles and expanded the infrastructure of aboriginal broadcasting (CRTC 1990). A more liberal advertising policy is in place, notions of Native language and culture are more flexible and regulations are minimal for aboriginal broadcasting in the North.

Obstacles to the implementation of policies fall into three areas: secure, long-term funding; high-quality training programs adapted to Northern regional conditions; and independently controlled distribution of Native programming signals. As federal allocation to Native broadcasting has decreased each year, the growth potential of broadcasting organizations has been blocked. Most communities are located in remote and isolated regions with little potential for economic development. Consequently, government pressure to diversify funding during a Canada-wide economic recession has resulted in staff layoff, rationalization of some operations and, in some cases, the cutting of entire units. Although they now produce fewer hours, production quality has not decreased. However, long-range planning has been compromised.

Training funds are negotiated on a region-by-region basis through Canada's manpower and training bureau or through private sources. Again, the unresolved issue is where to find long-term budget allocations to train new Native broadcasters. Given cutbacks, how much sense does it make to train new broadcasters when those experienced are having to grapple with diminished resources?

In 1983, the Northern Broadcasting Policy expected that two conventional broadcasters would carry Native programming as a social or public service in exchange for being granted their licenses. These were to be the CBC Northern Service and a private satellite distribution service called Cancom. Negotiations for access times to these services were difficult. CBC Northern Service television time slots, such as 3 a.m., were unpopular. Better time slots, such as 10 p.m., were often pre-empted for programs of national importance. Discussions with Cancom, a privately owned and operated distribution undertaking, were initially even more difficult. After years of frustration, Native broadcasters began lobbying for a separate satellite transponder for Northern programming.

At the cost of $10 million, the federally funded Television Northern Canada (TVNC) dedicated satellite transponder became operational on January 21, 1992. It is now the primary First Nations broadcasting distribution service to the North. Resolving the distribution problems which have plagued the Native Communications Societies, it delivers Native-language and English programming sponsored by territorial governments (the Yukon, Northwest Territories and Nunavut) and their local colleges to ninety-four communities and is pan-Arctic in scope, covering a market of 100,000 viewers (TVNC 1993: 5). TVNC management are now in the process of trying to convince the CRTC that their programming should be carried on Southern cable channels serving metropolitan areas.

Despite financial difficulties, First Nations Communications Societies' services remain outstanding examples of constituency-based broadcasting in the North. By contrast, the striking neglect of institutional support for first peoples broadcasting in Southern and urban regions is appalling, given the federal government's liberal record vis-á-vis Northern aboriginal constituency groups. Explanations are elusive. Perhaps it is because of the disparate and scattered populations of the first peoples communities in the South. Perhaps they have not yet felt compelled to organize around common information needs or are satisfied with mainstream coverage. This is doubtful. However, access to production and distribution facilities is critical in these times of economic cutbacks. Policy-makers must still address fairness in resource allocation for Southern aboriginal broadcasting.

POLICIES FOR COMMUNITY RADIO

As noted, Canada has a high number of community radio stations, most of which carry alternative forms of minority constituency programming. Community radio emerged in the early 1970s. It is based on the "principles of collective ownership, member access, and commitment to the community" (CRTC 1992: 2). It is:

> characterized by its ownership and programming and the market it is authorized to serve. It is owned and controlled by a not-for-profit organization whose structure provides for membership, management, operation and programming primarily by members of the community-at-large. Its programming should be based on community access and should reflect the special interests and needs of the listeners it is licensed to serve (CRTC 1992: 2–3).

Begun as a social experiment, community radio complements private and public broadcasting services and, as a voluntary sector, has contributed a great deal towards community cohesion in the North and in rural areas (Canada 1986: 491). Stations have fostered programs that reflect community concerns and carry the actual voices of community members to each others' homes. Success depends on the commitment of individual community members to participate in programming production. In communities where there are no newspapers or media outlets, community radio has provided an electronic billboard of useful information and entertainment. Even in large urban settings, the popularity of community radio has been notable.

THE POTENTIAL FOR INCLUSIVE JOURNALISM

Recent changes in broadcasting legislation mark a turning point in official recognition of collective over individual rights in broadcasting. The 1991 Broadcasting Act takes Canada's existing commitment to equality rights inscribed in the Charter of Rights and Freedoms (1982), the Multiculturalism Act (1988), the Human Rights Act (1976–77) and the Employment Equity Act (1986) and applies it to the broadcasting field. These equality rights include the right to express multicultural and multiracial differences; the prohibition of discrimination on the basis of race, national or ethnic origin, colour, religion, sex, age or mental or physical disability; and the right to equitable job opportunities. We cannot expect the broadcasting system to change overnight; strong legislative principles will enable minority constituency groups to gain opportunities to participate more actively in our broadcasting industries.

As a consequence of the debates around this legislation, and after three years of its implementation, the evidence already indicates that the Canadian broadcasting system has opened up to a multiplicity of new voices never before guaranteed access to a public medium of expression. In a democratic society, participation of minority constituency journalists within such powerful venues as public media represents a positive direction.

"INCLUSIVENESS" AND ETHICAL ISSUES ARISING FROM DAILY JOURNALISTIC PRACTICES

> I think that mainstream media still mostly represent the status quo—middle ground, middle class, white, male Canadian reality. Whatever is outside of that seems "other." Newsrooms are changing these days in terms of reporters, but the gatekeepers are still male white journalists, and the aboriginal world is outside of their reality. Visible minorities in the newsrooms know what's going on in those other communities. To have an accurate reflection of all the layers of a story, you need to have well-trained minorities working in the newsrooms of the nation. If you've never gone to Kahnawake or Kanehsatake, you'll have no idea of what's going on there (Loreen Pindera, television interview, October 10, 1993).

I would now like to turn to some of the more nitty-gritty aspects of the Canadian broadcasting system, its journalistic practices: objectivity, balance, fairness. Key themes emerged from my interviews and written responses to a request for anecdotes. Inclusiveness meant two things to journalists: inclusion of minorities on staffs at broadcasting institutions, and inclusion of minorities within stories covered by people outside of the community.

Journalists tended to adopt the Broadcasting Act's notions of employment equity and fairer portrayal or representational practices. Most of the journalists I spoke with supported the principle of equity to redress existing imbalances in employment opportunities for minorities. They had no problem with Section 3 of the Broadcasting Act of 1991 but raised issues of tokenism, reverse discrimination, objectivity, balance, professionalism and organizational cultural uniqueness. Among the hard realities they identified is the dilemma of implementing equity programs in a climate of economic recession and budgetary constraints. They also identified the classic problem of the "last hired first fired" as an obstacle to progress.

Two other problems emerged from the letters and interviews: the entry, acceptance and cross-cultural orientation of mainstream journalists covering unfamiliar cultural or racial communities; and the struggle of members of minority constituencies to gain acceptance *as journalists*, rather than as representatives of their cultural or racial communities. Let us turn to the first problem.

Negotiating access can be a difficult and alienating experience, especially if there is inadequate awareness of cultural differences. The experience of Pierre Mignault, a CBC News journalist who often covers Native "beats," can be helpful in this regard. This is a brief summary of his experience and his advice after working within Quebec first peoples communities for many years:

> I think that access comes with time and trust. Probably the most difficult story to do is the first one. After this, people will be able to read you a little better. But the idea is when you go into a community, you should be on Indian time rather than on deadline. Maybe you should actually take time to talk to people.
>
> When I started covering Native affairs, I went into it by accident. I followed a group of white men that were cross-country skiing and I did this sports event. And the last shot is when they arrive in the community. I went there for the arrival and that's where I met the Inuit and I just was stunned. So, I decided to get acquainted with the culture. That was my first real contact with Native culture. From then on,

I started getting drawn back in and back in. At one point, I realized that I was doing news coverage based on spokespeople like from the Band council. I went into Indian communities, but the only people I talked to were politicians. And also, I found that the clips were not that good in terms of what I was used to, because they spoke differently. So, my big problem was that I had no idea of the cultural values that I was facing there. I just had preconceptions. Obviously, I was raised to think what Indians are from books. Also, if I was drawn to the Indians, I was sort of maybe a little pro-Indian or paternalistic or something like that. I don't know if it's a guilt thing, but I think I just like Natives a lot for their spirituality. In any case, what I did was I dropped out. I took a sabbatical for six months and my only purpose during this time was to try to assimilate as much culture as I could, rather than look for contacts and sources and stories.

So I went on an archaeological expedition to Nunanguk at the tip of Ungava Bay, a site where Inuit presence goes back three thousand years. The expedition was organized by Avataq, an Inuit cultural organization. We were a group of thirty-five white people accompanied by three Inuit families. During the day, I shared activities with the Inuit. After this experience, I hitchhiked through the Northern communities with just a plane ticket and lived with other families and used my knowledge of networks like civil servants and things like that. And I think the most important thing I learned during those six months was that when you go to visit an Inuk, you just open the door and walk in. They don't knock on doors. Once you've understood that, you've established contact. So, that's what I tried to do.

My whole perspective on how they speak has changed and I can see where the clip is good now which I couldn't see as well before because I had these preconceptions that they should be just like us.

I think that what [journalists] have to do is basically take time . . . and start being interested in issues that are not necessarily constitutional issues. Just local issues and actually what people are really thinking about. I think the big thing is to get acquainted, take time. . . .

Language is very important when you're covering issues concerning a minority that is already seen with a bias . . . some words you can't use when you're describing a Native situation. I know that I check my language a lot more. . . . What I mean is that if you cover an issue that is happening in the Native community and you cover the same issue happening in a white community, you have to treat it differently. You have to be more cautious because the preconceived notions that people have of Natives make it that they're gonna blow it out of proportion.

You need careful language when you're dealing with Native issues because it's an explosive issue. You need careful language when you're dealing with black issues because portrayal of blacks on TV and in papers is always associated with crime basically. Therefore again, people have this bias—that's how I'm careful with Natives. Because I've seen reactions in newsrooms of the story I did, you know. Like people used to call me a moccasin licker. And people ask me very often, since I've done stories on Natives if I'm Native because they associate me with that. So, what I'm saying is that we need to use careful language when we're going to talk to our audience about something that's sort of foreign to them. . . .

> What I think in terms of advice for young people who are going to cover Native issues or ethnic minorities and things like that is that they have to know their audience. The real issue is who are we talking to and what is the language we have to use so that people will get information. In terms of covering Natives and ethnic communities, you have to take into consideration biases that are already built-in in your audience so that you will avoid traps like language. Well, I think the real answer and the easy way out for me, I guess, is this idea that if you do a story on a white man that's tipsy on the road, people will say, oh, you've had a bit too much to drink. Well, if you do a story of an Indian that's tipsy on the road, people will answer back, "Indians are all alike, Indians are all drunks." So, that's the idea. You're trying to put into perspective situations where, in order for it to translate what you really are trying to say to the people you are telling the story to, you have to take into account this process, how they already decode information regarding ethnic groups.

Like Pierre Mignault, CBC radio reporter Loreen Pindera has spent a great deal of time working with aboriginal communities. She is very critical of existing practices, especially those of "objective" journalism. Pindera argues that we need to take our time, study a variety of historical perspectives and find a common ground on which to build trust and respect with the people with whom we intend to work—in Canada, those whose lives are guided by behavioural, cultural and ethical codes different from dominant British and French traditions:

> From my experience with the justice inquiries in Manitoba, I have learned to listen, wait and watch. In aboriginal communities, we need to do this more than we are used to. So few mainstream journalists have any idea how things work. There is a need for a different time line and lots of patience. We have to let people . . . get their anger out before we get to the nitty-gritty of the story. Their point of view has to get out there. We can't use the quick-hit approach. It takes an awful lot more time to re-establish trust with community after they've been so frequently misrepresented by the mainstream media.
>
> There is an abhorrent lack of reponse to aboriginal issues by federal government leaders in (the 1993) election campaign. Almost no candidates have gone into Inuit communities in northern Quebec and this is always the way it is during elections. I spoke with William Tagoona (an Inuk CBC Northern Service reporter) this morning and he told me that the CBC sent out invitations to all leaders to send a tape for their free-time political broadcast. The only one that sent anything in was the Bloc Québécois. Few cared enough about the Inuit vote to send any stuff. The Inuit and Cree are in separate ridings—therefore, they don't have a large enough block of votes to have their interests represented. This is very frustrating to the Inuit I've spoken to. They know that their interests will never be represented. The last time an Inuk was taken seriously in Northern Quebec was when Prime Minister Trudeau named Charlie Watt to the Senate and then he became unavailable to us from then on.
>
> There is a great level of extreme anger about the fact that mainstream media ignore Northern Native issues. This resistance to mainstream media comes back to

> haunt anyone in the mainstream media who tries to get access to information. It is a long, slow process.

The non-Native journalist's frustration escalates when she or he expresses interest in Native or other minority issues, does appropriate historical research, takes the time to develop political spokespeople and grassroots contacts within the community and then is regarded as somehow having betrayed the tenets of "real" or "objective" journalism. Loreen Pindera, who with Geoffrey York of the *Globe and Mail*, stayed behind the barricades in Kanehsatake in 1990 after all other non-Native journalists had departed, experienced this consequence quite intensely. Theirs was an extreme case. They were accused of Stockholm Syndrome, in which the hostage identifies with the captors on whom he or she depends for security. From their perspective, Pindera and York were placed in an untenable situation, allowed to get only one side of the story. The Canadian army wouldn't talk to them and they had no access to the other players. Pindera said:

> The institution (CBC) had to make a decision—each journalist could only get and tell one side of the story—therefore CBC assigned journalists to one aspect of the whole story. The overall balance could only be achieved through a diversity of opinions from several journalists each getting only one side at a time. If the CBC expected to get the whole story through one journalist's perspective, they were not doing their job, because each was so limited in access to information. CBC reporters would have had to give up their jobs to the PR person at the army.

Because this is not a customary practice of journalists, when York and Pindera failed to bow to pressures for conformity, they were accused of extreme bias. Any outside journalist interested in the actual issues was seen as parti-pris by the majority of the other media. aboriginal media like CKRK (Radio Kahnawake) or *The Eastern Door* newspaper in Kahnawake are assumed to represent Mohawk interests. During the crisis, Miles Morrisseau of the aboriginal newspaper *Nativebeat* and Dan David, a freelance journalist, said they could not get their stories on the air because they were seen as being too cozy with the Mohawks. As Pindera says:

> As soon as journalists do get access to the community, the outside perception is that you are too close to accurately portray the issues. As a specialist on a medical beat, you never get accused of being too close to a story. But on a Native or racial issue, when you become informed and understand the issues, then people begin to slot you as being too sympathetic.

Given the current tendency to accuse journalists of bias and the preoccupation with political correctness, it is no surprise that many try to avoid the complexities of cross-cultural work. Add to this the controversy surrounding the Canada Council's recommendations for equality of access to the arts; of cultural trespassing; and appropriation of voice, ideas and stories, and it is easy to understand why "white" journalists are afraid of saying the wrong thing on the air and being accused of racism. In "risky" issues such as gambling in Mohawk communities or factionalism in black or Asian communities, this concern has led to self-censorship. Pindera's approach is to

> work slowly and patiently. I do bristle at political correctness that prevents us from doing critical stories of those communities. Journalists fear being labelled racists. These labels are thrown around too easily these days. Look at the coverage of black politics in Montreal. If there's one problem focused on one community, you *have* to talk about it. Or look at the Mohawks and cigarette smuggling. My biggest concern is that the media wait till violence occurs before covering an issue. This is a story about a million-dollar industry and communities that are forever changed. Yet, when mainstream journalists try to cover it, they are labelled as co-opted and when non-mainstream journalists try to cover it, they fear to tread because of the potential accusation of racism. Alternatively, they do slash and burn stories that place all Mohawks on the same boat and then the Mohawks get upset because they are unjustly labelled as cigarette smugglers.
>
> I think all of this has more to do with where newsroom priorities are than overt racism in the newsroom. For example, in Kanehsatake, until they reached a stage of violence, they were not covered seriously. And journalists ended up going into the community without knowing its history. The definition of what news is is problematic. News journalists never have time to look at historic factors that dictate how a situation is going to unfold. Some subjects require much advance preparation.

Another example of a problematic issue in Native communities is coverage of the subject of AIDS. Pindera notes: "A few years ago, one chief in Manitoba said about AIDS: There is no such thing as a gay Indian." Later on, she remembers watching the first television program on AIDS showing aboriginal victims and two Native politicians. She recalls one saying to the other: "Oh, he must be Ojibway." The other responded to the first one: "No, he must be Cree." Who would feel prepared to do backgrounders to these comments, to look critically at the issues behind the statements? As a result of putting herself on the line in the Kanehsatake issue, Pindera considers herself to be

> much less of a cultural relativist than in the past. Is it possible to be a cultural relativist and a feminist and a journalist all at once? For example, let's look at the issue of underground clitorectomies in Ethiopian and Somalian communities. Without a clitorectomy, women aren't marriageable. These often happen in Ottawa. Stories need to be done on these issues. We need education for women in these communities. We need to come down on the side of unwaivering human rights in these issues of cultural conflict.
>
> Or the issue of Sikhs wearing turbans in the RCMP or Rastafarians joining the RCMP and smoking dope before going on duty. These are real tough ones. In the name of political correctness and tolerance, we're not touching issues that should be dealt with. It's difficult. We can't be afraid to offend. Sometimes, you have to be prepared to offend.
>
> Another difficult case I've heard of lately is domestic violence within the Hassidic community in Montreal. Whose job is it to assure that people are informed of their rights? Do open-minded journalists take sides on these issues?

It is not the aim of this essay to answer these questions but to identify the complexity of cross-cultural journalistic issues. Let us now turn to the second point, the position of the minority journalist in a specialty service or within the mainstream. Particularly within large institutions, the burden of culturally representing an entire community has sometimes been laid on "ethnic" or "Native" journalists. In practice, this has meant that specific journalists are often expected to cover their own community's beat and speak about little else. The question of acceptance as professional journalists capable of maintaining critical distance from issues, but also struggling around their own cultural conflicts, is a difficult one. Take, for example, the case of Dan David, a Mohawk journalist from Kanehsatake.

As a CBC reporter working out of Regina in the late 1980s David wanted to become a generalist, covering police, health, labour issues and so on. Initially he was able to do this. Later he says he was slotted in as the "Native reporter" and told that if he did not agree to restrict his work to the Native beat, his contract would lapse. Very soon after, he left the CBC to become a freelancer rather than be limited professionally in this way (Doan 1993).

The interview with Dan David revealed other ethical issues around conflict of interest. For example, he feels that his knowledge of the complexities behind some of the Mohawk controversies has placed him in a particularly vulnerable position when it comes to covering the issues publicly. At what point would he align himself with a political position and at what point would he attempt to cover the issue journalistically, at least from a critical perspective? According to David, his affiliation with Mohawks (being himself one) became so public that mainstream journalists stopped considering him a credible witness to the events in Kanehsatake, his home community. Eventually, he says, he was denied access to mainstream radio because of this assumption of bias. How would his position in his own community be affected by the fallout of his coverage?

During the crisis of 1990 the broadcasters at the radio stations in Kanehsatake and Kahnawake found themselves in similar positions. On many occasions they had to decide between conventional journalistic practices and their own ethical codes. For example, how much information should be made public, keeping in mind panic levels and journalists' potential ability to help defuse public tensions? Should names of missing people be broadcast over the air? These and many other issues have emerged from the position of the broadcaster in crisis or the broadcaster moving out of conventional territory and crossing cultural and racial boundaries.[6]

What all this tells us is that journalists ought to take a good hard look at their taken-for-granted practices. A crisis or crossing into new cultural and racial terrain is an opportunity to identify gaps in conventional journalistic practices that should be taken up, deliberated over and resolved in an honest, open and sensitive manner.

In the complex context of multiculturalism, the notion of "objectivity" and bipolar thinking makes much less sense now than in the past. Where it is still espoused, I would recommend that the notion of "objectivity" be modified to one of "critical distance," with a recognition that balance and fairness can be attained by comparing and contrasting several perspectives on a single issue. There are multiple facets to any story or event, and the goal of journalists doing cross-cultural reporting should be to get at as many of the complexities as possible without confusing the audience.

This does not mean that stories will be "biased," but rather that multiple "situated" accounts can together become part of a coherent whole and provide for a critical balance of the many—not just one or two—existing positions. If journalists do their work well, these positioned accounts should be recognizable to members of minority communities as relevant to their perspectives.

CONCLUDING COMMENTS

In a pluralistic society, cultural and racial communities must be portrayed fairly and represented equitably throughout the broadcasting system. This chapter has shown that in order to open up audio-visual spaces to diverse cultural and racial groups, it was necessary to restructure Canada's legislative framework. Canada's 1991 Broadcasting Act enshrined employment opportunities, fair representational practices and aboriginal, multicultural/ multiracial and community/constituency groups.

Changing the legislative principles of broadcasting is the first step in meeting the complex information and entertainments needs and interests of Canadian audiences. Now that the principles of inclusion, equity and fair portrayal have been asserted in the overall media infrastructure, it is important that these become integral values informing the ongoing ethical practices of all journalists.

Appendix 1:
Ethnic, Native and Community and Campus Media in Canada

AM Ethnic Radio Stations

CIAO (Brampton, Ontario)
CKER (Edmonton)
CFMB (Montreal)
CJVB (Vancouver)
CKJS (Winnipeg)
CHIN (Toronto)

FM Ethnic Radio Stations

CHCR (Montreal)
CHIN (Toronto)
CIBO (Senneterre, Quebec)
CINQ (Montreal)
CIRV (Toronto)

Multicultural/Multilingual TV

CFMT (Toronto)—carried on the universal tier
CHEX-TV (Toronto; Peterborough, Ontario)
CHIN-TV (Toronto)
Chinese National TV Network (Toronto; Vancouver; Edmonton; Calgary)
CTEQ Télévision Ethnique du Québec (Montreal)
Rogers Multicultural Channel (Vancouver)

Vancouver Talent Vision
VISION TV (although licensed as a multifaith network, it reflects culturally and racially diverse populations)

Specialty Ethnic Television Services (carried by cable companies)

Cathay (Vancouver)
Fairchild Communications (Vancouver)
Telelatino (Toronto)

Native Media in Canada

Thirteen regional Native communication societies
117 Native community radio stations

Television Northern Canada

Dedicated Northern satellite transponder received in ninety-four communities, one hundred hours per week, English and Native-language programming; covers one-third of Canadian territory, north of 55° latitude.

Community and Campus Stations

Fifty-seven community radio stations—non-Native
Twenty-six campus-based stations

Appendix II: General Guidelines to Assist Journalists in Depicting Constituencies in the Media

Words, images and situations are the tools of journalists. In our coverage of (inter)national, regional or local events, issues and personalities, it is very important that we do not reinforce erroneous preconceptions or suggest that all or most members of a racial/ethnic group or nation-state are the same. What follows are some basic depiction guidelines from the government of Canada (Multiculturalism Canada 1982: 21–22). This is only a beginning. We should probably all develop our own lists.

Visuals

Constituency groups, particularly minorities, should be realistically depicted at all levels of society. This means that there is an attempt to show multiple aspects of cultural, racial, community and other constituency groups.

Guidelines

1. Reflect the presence of visible minorities at all levels in a broad range of occupations.
2. Portray visible minorities in pursuit of a wide range of interests, sports and hobbies.
3. Reflect the participation of visible minorities in all aspects of Canadian life.
4. Ensure that visible minorities are portrayed as equally capable, resourceful, self-

confident, intelligent, imaginative and independent.

5. Ensure that visible minorities are adequately depicted as both observers and participants in mainstream cultural events (music, theatre, etc.) as well as in festivities focusing on multiculturalism per se.
6. Be aware of regional population mixes when preparing material either regionally or at the national level, for regional distribution.

LANGUAGE

Oral and written communication in presentation and development should respect the principles underlying the guidelines for visual material. The following relate explicitly to the use of language:

1. Avoid words which cloud the fact that all attributes may be found in all groups and individuals.
2. Avoid qualifiers that reinforce racial and ethnic stereotypes. A qualifier is added information that suggests an exception to the rule. Substitution of the term "white" or an Anglo-Saxon surname may be used as a test for hidden qualifiers.
3. Be aware of language that, to some persons, has questionable racial or ethnic connotations, e.g., use of the term "culturally deprived," or color-symbolic words which have negative implications.
4. Be aware of the self-identification preferences of racial and cultural groups, e.g., "Inuit" is preferable to "Eskimo."
5. The use of individuals either as actors or as persons interviewing or being interviewed should not be precluded because of an accent, so long as the message can be understood. Deliberate use of accents which may reinforce stereotypes should be avoided.
6. Use gender-neutral words such as s/he and Ms.

Appendix III:
Interview with Rita Shelton Deverell, October 16, 1993

Rita Shelton Deverell: What happened was a casting call came up through the ACTRA [Association of Canadian Television and Radio Artists] union in 1983 for a CBC docudrama on farm suicide. This was to be one of the first of a series of programs that were planned for shooting in Regina. At first we were thrilled about this because ACTRA and Actors' Equity have lobbied and lobbied for more work. . . .

So I phoned up and made an appointment to audition, and when I got there, the script assistant gave me the parts of the two 40ish women to read. This seemed appropriate since the others were men or children. I went to the studio and the producer said, "Rita I would have you audition for this, but these people are white," and I said, "Are you sure?" And he looked surprised at that question, but he said, "Yes, I am, and so is the writer."

Now the writer was Barbara Sapergia of Saskatoon . . . so I couldn't query this. So I said to him, "I'm going to argue with you about this, but not right now". . . and then he had that look of revelation and he said, "but it occurs to me I could have you read for the psychiatrist." Now the psychiatrist had been listed as a fifty-year-old male, so he was having an interesting turnaround about my ability to read for the psychiatrist. He let me read for the psychiatrist. Subsequently, I was not cast as the psychiatrist nor was any other woman. . . .

When I got home, I phoned Barbara in Saskatoon and I said, "I'll just tell you what happened when I tried to audition for your script and I want to know if what the producer said is correct. Are the people white? Is there something that makes these people *irretrievably* white?" She was very shocked and said, "No these characters are an amalgam of newspaper clippings and I'd be quite pleased to have you audition for this script. I can't see any problem."

With that, we sent two of our local Saskachewan ACTRA members to meet with the producer and attempt to raise his consciousness on this problem. . . . Two middle-aged Anglo-Saxon men went to see him to tell him a couple of things. Our main problem was that we had a clause in our collective agreement . . . that the corporation does not discriminate against any performer on the basis of race, ethnicity, gender. . . . And the second thing was that as we were a very small region and, given that I was one of the qualified performers living there, I at least deserved a decent hearing and an audition. The two men came away from that meeting with the producer quite shocked because they realized that he couldn't see the problem. The image that he had in his head of the character was that of a white person. I'm not white. . . .

Also, on the basis of that meeting, the producer wrote a letter to the Saskachewan ACTRA group saying that he understood that we were upset about this, but that the picture that he had in his head of the characters was that they were white, that I was a marvelously talented performer, but that even someone as talented as me couldn't pretend to be white when I wasn't. He further claimed that we would be infringing on the producer's right to cast if we insisted that I or anyone else presumably could be considered for this.

We then learned that this letter had been invented by the CBC lawyers and clearly the cornerstone of the letter was the producer's right to cast. So, we then had a local grievance meeting where we asserted our right to audition. The grievance was denied. It then became a national grievance. I was at the national, though not at the local, grievance meeting. Here again, there was a long, protracted discussion where, with full confidence and many people sitting around the table, the corporation asserted that saying that I could not read for the part because I am black was not discrimination on the basis of race, that's not what it was. It was challenging the producer's right to cast, and that this would not be challenged. Producers have the right to cast. So they would not accept that.

The other reason that was being asserted by the corporation was that a typical Saskachewan farmer was white and therefore to put a typical Saskachewan farmer on the air as not being white would just befuddle everyone.

So, they denied that I was discriminated against on the basis of race, even though I couldn't read because I'm black and they asserted that we were challenging the producer's right to cast. ACTRA said at the end of the meeting that we did not agree with their decision and therefore it was to be taken to arbitration. Now, this seemed to shock the corporation greatly because an arbitration is a long, expensive process and I think that they did not anticipate that this matter was going to garner that much of the union's time and resources. I suspect, in fact, that if it were right now, it wouldn't. But at that moment for a whole variety of reasons, the union was ready to do that. The lawyers then started to get the arbitration together.

Lorna Roth: Why didn't the writer come in to speak on your behalf because she agreed that you should have had the audition?

Rita Shelton Deverell: Writers don't cast scripts, but she was definitely going to come in on the arbitration to testify exactly what she said to me over the phone. By the way, we learned subsequently that there were several attempts made to get the writer to change her mind about her statement. There was pressure brought to bear on the writer to somehow say that her vision was that these people had to be white. But she wouldn't say that, to her great and eternal credit, because it would have been a much weaker case if she had.

So, there were a couple of things. There was the writer. There was also the local of the national farmer's union in and around Maidstone, Saskachewan, which is largely black—that is, black farmers in Saskachewan. There are black farmers all over the Prairies.

The historic concentration of black people in Saskachewan is around Maidstone, as in Alberta it's around the Amber Valley. There was a wave of immigration from the early part of the century. These people are farmers, not to mention all of the Native farmers in Saskachewan and the sort of dark farmers of Slav origin. There is a whole group of people who are not white. But the union's argument was not about that. The union's argument was that the job that I was applying for was the job of acting, not the job of being a farmer. The issue was not whether there were any black farmers in Saskachewan or not. The issue was whether I was capable of doing this part and if there was anything in the part that meant that the person playing the part had to be white. For example, if you were playing Sir John A. Macdonald, most people know that he's white and, therefore, maybe that person should be white—unless you go into a form of very non-traditional casting. So that was the union's contention.

We're now into 1984 and about a week before the arbitration. CBC decided to settle out of court. I can't speak for them, but it is possible to suggest that they may have felt that they weren't going to win. Now, since they had presumably assumed they were going to win up until that time, the only thing that I can think that would have caused them to feel this way is that they had also had a seminar on racism for producers at CBC Saskachewan. Whether this was to be part of their argument about how they weren't racist, I don't know. But, I believe that the producer in question demonstrated at the seminar that, indeed, his attitude about this matter was racist, so that to testify that he was not racist was going to be problematic. . . .

The settlement was that every casting director and every producer in the entire system be written to that this matter had violated the collective agreement; that people had the right to audition as the collective agreement says and that a small cash settlement had been awarded to the griever—that is, me—which came out of the producer's production budget. The message was that if you make these kind of mistakes, they can cost you money. . . .

Now, I suppose that if I wanted to devote my entire life to this, I could have insisted that the thing be reshot with me in it or something like that. But that would have been a little bit too much, you know, life was moving on in the meantime.

Appendix IV: Letter from Joan Beatty, CBC Television, Regina

October 14, 1993

Lorna Roth
Concordia University
Journalistic Ethics Project

Two stories stand out in mind which would fall into the research you're doing.

1. Honouring aboriginal elders

This involved doing a medical story on an aboriginal reserve. One element of the story involved talking to an aboriginal elder who used traditional medicine.

For years, I've been trying to get someone to talk to me on camera about this. Aboriginal people are very touchy about things like this. To them, it's sacred and not to be shared with just anyone. Even young aboriginal people are usually not shown these medicines and how to apply them unless you have been chosen to do so. Never mind white mainstream media filming.

This lady only spoke Cree. I speak Cree, so I was able to break down that barrier. She agreed to show me the various herbs she works with and to allow us pictures after I explained why we were doing the story. She saw our story as a teaching tool.

But there is another tradition common to many aboriginal communities, especially those who still follow traditional customs. And this is the point I want to make. Elders are held in high esteem in traditional aboriginal communities because of their wisdom, skills and knowledge. They are the teachers, the keepers of aboriginal culture. If they help you, you show respect and honour by giving them gifts. In some communities, that gift is tobacco. In other areas, like the North where I'm from, where we did this story, gifts vary.

In some communities, it's customary to present your gift prior to the elders helping you. In this case, I did it after we had completed shooting.

CBC policy says you are not to pay for your stories. What I did was I bought this old medicine lady some thread (it had to be a specific strength for tying herbs together) and a large scissors for cutting them. She lives far from a general store, so she was very thankful. I told the producer what I was doing. He didn't see any problems with it.

But there are times when I want to show my honour and respect of elders when I do aboriginal stories and they agree to work with me. I don't always give them anything. Every time I do present a gift, it's out of my pocket; and usually after the fact so as not to appear I'm paying them.

There are times I wonder why it always has to be the white man's or the CBC's way all the time, with little or no regard to aboriginal customs or value systems.

2. Power of the Chief

In a small Northern aboriginal reserve, five teenage suicides occurred in seven months, with thirty suicide attempts a month. It's still happening.

In aboriginal communities, death is a very sensitive topic. It's not to be treated lightly, especially when you are talking about someone who has passed away. Visiting a graveyard is done with utmost respect. You do not step over the grave for example.

I could only do the story with help from the health workers because I know them and they trust me. Earlier, other television reporters had been prohibited from going into the community. These health workers are younger and believe one way of dealing with these deep-rooted problems is to talk about them openly, to get professional help through workshops and individual counselling.

I wanted to do the story, the health workers wanted to talk and even those directly affected wanted to share their pain. A former volunteer worker, fairly young, was elected to the Band council. He wanted us to do the story too. That was our big link to the community.

I phoned the Chief to tell him the kind of story we wanted to do; talking to the families affected, why it's happening and what the community is doing about it. He agreed. Permission was also cleared by the health coordinator. This took more than a year to coordinate because it is so sensitive.

With help from one Band councillor and the health workers, we line it up. People agree to talk, including an aboriginal minister and elder who went to the grave site with us. We go there and begin shooting. On the third day, we are told by another Band councillor to stop shooting under orders from the Chief. We were told this councillor didn't want us in there. He said it would hurt the community. A fax was also sent to CBC regional director and the executive producer not to air the piece.

We completed the story. It will be aired, but now the Chief has banned his staff from talking to me or other CBC staff unless it's been cleared with him.

On my own, I spoke to an elder from that community to ask his thoughts on the matter. He said the story has to be done. I also spoke to the staff who worked with me on the story. They said I would be letting down those individuals who shared their stories in hopes of helping others if we didn't do it. One staff said there's an undercurrent of young people trying to make changes who are also fighting the old establishment.

Still, it was one of the hardest pieces I have ever done because I pride myself in understanding and doing aboriginal items fairly and honestly because I am one. I found this very difficult to do because of the sensitivity of the story, but I felt it had to be told.

But I also question the power of the Chief to try and muzzle his own people. Where is the freedom of the press when it comes to aboriginal reserves?

For years, it's been the custom of aboriginal media outlets not to do hard news stories which would put their own leaders and people in a bad light. If you did, you didn't last very long because most were tied to aboriginal political organizations.

Perhaps what's happening is that more aboriginal people are starting to question what aboriginal leaders are doing about the many problems in their communities, including aboriginal journalists like myself. Only time will tell how many of these kinds of stories I can do without being totally blackballed from the aboriginal community. Do white journalists go through the same thing?

In terms of my own peers here, not much was said about this story. My field producer, I think, understands what I went through. He was supportive and very sensitive to how we approached people and how we shot the story. There was never any question whether we would air the piece or not.

Appendix V:
Letter from Conway Jocks, former manager, CKRK, Radio Kahnawake

Dear Lorna/Daniel,
As the former station manager for CKRK-FM and presently a freelance contributor, I'm more likely to remember problematic incidents at a scale equal to the small size of my community and its radio station. Almost every media-related dilemma in a tight little town can have a personal repercussion for its author. Add to that this community's unique ethnicity, if I can use that word, then the problem is geometrically more profound.

To answer your question, there is one specific incident I can recall, but there is also a continuing problem that nags me, morally and ethically.

First, the one specific incident. During the days immediately following the re-opening of the barricades after the Mohawks' 1990 confrontation with the police and army, there was a great deal of resentment towards the SQ [Sûreté du Québec, the Quebec police] which patrolled the entry points to the reserve. For our part, we erected checkpoints manned by the Warrior Society at all the five "gateways." They soon turned out to be potential flashpoints for more trouble.

One night, the deejay on duty phoned to tell me the Warriors and their supporters had massed in front of the station and the "War Chief" was in the building, demanding air time on behalf of "the people." When I arrived I found I couldn't get in through the front entrance, so I took a detour and came into the station through the fire door. After some verbal sparring with the War Chief we sat down together to discuss his demand.

According to him, a boy of about ten years was at one of the checkpoints and was sideswiped by an SQ car and hurled into the nearby bushes. I met the boy, looked at his bandages and asked him to take a few steps. Then I went on the air with the boy and indulged myself in some fine indignation towards police who would do such a thing.

It wasn't until a few days later that I found I had been had. But in the meantime I realized I had unconsciously escalated the community's bad feelings toward the SQ. In retrospect, I think I should have made a better evaluation of the facts before I committed the sin of sensationalism and compromised the station's integrity.

Now the ongoing nagging problem. Unquestionably, the radio station serves a vital community service through its daily talk show, "Party Line." This is where all the factions can give voice to their disparate credos. Sometimes I think the show would be better named "Free For All." As the show's host, I must demonstrate complete neutrality. For that reason, I can no longer attend the Longhouse of my choice since each of the three Longhouses espouse opposing philosophies. The penalty for going to a particular Longhouse would be to be branded as being obviously partial to their philosophy, and my audience would be reduced to a third. In effect, I've surrendered a degree of personal freedom for the sake of the public good, as I see it.

I hope this can be helpful to your inquiry, but as I said earlier, problems and dilemmas in small towns are small problems and dilemmas. But the effects are big time.

9. Journalism and First Nations

Bud White Eye

During the week of the O.J. Simpson pretrial, at least 450 other felony hearings were held in Los Angeles alone.[1] Most likely, some were brutal murders. Every journalist knows that if they don't live up to the standard way of selling the news, they're out of a job. That means covering murders, or anything else horrific, that can be made sensational with as much gory detail as possible. In the 1950s murder shocked us. Now only multiple murders catch our attention. We seem to be shock-proof because of the number of murders reported. Is it all the journalist's fault?

Some of the responsibility belongs to the news organization. Cocaine isn't good for anyone but millions buy it. If no one offered it for sale, no one would buy it. If the media did not offer sensationalism, the public would read, hear or watch something else. But is there money in "something else" if you can't sensationalize it?

So we know that ethics doesn't play a big role in reporting the news. Perhaps reporting does have a minor role in alerting the public to significant events, good or bad. However, ethics in journalism, or the lack of ethics, profoundly affects people whether or not they read the paper or watch or listen to the news. They tend to pass off what they read as a societal norm and talk about it in coffee shops and bars, often mentioning where they read it as "not being wrong."

Journalists have to assume blame somewhere, somehow, sometime. If they're going to write and report, they *must* know that the way they see something may not be the way others who have a stake in it will see it. And journalists can change or influence the thinking of those who are mere bystanders or news followers. For example, a couple of years ago two murders were committed in the London, Ontario, region. One of the victims was a white student attending the University of Western Ontario. The other was a First Nations youth living in London. There is no indication that the two incidents were connected. The first victim was presumed to have been abducted and killed after stopping her car on Highway 401 to check on the condition of her vehicle. The second victim is presumed to have been abducted and later killed; his body was found some miles east of the city along Highway 2.

In the case of the white victim, the initial reports were headlined and the story was carried for many days and continued periodically for months after. In the meantime the reporting on this case led to much public outcry deploring violence. Women's groups became involved and police set up a hotline and asked anyone with information to come forward. Two years later, the police released more evidence, hoping people would be able to give them help with their investigation. All of this was done through the media.

The First Nations victim didn't make the headlines. There was one follow-up story and another story a year-and-a-half later saying police had reported that the case was still a mystery. There was no mention of a hotline or a continuing investigation nor a plea for help from the public. Even if the police handled the two murders in the same way, this was not reflected in the media.

First Nations community members and family easily recognized the different treatment and the subtle message that was conveyed: the white woman's case was worth expanded coverage, the case of the "dead Indian" had little chance of increasing news sales and did not merit continuing coverage. First Nations children in school playgrounds and high schools suffer from the belief that their lives are of far less worth than those of others, a belief perpetuated by the media in the handling of First Nations stories.

Even if a journalist is a member of a First Nation and is available to advise on news coverage, there is no guarantee that news outlets will get their reporting right or that they will even want to. Not long ago, CBC Radio had a First Nations associate producer on one of its afternoon shows. The radio station, in Windsor, Ontario, has several First Nations communities in its listening area. It regards its coverage as "tri-county" and comprehensive, including the First Nations communities in that "tri-county" area. One morning, as the First Nations associate producer, I proposed a story originating at Walpole Island. The producer's response was, "Bud, we have already done two Native stories this week." Surprised and angry, I replied, "How many white stories have we done this week?" She said, "You know what I mean." I know she knew what I meant, but I still don't know what *she* meant, because she refused to talk about it anymore.

During a training period at CBC's "Morningside," Canada's premier radio show, I was introduced to script writing. The first couple of weeks were heavy in "intro" (lead) writing. None of my intros was accepted. This was fine, I was new. After a time, I started comparing my intros with those of other producers. Soon I was at a stage where I thought they were as good as anyone else's, yet they were still being sent back to me.

I asked veteran producers to check my work and they said the intros were fine. So I told the desk editor/producer I would seek help from the show's veteran producers before turning my work in. Things started to go well and my items began to get broadcast. Not long after, I quit asking for help and informed the editor/producer I was doing my own work.

My next item was immediately criticized and sent back. Once another producer had checked it, it was accepted. I soon learned that all I had to do was to say someone had helped me (whether or not they did) and my work would be accepted. So I did. For the better part of a year at "Morningside," I turned in my scripts along with "So and so helped me with the lead," and bingo! Once, it got so ridiculous that the editor/producer reworked my intro with his own pen and sent me back to redo it. I did. Then I took it back and he said it was unacceptable, I said, "But sir, those are your notes on my intro, you rewrote it." He said, "I did?" I said, "Yeah, you did it with your special pen." And I showed him the intro with his notes. He then said, "So I did. Okay, throw it in the basket." The "basket" holds all the material for the next morning's show. In other words, my work had been accepted for that day.

In the year, I produced seven or eight Native stories. I did one on the Eagle Heart Drum, from Toronto, brought them right into the studio. I did a story on the purple murrelet, a bird which can only survive high in the old growth trees of Victoria Island and is now disappearing. I did the Gerald Bull story about the man who designed the big gun but was assassinated in Belgium for his efforts. I did a story about a Native flutemaker from Buffalo, New York, who designed "love" or "courting" flutes that really work. And I produced a major story I felt really good about. I went to Walpole Island, did the research and set up a two-day taping. Using our Walpole material, Peter Gzowski broadcast on "Morningside" back in the studio during the Oka/Kanehsatake crisis.

We had a big meeting at Jackson Point, Ontario, where we all made initial proposals for the coming year. I told them they didn't need to "ghettoize" me into First Nations stories. I said there was no shortage of Native stories. I said that, with over 2500 reserves in Canada, each with a few hundred stories of its own about life, politics, heritage, arts and so on, we would never run out of First Nations stories. One of my proposals was to set up a panel with people talking from different parts of the country at the same time, giving a "window" on the communities. "Morningside" still does a weekly panel like that, every Monday morning. I suggested doing it in a First Nations context.

I said First Nations communities were full of stories if you had the courage, or the conscience, to go and do them. I stood up and talked for about twenty minutes. At the end they asked me how they could get a good window on one of the communities. I suggested Walpole Island because of its size and its cross-section of people, from fairly affluent to poor.

This was during the Oka crisis, during the time when the army had the people at Kanehsatake squeezed into the treatment centre. Peter Gzowski wanted something to happen while we were there, so he could get public reaction from Band members. They were looking for some big community hall with the whole community looking at one television set, waiting for things to happen. I told them, "You're not going to find that. They're not gathered around one TV someplace." To find something like that seemed to be worth a big score to them. I told them, pretty well everyone had their own TV set and was probably watching the Kanehsatake situation "but if they're going to talk about it, it would be over coffee tomorrow, just like everyone else does when some major news event catches their interest or disturbs their morality."

I did all the advance work. I wrote the script. I thought they gave me a lot of liberty on that. I wasn't restricted in any way. Then, a few months after doing the Walpole thing, back at "Morningside," I was told to stop offering up First Nations stories. They wanted me to "show my ability" to discover other stories.

Because of this, there was a big conference call among First Nations CBC journalists from across the country and one of the higher-ups at the CBC who had heard that Native employees were complaining of being stymied in their efforts to produce Native stories. That "higher-up" from personnel said she would take it right to the top and they would get to the bottom of it. She seemed so sincerely interested in doing something that seemed to be against CBC policy and to be interested in how it affected us. She said she had been after "Morningside" for a long time, for a variety of complaints from across the country regarding the CBC and its treatment of First Nations producers and staff. That was the last I heard. Nothing happened.

At "Morningside," they went back to the non-First Nations producer who had done First Nations stories before I got there. I worked with him closely in the beginning. He was an excellent producer and is still a good friend of mine. But when they saw that I was bent on doing First Nations stories, I was called into the office and told to stop. At the Jackson Point meeting, they rejected my proposal for a First Nations panel. They said it probably wasn't a good idea. Less than two years later, they tried it. I was long gone. It had become "somebody else's" great idea.

I first felt the lack of trust at "Morningside" but the worst experience was in Windsor. The producer and I went into the back room about every other day and argued over my stories. I was producing stories from all over because I knew the counties really well and all the reserves in the area. The first story I tried to sell was about Walpole Island. That's when the producer said, "Bud, do you have anything else on your list? We've already done two Native stories this week."

When I asked how many "white" stories we had done so far, she slipped right off the handle. She said, "Come on, Bud, you know what I mean. Never mind . . . later." We argued my approach to stories and hers. She never threatened to fire me. We'd argue for half an hour and she'd say, "Let's go back out there and go to work," and we did. But the message was that if you did too many First Nations stories, they would be thrown out (and they were). How many is "too many" in terms of good stories, First Nations or not?

Then I brought up a story idea about (non-Native) Manitobans who migrated to Mexico, lived there for fifty years and migrated back to Ontario. I did the pre-interviews, got the background, pitched the story. There was a sort of clearing house, complete with an interpreter, counsellor and liaison for housing, food, etc., in Chatham, Ontario, for the immigrants whom Canada was accepting because they were originally Manitobans. They had gone to Mexico looking for peace and tranquillity. Now destitute and starving, they had somehow made it back to Canada, through Windsor to Chatham, where the special office helped them find assistance of many kinds.

When the producer said, "So what's the story?" I really got mad. "What do you mean, 'What's the story?'" I asked. She replied, "Well, that's too bad. I don't think it's a story." I felt like quitting. I was told that producing radio was demanding and often frustrating. But this was just plain mean—it had nothing to do with a "difficult job." There was just too much to do to be bickering like that, but there had to be time to discourage First Nations writers and producers.

Media say their budgets are tight. But if you stand by the door long enough, you'll see a new face come in, and it won't be "Indian." I got hired at CBC Windsor in November 1991. I had worked there about three months when another journalist came in, a white producer. When they made the big cuts, they cut everybody, including me. I was there three months, she was there three weeks. When the cuts came, she didn't go, I did. They said she was there "for training" and my contract was up, and because of the cuts they couldn't renew it. But she stayed on. Six months later, I was doing some work on Walpole and there she was, phoning me up for story ideas about the powwow on Walpole Island. As far as I know, she's still there. Why didn't they call me back? Why didn't they keep me and send her home?

I was surprised when the *London Free Press* asked me to review the November 1992 Harry Rasky documentary, "Wars Against the Indians." I thought this was great. They gave me short notice, I wrote the review and they liked it. But they didn't tell me they had also asked a white journalist to write an even bigger piece. They put his review on the front page of the arts and entertainment section with a bold headline. They stuck mine on the third page, so it looked like a filler piece.

When I saw the paper the next morning, I thought, "They didn't trust me enough to do a decent review so they hired someone they trusted." But I don't think it's just about trust. It's also the idea of the "critic," their idea of what a "real review" is. I think it's also about the authoritative voice. Each week there are several reviews of films, books and arts events but they don't double them up. For "Schindler's List," did they hire someone non-Jewish for the "real review" and hire a Jewish person to do a "Jewish" review?

I went to cover an "Indigenous Peoples" workshop at Kings College in May 1991 and brought my story to the *Free Press* on a Friday afternoon. One of the editors looked over my piece, went back to the top and all of a sudden started adding things and taking things out. I was *there*. He couldn't change the events, but he was taking out big chunks and putting in big chunks. After reworking the story, they didn't just print it with the usual byline, they added a box with my photograph and an explanation:

> Native journalist Bud White Eye is a guest reporter contributing to Free Press coverage of this weekend's Indigenous People's Conference in London.
>
> A graduate of the University of Western Ontario's native journalism program, he has written for the CBC's national radio program "Morningside." He has also been associate producer of morning and afternoon programs at the CBC radio station CBE in Windsor (White Eye 1991).

Later in a story meeting, I told them that if I do a story, I want it done the way I do it. I'm a First Nations writer, this is a First Nations perspective, a First Nations writing style. If you change it to your way, there's no sense having me. You might as well go out and do it yourself. After 145 years of existence, I don't think the *Free Press* had ever had a First Nations writer before I got there. To finally have a First Nations writer and say, "We want your style, we want your perspective," then go back to the office and start making major changes—how on earth can you edit a First Nations person's style or content if you've never worked with one before? How can you get that different flavour if you start changing things? Editing has to be based on understanding and experience. If you worked with Ojibway writers over many years, you could edit an Ojibway writer's work because you know that it flows a certain way and you know your readers. But with a first-time writer, when readers have yet to know if they like his style or not, the editor has no business making major changes.

Unless you come out of a school of journalism assimilated and write like mainstream white journalists, they don't want you. When the crunch comes, some of the least innovative people are the ones who stay. If you want a good cross-section of the communities you serve, you need to make it happen. Money shortage or not, there are still many white people working at the *Free Press* and no First Nations people. For that matter, I haven't seen any black journalists there either. They say, "As soon as we get some money, we'll do that." When they had lots of money, when times were good, they still didn't hire First Nations people.

I've conducted a little survey of newspaper coverage. In breaking "hard news" stories involving Native people, the first one to get interviewed is the white guy and he gets about ten paragraphs.[2] The reporter drags the chief in at the bottom, in a one-paragraph interview, or the story has no First Nations interviews at all.[3]

A couple of years ago, a "shooting" at Camp Ipperwash blazed on the front pages, yet even today no one knows whether there *was* a shooting. A helicopter landed, people said someone took a shot at them and they found a bullet hole. Fifty Ontario Provincial Police (O.P.P.) officers surrounded the Stoney Point First Nation encampment where people were protesting the army's refusal to return the land to the community. The next day they raided and tore houses, tents and trailers apart. They didn't find any guns. Guns are there because the *army* has guns. The news showed the army on one side, the O.P.P. on another and the small Band of Stoney Point people in between. Across the country, people got the "news" of a "shooting" and the idea that First Nations people had done it (Mathewson 1993:1: Dobson 1993:1).

In another case, an off-duty policeman left his car running while he went into a Becker's store. While he was in there, somebody stole his car. The news report said they had captured the thief on a reserve.

> He followed the suspect, who drove at normal speeds through the city before heading out onto Highway 401. At one point, Glenn stopped briefly to ask a cab driver to notify police before continuing his off-duty surveillance.
>
> Glenn lost sight of the thief when the driver pulled off onto Highway 4. But OPP officers were on the lookout and soon came across the car and arrested a man on the Oneida Reserve.
>
> Charged with car theft is Cary James Wojtkowski, 18, of RR 1, Muncey (Massecos 1993).

The alleged thief was not even a First Nations person. If the stolen car had been taken to another nearby community, it would not have been a news story at all. Car robberies happen in this city all the time. It was the "Indian reserve content" that made it a story. Someone asked me how to cover this kind of story. The answer is, you don't cover it unless you are covering all auto thefts.

If I'm a white editor and I see a car theft, I don't see "crime," but if I see a First Nations person and a car theft, I see something to put in the paper. So how do we get to people? First of all, you need to hire Native writers. Let them write the stories they feel are important and let readers decide if this is what they've been looking for all these years. How can the public judge, if they never have a chance to read? Readers might say, "We're finally getting a look into the community, getting a feel of the people. Having a Native journalist is finally breaking down some of the barriers, some of the secrecy is lifted from the community."

10. The Rashomon Principle: The Journalist as Ethnographer[1]

Valerie Alia

> I do not feel myself to be . . . a cold recorder of what I see and hear. On every professional experience I leave shreds of my heart and soul; and I participate in what I see or hear as though the matter concerned me personally and were one on which I ought to take a stand (in fact I always take one, based on a specific moral choice) (Fallaci 1976: 9).

> Ethnographic studies can make important . . . contributions to our understanding of morality. . . . Ethnographic work reveals that morality must be understood contextually, and once that broader, more realistic perspective is adopted, it provides a sobering appreciation of the prospects for moral reform (Hoffmaster 1992: 1425).

In the process of rethinking how to educate the next generation of journalists, I have had to re-examine my own work. After twenty years as a journalist and teacher, I am just learning how little I know of the depth and intricacy of other people's politics, cultures and traditions. I am deeply dissatisfied with the well-intentioned inaccuracies that persist in news coverage, bolstered by inadequacies in journalism education.

Some of my colleagues see ethnographic/cross-cultural training as a distraction from the "real" business of journalism and journalism training—the reporting of "facts" in an "inverted pyramid" style. I have always believed, with Oriana Fallaci quoted above, that journalists must put more than mere information into their work. They must also put in "heart and soul" and conscience. One way to do this is to borrow techniques from ethnographers.

While journalism and ethnography are not identical, the similarities are striking. The obvious difference is the deadline. Journalists are adept at becoming overnight experts while "an anthropologist is a journalist with a two-year deadline (Grindal and Rhodes n.d.)." Although the journalist's deadline may be closer to two hours than two years, investigative journalism and news analysis often use ethnographic approaches to research and reporting.

I use the term *ethnography* in its broadest sense to refer to the process of describing a culture. The journalist must learn to ask ethnographic questions which include the traditional five Ws and H (who, what, where, when, why and how). The next task is to understand and report accurately from one experience or culture to another. Regardless of where reporters do their work—at home or abroad, in large cities or remote regions—they almost never receive the kind of basic training given as a matter of course to diplomats, sociologists, anthropologists, politicians and businesspeople. The result is reportage with a level of ethnocentrism long held unacceptable in other fields. Despite growing awareness and increasing respect, people and events are still reported as cross-cultural kitsch, and journalists frame their work with a pretence of nonparticipation.

James Clifford (1987) says the ethnographer is an *active* participant who, in effect, tells the reader, "You are there, because I was there." James Spradley demonstrated this in his famous study of skid row men: "Listening, watching, and allowing these men to become my teachers, I discovered a complex culture that gave shape and meaning to the lives of men most people wrote off as 'derelicts'" (Spradley 1980: vi). Because he was an ethnographer and not a journalist, Spradley had time to live in the community. Following his principle of starting from a position of "ignorance," he behaved as a learner, not as a teacher, in an unfamiliar community.

Ethical journalism and ethical social science have many of the same characteristics, and similar research methods serve both fields. Like social science, journalism requires a certain humility, a willingness to learn new information and an awareness of one's limitations. In 1993, I attended a holiday celebration at the London, Ontario, office of Canada's New Democratic Party. In the previous weeks, there had been bomb threats and a demonstration by labour union members. People who arrived at noon saw Royal Canadian Mounted Police officers and a demonstration. Those who arrived five minutes later saw a quiet coffee party, with friendly chatter, people sipping tea and coffee and nibbling cookies. If one reporter had covered this event at 12:00 and another at 12:05, who would have the story?

I call this the Rashomon principle: "Truth" is really "truths" and is always based on multiple realities. It takes several reporters' voices to tell the whole story. Sometimes it takes the combined voices of insiders and outsiders.

In the early days of defending the "scientific" validity of social science, the core of "respectable" research was quantitative. Any self-respecting professional in almost any field knew how to collect quantities of data and assess and present the results as a contribution to knowledge. The obsession with numbers did not always lead to understanding, however, and, when it did, the understanding was limited. Missing were the human dimensions, the depth and nuance of experience. Today, people in many fields are adding qualitative components to quantitative methodology, studying atmosphere and context, considering the impact of "soft" data on "hard" information. Researchers are learning to ask new questions or to ask old questions in new ways.

Frederick Fletcher notes the growing importance of "participant observation" and descriptive techniques for opinion pollsters whose work has long been a major resource for journalists. These prototypical "bean counters" have radically changed their ways. To learn about television audiences, they used to set up an attachment to the family TV set and count who watched what. "Now they sit in people's livingrooms, watching how people watch TV" (Frederick Fletcher, personal communication, 1993).

LEARNING JOURNALISM

Reporting is not just about collecting "facts" and accumulating "sources." It requires descriptive powers, investigative skills and an ethnographer's attention to context. It often involves participant observation, removing the pretence that the researcher (or journalist) can or should stand antiseptically aside. Melvin Mencher told me (1981) he always included participant-observation exercises when he taught journalism at Columbia University.

Serious deficiencies in training leave journalists unprepared for many of the realities they encounter in the field. Reporters are taught to find "the truth," control the gathering of information and avoid, ignore or challenge the surprises. Some of my colleagues tell students to go out with the story firmly in hand, "stick to the outline," pick "authoritative sources" (i.e., elite "experts") and "always keep interviewees on topic."

In my view, that is a dangerous way to teach the next generation of journalists and a way to prevent accurate information from reaching the public. I ask students to write copious descriptions of a staged "event" and discuss the limitations of each person's vantage point, starting from the premise that no two people can *physically* see or hear the same event. I suggest that they look for "sources" "bottom-up," talk to people *affected* by decision-makers and "experts," listen for the questions they didn't know to ask and follow Spradley's principle of starting with a conscious attitude of near-total ignorance. The journalist should expect the unexpected, not write the story in advance; to understand and report the story, the journalist must be meticulously descriptive, incisive, investigative and critical. An honest reporter will almost always change the outline or the story; advance preparation is necessary but always insufficient.

Journalism is ethical to the extent that it tells as many truths as possible and avoids pretending that one reporter can ever have all of the information. It avoids ethnocentric biases that skew truthtelling. Some people construct a fictional dichotomy between "real," "fact-based" journalism and journalism that pays attention to cross-cultural communication. Such fictions miss the point: accuracy (the one principle everyone agrees on) requires that we research the cultural context. Sometimes it also requires more than one voice.

AN OVERVIEW OF TRADITIONS AND APPROACHES

An ethnographer does not only learn about "other" people: "No longer relegated to . . . cultures in far-off places, ethnography has come home, to become a fundamental tool for understanding ourselves and the multicultural societies of the modern world" (Spradley 1980: v)

The "first real research tradition" in American sociology emerged in the 1920s, led by Chicago sociologists W.I. Thomas and Robert E. Park. The "Chicago school" applied principles anthropologists had used to study "others" to the study of the researchers' own cultures (Collins 1985: 199). Their view of life as fluid and full of rapid changes is crucial to the reporter who must be prepared to record sudden shifts and unanticipated events. Like good reporters, they watched events unfold in their natural setting.

Then came the "symbolic interactionists," who emphasized change and spontaneity. Herbert Blumer said that any institution could change, any society erupt into revolution (Collins 1985). His principle of anticipating the unexpected is a crucial component in journalism training. The "down-to-earth approach" was not without contradictions. Randall Collins (1985: 2) reminds us that, along with an "interpretive, subjective study of human experience," they wanted to develop "an objective science of human conduct" that would reflect work in the "natural sciences." Symbolic interactionist Erving Goffman (1959: 128–29) applied the Rashomon principle in his work on "multiple social realities." He called day-to-day behaviour "performance," and looked at "informal or backstage . . . behavior" in private settings and formal "front" stage behaviour in public settings. For example, kitchen and serving staff behaved irreverently towards customers behind their backs but were very polite to their faces. Goffman and his colleagues said that, to interpret events, we must learn to read nonverbal language and look for backstage clues and meanings.

Too often, journalists are trained to read only front stage cues. According to William Boyd (1992), this has caused inaccurate reporting: white reporters misunderstand and misreport the everyday high-energy and loud talk and exuberant body language of African Americans as "aggressive." Similarly, some Anglo-Canadians misinterpret my own European-American-Jewish talk style (high energy talk punctuated by word play and hand and arm gestures) as "confrontational."

Sometimes misinterpretation is a life or death matter. In Hartford, Connecticut, a crowd of about one hundred attacked three policemen who were giving heart massage and oxygen to a woman having a heart attack. They thought the policemen were beating her. She died. To report the story accurately, the reporter needed to understand two sets of behaviour: the policemen's and the crowd's. The confusion may have originated in cross-cultural miscommunication: the police were anglophones and the crowd, mostly Hispanic neighbourhood residents were used to rough treatment and intercultural conflict and perhaps unaware of CPR techniques (*Hartford Courant* 1973: 6–7).

On the other hand, Geoffrey York's (1992: A14) incisive account of the arrival of Canadian troops in Somalia calls upon nonverbal description to interpret breaking news:

> Taking no chances, 58 Canadian soldiers kept their guns at the ready yesterday as they jogged off their transport plane into the blazing Somali landscape. . . . The soldiers . . . immediately formed a protective circle, keeping their C-7 automatic weapons poised for action, as they moved into position at Bela Dogle airport. For a full hour, the Canadians maintained their defensive position.

There is no need for briefings or verbal explanations of this behaviour; the description says it all. Later in the story, York includes background information, interviews and other details. The story shows us that the social scientist's insistence on long-term research need not limit the usefulness of ethnographic approaches in daily reportage.

The approach known as ethnomethodology was developed by Harold Garfinkel. Non-social scientists sometimes mistakenly use "ethnomethodology" as a synonym for ethnography, unaware that it is merely one of many ethnographic schools. The name comes from "ethnography", the "observational study of"; and "methodology", "the methods that people use to make sense out of experience" (Collins 1985:211). Ethnomethodologists (nicknamed "ethnos") criticized survey researchers for merely asking questions and mistaking answers "for the real ways people handled their lives" (Collins 1985: 205). They said symbolic interactionists stayed too close to the surface of human behaviour. The same criticism applies to reporters who rely on press releases, press conferences, surveys and opinion polls rather than careful investigation and observation. The growing reliance on what Pierre Mignault calls "melt-down" reporting works against this (see Chapter 13). As Tuchman (1978: 182) puts it, "newsworkers cover, select, and disseminate stories about items identified as either interesting or important . . . news reflects society [and presents] a mirror of its concerns and interests." Without news accounts, events such as Watergate or the My Lai massacre would be merely "personal troubles.'"

> News accounts indicated what was happening . . . in the everyday world . . . [and became] active participants in the sociopolitical processes. The military tried to bury the story of My Lai; the President's associates tried to bury the stories about Watergate. The media were part and parcel of the drama of structuring and releasing

information that would become the basis for the shaping of knowledge (Tuchman 1978: 189–90).

Garfinkel's methods were extreme. He became notorious for sending students out "to do 'experiments' that involved 'breaching' the taken-for-granted surface of everyday life." They were told "to act like strangers in their own houses, politely asking if they could use the bathroom" or "to go into a store, pick out a 99-cent tube of toothpaste and see if they could bargain the clerk into taking 25 cents for it" (Collins 1985: 212–13).

Edward T. Hall's work on time and space added important new tools for cross-cultural understanding. His work on "proxemics" is essential for journalism education. Each culture has its own unique time frames. To interpret across cultures, "it is just as necessary to learn the language of time as it is to learn the spoken language" (Hall 1983:2). Hall labeled the North European system of doing one thing at a time "Monochronic," or "M-time"; "Polychronic" or "P-time" stresses "involvement of people and completion of transactions rather than . . . preset schedules." In P-time cultures, appointments are taken less seriously and are often "broken." As a journalist and social scientist working with Inuit in small Arctic communities, I learned this the hard way. The local research assistant often made appointments with me but not with interviewees, forcing me to learn a new way of conducting unscheduled interviews and adapting tothe Inuit way of visiting (open doors, open schedules).

Polychronic peoples seldom experience time as "wasted"; monochronic cultures make a "fetish" of management and view polychronic people as always in flux with nothing "solid or firm" and no sense of planning "for the future" (Hall 1983: 46–47. A Middle Eastern or Latin American administrator diagrams the components of a job on elaborate charts, checking off each task as it is completed but leaving the employees to do the scheduling. A North American or European administrator does the scheduling and leaves analysis of the job's components to the employee. Hall identifies four levels of social distance: intimate, personal, social and public, each with a close and a far phase. To correctly interpret people's behaviour, we must understand the meaning of such distances for the people involved and the ways spaces are identified. Sometimes we need this understanding just to get to the event. The Japanese name intersections and not streets— each corner has a different name. Even Tokyo taxi drivers must ask police for directions in a city where houses are numbered in the order in which they were built. I have had similar problems locating houses in communities in the Canadian eastern Arctic, where streets have no names, and houses are numbered in different ways (for example, the Igloolik home which uses the owner's former "disc" identity number and has no numerical relationship to other homes on the same street).

Like many journalists, ethnomethodologists replaced the "objective" and distant observer with the interfering observer who "makes trouble" to get more information. Garfinkel challenged everyday assumptions about familiar situations. By multiplying "the senseless features of perceived environments" and observing the "disorganized interaction"—the "bewilderment, consternation . . . confusion . . . anxiety, shame, guilt, and indignation," we might learn more about how "structures of everyday activities are . . . produced and maintained" (Garfinkel 1967: 38). Some have criticized the ethics of his intrusive method.

Janet Malcolm (1990) embraces this trouble-making principle wholeheartedly with nary a glance at its problematic aspects. In a much-quoted essay, she insists that the ways journalists conduct interviews are always "morally indefensible" and calls the journalist "a kind of confidence man, preying on people's vanity, ignorance, or loneliness, gaining their trust and betraying them without remorse." For Malcolm, deception is required. Not everyone agrees. In the case of Watergate,

> Certainly, the situation was one of mounting crisis for the nation and of potential danger for investigating journalists.... It is certain, too, that there was great pressure to be first.... The desire to advance professionally and to gain fame formed no small part of the undertaking ... a whole fabric of deception arose.... It is not clear that, beyond the secrecy which had to surround the investigation, deception was actually needed (Bok 1978: 120–21).

It is not enough to say a practice is "accepted" or expedient. We need to examine the obvious contradiction of "accepted" deception in the interest of our assumed goal of truthtelling.

Journalism students and young professionals are taught to start their research "at the top," to go for the "experts," the "leaders," the officials. In 1965, working in an Appalachian community, George Hicks discovered that the best information didn't come from the top. "Stores and storekeepers were at the center of the valley's communication system" (Spradley 1980:3). Visiting each store daily, he gradually pieced together the understanding he was looking for. I have often told students to start at the general store. With others saying they should start with "primary" locations and sources, they rarely believe me and proceed immediately to somewhere official. They get frustrated. They come back and say, "We went to the offices, but no one had any information and the interviews were boring. We found the real story at the general store."

The news happens in people's daily lives. If you want maximum information, you go to a place people frequent where their guard is down and the gossip flies. For the official version, you go to municipal offices, courts, police headquarters. To learn what is going on, what people think, to get the *story*, you go to where people hang out or drop in.

As a reporter covering remote regions such as the Arctic or rural Vermont, I learned to loiter long and often in stores, pubs and coffee shops. Assigned to find out why a tiny Vermont town remained "dry," I was stymied. My editors assumed the town was "backward," driven by fundamentalist beliefs, opposed to "progress" or out of touch with "reality." In vain, I sought information. I wandered into the general store for a soda, started chatting with customers and the proprietor and got a very different, front-page story. It turned out that our assumptions were wrong. Townspeople had spent years studying a politically, environmentally, socially and economically tricky situation. Going "wet" could endanger a delicate environment. The decision was based on astute and complex thinking, not on unquestioned or old-fashioned beliefs.

Reconstructing Method

Psychiatrist Robert Coles found that the conventional wisdom he learned at university did not work with real people. When the "correct" methodology failed to help his patients, he found an unconventional mentor who told him:

> The people who come to see us bring us their stories. They hope they tell them well enough so that we understand the truth of their lives. They hope we know how to

> interpret their stories correctly. We have to remember that what we hear is *their story* (Coles 1989: 7).

Coles abandoned the abstractions intended more to impress colleagues than to help patients and began to *listen* to patients' stories. He helped one person out of an impasse by asking her to "begin at the beginning again" and tell some stories about her life (Coles 1989: 11). What was radical was not the idea of hearing someone's story, but the idea of allowing the storyteller's agenda to take over and the professional to "become bogged in a mass of circumstantial detail" (Coles 1989: 13).

In journalism, as in psychiatry, conventional wisdom—and teaching—tells us to avoid the subject's agenda, impose and maintain order (control the interview), avoid "superfluous" detail in the interest of meeting requirements of deadline, column inches or air time. The journalist-ethnographer knows that following those rules often means missing the story. Forecasting Coles' new psychiatry, Spradley (1980: 3) advocated an ethnography "based on the principle of *learning from people*, rather than *studying people*." That principle is especially important in covering First Nations as an outsider.

I have heard over and over again that non-Native journalists are afraid to go into First Nations communities to research stories first-hand. This fear comes from stereotypes, often perpetuated by the news media themselves. During a four-month research stay in the Yukon in 1991, I was repeatedly warned not to go into First Nations communities.

Insider-outsider teamwork encourages us to question whether the ethnocentric (and perhaps gender-centric) tradition of aggressive news-gathering is always the most effective way to get the story. Softer approaches—"hanging around"—and quieter and less obtrusive ways of presenting the journalist's self in the world she or he is observing can lead to greater trust and improved access to information. Stevie Cameron is known for her sharp, take-no-prisoners investigative reportage on Canada's most powerful people. She says her early "training in good manners" and less "testosterone-driven" interviewing style often lead to information more aggressive (usually male) colleagues miss. Sometimes, key information comes from sources conventional journalists ignore. She has learned much from hairdressers and cooks (less surprising if you consider that her early work was ghettoized in "women's" pages) (Cameron 1993).

Investigation is not the only way to serve the public. A journalist can be a cross-cultural guide, providing insights into one culture by explaining another. Kiri Nesbitt found a new way to write about abortion in Canada by starting with Japan. The Japanese do not view legalized abortion with the "moral outrage" expressed in Western countries. "Contrary to what anti-abortion proponents have suggested," Japan's provision of abortion on demand has not led to "multitudes" of abortions. One explanation lies in use of the same word, *ryuzan*, to mean either spontaneous or induced abortion. Another is the Buddhist understanding of karma which has led to the development of rituals to commemorate and apologize to "the spirit of the aborted fetus," called a *mizuko*. Some temples are primarily for aborted and miscarried fetuses. Toys are left, and "piles of flat stones so that the *mizuko* [can] climb to heaven."

> Thus, Japanese people both respect and remember the lives of unborn children and permit the termination of unwanted pregnancies. . . . Westerners should not be so arrogant as to assume that their [own] culture has all the answers (Nesbitt 1994: A22).

To find a solution to our "moral dilemma," we "need a much broader definition of what it means to be human. Examining attitudes in another culture . . . will not only provide us with a new insight" but may "help us come to terms with abortion" (Nesbitt 1994: A22). While the best journalists are, like Nesbitt, instinctive ethnographers, it is rare for them to receive formal training in ethnographic method. I believe that this methodology belongs at the core of journalism curricula.

WIDE ANGLES, CLOSE-UP LENS

Often, we can best show the broad picture through small details. Missing these details can mean missing the story. I.F. Stone (1970: xiv) spent his whole career taking material in the public domain and finding *more* than others found: "I sought [what Galsworthy] called "the significant trifle"—the bit of dialogue, the overlooked fact, the buried observation which illuminated the realities of the situation." Concerned that reporters "tend to be absorbed by the bureaucracies they cover," he stayed outside the pack. With a keen eye for text and an ethnographer's understanding of the cultures of journalism and government, he found "significant trifles" in dialogues and documents. Among other "coups," he forced "the Atomic Energy Commission to admit that its first underground test was detected not 200 miles away—as it claimed—but 2600 miles away" (Stone 1970: iv–v).

Tony Hillerman's novel *The Fly on the Wall* is both an ethnography of the Washington press corps culture and a demonstration of the uses of ethnography in investigative journalism.

> Whitey Robbins had just asked the usual question about Roark's political plans and Roark was giving his usual noncommittal answer. . . . "Governor," Cotton said, "were you surprised by the move in the house . . . ?"
>
> "I was surprised." His smile denied the statement (1971: 56).

Another angle on the culture of journalism (as well as on reporting across cultures) comes from a report by T.D. Allman who, in March 1993, went to Serbia to learn more about the killing euphemized as "ethnic cleansing." Allman and NBC correspondent Tom Aspell went in search of "life among the ruins."

> The only signs of life are occasional clumps of men—some armed, some not—sitting out in the sunshine, in front of bombed-out buildings, drinking.
>
> Then we see an elderly couple working in their garden. May we visit them? She rushes to make coffee, while he shows us the garden—tomatoes, pumpkins, plums. After serving the coffee, the old woman sits down in front of Tom's camera and is asked to describe what happened here. Immediately, she starts crying. She tells us that she and her neighbors spent nine weeks huddling in her basement. . . . Sometimes, when one of them went for water, she didn't make it back. . . .
>
> This couple, whose house and life were destroyed by Serb artillery, happen to be Serbs themselves (Allman 1993: 114).

Allman interviewed the couple, a professor and a succession of presidents, most of them not officially recognized—for example, Albanian President Ibrahim Rugova, a literary theoretician whose first love is Edgar Allan Poe.

It takes a watchful eye, and a readiness to interpret divergent cues and signals, to get the story. I tell students to watch for contradictions between "front and back stage" words and gestures and for small things that reveal large patterns. As we will see, journalists like Oriana Fallaci, Seymour M. Hersh and Mary Anne Weaver have elevated such observation to high art.

Hersh took readers on an ethnographic tour of the U.S. National Archives to explain the convoluted process and political importance of former President Richard Nixon's "last cover-up." To understand Nixon's suppression of tapes in a so-called "public" archives requires detailed analysis of the people and culture of the archives, as well as a chronology of events.

> Within a year of the tapes' arrival at the Archives, a small group of specially selected young archivists, who had spent their apprenticeship sorting through President Ford's gifts or Mrs. Nixon's office correspondence, was in place. . . . "Day in and day out it wasn't thrilling, but there were moments. It was a status thing. You knew secrets" (Hersh 1992: 82–84).

The political neutrality of the National Archives was a fiction: a carefully selected team of Nixon protectors remains in place, bolstered by a Justice Department ruling allowing Nixon to restrict any document of his choosing, unless challenged by the archives. "The Archives had now given Nixon what the Supreme Court and Congress would not: a blanket claim of executive privilege (Hersh 1992: 86). Rick Salutin says major insights bear little relation to the interview which is inherently "abnormal" and stilted. "Insights of [the] murkier sort are unlikely to occur during the profile process. They're more inclined to come out incidentally, when people are just living their lives . . . the best stuff happens when you turn off the tape or shut your notebook. . . . Everything important happens at the door" (Salutin 1993).

In my experience, the first reply to a question about a contentious issue is often, "no problem." I have learned to listen for subtexts and turnarounds, spaces and gestures between words, and to take my time (something journalists seldom do). Often the contradictions are not lies but evidence of "front and back stage" behaviour. Fallaci watches for shifts in tone, position, methods, motivations. She takes control of interviews with people who are used to managing their interviews. To penetrate their carefully constructed public personnae, she must watch for the smallest detail.

> I saw [Henry Kissinger] arrive out of breath and unsmiling. . . . He said, "Good morning, Miss Fallaci." Then, still without smiling, he led me into his elegant office, full of books and telephones and papers and abstract paintings and photographs of Nixon. Here he forgot about me, turned his back, and began reading a long typewritten report . . . it was a little embarrassing to stand there in the middle of the room, while he had his back to me and kept reading. It was also stupid and ill-mannered. . . . However, it allowed me to study him before he studied me. . . . After reading the . . . report—meticulously and carefully, to judge by the time it took him—he finally turned to me and invited me to sit down on the couch. Then he took the adjacent armchair, higher than the couch, and from this privileged and strategic position began to ask me questions in the tone of a professor examining a pupil. . . leaning back in the armchair with his right arm outstretched . . . crossing his legs .

> . . his jacket was so tight over his stomach that it looked as though the buttons might pop (Fallaci 1976: 20).

The details and the positioning of the reporter in the interview help to build a portrait of power. However carefully he manages the interview and Fallaci's place in it, Kissinger reveals himself through body language, the architecture of his office, his manner and manners. Merely quoting would suggest that the man equals his words and is no more than his rehearsed text. We see this kind of press conference-driven journalism all the time. It seldom tells us much about the issues or the people behind them (except for fueling critical evaluation of their "front stage" performances).

To make his radio documentary about theatre in Vilnius entitled "There Is No Death Here," William Law had to look beyond the official source-driven news machinery. Months before the fall of the Soviet Union, he saw the changes. To get the broad political picture, he narrowed his investigation to a particular community, interviewing artists, not politicians. What he learned did not make the newscasts until months later. There are ironies and lessons here. When he arrived in Vilnius, Law was suddenly faced with a new decision.

> We got in by train and [after hearing news reports] expected to see evidence of Soviet troops. At 6 a.m. we drove through the streets of Vilnius. We stayed at the Intourist hotel, twenty stories high with a view of the whole downtown. I got to my room on the nineteenth floor and turned on the TV. There was Sky TV, with a story of tanks moving through Vilnius. They showed footage of the tanks, at night. I stuck my head out the window—tanks make noise. All I could hear was the twittering of birds. The rest of the world was reporting a tense military situation. It wasn't happening.
>
> Sky TV was saying "we're there, in the streets," instant coverage. . . .

Around the world, people saw and heard a "truth" contradicted by on-site observation. Law's team discovered they were alone: all the other film crews had been kicked out of Vilnius. Then they received a phone call from the executive assistant to Lithuanian president Landsbergis.

> He said, "You're the only news crew left in the city. We're prepared to give you an interview with the president." I asked if the phone was being bugged . . . probably . . . . My unit was in the hotel room together; we were writing messages in case the room was bugged. Our agenda was to talk to artists and get a take on the realities as they saw it. Here we had what a lot of journalists would consider a big scoop. We had to make a judgment call.

Gorbachev had given Lithuania an ultimatum. The Lithuanian government had its own agenda. Law decided not to "buy into the agenda of the Lithuanian nationalists." His decision was grounded both in ethnographic instinct and production reality.

> We said, "We're a documentary unit, not a news unit." We were only there for twenty-six hours. We were already lined up to shoot the play, "There Is No Death Here." We said we were willing to interview the president as a theatregoer, if he came to the theatre. He didn't come.

The decision was that "it wasn't an important story," even though in conventional journalistic terms it would have been a scoop. Ignoring the pressure to do the story, Law produced a remarkable documentary which in effect forecast the political events to come. Although it provided far greater insight than could be gained from an official-source interview with the president, it remained an "arts" story. A more enlightened news department would acknowledge the broader news value of the documentary.

One of the finest examples of ethnographic journalism is a story by Mary Anne Weaver about a Pakistani bird. Her chronicle of the annual hunt by Saudi Arabian sheiks and princes for the houbara bustard reveals global concerns through the tiniest details. On the surface, it looks like a tale of regional environmentalism, but the reporter weaves a tale of international politics and conflicts among cultures, unravelling tangled strands of information.

To understand the politics, we must understand the cultural reasons the bird is so highly valued (by Saudi aristocrats, for its power-giving meat; by the Pakistani, for its right to exist and its potential for revenue production). We must understand the configurations of prestige and power in Pakistan, the economic tug-of-war that drives the hunt to its annual grim conclusion. Weaver takes us hunting, takes us to dinner, takes us into the realms of falconry and animal husbandry. Every detail counts.

> Saudi hunters would be led by one of the Prince's sons . . . the Ambassador in Washington, or Prince Khalid, who had commanded Saudi forces during the Gulf War. . . .
>
> "In the old days, we would hunt the houbara on foot or camelback . . . try to outsmart it. . . . Now customized vehicles have replaced camels. . . . They use radar, computers, infrared spotlights to find the bird at night. . . . The poor bird doesn't stand a chance anymore. . . ."
>
> [Officials said the] Saudi royal parties—which usually hunted two to three thousand birds during their monthlong stay—had no beneficial impact on the local economy.

She is told:

> "The Prince doesn't want to meet any women at this time."
>
> "I'm not a woman. I'm a journalist."
>
> He shrugged. "It's all the same," he said.
>
> Prince Fahd, dressed in a camel-colored woollen robe embroidered with gold thread, sat cross-legged on an Oriental carpet, receiving his guests. The floor of the *chamiana* was covered with exquisite Kashan and Persian antique carpets. . . . In a far corner, there was a network of cellular phones, and other communications equipment hooked to a satellite dish. Behind the Prince, like a ceremonial guard, thirty-five hooded falcons stood at attention [perched on] stools etched with ivory and gold (Weaver 1992: 60–61).

The ethnographer-journalist—a Weaver well-named—weaves a tale of intrigue, of a centuries-old quest for sexual and political power, of poverty and extravagance, deprivation and excess. We learn why a small bird in Pakistan is the subject of an international controversy the United Nations may have to resolve, and why the political consequences affect North Americans. Weaver brings us new information, new understanding, multiple perspectives, complex truths—ethnography and journalism, serving the Rashomon principle and the public.

Part Four

Journalistic Codes and Conflicts

11. Codes of Ethics: Who Needs Them?

Brian Brennan

British pirates had a code of ethics. In 1640 they loosely banded themselves into a democratic fraternity and adopted a set of vows collectively titled "The Custom of the Brothers of the Coast, or the Pirates' Creed of Ethics." It was signed by the whole ship's company before every departure and served as the social contract of the expedition. Every decision of importance was discussed and a vote taken. Courage alone conferred distinction. A pirate ship was an extremely well-ordered floating community.[1]

Journalists are less orderly than pirates. Of the two hundred countries in the world with developed systems of mass communications, fewer than fifty have national codes of ethics for journalists. Many of the remaining countries indicate some desire for ethical guidelines, but few seem to know what criteria to adopt or who should accept responsibility for establishing and enforcing such guidelines (Swedish Press Council 1991).

Canada is one of the majority—it does not have a national code of ethics for journalists. Should it? In 1993, I put the question to members of the Canadian Association of Journalists (CAJ), the largest group of journalists in English Canada.[2] Although the response rate was too low to constitute a statistically valid sampling of Canadian journalistic opinion, the response—mostly in favour of an ethics code—did mirror the results of more comprehensive surveys in Canada and the United States.

Defining Codes and Their Functions

Before presenting some of the published arguments for and against ethics codes, I should pause and define what I mean by a code of ethics for journalists. For the purpose of this essay, I would describe such a code in general terms as a declaration of the standards, ideals, practices and accepted behaviour of the journalistic profession, articulated by its practitioners and designed to shore up what Earl A. Molander (1987) calls "the middle ground between internalized societal values on the one hand, and law on the other." Because outside control might lead to a violation of the constitutional freedom of the press, I would expect such a declaration to be adopted internally by the practitioners of journalism, not imposed externally. Finally, I would define "standards" as everything ranging from minimal expectations of conduct for all journalists to the perceived ideals towards which journalists should strive.

What would a code of ethics for journalists contain? There is no simple answer. Because there is no such thing as a "standard" code, it would be difficult to find a common position on how journalists should deal, for example, with such matters as outside employment or acceptance of free books and CDs for review. Many codes, however, do reflect broad areas of agreement about journalistic conduct. Most contain, for example, declarations on accuracy, fairness, right to privacy and media responsibility.

What functions might a national code of ethics for journalists serve? Data collected by the Swedish Press Council (1991) on behalf of the World Association of Press Councils from codes developed in the United States, Norway, Australia, New Zealand and other countries identify three principal aims:

1. To protect the consumers of news, the mass of the population, from any irresponsible anti-social or propagandistic use of the media.
2. To protect journalists from being forced to act in ways that are irresponsible, humiliating or in any manner contrary to the dictates of their consciences.
3. To keep open the lines of communication between journalists and informational sources (state security matters excepted), and between the media and those who want to indicate through the media how they feel about what is being done in their name.

To the above main aims, I would add that codes might also serve the secondary functions of providing guidance for journalism students, helping journalists identify potential conflicts of interest, providing guidance for journalists faced with pressure to commit unethical acts, providing support for ethical behaviour and showing the public that journalists abide by certain moral values and principles.

RESULTS FROM THE CAJ SURVEY

I conducted the CAJ survey to get a sense of what Canadian journalists generally think of ethics codes. I knew that certain individual CAJ members have been voluble over the years in their denunciation of codes.[3] But I had no idea how representative this anticode sentiment was. I also was curious to know how Canadian journalists felt about their public image. Polls in the U.S. had shown that a growing segment of the American public considers the media arrogant, unreliable, unfair and increasingly unbelievable.[4] Did the Canadian public feel the same way?

Questions had been raised about the use of "drama techniques" in the Canadian Broadcasting Corporation's Second World War documentary series, "The Valour and the Horror." A Vancouver columnist had been publicly accused of mixing fact with fantasy in a column about an assisted suicide (Ouston 1991). *Maclean*'s magazine had been criticized by its readers for following the lead of U.S. and British news organizations in naming the "alleged victim" in the William Kennedy Smith rape case (Funnell 1991). Would some of these controversies—followed by incidents after the survey such as the Toronto newspaper bidding war for photos in the Paul Bernardo–Karla Homolka murder case, and Canada's rush to join the international media feeding frenzy surrounding the O.J. Simpson affair—have been avoided if Canadian journalists had an agreed-upon set of standards governing how they do our job? Clearly, the survey, because of its limited scope, could not definitively answer this question. But it might show which way the wind is blowing.

The response rate was disappointing. I sent out 1300 surveys and received back only 148—a mere snapshot of Canadian journalistic opinion. But even that limited response could be seen as having some value; the results parallel those obtained from post-Watergate surveys in the United States showing that more than 60 percent of newspaper journalists favour written codes of ethics (Meyer 1987: 38; Gordon 1979). The results also support the conclusion drawn by Nicholas Russell of the University of Regina. His 1990 survey of 156 Canadian newsrooms showed "that codes of ethics were not widespread in the Canadian news industry, but were evidently increasing fast" (Russell 1994: 424). More than 70 percent of the respondents to my survey (105 of the 148) answered yes to the question "Should Canadian journalists have a self-imposed code of ethics, effectively designed and implemented, setting out general precepts to guide professional conduct?"

A broader examination of the topic has taken place in the United States where the debate over ethics codes has been under way since Benjamin Harris published the first and only issue of his newspaper, *Publick Occurrences Both Foreign and Domestick*, in Boston in 1690. Harris has been dismissed as a trouble-maker, a wretch and a "scatter-brained opportunist with poor judgment and worse luck." But his short-lived newspaper's statement of purpose has stood the test of time. It has also proven to be remarkably similar to statements about the role or responsibility of the press issued in this century by major American and Canadian news organizations (Skaggs 1985: 37–42).

Harris's statement of purpose was the first written code for newspapers to be published on this continent. It was followed by many more. A 1992 survey by the U.S. Society of Professional Journalists, an organization similar to the Canadian Association of Journalists with membership totalling more than twenty thousand, found that of the 304 media outlets polled 42.5 percent of newspapers and 31.3 percent of television stations relied on written codes of ethics. In an analysis of the survey results for the Society of Professional Journalists, Jay Black (1992) concluded that codes served a useful "red light" purpose for newspaper managements that wanted to stop reporters from stepping across boundaries of propriety while gathering the news, but he offered no opinion on how the codes might affect the performance of individual journalists. For that determination, I reviewed some of the other articles on the subject published in the U.S. since 1926, the year the Society of Professional Journalists first adopted its code of ethics.

ARGUMENTS PRO AND CON

My examination of the literature from the United States showed that the arguments advanced against journalistic ethics codes were numerous and often persuasive. Here, in point form, are six of the most common:

- *Codes are nothing but PR.* Codes are largely an exercise in public relations, designed to show the public that journalists are accountable, but they are ineffective in eliminating unethical practices and they do nothing to instill public confidence in the media.
- *Codes are no substitute for gut feelings.* Codes can never replace "newsroom learning" as a way to shape ideas about journalistic ethics. There's no evidence that codes directly affect the decisions journalists make in situations involving ethical issues.
- *No consensus is possible.* There never can be a consensus on what constitutes ethical behaviour. In the absence of accepted moral principles, subjective judgments will always take precedence.
- *Codes provide legal ammunition.* Codes provide lawyers, judges and juries with ammunition in libel and defamation suits. The codes can backfire if the courts ever use them as standards against which to measure media actions.
- *Codes undermine press freedom.* Codes restrict the constitutional freedom of the media. If only certified journalists are allowed to practise, the press wears a ready-made gag.
- *Codes are never complete.* Codes can never be sufficiently comprehensive to cover all

possible ethical dilemmas. Some journalists will always feel anything not covered by the code is acceptable behaviour.

Notwithstanding the cogency of the above arguments, the resolve of numerous news organizations to adopt and strengthen ethics codes in the late 1960s and 1970s shows no signs of weakening in the 1990s. In June 1993 for example, the *Winnipeg Free Press* phoned me to say it was thinking of developing an ethics code for its newsroom and asked where it might go for help. In 1994 the Féderation professionelle des journalistes du Québec, the largest group of French-language journalists in Canada, adopted a draft code of ethics at its annual general assembly. And as I looked elsewhere around North America and across to Europe, I detected a heightened interest on the part of news organizations to advance their credibility through written codes of professional conduct. The Canadian Broadcasting Corporation appointed one of its senior executives to be vice-president in charge of "media accountability."

Forty percent of the U.S. newspapers surveyed by the Society of Professional Journalists amended their codes during the 1990s (Black 1992: 32). Basic guidelines for an international code of journalistic ethics were accepted in October 1992 by delegates to the World Association of Press Councils' third international conference held in New Delhi. Towards the end of 1993, Canada's private broadcasters adopted a code to curb TV violence. And the editors from nineteen of Britain's national newspapers, in a rare spirit of collaboration, agreed to adopt a code of journalistic practice when it became apparent to them that politicians were ready to respond to public pressure and draw up legislation to curb the sensation-seeking proclivities of the Royal-baiting tabloids (*Times* 1989).

It is unlikely that any of the news organizations referred to here ever sat down in isolation to deliberate pros and cons before adopting an ethics code. More likely, many of them simply responded to the threat, real or imagined, of government regulation. The essential work of journalism involves reacting to the events of the day, and there's nothing like a warning from a public official to make the press start beating its breast and showing that it is principled, socially responsible and committed to professional standards.[8] It is interesting to note that if these organizations had examined the literature on the subject, they would have found an effective counter-argument for every argument put forward against ethics codes. Here, taken in order, are brief summaries of the counter-arguments I found for each of the arguments mentioned above:

- *Codes are nothing but PR.* Molander (1987: 623) says codes are only ineffective when they are created simply for the sake of having them, and when they contain little more than platitudes. A well-written ethics code effectively designed and constantly consulted by journalists for guidance in making ethical decisions can go a long way towards eliminating unethical practices, relieving ethical dilemmas and demonstrating a serious commitment to ethical conduct.
- *Codes are no substitute for gut feelings.* "Newsroom learning" is a term I use for anecdotal knowledge of past behaviour, otherwise known as the unwritten rules or internalized parables of the newsroom. Such knowledge presumes that junior or middle managers are conditioned by the actions of their superiors and peers. The superiors in turn are conditioned by their superiors, right up to the top of the organization. The ethical tone,

therefore, is set by top management. However, top management, as Steven Brenner and Earl Molander note, cannot communicate continuously and directly with subordinates. Nor can it open up all manner of corporate decisions to subordinates to show how ethical considerations are incorporated into the decision-making process (Brenner and Molandes 1977: 62). A more structured form of communication must be employed, and this is the rationale for an ethics code. If the code identifies specific practices and sets out general precepts to guide conduct, it will eventually affect journalistic ethical decision-making in the same way that a style guide affects the way stories are written and edited.

- *No consensus is possible.* There can, in fact, be a consensus on minimum standards governing how journalists should act. Moral principles can be drawn up, subject to violation only when adequate justification—determined by impartial, rational people—exists. Subjectivity can be eliminated if decision-making models are created for dealing with ethical dilemmas.[9]
- *Codes provide legal ammunition.* Ethicist Deni Elliott (1990) says that when journalists find themselves in court, *something* tells the judge how reasonable journalists act in similar situations. Far better for that *something* to be a well-conceived and well-written ethics code than the opinion of some disgruntled journalist or journalism-school professor who can't separate lofty ideals from the conventions of journalistic practice. If the well-written code comes back to haunt the news organization that violates it, so be it—the enterprise of journalism will come closer to the public's legitimate expectation of accountability. The public nature of journalism means that ethical breakdown in one organization raises questions of credibility for all.
- *Codes undermine press freedom.* Constitutional freedom only becomes a factor in cases where journalists find themselves subject to penal action by governments. Efforts by journalists to provide guidelines for their own ethical conduct cannot be said to threaten constitutional freedom. Neither can efforts by journalists to make themselves answerable to the public through devices such as press councils, ombudsmen, letters to the editor and explicit principles for correcting mistakes.[10]
- *Codes are never complete.* Codes may never be fully comprehensive but an accompanying casebook of ethical decisions, gradually built up over time, will eventually provide a set of guidelines to cover all possible dilemmas. Such a manual is currently being developed by the Society of Professional Journalists (SPJ) as a companion to its code of ethics which has been revised three times (in 1973, 1984 and 1987) since the society first adopted it in 1926.[11]

THE SPJ CODE AND ENFORCEMENT

When Canadian journalists say, as they increasingly do nowadays, that they want to be seen as principled, socially responsible and committed to professional standards, they echo a sentiment first articulated by the U.S. Society of Professional Journalists, then known as Sigma Delta Chi, in 1926. Much of the early impetus, says Clifford Christians (1985), came from status-seeking journalists comparing themselves to lawyers and doctors and wanting to upgrade their profession's honour. This led to accusations that the SPJ code is essentially a self-serving document, bland and over-generalized; and it also gave rise to a parallel contention that, when viewed solely as an exercise in writing, the SPJ code turns out to be nothing more than vacuous rhetoric.

It is not my purpose to take sides in this ongoing ethics codes debate. I have summarized above the principal arguments, pro and con, that have been articulated and discussed in American journals, and I feel that more blood will have to be spilt on the floor before one side begins to make more sense to me.

One aspect, the enforcement question, bears examination in Canada because it has been a focal point of disagreement among American journalists since the beginning. It also seems to be the rock on which the ship of American journalistic accountability invariably founders. The history of the SPJ's code of ethics is a saga of newspeople self-righteously embracing ethical principles, then struggling with the dilemma of how to live up to these principles in ways that might instill public confidence in journalism.

In 1973, the Society of Professional Journalists revised its 1926 code of ethics to give it teeth. A "censure" clause was written into the code so it would not be, in the words of code author Casey Bukro, "just another document of high-sounding principles that could be ignored" (Merrill 1981–82: 14). Not until 1983, however, did the society consider the next logical step: code enforcement. Efforts at implementation since 1973 were almost exclusively educational. Bukro headed a task force that recommended to the SPJ board that the society's chapters be authorized to investigate ethical complaints filed against its members. The process would begin with a hearing at the chapter level and continue on appeal to the national level. It would provide for a wide range of disciplinary measures, including expulsion from the society. "Good journalists should point out bad journalism," said Bukro (see Bukro 1985: 10–13).

His proposals were rejected by the SPJ board which later decided that, in the absence of a formal procedure for handling ethics violations, it would eliminate the "actively censure" clause from its code and replace it with this meaningless statement: "This society shall by programs of education, and other means, encourage individual journalists to adhere to these tenets" (Sutherland 1987: 4–5). In the process, the SPJ board turned into a retreat what might have been a significant march towards making a major decision on journalistic accountability. The SPJ rallying cry to have framed copies of its code placed on every newsroom wall seemed more like a call for interior decoration than a move to advance the cause of responsible journalism.

In Canada the enforcement question could prove to be similarly thorny. Codes of ethics seem to be easier to sell when they remain theoretical. Most respondents who said yes to my limited survey, for example, agreed that compliance should be mandatory. Experience shows, however, that Canadian journalists, like their American counterparts, are invariably at a loss when it comes to punishing colleagues whom they consider unethical. Witness the dilemma of the Parliamentary Press Gallery when it penalized one member for unethical conduct, i.e., using the gallery facilities to obtain non-journalistic benefits, but then discovered that other members were doing the same thing (see Chapter 12).

Many of the ethics codes adopted by Canadian newspapers began as codes developed by other organizations, e.g., provincial press councils. For the most part, these generic codes contain no enforcement provisions. Enforcement does, however, take place at many newspapers when serious breaches of ethical misconduct are identified. At least four reporters in Canada have been suspended or fired for plagiarism in cases widely publicized internally in the business. One was a sports columnist for the Saskatoon *Star Phoenix*; the others included a Toronto sports writer, a Calgary film critic and a Toronto book-page editor.

Plagiarism—stealing another person's copy and passing it off as one's own—is the one ethical crime which all journalists agree is unacceptable. They may have great difficulty defining plagiarism—when is it stealing? when is it research?[12]—but all agree that, once proven, plagiarism should not be tolerated. Honesty in the practice of journalism is as important as telling the truth.

Other crimes are harder to weigh in terms of relative seriousness. One journalist's mortal sin is often another's minor misdemeanor. That, inevitably, becomes one of the big stumbling blocks when journalists, as a national group, try to adopt an ethics code. Some journalists see nothing morally wrong in accepting free travel and other gifts from people they write about. Others believe that accepting "freebies" poses a conflict of interest. How can a code reconcile the two? The answer is that it can't. It can provide decision-making models for behaviour and set out general moral principles, but it will always hit a stumbling block if it tries to narrowly define these moral principles for enforcement purposes. Movie critics employed by the *Toronto Sun* chain will never give up their coveted junkets to Hollywood and their brandy-drinking bosses will never make them try.

IMPACT OF CODES ON JUDGMENTS

Suppose, for the sake of argument, that Canadian journalists were to adopt a code of ethics similar to that of the SPJ. Is there any evidence that such a code would shape decisions made in situations that raise ethical issues? A cursory review of the literature reveals the available evidence to be slim, anecdotal, contradictory and generally inconclusive.

Newspaper managers, according to the SPJ's 1992 survey of 304 U.S. media outlets, believe that written codes serve a useful regulatory purpose. The codes also provide an opportunity for managers to discuss ethical values with new employees during the hiring process and thus set the tone for their behaviour while on the job (Black 1992: 32). Some academics agree. Molander (1987: 623) says that while ethics codes are not a panacea for the reform of unethical behaviour, they can make an important contribution towards this goal. He cites a 1977 study of business ethics that notes that, when faced with pressure to commit unethical acts, executives usually refer to formal company policy for guidance (Molander 1987: 629).

Others disagree. From their "natural experiment" with fifty-six newsroom staffers at the jointly owned Indianapolis *Star* and Indianapolis *News*, David Pritchard and Madelyn Peroni Morgan (1987: 941) conclude that there is no support for the common assumption that ethics codes directly influence the decisions journalists make. They presented six hypothetical situations and asked staffers how they would each cope with the ethical issues. They then measured the answers against the guidelines contained in the ethics codes of the two newspapers. They could find no evidence that the codes had any direct influence on the journalists' decisions. "If there is a link between the content of newspaper ethics codes, and the behavior of journalists faced with ethical decisions, the link is almost certainly indirect, and mediated by a wide variety of other factors." They conceded that the antecedents of journalistic behaviour were complex: "It is likely that formal norms are only one ingredient in a rich stew" (Pritchard and Morgan 1987).

The study focused only on journalists who work for the same company in one U.S. city; Pritchard and Morgan are therefore on weak ground when they extend their findings to suggest that, more generally, ethics codes do not directly influence journalistic behaviour. In the absence of a more wide-ranging survey, the jury remains out.

It may well be, as Pritchard and Morgan and others have speculated, that the most important effects of ethics codes are symbolic rather than behavioural, that they exist to persuade various constituencies (newsroom staffers, advertisers, the public) that a news organization is acting in a professional and accountable manner. It may also be true, as many editors maintain, that ethics codes serve a useful practical purpose in helping practitioners deal with the details of journalistic practice that often cause problems: freebies, moonlighting, political activity, plagiarism and related matters. As William Brown of the *Montgomery Advertiser* and *Alabama Journal* says, "Our code does not answer every question, but it does help establish the tone we want, and helps staffers recognize situations they ought to ask questions about" (quoted in Hartman 1987: 7).

Conclusion

Should Canadian journalists, as a national group, have a code of ethics similar to those adopted by their counterparts in other countries? The answer will depend in part on how they can balance public demands for answerability against their own fears of formal regulation and erosion of press freedom.

Some respondents to my limited survey suggested that Canadian journalists do not constitute a uniform national group and therefore have no way of taking the kind of collective action required to adopt a code of ethics. This argument fails to account for the existence of such national journalistic organizations as the Radio-Television News Directors Association of Canada, and the Canadian Theatre Critics Association, both of which happen to have codes of ethics. If the Canadian Association of Journalists were to adopt an ethics code, it would de facto become the code for Canadian journalists because the CAJ is the organization to which most English-speaking journalists in Canada belong. As for French-speaking journalists, they have collectively laid the groundwork for adopting a code of ethics. At the time of this writing, the Féderation professionnelle des journalistes du Québec (FPJQ) had accepted a draft code prepared by Louis Falardeau, president of the journalists' union at Montreal's *La Presse*, and started reviewing it during the FPJQ's annual assembly in the spring of 1994; continuation of that review was planned for the FPJQ's assembly in November 1995.

Respondents to my survey also said that any concern with journalistic ethics must begin with an examination of the corporate behaviour of the companies that own the newspapers and broadcast outlets. This is certainly a valid consideration, especially at a time when the ideals of the free press are being sacrificed at the altar of profit, and when the two largest newspaper groups in Canada, Southam Inc. and Thomson Corp., choose not to have codes of ethics binding on their individual newspapers. However, this fact hardly relieves journalists of personal responsibility for their own ethical behaviour.

If their assurances of responsible behaviour and accountability are to have any trustworthiness, journalists must agree on a tangible model for demonstrating their commitment to such pledges. Accountability is vital for credibility; and with declining credibility come public demands for the limitation of press freedom. Those with power have an obligation to the public they serve. They have to be answerable when the public questions their conduct. If their answers prove unsatisfactory, the media may be accused of neglect or irresponsibility and punished by scorn or indignation. And if a diminishing segment of the public finds the media competent, as evidenced from polls in the United States,[13] then it is only reasonable to speculate that in time such scorn and indignation might be transformed into inhibiting legal decisions, press-controlling laws and other media-paralyzing initiatives.

Even without such unsettling possibilities, Canadian journalists must still find a way of showing the public that words like "accountability" and "sacred trust" are more than just the clichés of the profession. In practical terms, ethical codes may be structurally flawed as devices for producing accountability, especially when they contain no enforcement provisions and are seen by certain members of the public as mantles of arrogance, self-protection and status quoism. They may also promote weak and inadequate journalism because of their traditional emphasis on "don'ts" rather than "dos," and their tendency, as University of Minnesota ethicist Arthur Caplan says, "to equate morality with prohibitions and taboos" (Fulford 1994). But if one accepts the notion that no accounting can occur without a visible process whereby agreed-upon principles function as arbiters of obligation, then one must also accept that such a visible process can be the enforcement of an ethics code containing explicit directions for correcting mistakes.

The public will always expect more of journalists than they can deliver because the public can never fully understand how haphazard the process of gathering and preparing news for publication is. If the public knows that Canadian journalists care enough about their own integrity to nail their ethical colours to the mast, then it also knows that these journalists are making some attempt to meet the public's legitimate expectation of accountability. Producing a newspaper or newscast has often been described as a daily miracle. Being answerable for the mistakes that are made before the miracle occurs should be taken as a matter of honour, not as an admission of failure.

12. Conflicts of Interest and Codes of Ethics in the Parliamentary Press Gallery

Frank Howard

For much of 1990 and part of 1991 the Parliamentary Press Gallery in Ottawa, a clubby institution dating back to the first years of Confederation, found itself entangled in a messy and embarrassing struggle with its professional conscience. In the end, the Gallery decided that life would be simpler without a system of codified scruples. Even those journalists in the Gallery who had fought for a group conscience or, at the very least, more transparency in areas where conflict of interest or capture by sources was possible, came to believe that the Gallery had neither the will nor the power to do much about ethics.

In the end it had also become apparent that the only institutions willing and able to impose professional standards were employers and not the journalists themselves.

The Gallery's year of conscience started innocently enough in the late winter of 1990 with an attempt by its executive to expel an unpopular member by using an obscure segment of the Gallery's by-laws which seemed to prohibit members from getting paid for work done for politicians or government departments. It ended in February 1991 with a cynical retreat. This retreat came as no surprise to those who knew the history of the place. The Gallery, since its founding in the nineteenth century, has always been more of a private club for the established media of the day than a guardian of professional standards. It has seen itself, in the words of one of its older members, as an "adjunct to Parliament," as a protector of privilege rather than a journalistic conscience.

The style and ethic of the place was something like one imagines a middle-ranked college frat house might have been in the 1930s: pretentious in its self-awareness, sophomoric in its taste and, above all, irreverent and messy. "Pictures of early Gallery Members are hung haphazardly around the room," wrote former *Telegram* reporter Peter Dempson (1968) in his memoirs.

> One, taken in 1882, shows 32 members, nearly all of them with beards, sitting around a desk.... Another picture is of such well-known [sic] Canadian newsmen as Senator Grattan O'Leary, who represented the Ottawa Journal; Senator Charles Bishop, a member of the Gallery for more than 40 years, who was employed by the Ottawa Citizen; Arthur Ford, editor-in-chief of the London Free Press; and John Bassett of the Montreal Gazette, and father of John Bassett, publisher of the Toronto Telegram.
>
> The Gallery abounds in squalor and filth.... Empty beer bottles are to be found everywhere. Empty glasses, with the remains of scotch, rye or gin, clutter up the room.... A cuckoo clock at one end of the narrow Gallery pops out on the hour, startling visitors who happen to drop in.

Dempson, a past president of the Gallery, knew something of its financing. The fees he and others paid in 1968 were a mere $10 per year. None of that money went to the upkeep of the facilities used by members; that was paid by taxpayers:

> The Gallery is maintained at an annual cost to the Government of about $52,000. If rental were charged for the space occupied, it would entail that much again.

In addition, there was a staff of clerks hired "at the Canadian taxpayers' expense" (Dempson 1968).

The privileges were and still are impressive: access to the government's free long-distance network, parking on the Hill, subsidized meals in the elegant Parliamentary restaurant, messenger services and many small perks such as cheap haircuts, low-cost fitness centres, free photocopying, telephone-answering service by permanent Gallery staff and, of course, a desk in the "Hot Room," in other words, free office space for those, mainly freelancers, who could not afford private space in pricey downtown Ottawa.

Fees still come nowhere close to covering Gallery operating costs. Until 1992 the Gallery charged $50 per year for membership. Until recently most of its annual spending of $20,000 went into social events, the Christmas party and frequent "muggings" or spontaneous parties called by the executive to mark the departure of some member or maybe just the arrival of spring. The social budget used up $12,000 annually or 60 percent of the total.

Another big chunk of budget in recent years went into lawyers' fees to fight off suits of applicants claiming they were unjustly refused full membership.

The clubbiest event of the year was the Parliamentary Press Gallery dinner, a huge shmooze and booze session where hundreds of reporters, ministers, MPS (Members of Parliament) and bureaucrats, mostly men in tuxedos, mingled at free bars and at dinner tables in the Parliamentary restaurant. They were entertained by party leaders and the governor general who made off-the-record and sometimes funny speeches. And after dinner there were off-colour sketches and more booze until dawn.

In recent decades there have been attempts to break from the frat house traditions that still linger around Gallery membership. In the 1980s some reporters, led by Southam News Services' Don McGillivray, broke the embargo on reporting on the annual dinner and were banned for their efforts.

In the idealistic 1970s, a handful of activists had inserted an ethics clause in the by-laws of the Gallery. It said that members could not do paid work for politicians or government agencies. At least that's how it was interpreted. McGillivray's campaign to open the dinner to the outside world has had its effect. In the penny-pinching 1990s, more and more employers were refusing to pay the cost of renting tuxedos, renting hotel rooms for "hospitality" and buying tickets for their guests and employees; and many fixed on the "off-the-record" issue as an excuse for backing out.

Politicians, including then Prime Minister Brian Mulroney, began backing out too and in 1992 the dinner was cancelled. But although the coziness of the annual dinner has been disrupted by a combination of journalistic conscience, cost-cutting and growing apathy, the practice of some Gallery members of picking up cash and contacts through freelance government contracts has survived virtually intact. The ethics clause which seemed to ban that form of commercial concupiscence between reporters and their subjects has not fared well.

At the 1991 annual general meeting held on February 13, the membership voted to remove this troublesome reference to ethics in its by-laws.

After almost a year of rambling debates and embarrassing disclosures about the ethics of its members, the Parliamentary Press Gallery decided that it had no business telling members they could not take money from government, parties or lobbyists. The section (article 10) had been used the previous March to temporarily impeach Steve Hall, editor of an electronic newsletter, because he had worked on a job for which a government department had paid his employer, Informetrica, a consulting firm owned by economist Mike McCracken.

Hall's admission to membership in the Gallery had always been problematic. The executive did not like the fact that they were letting in a representative of what they regarded as fringe media, an electronic newsletter, owned by a consulting firm and not available to the general public.

The Gallery membership was already too large at 450 and was dominated by the traditional electronic media (radio and television) and their large contingents of non-journalists or para-journalists (technicians, camerapeople and the like). Hall also was sometimes abrasive and had few friends among the Gallery's executive members. So when it was discovered that he had helped his employer, Informetrica, with a non-journalistic project for which the government had paid, the Gallery executive, which had not shown any great interest in questions of conflict of interest until then, suddenly found a use for its political conscience. They unearthed a by-law passed in the more idealistic seventies and found a clause in it which seemed to prohibit Gallery members, on pain of expulsion, from working for government departments.

The executive called a special meeting of the membership to ratify a motion to expel Hall from the Gallery. Membership was queasy about the expulsion order but feelings were mixed. Some of those who agreed with the aims of the ethics clause thought expulsion was too severe and questioned the motives of those who wanted to ban Hall. Some of those who felt that allowing Hall to join the Gallery had been a mistake in the first place were not interested in raising the question of professional ethics through the Gallery.

At the meeting, membership backed away from expulsion and only approved only a three-month suspension. During the special meeting, Hall had argued that any suspension of his membership in the Gallery could put him and his newsletter out of business. This turned out to be one of many examples of hyperbole that got published during discussion of his case and Gallery ethics. Deprived of Gallery accreditation, Hall was granted a special pass by the office of Speaker John Fraser and he used this pass for the duration of his suspension. Neither he nor his E-mail newsletter "Publinet" had suffered any substantial damage from the incident but the Gallery emerged from the fray with its moral authority slightly tarnished.

Some members who had doubts about the motives and justice of the particular case welcomed the chance to explore the practical implications of the Gallery's decision, but it soon became painfully obvious that those who fully understood the implications of an effective professional conscience in the Gallery were a very small minority.

In my column of March 16, 1990, I gave my version of the implications: "One can only welcome the Press Gallery's ruling this week which makes it clear that contract work for a government department by a member of the Gallery is unethical."

Hall's newsletter is published by Informetrica. Specifically, Hall had been charged with two things: (1) his name had appeared as co-author of an Informetrica study on free trade commissioned by the government, and (2) he had also allowed himself to be identified regularly on the CBC news network as a spokesman for Informetrica. Hall admitted that both of these things had happened, although, he claimed he had not considered them to be "unethical."

The Gallery's ruling of March 13, 1990, until the by-law was amended nearly a year later, created two precedents. Informetrica's president had (1) appeared at the meeting and (2) submitted a written set of guidelines designed to ensure it maintained an arms-length relationship with its subsidiary, "Publinet."

If the ethics clause had stood unamended, one might have expected the same sort of rules to apply to publishers and broadcasters who own more traditional media. It would have also made clear that any work done for a government department or agency would result in censure of the Gallery member who receives a direct or indirect financial benefit. (Hall had claimed he was not directly paid for the work he had done on the government-paid study.)

Here was a first practical application of the ethics clause in the Gallery's by-laws. Section 10, as it then existed, listed the reasons for expelling a member and these included:

> [Using] his [sic] membership or the facilities of the gallery to obtain a benefit other than by journalism or [engaging] in unethical conduct. Members shall be deemed to have engaged in unethical conduct [by taking part in] activities such as the representation of political parties, governments, extra-parliamentary groups or clients other than those defined in Bylaw No. 4.

Bylaw No. 4 restricted the permissible clients of a member to newspapers, broadcasting enterprises and magazines.

I decided to test the new dispensation by searching out and publicizing payments made to Gallery members by departments and agencies.

The first responses (under access law) involved two *Globe and Mail* reporters, Hugh Winsor and Jeffrey Simpson. Winsor had received $350 and Simpson $500 from the Center for Management Development for giving classes on media relations to groups of assistant deputy ministers. Later access responses would show that Simpson had also received many other payments for government work, including $1500 from Finance for talking to departmental managers. The Press Gallery executive had no comment following the publication of news that the two *Globe and Mail* reporters had apparently violated the ethics clauses.

Gallery President Guy Gendron promised to bring the information gathered under access-to-information law to the next executive committee meeting in two weeks. He did, but there was never even a suggestion that the two would be disciplined the same way Hall had been. In fact, no action was taken then or later when other revelations followed over the next few months. Simpson, Winsor and others whose names were published later dismissed the whole idea of a conflict of interest.

On the day I first published names, I wrote:

> There are at least three different opinions among the members about the ethical rigor with which journalists should be judged.
>
> There are those, myself included, who believe it is wrong to accept money from people about whom one writes or reports, especially political parties, elected officials, appointed officials, lobbyists or unions.

> Simpson, who took $500 for talking to a group of mandarins at the government's Center for Management Development, has a different rule.
>
> "My personal rule," [Simpson] said, "is that I don't do it for partisan organizations."

I added:

> There is also probably a third faction who believe their integrity is not affected by extracurricular cash, even if it comes from a partisan source. Nobody has come forward to defend that view yet.

I might have added that when I began reporting in Quebec in the late 1950s there were many reporters who accepted money from political organizers and claimed it did not affect what they wrote. A lot has changed in Quebec politics since the death of Premier Maurice Duplessis. That column continued with an anecdote from my four years in the federal bureaucracy:

> My own view was formed in part by my experience as a government flack in the '70s.
>
> I found I could get the attention of journalists by hiring them to do "non-partisan" work for my department. I even got one reporter interested in a neglected native program by commissioning an article for a non-existent publication.
>
> That reporter subsequently wrote something for his own paper, the *Montreal Star*.
>
> I am not particularly proud of the tactic, but it worked.

The reference was to a period at the beginning of the Trudeau era when I had worked as director of information for the Secretary of State, a catch-all department that gives out grants to citizens' groups; the program I was promoting provided funding for non-status Indians.

Over the next few months the subject of Gallery ethics kept coming up as access responses and anonymous tips trickled in. Here are a few items:

- a member of the board of directors that had ousted Hall, Manon Cornellier, was paid $750 for an article written for the Canadian International Development Agency and had accepted free trips overseas;
- Michel Vastel, a reporter for the Unimedia group of papers, got $450 for doing work similar to that done by Winsor and Simpson for the Canadian Centre for Management Development (CCMD); and
- W.A. Wilson, a freelancer, revealed in a letter to me that he got $3000 for writing speeches for Simon Reisman when that government official was negotiating the U.S.-Canada free-trade pact.

Wilson, a former correspondent for the *Montreal Star*, defended his action in a curious letter in which he developed the theory that, if you agreed with a government policy, it's not unethical to accept money from the government. He also attacked my journalistic ethics, saying, as Vastel had also done, that I was involved in a smear campaign:

As the paper's long-time bureau chief and then its Ottawa editor, I object very strongly to the way in which you referred to the now-defunct *Montreal Star* in your column of April 16 (see above).

First, however, I must declare an interest: you will in due course receive an Access to Information return showing that in 1988, I received payment of $3,000 from the Department of External Affairs for drafts of two speeches for Mr. Simon Reisman, then chief trade negotiator, explaining and supporting the free-trade negotiations. For the reasons which follow, I reject as forcefully as I can, your proposition that this sort of activity is unethical:

1. I had been a strong supporter of the free-trade policy in my column from 1984 onward, i.e., from the point when the Americans informally indicated that they would welcome a trade initiative from the new Canadian government. My support for the idea pre-dated by several months the government's decision the following year to seek such an agreement with Washington.

When Mr. Reisman approached me, he explained that it was because of my long-standing support for free trade. These speeches were delivered, in somewhat revised form, to entirely non-partisan and non-political audiences. I had no connection whatever with the speeches Mr. Reisman delivered during the election campaign later that year.

Since you began your campaign, I have considered this work as dispassionately as possible. I hope I am not being self-serving but I can see no grounds at all on which it can be considered unethical for a columnist to support, through other work, a viewpoint he has been expressing in his column over a period of years. The idea that support for your ideas in secondary ways is improper strikes me as preposterous.

2. I made no use whatever of my membership in the Parliamentary Press Gallery in connection with this work. I did not approach Mr. Reisman. He approached me.

I have very rarely made use of Gallery facilities since the demise of the *Montreal Star*, and I maintain my membership in that organization only because the Gallery is effectively the accreditation agency for both Parliament and the entire government of Canada.

There is no way in which overall continuing accreditation to the Canadian government can be secured, except through Gallery membership.

This has never seemed to me an arms-length relationship on the part of the Gallery, which receives extremely valuable real-estate and staff benefits from government entirely without charge.

The relationship has always supported (former) prime minister Mackenzie King's description of the Gallery as an "adjunct of Parliament," which the Gallery has never rejected, disavowed or sought to alter. . . .

I question the ethics of any body composed of journalists when it attempts, as the Gallery did in March, to bar any other journalist from access to news sources.

Unlike you, I regard that Gallery action as highly unethical: to me, blocking access to news is the ultimate journalistic offence.

In your April 16 column you relate having duped a *Montreal Star* reporter into writing a story for our paper by first arousing his interest in an issue by commissioning an article for a non-existent publication.

> It is clear to me from the way this part of the column is written, and from your campaign, that you intend this to be critical of my unknown colleague.
>
> I am not sure that the item is as damaging to the journalist as it is to yourself, but since you clearly intended it in a derogatory way, I have to point out that you have applied it to every *Montreal Star* reporter of the 1970s.
>
> You applied an identical approach in your column of 6 April when you announced that you expected to receive the names of two *Globe and Mail* reporters whom you did not name at the time.
>
> By this technique, you extended your disparagement to every member of the *Globe's* Ottawa bureau. I doubt that you actually damaged any of them and certainly neither Jeffrey Simpson nor Hugh Winsor in your later identification and re-identification of them.
>
> Both are far too highly regarded as skilled and honorable journalists for your smear to be taken seriously. It is your intention, rather than the result, that disturbs me (Howard 1990c).

The Wilson letter had a scandalizing effect on some members and convinced the executive that something had to be seen to be done. (Wilson has turned out to be one of the few real victims of the ethics debate: he was subsequently denied a life membership in the Gallery, an honorary status that is usually granted automatically to Gallery veterans. His treatment contrasts with that of Corneiller—she went on to be elected president the year after.)

Faced with this embarrassing development, the executive did what the people they were supposed to cover would have done. They ordered up a study headed by a journalism professor (for $1300) which produced the rationale for doing what had to be done.

After months of discussion with a panel of elders (former Gallery presidents), Carleton University professor Stuart Adam concluded that the Hall case was badly handled from start to finish. But the errors were mainly errors of process rather than of ethical substance. Shorn of verbiage (about 2500 words) the report said: (1) that Hall should have been censured not because he had done a little work on a government contract, but because the consulting firm Informetrica, which owns "Publinet," was not a bona fide news organization, and (2) that section 10 of the by-laws (the ethics clause) should be rewritten so it could no longer be interpreted as banning occasional government jobs done by Gallery members for pay.

As the report noted, with a good larding of euphemism, the rule as written could be interpreted to mean that a Gallery member "cannot share for payment his/her experience and understanding of the world of politics and government with politicians and representatives of government" (Howard 1990e). With that gloss put on the business of giving advice for pay, the report urged the Gallery "to delete the reference to unethical conduct since it conveys a meaning and stigmatizes an individual for actions which are a good deal short of being unethical" (Howard 1990e).

It was obvious from the beginning that, except for Hall and Wilson, the people who had taken money for government projects would not be disciplined. Gallery members would not attack popular or prominent fellow members unless, as Wilson had done, they confessed to having engaged in a clearly partisan activity.

The problematic thing, according to this report, was not the behaviour that seemed to violate both the letter and the spirit of the ethics clause, but the ethics clause itself. Therefore, the law had to be amended after the fact to remove even the suggestion that journalists picking up cash from government contracts were compromised by their special relationship with the government paymaster.

A poorly attended special meeting which followed did just that. At a rambling meeting on the night of October 23, 1990, a group of members discussed a proposal to remove the word "unethical" from its by-laws. The meeting, held in the National Press Theatre, never had enough members to make a quorum of thirty-six. But it voted fourteen to one, at one point, to accept a proposal by director Don McGillivray which would remove the offending word from section 10 of the by-laws.

That had been the section cited in March when the membership had voted to suspend Steve Hall because he had worked on a contract commissioned by the international trade section of External Affairs. A proposal presented by freelancer Richard Cleroux and myself that a disclosure mechanism be adopted that would require members to report paid work done for government, political parties and others who might benefit from Gallery members' attentions was rejected by the same margin that favoured the removal of the ethics clause.

The by-law proposal was adopted at a general meeting early in 1992 and Manon Corneiller was elected president. The Gallery membership wanted to put the ethics debate back into a dark closet. But outside interests were to force the closet open again. And a cynic would conclude that, in the end, money spoke louder than consciences.

Two issues had been bothering some members for longer than the moonlighting for government departments issue. Many people in the media, most of them not members of the Gallery, felt uneasy or even envious about the perks of Gallery membership. Parliament Hill bureaucrats forced a debate about the perks by suggesting that the Gallery might pay part of the cost of providing free parking on the Hill for members and free access to the government's long-distance telephone network.

The outrage of many members, especially freelancers, was spectacular. Where it had been impossible to get a quorum for debate on the enforcement of the ethics clause, the opponents of any restriction on perks (led by columnist Clare Hoy) arrived in force to defeat any discussion of what they portrayed as an assault on freedom of the press. Their victory was not complete. But they managed to divert the discussion of the Gallery's budget and the suggestion that the Gallery might pay for its own phones off into yet another study.

The idea that Gallery members might pay for some of their perks got more support off the Hill. A group of employers, my own paper among them, forbade their reporters in the Gallery to accept free parking and urged the Gallery as a whole to pay its own phone bills. Many large employers also refused to pay for the annual Gallery dinner at which hundreds of journalists, politicians and bureaucrats dined and drank while listening to off-the-record and frequently off-colour speeches and skits.

The employers' cash strike—as much as Brian Mulroney's last-minute cancellation of his speech—forced President Corneiller to call off the event in the spring of 1992.

By 1993 the Gallery's interest in journalistic issues had clearly waned. Reporters seemed to have lost interest in the Gallery as a professional institution. A sign of the times and the changing demography of the Gallery was the election of CTV cameraman Giancarlo Ciambella as president.

In the past, camera and technical crews have had virtually no role in discussions of journalistic ethics in the Gallery. In fact, in the past, they were not even considered to be journalists. But the power of non-journalists in the Gallery may have peaked.

By the end of 1993, cuts in media budgets had reduced the size of the Gallery to about 365, according to chief clerk Terry Guillon. Technical support staff was being displaced by lighter, more automated technologies. Reporters from newspapers were also being cut. But there was a compensating phenomenon from an unexpected source: more foreign journalists were asking for membership. In the last months of 1993 the Gallery received applications from organizations in Kuwait, Bulgaria, Switzerland, China, Russia and Mexico.

Canadian Press, which had been drawing back from the Hill, started coming back as member papers reduced their staffs. Four more staffers were assigned to the Center Block Gallery spaces assigned to the cooperative news agency. Bureau Chief Kirk Lapointe said it was the first time in four years that the Hill offices had been fully staffed.

At the same time, papers like the *Montreal Gazette*, the *Toronto Star, Hamilton Spectator* and the *London Free Press* were reducing staff.

What was emerging was a new Gallery demography. Agencies like CP or Southam News Services would stay or even increase, but the familiar bylines of star reporters working for individual newspapers would be less numerous. The same sort of shrinkage would happen to broadcasting. Networks and large local stations, faced with shrinking audience shares, cut staffs and relied more and more on satellite feeds mixed in central locations far from Ottawa.

The Gallery of the 1990s would have fewer stars, would be much smaller and would have its output dominated by large telecommunications and publishing organizations tied into global networks and information distribution systems. In that sort of environment the ethics of the Gallery becomes marginal: the fact that large organizations like CP, Southam and the Canadian broadcasting networks can make rules about employees accepting outside work, gifts or free trips has considerably more impact on the behaviour of members and the institutions they have been assigned to cover. But it won't stop there. The big news-gathering companies are also in transition and their role as major ethical arbiters may be transitory.

In the shifting sands of journalism in the last years of the twentieth century, the prestige and moral authority of the Canadian Parliamentary Press Gallery is clearly declining. But it's also clear that large organizations are "rationalizing" reporting staff; they will have fewer front-line observers in the future and will rely more on people at nodes (newsdesks) on the electronic information net who can read material coming in from many sources and package it for clients.

As the capacity of the "information highway" increases, especially at the client's outlet, there will be intense competition for an increasingly fragmented market. In a system that provides the equivalent of five-hundred channels to households, few competitors will survive unless they have access to markets that are at least continental. And with advances in software at the receiving end, the client will have a greater capacity to find and retrieve information without the intervention of "reporters." At the turn of the millennium, the future of reporters themselves is more problematic than the future of reporters' ethics. Questions about journalistic ethics will have been transformed not by new codes or laws, but by the widespread removal of significant numbers of professional journalists from direct contact with news. When the dust has settled after the current transformation of news-gathering organizations, what may emerge may be large "information utilities," but not news organizations in the sense that we saw them evolve with the development of mass circulation papers in the nineteenth century and large broadcast networks in the twentieth.

In the "information utility" model, users become more like journalists; and the owners of the distribution system become more like common carriers, more like telephone or cable companies and less like broadcasters and publishers. This will transform and perhaps eliminate current concerns about journalistic ethics.

In a world where anybody may become a "journalist," there's not much special about journalistic ethics. It is not a professional problem, but a problem of public order and personal morality.

Part Five

Ethical Issues in Contemporary Journalism

13. Pictures, Packages and Public Trust: The Seamless Byline and Instant TV[1]

Pierre Mignault

Public confidence in journalists is based on a simple premise: "Trust me, I was there, I saw what happened, I heard it from the horse's mouth." That confidence is the only reason the public bothers to read a newspaper or watch the news. People depend on journalists to be there and to report on what's going on, not only at home but around the world. It's not an easy task.

Here I focus on the impact of changes in modern news-gathering on this trust relationship between journalists and the public. The research for this chapter was three-fold: aside from the very scarce academic literature on this subject, I have relied on my personal experience over the past twenty years and on interviews with several practising journalists. Three of them have agreed to go on record: Neil MacDonald of CBC TV, Jean-Michel Leprince of Radio-Canada and Normand Rhéaume from TVA, Quebec's private French TV network. In my opinion, their reflections on modern newsmaking ably describe the ethical problems inherent in the modern electronic news-gathering process.

In 1982, A.W. Johnson, then president of the CBC, wrote in the foreword of the CBC's journalistic policy book that

> the matter of trust in the media is of crucial importance. In the complexities of contemporary life, the distance between what we know and what we need to know, for proper comprehension and correct decision-making, seems to be greater than ever. It follows, therefore, that there has never been a greater need for truly effective media and for public confidence in the media. . . . The journalist has become an "agent" for the citizen in the gathering of information and knowledge—which is a position of trust and great influence. . . . It must be recognized that in today's complex society, it is becoming increasingly more difficult to meet challenges of responsible journalism. The sheer volume and complexity of what has to be covered is a measure of these difficulties. The amount of information to be put before the public has grown enormously, in national, provincial, local and international affairs. The issues have proliferated—economic, social, environmental, cultural, political—and the complexity of the issues has been compounded even as our capacity to understand and analyze them has grown. Faced daily with a multitude of options as to what to present, the media must be selective and can show only slices of reality, not the whole (CBC 1982: i–ii).

If the media must be selective, a journalist's first duty is editorial. In some way, he or she has been granted the authority by the public to decide what should be printed or broadcast so readers or listeners will be well enough informed to make up their minds about important issues. The reasoning here is simple: as ordinary citizens, we simply don't have the time to be everywhere all the time and to process first-hand information. Rather than hearing it from the horse's mouth, we put our trust in a secondary source, the journalist.

I have been involved in television newsmaking since 1975. Back in those days the television journalist's job was still similar to that of the print journalist. We would both be assigned to eye-witness an event and, while the cameraperson would take some pictures—not too many because of the high cost of film production—we would both be taking notes. I would rush back to the office and the film would be sent out for processing. While I wrote my text, a film editor would splice together some pictures of the event and we'd run a voice tape along with the item. What happened in those days was that TV news closely resembled newspaper stories, with mildly relevant pictures running alongside. For both TV and newspaper journalists, that meant competition in terms of deadline but little competition in the gathering of facts. We were both in the field, covering events.

Even if journalists are still the next best thing to being there, there has been a significant change in news-gathering with the coming of videotape, satellites and live broadcasts. Is the journalist still a first-hand witness of events? Does he or she really get it from the horse's mouth? Is the journalist still a secondary source? Modern technology and means of production are as pervasive in journalism as in other areas of life, if not more so. Satellites can relay the news anywhere, around the clock, with the speed of a radio wave. Bureaus can be set up overnight and then pulled out just as quickly. Cameras travel everywhere, and there are more of them than reporters.

These innovations are not just ways of facilitating the job journalists have always done. They are changing and have already changed the way journalism is practised.

Turn on the TV set; Zap, you're there. That is also true for journalists during the course of their work. Both the National Assembly in Quebec and the House of Commons in Ottawa are loaded with government cameras. Any press-gallery journalist covering these capitals, whether for the print or electronic media, could spend an entire career sitting at his or her desk, zapping from one Parliamentary commission to another. Or he or she can watch question period while making phone calls.

More alarming, though, is the fact that the cameras covering the "in-house live events" are government-controlled! Government employees produce and broadcast these happenings. They select the pictures that will later be used in the news reports broadcast by the networks. That is why television audiences never see the wheeling and dealing that goes on when the cameras are pointed the other way. Similarly, we rarely see that a lot of the time half the seats are empty or filled with members reading the newspaper and ignoring the debate.

Not only are journalists not on the scene in this situation, they are relying on a government source to show them what is going on in government affairs. During the six years I worked out of the National Assembly in Quebec City, numerous attempts were made by all of the television networks to get the government to allow news cameras in the House. None of these initiatives succeeded. After all, why would the government give up such an important media manipulation tool?

> I guess what happens is that the reporters who are there are there for their story-telling ability. And you tell a story from what you've got. That's TV (Mignault 1994b).

Neil MacDonald works for the CBC's network news show, "Prime Time News." During his career as a journalist, he has also covered Ottawa for the print media.

> People think that when they read a newspaper: you would think a newspaper reporter, when he takes quotes from the Prime Minister, he was there. But the way technology has evolved, most print reporters in Ottawa don't cover question period anymore: they watch it on TV from their offices. And it's getting to the point where they can get feeds on scrums from a press gallery camera outside the House of Commons. So they can sit there and take notes. . . .
>
> So the print reporters barely have to move their asses out of the office and go across the street. . . . They claim that this frees them to make phone calls. There is some merit in that. John Turner used to call question period "bullshit theatre." That's what it is. It's all for the cameras, it's all totally controlled, we don't control the cut-aways, we can't take reaction shots, we take a feed from a government camera and [all the journalists realize] that that's what it is (Mignault 1994b).

It could be argued that using government-supplied pictures is a lesser evil than having no pictures at all. But the fact remains that, in the process of relying on a government TV feed, the reporter has been further removed from the event than if he or she had been there in person.

Today's media are faced with another important challenge: covering "all the news" on ever-tightening budgets. Modern technology has made instant news possible but it has also brought along escalating costs. Because the public demands to know everything, the media have no choice but to follow the wealthier news-gathering organizations, those who can afford to be everywhere at once. Today the fastest growing technique in TV news is called a "melt-down." Under specific agreements, media are allowed to use each other's material—whether they be pictures, interview clips or news reports—and to "melt them down" into one single report narrated by their own reporter.

The overwhelming presence of NBC, CBS, ABC and CNN all over the world allows these American networks to operate as international news agencies. Their television crews are everywhere while much smaller Canadian and foreign media can usually depend on only one crew. Let us consider the case of Washington, D.C.

The story of the day is the defence budget. Press conferences have been announced at the White House, the Senate and the Pentagon. The American networks will dispatch three crews and get the whole story. But less-resourced journalists, from networks that can't afford to be everywhere, end up staying at the office watching the press conferences on television and in the American networks' newscasts. Through agreements negotiated with the American networks, these journalists can write their own story to the pictures the American networks have already edited in their reports. As in the press galleries of Quebec City and Ottawa, the journalist relies on a secondary source: in the first case, government cameras provide the pictures where there is no access given to media and, in the second case, American networks provide pictures where access is curtailed by financial limitations.

> Only American networks can afford to cover everything! . . .
>
> The biggest constraint is that there are not enough journalists and you can't be everywhere. When you have to do a melt-down, its borderline, it's a litle more

> complicated. You have the material you shot yourself and the rest shot by other journalists. It doesn't bother me. We do it for practical reasons. An important or complicated story happens and it's my job to use the means at my disposal to let the public know. . . . It's similar to a situation where my cameraman goes out and shoots something for me. It's teamwork, and for me that extends to all those who feed us pictures, like the American networks (Mignault 1994a).

What about when you have do a melt-down on a story that happened somewhere else, a story you haven't covered?

> That's more complicated. You stand to lose credibility when that happens. There have been a few situations where I was asked to do a report from Washington on a *fait divers* that occurred somewhere in the United states. I try to avoid that, because I don't find it credible, nobody is credible in a situation like that. We were not on the scene, we didn't see it first-hand and we use someone else's pictures right off the TV set. It is not something that calls for your competence since you have no knowledge of the issue. . . . On the other hand, there are situations in which I feel comfortable doing melt-downs. I was assigned to go to Somalia and Haiti to do a series of reports in the field. When I got back to Washington, it happened very often that these two countries were in the news. It was my job to update the story and do melt-downs. I knew what I was talking about because I had been in the field (Mignault 1994a).

Only the wealthier media can afford to have correspondents in Washington and, for the most part, their organizations have gained control over editorial content through their monopoly on the gathering of images.

> The American eye filters the national news that reaches Quebec, and our coverage of other realities is essentially Western-based and event-driven. Our television industry is totally dependent on American coverage for international news—except for Radio-Canada which has five offices abroad (Washington, London, Beijing, Paris and Moscow)—because it purchases American pictures for its newcasts. The choices made by the Americans therefore determine the news that our stations will broadcast. . . . Our newspapers are also dependent on agencies and offer international coverage that contains an American bias (Beauchamp 1987: 69).

The melt-down technique is used in newsrooms around the world. When the events of one story happen at different locations at the same time, one reporter somewhere becomes the storyteller. He or she will gather facts from each of the sources and then write the final script. A reporter could be using pictures and clips taped by government cameras or other networks, or pre-edited material from local stations throughout the country. All these sources are secondary sources that provide pre-edited material. This has a significant impact on the editorial process.

When journalists do melt-downs, they are working with pre-edited material. That means they have to decide on the relevance of a fact or clip based on someone else's appreciation. The local reporter does an interview and selects an eight-second clip. The national reporter assigned to do the melt-down will then take all these eight-second clips and pass editorial judgment on the ones that best reflect the story. This national reporter has to trust that everybody down the line has made the correct editorial judgment on which clip best illustrates the subject's point of view.

> There is room for monumental fraud, if the reporter chooses to go that route. And we are not regulated, we are not even a profession, we are a trade. The CBC's got a policy which sets it apart, but by and large we have no code of ethics, no regulation. The only thing governing us is the civil remedy of libel laws. . . .
>
> I take fairly great care to make sure that—as much as I am allowed to within the confines of this medium—I know what I am talking about. . . . Television being the extraordinarily cumbersome tool that it is . . . to get everything on the record you have to run around with that big heavy camera and a car and that's just not feasible a lot of the time. So the reporter becomes a clearing house for the information, and I guess you just try to use your best instincts. You try to use whatever experience and skill you've got to make sure that the information you are passing on is not passed on in questioning. . . .
>
> It's not very pleasant to do melt-downs. Whenever reporters talk about melt-downs in TV, they all look at each other as if it's a big headache. . . . You've got to basically count on the honesty of the people putting forward the information (Mignault 1994b).

In the final analysis, it all boils down to a question of trust. But how much can journalists trust their sources? And what impact does that have on the trust relationship pre-established with the reader or listener?

One of the best illustrations of the limits of that trust was the coverage of the Gulf War. Pictures of Saddam Hussein broadcast by North American media were accompanied by commentaries explaining at great length that the pictures originated from Iraqi TV and should be judged with caution. The same thing didn't always happen when the information originated from Washington. Leprince explains:

> I think in terms of melt-downs, everybody fared badly during the Gulf War. But there was no other choice. I was working out of Washington and that meant depending on press briefings that were happening thousands of kilometres away. We had to depend on the Pentagon. So we'd go on the air and specify to the listener: this information comes from the Pentagon, we do not have Baghdad's side of the story (Mignault 1994a).

Eventually the Gulf War ended. It soon became clear that the Pentagon had sometimes bent the truth. Facts had been released to the press prior to being checked. But, all in all, the public had been warned that the facts relayed by the journalists had originated from a partisan source and had not been gathered first-hand by the reporter. Journalists had decided, during the editorial process, that identifying the source of the news was an important element to the story.

But such is *not* the case in daily news. Although the journalist uses multiple secondary sources, both governmental and journalistic, these sources are rarely identified as such. Satellite feeds are bought and packaged without mention of who gathered them because there are no contract requirements to identify the source. If it seemed important during the Gulf War to identify Iraqi TV and the Pentagon as sources because this indicated more or less how reliable the source was, then it follows that any second-hand source should be clearly identified.

> The transmission of news and different messages through media networks is an ongoing process of multiple interpretations, whether intentional or unconscious. From the wire agency where a journalist has originated the story, the information goes through a web of interpretations obeying to various forms of motivation: technical restrictions, broadcast urgency, limited writing space but mostly different orders of interest: audience targetting, advertising support, power or pressure groups. Under these conditions, pure objectivity in information gathering is utopia (Oliveira and Beguin 1983: 30–31).

Relative objectivity is one of our goals in the news business. Trusting a journalist's view of issues is often the result of a direct relationship established between the reporter and the public. This is why journalists warn the public when they have doubts about a source. They are also protecting their credibility in case something goes wrong. It is this same credibility that they work so hard to establish which is at stake when they fail to mention secondary sources. There are, of course, still some journalists who work in the field who dig for stories, investigate issues, shoot their own pictures and produce their own material. But in this modern age of ever-advancing technology, the melt-down has become a popular and increasingly accepted tool.

> I think above all the pressure is economic. Media owners are looking for new and cheaper formulas to cover events. . . . So they are squeezing the lemon, and the journalist is the lemon (Mignault 1993).

It is noon and I am having lunch with an old colleague. It's smack in the middle of the federal election campaign; Normand squeezed me into his very tight schedule. He is the parliamentary correspondent for Montreal's private French TV network, TVA. He has been assigned to be a one-man band for the election campaign coverage. He's been working seventeen hours a day. He tells me, "In Quebec nobody but the publicly funded networks can afford to do an all-out coverage of an election campaign" (Mignault 1993).

TVA has devised a new formula to cover the campaign. Rather than assign reporters to cover the leaders on the trail, it has decided to buy pictures from different sources: ASN network in the Maritimes, Global-TV for Ontario and for the western provinces, CTV and its affiliates. The editorial desk surrounding Rhéaume is in Montreal, where he will produce the melt-down. On top of the feeds from other networks, he relies on his network's affiliates' reporters in Quebec and on newspapers, newswires and radio-station coverage.

> At first I hesitated before taking the job. Not only did the sources gathering the information escape my control, but there were also cultural and linguistic considera-

> tions of significant importance. Most of the reporters we depend on work for English media. That means they have a different view on issues at stake. . . . The further you are removed from the event, the more details you lose (Mignault 1993).

Normand Rhéaume is on the air three times a day, five days a week. During all that time he depends on his experience in political coverage and on secondary sources to deliver daily analysis of the leaders on the campaign trail. During the weekend he does field work to keep in touch for the coming week.

> Once in a while you have to go out in the field, otherwise you're totally disconnected from what's happening. You need to feel the pulse. Without it it's an impossible task . . . . When you have to analyze something a little touchier it becomes uncomfortable. For example, when Prime Minister Kim Campbell made public her plan to reduce the deficit. I could have done a better job if I had been there. Because it's not only what they say that's important, there's the context, the body language. Was it improvised for a speech? Is the political personnel surrounding her nervous, are they panicking? I don't know that. I wasn't there to evaluate that and it has impact on the subject matter and how I will report on it. . . . In theory a journalist should only report on what he has witnessed, but in real life that's not how it works (Mignault 1993).

With the melt-down, however, comes a distressing change in the relationship between the journalist and the public. The practice of journalism has grown more and more sophisticated with the advent of technological tools that guarantee instant access to information from around the world. If viewers were at least aware of what's actually going on, one could argue that the relationship of trust had not been compromised. But this is often not the case. It may be unrealistic to expect a television reporter on a major newscast to say, "I pieced the following story together from assorted reports on American networks, what I heard at a press conference and a telephone call to a contact in the State Department. I have not sought independent verification of the claims made by the Secretary of State. So, take it for what it's worth. John Doe, XYZ News."

That sign-off may be slightly exaggerated, but it is becoming increasingly necessary. It identifies the secondary sources to the audience, helping them to process the information they have heard. Sources are always partisan, or subjective, at the very least. The journalist takes that into consideration when he or she writes the text. The journalist will be affirmative when he has first-hand information and prudent when she relies on a secondary source. Neil MacDonald continued:

> Yesterday there was a story in the *Gazette* about a rape case. There were few media, no cameras. You were not there, what can you do? We are not a regulated profession. We are not like the medical profession, there are no regulations that govern us. We can say anything we want. So what I did is I took the quotes from the *Gazette*, I couldn't get the court transcript. I went to the courtroom and asked the people who were in the courtroom at the time if these quotes were essentially accurate and, more than that, were they an accurate depiction of the context of the courtroom.
>
> The answer was yes, and, on top of that, I said, "The judge is reported to have

> said. . . ." Now it's a subtle distinction, and I admit that it's perhaps not one the viewer will catch, but it's one that at least I can say if there is fault picked with it, well, I said, "was reported to have said."
>
> Unfortunately in television a lot of what we do is covering our asses that way. You know we'll put a qualifier here, a qualifier there, so that if somebody points a finger at us we can say, well, technically we are accurate (Mignault 1994b).

Leprince believes

> that people know the pictures are American even if we don't say so every time, and I'm not sure it's an important issue. The pictures are there and we use what it takes to inform the public correctly (Mignault 1994a).

The goal is certainly noble but the means remain questionable. There is no doubt that journalism must adapt to changing times. Melt-downs have become a necessary tool to broadcast information at a faster pace than ever. But how is the public to judge the information it receives if it's not in on the rules of the game? And where does this leave trust, as implied in the basic understanding, "Trust me, I was there, I saw what happened, I heard it from the horse's mouth"?

If the journalist's relationship with the reader or listener is that of trust based on first-hand information, then it goes without saying that, in order to maintain that trust relationship, the journalist must caution the public on any information that is second-hand by at least quoting the source or identifying it. Otherwise, the formula must be changed to "Trust me, I wasn't there, these are my first-hand facts and these are the facts I *didn't* hear from the horse's mouth!"

14. Journalism in a Fish Bowl: Ethical Dilemmas in Campaign Coverage[1]

Frederick J. Fletcher

Election campaign coverage—described by one veteran of many campaigns as the Olympics of political journalism—is journalism in a fish bowl. Reporters face not only deadline pressures but exhausting travel schedules, sophisticated manipulation by "spin doctors" and high expectations from media critics, voters and their news organizations. There is the ever-present risk of "flak" from parties and candidates, and pressure from news managers who expect compelling journalism in return for the high and increasing costs of covering national elections. In this high-pressure context, ethical and professional dilemmas are inevitable and controversies are highly visible.

Although some basic ethical concerns are common to all forms of journalism, some are unique to campaign coverage, or at least more sensitive. For example, issues of fairness, balance and privacy that would normally remain personal to individuals or groups become politicized in the highly partisan context of election campaigns, placing reporters under unusual pressure. The boundary between public and private takes on an added dimension when the private life involved is that of a public figure. Politicization of issues can take place in other contexts but a campaign focuses the process. For example, the appropriate role of so-called "character issues" in election coverage has been a matter of controversy in recent elections in both Canada and the United States. The coverage of these matters in the two countries remains quite different with Canadian news organizations showing much greater restraint, as will be seen (Taras 1993).

Because the rationale for press freedom derives from the central role of autonomous journalism in a democratic society, election coverage has a "sacred" aspect that brings other ethical considerations into play (Taras 1990: 176). An election is not only a struggle for power but is also a public debate and a democratic ritual. The right to vote can be seen as a right that includes the right to be informed, thus giving the media a central role:

> In modern industrial democracies, the media are major participants in the electoral process. Like political parties, they have a public as well as a private dimension. As Judith Lichtenberg has put it: "The seeming undeniability of the idea that the media are agents in the political process and not simply observers of it provides one important reason for rethinking the traditional responsibilities and prerogatives of the press" (Canada 1991, quoting Lichtenberg 1990: 1).

Few would argue any longer that the coverage decisions made by news organizations during campaigns "merely reflect reality" or have little influence on the process and outcome of electoral contests. The weakening of political parties has increased the importance of the media in leadership selection and election campaigns (Taras 1990: 26–33 and 233–38).

Identifying the most important ethical issues of concern to campaign journalism is not an easy task. Potential issues cover a wide range, from partisan bias and conflict of interest to matters of professional autonomy and respect for public institutions. Because elections are so important to democracy, many major news organizations have developed special rules for covering them that supplement and in some cases supersede normal standards of newsworthiness. Although some news organizations deny the existence of standards for news judgment unique to elections, numerous studies have demonstrated their existence (see, for example, Fletcher 1987).

It is clear that many news organizations devote more resources to election coverage than newsworthiness alone would dictate, that they establish rules of access (whose views should be covered) and balance (especially among established political parties), and that they take special care to ensure the accuracy of controversial stories (Fletcher and Everett 1991a). Broadcasters are required by law to ensure that all reasonable viewpoints are communicated and that parties and candidates are treated equitably, and all responsible news organizations endeavour to ensure that voters have the opportunity to make an informed choice (Canada 1991). In specific coverage decisions, tension exists between everyday standards of newsworthiness and the special rules of election coverage.

A central reason for the development of special professional practices for campaign coverage is the immediacy of the consequences that might flow from editorial decisions. Decisions about whether or not to cover a story and how to present it might well affect the outcome of an election or, at least, alter the nature of a campaign. In non-election periods, errors of fact and interpretation are limited in their impact because corrections can be made, politicians can make their disagreements known and other journalists can contribute alternative perspectives. (That the ideal plurality of views is often absent in political coverage outside election periods is a subject for another essay.)

In campaign coverage, however, the opportunity to respond is foreshortened by the brevity of the campaign, and there may not be time for other news organizations to offer alternative versions of events. Thus editorial decision-makers bear a special burden during campaigns.[2] This burden may be seen as part of the larger responsibility: that the media must play a constructive role as part of the justification for constitutional guarantees of press freedom.

Types of Ethical Concerns

When examining the ethical dilemmas of campaign coverage, it is important to distinguish between two kinds of ethical concerns. The first involves clashes of principles within the context of journalistic practice. Here, reporters must decide which of two competing principles should take priority. Outside of campaign coverage, journalists must frequently balance demands for speed with accuracy (verification often consumes valuable time). In campaign coverage, a tension between the requirements of partisan balance and the normal standards of newsworthiness is common. In order to maintain partisan balance, many news organizations have chosen to present material that falls short in terms of audience interest or is not new.

The second category involves ethical concerns raised by journalistic practices themselves. Here, journalists must be prepared to explain their decisions to other stakeholders—parties, candidates, citizens—who see themselves as treated unfairly or view conventional journalism as failing to meet the challenge of changing times. This category includes concerns such as the marginalization of some groups—whose voices should be heard during campaigns—or the negative tone that has pervaded much recent election coverage (Fletcher and Everett 1993; Saunders 1991; Comber and Mayne 1986).

In almost every modern election, at least one major news decision has raised questions about ethics. Many of these decisions involved the reporting of statements politicians believed were off the record (Levine 1993: 260, 292, 300, 311–12 and 320–21). Journalists are frequently faced with issues involving use of confidential sources, reporting of casual or overheard conversations or participation in off-the-record briefings. For example, during the 1984 Canadian federal election campaign, both Brian Mulroney and John Turner felt betrayed by the reporting of comments made to journalists that they thought were off the record. Norms have changed in this regard from an earlier period in which there was a more personal relationship between politicians and journalists. These issues, common to many forms of journalism, can usually be sorted out by clear understandings between journalists and sources, and judicious and limited use of non-attributed sources, informed by the test of public interest—does the public interest require that this information be reported? Therefore these issues are not examined in detail here.

ETHICAL DILEMMAS IN CAMPAIGN COVERAGE

MAINTAINING JOURNALISTIC INDEPENDENCE

The autonomy of the journalistic enterprise from external, or at least political, control is not only a highly prized value in the Canadian journalistic culture but also an important foundation for the unique contribution that the news media make to democratic elections.

> The unfettered editorial judgement of the media makes an important contribution to the campaign process and has the potential to provide an autonomous critique of those seeking power (Canada 1991b: 474).

However, there are a number of persistent challenges to this autonomy, not so much from government regulation or payoffs as from the social milieu of senior political journalists and their need for access to information. (There has been a history of threats to journalistic independence from government pressure and payoffs—even in Canada—but this is not a matter of current concern for election coverage.)[3]

As Allan Fotheringham has put it in his usual offhanded eloquence, politicians and journalists are "birds of a feather" who share interests and watering holes in Ottawa between elections and travel together during election campaigns. He argues that much essential information is acquired by journalists in their after-hour socializing with politicians and political strategists. According to Charlotte Gray, "the key to covering Ottawa has always been sources, and every lunch-time you see journalists taking politicians and civil servants out to lunch."[4]

However necessary this process is, it raises difficult questions of personal loyalties and journalistic independence. The issue is compounded by the number of journalists who have personal relationships (through marriage, for example) with senior public officials and political staffers. These linkages raise questions of conflict of interest—which are rarely discussed in the media—and dependence. Many journalists are concerned when political journalists get "too cozy" with their sources (Kiefer 1994c).

Contemporary media criticism—including self-examination in memoirs—contains references to many journalistic "sins," including partisan bias, sensationalism and pack journalism, but few references to direct conflicts of interest. However, most people in Ottawa are aware of these conflicts, and journalists do come under pressure because of them, as Charlotte Gray of *Saturday Night* told us.[5] Reporters may overcompensate by being aggressive or may decide to avoid certain topics for fear of compromising a partner. There are occasional allegations, but there is little direct evidence of undue influence. Nevertheless, such potential conflicts of interest must leave journalists who report on conflict of interest in government feeling vulnerable.

The more significant problems are perhaps even more subtle: the emergence of a common worldview or relationship of interdependence. Much has been written about the phenomenon of "pack journalism" or "identical inspiration." It is certainly an issue in campaign coverage. The highly politicized situation produces a strong temptation for reporters to take on the protective colouration of the group. "The news business is a collective hunch about what matters to most people in any given day," according to Pamela Wallin (Kiefer 1994b). Journalists worry about the influence of the pack but find it difficult to resist (Kiefer 1994a).

It is fairly easy to demonstrate a kind of "narrative line" regarding a campaign or, more particularly, a party or leader who emerges in a campaign. This "line" influences subsequent coverage. In 1993, for example, the NDP was never taken seriously—regardless of the newsworthiness of its ideas—because of its standing in the polls. This raises the question of news values: public support is taken to be a measure of the level of audience interest in the ideas of the party. Is this equation appropriate? The answer depends in part upon whether or not an election campaign is viewed primarily as a public debate about the future of the country or a contest for power.

More insidious is the Ottawa-centric view that sometimes unites political leaders and journalists in a common perspective. David Taras (1989) has demonstrated its effects in the coverage of the Meech Lake Accord. Journalists feel "manipulated" by the parties and their public relations people. The failure of politicians and media alike to raise issues deemed insignificant by national elites has been commented on extensively in the case of the 1992 Canadian constitutional referendum. Yet, with the very limited exception of the *vox populi* and town hall features in 1992, dissident views tend not to get much of a hearing during campaigns. Journalists are likely to ask about smaller parties or groups not "How interesting are their perspectives?" but "For whom do they speak?"

CLOSED SYSTEM

In election campaigns the information that becomes news emerges from a kind of closed system in which journalists are dependent for information on a small circle of sources in each of the political parties. This dependence, like the emergence of a shared worldview, can result in a loss of perspective. As Pamela Wallin told us, "In the exchange of information, you are always going to be serving somebody's cause" (Kiefer 1994b). To avoid becoming mere conduits for party propaganda, reporters must maintain a "critical distance" while maintaining close ties with key sources. News organizations attempt to keep reporters from becoming too close to their sources during campaign coverage by rotating reporters among parties and candidates. This, too, results in a loss of perspective, as recently rotated reporters lack a sense of the development of a campaign and strong ties of trust with key sources.

In addition, there is a risk that reporters will develop a stake in the standing of a particular candidate or party. This can arise from sympathy with a person or cause but comes perhaps more often from an attachment to one's own predictions. Reporters spend a lot of time handicapping political races, and their performance as forecasters influences their professional status, as does their access to "inside dope" (Fletcher 1994b). These weaknesses are entirely human and are shared with others who follow politics. The danger here is that reporters may start to unconsciously shade their coverage to support their predictions. For example, a journalist who has reported earlier on the strength of a party's campaign organization might well overlook later evidence of weakness.

There are a number of instances in the history of Canadian campaign coverage where journalists have selected an image or emphasis in reporting that reflects the consensus or "narrative line" popular among other journalists about a particular candidate. For example, the image of Robert Stanfield fumbling a football which appeared in many Canadian dailies during the 1974 campaign underscored a widespread feeling among reporters that he was fumbling the campaign (Levine 1993; Fletcher 1975). Similarly, the proliferation of negative images of Joe Clark in 1979 and 1980 reflected reservations that influential political journalists had about him. Many journalists felt Clark was unprepared to be prime minister, but they communicated this by focusing on verbal gaffes and physical awkwardness rather than by a substantive analysis of his statements (Levine 1994; Fletcher 1981).

The Stanfield photo is an interesting case. CP photographer Doug Ball took a series of pictures which included the sixty-year-old Stanfield catching, tossing and fumbling the football. CP transmitted several pictures but editors across the country chose to feature him dropping the ball. This choice is usually defended by saying it was the more newsworthy photo, but it could be argued that an aging politician successfully catching a football was equally interesting. Stanfield himself was amazed that such a trivial matter became an issue. This incident suggests that political journalists who wish to avoid having undue influence on campaigns should consider images as well as words. Perhaps the symbolic interpretation suggested above is worth taking seriously. Stanfield strategists argued that the photo was misleading because the Conservative leader actually caught most of the balls tossed his way—and unfair. In interviews after the fact, a number of journalists argued that the photo crystallized for voters an accurate perception that Stanfield was "fumbling the campaign."

CONFIDENTIALITY AND THE TRADING OF INFORMATION

The closed circle of interaction that characterizes campaign coverage exacerbates the ethical concerns surrounding a common journalistic practice: trading information. Reporters regularly trade information among themselves as a way of keeping on top of complex situations and expanding their network of sources. It is an axiom of political journalism that the best questions in news conferences come from reporters who already know the answers. This practice poses no professional or ethical problems, as long as information is properly verified and confidentiality is maintained. Similarly, reporters routinely trade information with party sources, especially in the campaign loop where information is the currency of influence for party strategists as well as journalists.

Problems arise when confidentiality is breached. This can happen when reporters are rotated from one party to another and carry with them confidential information about the plans of a rival party, information that could have important repercussions for party strategies. Information can cross over directly when a journalist uses knowledge of one party's strategic plans to get a response from another party or provides information in an exchange. More commonly, information shared with another reporter will enter the market and be passed along to party officials second-hand. The problem is that, by sharing this information, the journalist becomes part of the electoral game and could potentially affect the outcome. This is especially important in the current strategic situation where events move quickly and rapid response is important. For example, the fact that Liberals were ready to respond quickly to the Conservative advertisement in 1993 depicting Jean Chrétien as an "embarrassment" as prime minister was important in the campaign. In several recent elections, there have been allegations that one party had been "tipped off" by journalists about a rival party's plans.

THE ETHICS OF INFLUENCE

The predominant professional norm among political journalists may well be: "Thou shalt not be a participant." Indeed, some journalists refrain from voting in order to maintain a clear line between journalism and politics. However, in the course of any election campaign, journalists must inevitably make decisions about coverage and interpretation that might affect the outcome. (The comforting myth that news coverage has no clear consequences has been abandoned by most experienced political journalists. Many, however, prefer to leave these difficult decisions to news managers.)

In an election campaign, many journalists believe the parties should be left to set the agenda because there is a structure of government and opposition intended to ensure that major issues are debated. Others, however, take the view that journalists have an obligation to raise issues neglected by the parties, serving the time-honoured role as tribune of the people. On the whole, research suggests that journalists do leave the field largely to the politicians, but many larger news organizations have tried over the past several elections to develop acceptable ways of supplementing the party-dominated debate. Some news organizations established issue teams to dissect party positions, and these were the forerunners of the "reality check" features of 1993. There have also been various attempts to involve "ordinary voters." Along with public opinion polls, these are vehicles to raise neglected issues without direct intervention by journalists, relying on the public or non-partisan "experts" instead (Fletcher and Everett 1991a).

TO PUBLISH OR NOT TO PUBLISH

Recent elections have produced a number of cases in which the editorial decision to proceed with a story raised difficult professional and ethical questions. Perhaps the most discussed case took place in the middle of the 1988 Canadian federal campaign when the CBC broadcast an extraordinary report on divisions with the Liberal organization. On October 19, the CBC presented a report by Peter Mansbridge that was unusual in several respects: (1) it was presented by Mansbridge and not a regular Ottawa reporter; (2) it was four minutes in length, more than twice as long as most major CBC television news items; and (3) it was very carefully written and, as it turned out, had involved far more verification and internal debate than any other campaign story in living memory. After a transitional reference to a previous item, the report began:

> For the last several days, there has been some astonishing manoeuvring at the highest levels of the [Liberal] party. Some of the most senior people in the party thought the unthinkable. Deep into this election campaign, they though about putting pressure on John Turner to quit. But CBC News has learned they've pulled back and are now prepared to work to salvage the campaign (Frizzell and Westell 1989: 80–82).

The story reported accurately, it appears, that there were significant divisions within the party and concern about the leader's public image, but the report left the misleading impression that there was some sort of plot to oust John Turner as leader. Indeed, other news organizations summarizing the CBC report used terms like "plot" and "coup." Even today, it is difficult to get at the truth. Certainly, there were internal divisions and discussions of replacing the leader, possibly in the context of Turner's difficulty with a pinched nerve in his back, but there is no confirmation of an actual plan to force him out (Caplan, Kirby and Segal 1989: 138–44).

In any case, the report raised a series of ethical dilemmas. To begin with, it was the subject of unusually careful verification and, in the end, appears to have contained only minor errors of fact, yet none of the principals were contacted for their side of the story (Levine 1993: 350). But the real issue for internal debate revolved around whether or not it was appropriate to break a story likely to deal a devastating blow to the electoral chances of one of the parties in the middle of an election campaign.

According to John Owen, then head of CBC News, CBC news managers finally decided it would be" irresponsible" to withhold the information from viewers. In general, journalists take the view that significant information should be made available to the public whenever possible. Wallin, who was not then with the CBC, takes this view: "I always err on the side of making information public. The benefits usually . . . outweigh the costs, and if they don't, then that's just the price of a democracy" (Kiefer 1994b).

The internal CBC discussion focused on two elements: accuracy and possible consequences. Certainly the report did harm Liberal election chances, though its most possibly adverse effects were overcome by a damage-control exercise and Turner's strong performance in the debates. However, some Liberals still maintain that it set the stage for the subsequent Conservative attack on Turner's credibility that did have a substantial effect on the outcome (Levine 1994: 351–52; Caplan, Kirby and Segal 1989: 138–44; and Fletcher Everett 1991: 317–22).

Perhaps more important, however, was the nature of the item. It was a report not of a specific event but rather of a situation—internal division within the Liberal party—and a hypothetical possibility—the replacement of Turner as party leader—that had been rejected by the time the story aired. Allan Frizzell and Tony Westell (1989: 83) report that

> there were those in the CBC who questioned whether the corporation, with its large audience and semi-official status and credibility, should broadcast in the middle of an election a devastating political story based in part on leaks and rumour and that could not be known with confidence to the whole truth of the matter.

Inevitably, the report was not the whole truth which was simply too complex for even a four-minute (or 830-word) item.

Whether the story was pieced together by CBC reporters or inspired by a leak—perhaps by someone who wanted to pre-empt a move against Turner—is not clear. What is clear is that no specific event had actually occurred that needed to be covered. It has been suggested that the CBC had learned that the *Globe and Mail* was preparing a similar story and, having been scooped as a result of its caution on previous stories, CBC news managers decided not to let it happen again (Levine 1993: 51; Caplan, Kirby and Segal 1989: 138–44). The scoop, it may be argued, is an obsolete form of journalistic competition that should not be a major factor in decisions about campaign coverage.

One key figure in the discussions, former Ottawa bureau chief Elly Alboim, has observed that, in the end, stories of this sort must be subjected to a public interest test (Fletcher 1994b). Was the public interest served by the broadcasting of this item? Are the internal conflicts of political parties essential information for voters? Is it news that a dramatic move might have been discussed but rejected?

The story raised other, more conventional ethical concerns as well. The dramatic presentation of the story overwhelmed its careful wording and left a misleading impression with viewers and, as noted above, other journalists. For television, the overall impression is probably more important than the words. In this case, the text implied that a memo had been sent to Turner outlining the issues and that he had decided to fight on. The words were illustrated by a visual that many viewers took to be the memo in question. The CBC admitted subsequently that it did not have the memo and that the visual was merely a "graphic representation." Alboim commented later that this was a mistake (Fletcher 1994b). Yet the "representation," as well as the use of Mansbridge to present it, added credibility to a story that was more speculative than the image would suggest (Caplan, Kirby and Segal 1989: 134–39). Careful wording is not enough for television.

From a broader perspective, the story probably appealed to CBC journalists and others who took it up because it encapsulated their feelings about John Turner and the Liberal campaign. There had been rumours about Turner's personal problems in the period prior to the election that journalists had hesitated to report. Since these matters were widely known in the Ottawa press gallery, the information and perceptions about Turner provided a context for the CBC story that was unknown to the general public (Kiefer 1994b; also see Levine 1993: 34b). This view illustrates the problem of the common Ottawa perspective that defines some information as appropriate for public disclosure and some as suitable only for internal gossip.

This example illustrates the dilemmas faced by news organizations in campaign coverage. It is now widely accepted that voters need context as well as reportage of election events. To add context, however, risks criticism and raises ethical concerns because subjective elements inevitably enter such coverage. The public interest can be seen to require that journalists raise issues neglected by the parties and investigate matters that politicians would prefer to have ignored. To do so, however, requires the exercise of judgment and raises concerns about possible effects on the campaign. The extensive debate within the CBC regarding the Turner story involved difficult issues such as these.

CHARACTER ISSUES

The ethical concerns that arise from news reports that attempt to provide citizens with insight into the "character" of politicians are even more subtle and difficult. The central dilemma involves determining what information about the private lives and personal characteristics of party leaders and other candidates are relevant to their public performance and potential as leaders. For example, the majority of political reporters would not disclose the fact that a politician is gay unless the information was directly relevant to a major policy issue or disclosed by the person in question. A minority might disagree under some circumstances but the question is where to draw the line. When the issue bears directly on sexual orientation, some might feel disclosure would be appropriate.

As with other matters of personal behaviour, to take another example, evidence of past domestic violence might be reported under certain circumstances. The key is the perception by journalists of what is in the public interest. In such cases, journalists are required to balance competing ethical principles.

In general, David Taras (1993: 338) found that Canadian journalists believe "that reporting on the private lives of politicians is out of bounds unless the story has a direct bearing on a matter of vital interest to the public." This view is held most strongly among Francophone journalists. Unlike in the United States, in Canada character issues are covered in restrained or veiled terms. Canadian journalists often try to convey their views of a politician's fitness for office as a kind of subtext to the day-to-day coverage of the campaign. *Toronto Star* columnist Carol Goar confirmed this perspective in a 1987 interview, noting that personal foibles are overlooked unless they represent some deep-seated characteristic that the reporter deems relevant to the public life of the politician involved (Gilsdorf 1987).

The coverage of Kim Campbell in 1993 provides some support for this perspective. Many observers detected a subtle questioning of her fitness as leader underlying the coverage. The focus on her inconsistencies and incautious statements was intended to raise questions about her personal stability. Is a person who exaggerates her accomplishments fit to be prime minister?

During the 1993 campaign, an undertone of distrust of Campbell developed among key reporters, illustrated by the considerable attention given to an allegedly secret blueprint for reform of Canada's social programs that presumably involved deep cuts in line with her deficit-cutting rhetoric (Fletcher 1994b; also see Levine 1993: 364, Taras 1993: 330 and Campbell and Pal 1994: 295). Aside from some contingency plans prepared by civil servants, however, there appears to have been no such blueprint. Nevertheless, the suspicion of a "secret plan"—which gave substance to quite plausible speculation about her probable behaviour if re-elected—dogged her for much of the campaign and triggered her damaging remark about forty-seven days being too short a time for debate on social reform. The reports themselves appear to have been inaccurate but they reflected real concerns by journalists. Would it have been more ethical if their projections had simply been presented as such?

There was relatively little actual "muckraking" in the profiles and background pieces on Campbell or other leaders and leadership contenders. The most controversial journalism about Campbell derived from an interview she did with Peter C. Newman that appeared in the May issue of *Vancouver* magazine (Levine 1993: 364). The controversy flared during the Conservative party's leadership campaign, following a story published in the *Toronto Star* on May 18. William Johnson (1993) describes the report in these terms: "Patrick Doyle, a parliamentary reporter for the Toronto Star culled the lengthy profile for all the unfavourable items he could find, removing the context that gave the words their meaning." Although rebuttals appeared quite quickly, other reporters and commentators picked up the distortions and they became part of the discourse regarding Campbell's fitness for leadership.

The Newman interview story raises several important issues. First, the origin of the item is of interest. It appears that staff from the camp of leadership rival Jean Charest brought the magazine article to the attention of Parliamentary reporters, with the controversial phrases conveniently highlighted. The *Star* apparently based its story on the magazine piece without delving further into the matter. Does the fact that the interview was published excuse subsequent coverage from the responsibility of verification and clarification?

More important, perhaps, the *Star* article and many others that took the same line illustrate a widespread tendency in contemporary campaign coverage that has two main elements: (1) constant surveillance for controversial or damaging words or phrases (especially contradictions or inconsistencies) and (2) a focus on phrases or images that further a pre-existing story line. This tendency promotes a political discourse that leans towards the cautious and trite because leaders risk a punishment by negative publicity if they step outside expected patterns of campaigning.

Journalists expect politicians to play the campaign game according to established rules and they also expect them to make news every day during a campaign, reflecting their own deadline pressures. This places politicians under a rather unrealistic form of pressure and produces a focus on specific words and phrases as reporters search for a fresh lead or angle. This pattern raises concerns not only about fairness to candidates but also about the utility for democracy of a campaign discourse that discourages innovation and a search for the real meaning of politicians' statements and views.

BROADER ETHICAL ISSUES

Beyond the issues of balance, fairness and privacy is a series of ethical issues about the nature of political discourse encouraged by campaign coverage during Canadian elections. Several broad trends illustrate these concerns:

- election news has become steadily more judgmental and negative in tone;
- journalists have supplanted candidates as the main sources of statements in the coverage;
- the framework of election coverage has shifted from a policy- or governance-centred orientation to a strategic-game perspective; and
- smaller parties and groups are largely shut out of the coverage.[6]

These trends, which can be found in other industrialized democracies as well, impoverish campaign dialogue and weaken the capacity of campaigns as presented in the media to prepare citizens for social and economic change. These tendencies also privilege certain voices in campaign debate and marginalize new social movements and other groups that challenge the conventional wisdom. In addition, the strategic-game perspective focuses debate on campaign strategy rather than on substance and communicates a cynical view of politics that may actually do politicians and citizens a disservice. It overlooks the possibility that politicians shape their policies not only for electoral advantage but also according to their own assumptions about the public interest. The latter may prove to be as good a source of predictions about their behaviour in office as the former, perhaps better.

Though these practices are well within the norms of contemporary campaign journalism, they raise ethical questions in the context of democratic politics. The cynicism of the strategic-game perspective, for example, may be unfair to politicians as a class. The focus on established voices is unfair not only to the groups left out of the dialogue but also to the citizens who might be interested in their ideas. The traditional norms suit the established system of party competition but new developments in our society, including increased social diversity, the proliferation of activist groups and the weakening of the linkages between party and society, suggest the need for new thinking.

CONCLUSIONS

The fact that major electoral consequences might flow from the decision to expose certain facts or present certain interpretations instead of others puts a significant ethical burden on political journalists during election campaigns. This burden is made heavier by the highly public nature of the work and the pressures it places on journalists. It is not enough that campaign reports be factual, they must also be appropriate and not misleading. Indeed, one might go further and suggest that the new media have an obligation to present competing interpretations of key events. In the brief period of an election campaign, news organizations may not be able to rely on other outlets to provide the necessary plurality of interpretation and may themselves have to bring an appropriate degree of honest doubt to their own work. This might mean, for example, asking whether it is appropriate to say a party's public standing is "surging" instead of "increasing" or "declining" rather than in "free fall."

With respect to character issues, David Taras (1993: 340) asks "whether the decision not to act strongly on [such] issues actually constitutes an intervention on behalf of those politicians whose behaviour and characters are inappropriate?"; failure to disclose relevant information could be seen to deprive voters of "information that could be vital in making an intelligent assessment of the leader and in weighing how to vote." This is in line with the view expressed by Pamela Wallin and others that journalists have an obligation to disclose as much as possible. However, it begs the hard ethical questions: What is "inappropriate" behaviour or character? Does disclosing information about one candidate unfairly benefit others whose vulnerabilities have not come to light? It seems necessary to proceed with a degree of humility, to apply public interest tests and attempt to place information in context.

In the end, electoral democracy must rely on the good sense and good offices of news organizations and individual journalists. However, it may be time for journalists to step back and consider what citizens need to know and how best to present it. Many thoughtful voters would feel more confident if journalists revealed their own conflicts, doubts and concerns and if they knew journalists took the consequences of their actions seriously (as most do).

No code of ethics or professional standards can provide detailed guidelines for dealing with these issues but in journalism, as in other professions, the usual post-mortem dissections can be more productive if key ethical dilemmas and issues are identified. Codes, after all, are simply statements of principle informed by the practices and precedents that have emerged from experience. As CBC anchor Pamela Wallin notes, for experienced journalists, questions of ethics are personal and subjective (Kiefer 1994b).

15. Slings and Arrows: The Editorial Cartoonist

Conway Jocks

> You have to be a political analyst, an artist, a caricaturist, a humorist and a journalist—all five. The only difference between *New York Times* columnist James Reston and an editorial cartoonist is that Reston doesn't know how to draw—Israeli cartoonist Ranan Lurie (1975)

My first editorial cartoon appeared in my high school newspaper in the 1940s. I can say without fear of contradiction that there were few, if any, conflicts in editorial direction while I was editor. But any thoughts of entering that career upon graduation were nipped in the bud when I was drafted into the United States Army. Throughout my ensuing career in the army and air force, I managed to wrangle occasional off-duty jobs as editor or cartoonist on various local service papers, beginning with the scrounging of a private cabin on board a Pacific-bound freighter and troopship because I "needed" space to edit the ship's paper.

Early on, I evolved a personal, one-line, code of ethics: No one tells me what I can or cannot draw. My self-admitted bull-headedness—a sense of righteous independence rather than arrogance—eventually cost me my syndicated comic strip (and offers to go air force–wide) for the USAF Strategic Air Command. But I never regretted it. I had experienced the ethical challenge of confronting not the the editorial line, but the publisher's politics. I did what any cartoonist would have done: I bailed out. Unwittingly, I had followed a principle which was already the ongoing ethic of most editorial cartoonists for the world's newspapers.

The Premise

> Editorial cartoons are, by nature, overstated, oversimplified and therefore unfair. So they are, and more power to that in this cautious, double-talking world. More power to Szep's bosses for turning him loose on all the hypocrites, liars, dimwits, con men, parasites, fatcats and crooks that surround us—Tom Wicker

The accompanying "editorial cartoon" by Jennifer Berman appears in a handout published by FAIR (Fairness and Accuracy In Reporting) as part of a facsimile newspaper in which the various departments are taken over the coals for misleading and/or biased reporting. FAIR is a

> national media watch group offering well-documented criticism in an effort to correct bias and imbalance. FAIR focuses public awareness on the media's allegiance to official agendas and their insensitivity to women, labor, minorities and public interest constituencies. FAIR seeks to invigorate the First Amendment by advocating

Jennifer Berman, "An editorial cartoon about editorial cartoons"; FAIR.

for greater media pluralism and the inclusion of public interest voices in national debates. FAIR is located at 130 West 25th Street, New York 10001.

Although I think Jennifer Berman created that cartoon as a critique of the daily editorial cartoon, most working cartoonists would see it as a positive comment on their work. All the working elements are there: the recognizable stereotyped images, the targets and the "stinger" in the bottom right corner. The odd side of this "editorial cartoon" is that the obviously liberal-minded folks at FAIR have turned on their potentially staunchest ally.

But there is another side to this moral coin. I hesitated before undertaking this review of encounters with journalistic ethics. I came to the table as a rabid liberal whose holy grail was fair play and balance. However, closer examination made me realize that absolute "fair play" was not part of the editorial cartoonist's rules of engagement which begin with "A for Ambush." My dilemma had to be uncompromisingly resolved in favour of the cartoonist's point of view, "fair play" notwithstanding.

FAIR PLAY

Assuming Ms. Berman's cartoon represents the opinion of the editorial critics, her point is that there is no fair play. Fair play means "balance," showing the other side of the story, the rule for straight news reporting which must avoid any hint of editorial bias.

Some will say, "But there should be someone who speaks for us!" The response involves the politics of the publisher. A conservative owner/editor would find it untenable to display a liberal-minded cartoonist next to his editorial piece. The publisher knows the paper's readers. It is a fact of life and part of the freedom of speech argument.

Editorialists operate from a position of bias or, editorially speaking, "righteous bias"—they fight against perceived wrongs. Theoretically, everyone is free to publish their own prejudices in their own paper or at least contribute to the "commentary," op-ed page. The cartoonist, by rights of tradition and usage, operates under the same rules except that his or her methods approach those of a waylaying mugger. The editorial cartoon is biased and opinionated. Its no-rules approach makes it the rogue of journalism. As one observer said, the cartoon, unlike the editorial piece, doesn't say, "on the other hand," which distinguishes it from the broader "political" cartoon.

If "fair play" followed the liberal hard-liners, ridicule would be banned. Ridicule includes caricaturing people, situations and mores; caricature and analogy reinforce the reader's understanding of the premise. The far left and right use the same weapons to call down their foes in their literature and when flying three-dimensional caricatures at protest demonstrations. In the end, to get their point across, FAIR and Ms. Berman resort to the tools of the cartoonist's trade to present their case.

STANDARDS

The editorial cartoonist works like a political columnist: both are generally free of editorial influence, both represent their personal agendas and the publisher buys their work. Cartoonists work on the cusp of self-service and get away with it.

However, standards for cartoonists and columnists are different. Depending on the paper you buy, you find cartoons carrying sombre messages of impending gloom and doom—more often than not, comical or titillating nevertheless. You won't find such a range among the serious political columns with which they share editorial space. Cheap shots are not uncommon in cartoons. Cheap shots sometimes pay off—for example, when the call goes out for party spin doctors to put a cap on it. Cartoonists are then as quick as columnists to spot the developing spin.

Cartoonists have their constraints. Most concern community taste and libel. But tastes change, and the limits of libel concerning political figures in a democracy recede as the courts redefine the limits of "fair comment." As far as personal guidelines are concerned, it is the rare cartoonist who doesn't value his or her reputation for honesty and integrity.

In the fall of 1993, I bantered with editorial cartoonist Terry "Aislin" Mosher of the *Gazette* for almost an hour, shamelessly nodding at each point of his thesis: yes, for the editorial cartoonist there are almost no ethical boundaries; yes, the editorial cartoonist is not a hired gun; yes, the cartoonist is a crusader who assumes the cloak of the avenging angel, such dramatic disguises used to cover one's true identity as storyteller and stand-up comedian.

THE EDITORIAL CARTOON

> In trying to ridicule those set in authority over us, one was constantly frustrated because, as it turned out, they were themselves infinitely more absurd in what they did than in one's wildest inventions—Malcom Muggeridge

To look at the ethics of cartooning, we should examine the purpose of the cartoon, how the art is created and why the editorial cartoon has prospered since the end of the nineteenth century when it moved from the illustrated magazines to the daily newspapers.

The late C.D. Batchelor, Pulitzer Prize-winning cartoonist for the *New York Daily News*, saw the editorial cartoon as a force in forming public opinion. He said North American newspapers used cartoons to supplement political editorials because a cartoon can encompass the thesis and argument of a whole column of writing in a self-contained, self-explanatory unit. The cartoon's power lies in its brevity and clarity. The approach depends on the artist's personality, Batchelor wrote. Some use humour, some satire, sentiment or pity; some even appeal to reason. Invariably, all employ caricature (Byrnes 1953).

Roy Nelson (1975), professor of journalism at the University of Oregon and a former cartoonist, said editorial cartoons are intended to sway public opinion. The weakest merely restate the news in graphic form but the strongest depict a political, social or economic problem and imply a solution. Nelson quotes Allan Nevins's comment on Hamilton Fish, a member of President Grant's cabinet: "He sometimes chipped the cube of truth to make it roll."

Stefan Kanfer said cartoons satirize events and event-makers, refining the material until only the ridiculous essence remains (Nelson 1975). How do they do that? The loaded answer: through satire, caricature, analogies and humour. As Kanfer says, the usual tangible, problematic result is ridicule. Is ridicule fair? Is it libelous? Are all politicians dishonest, scheming fat cats? Are all police officers brutes? Are all taxes unfair? No. But *some* politicians *are* dishonest, some police officers brutes, some taxes unfair. To get the point across in a single panel with minimal dialogue, the message is written large and plain, with lots of shorthand stereotypes.

The cartoonist uses satiric analogy, parody or simile to reduce a problem or situation to an easily understood picture, somewhat along the line of a biblical parable. When the cartoon is on target, the reader who is on-side feels satisfied. Don Wright (1971) of the *Miami News* said, "The editorial cartoon has become a welcome relief from some of the ponderous, elitist, overwritten property that typifies so many editorial pages today." Aislin says:

> You can't go farther than public opinion. Cartoons are often thought of as a vehicle to say things people are thinking but you can't sort of say it in correct society. That's what a cartoon is supposed to do.
>
> The momentum of a cartoon or a caricature of an individual, how it evolves, depends on public perceptions of the individual. But there's no point in that first year [in office] if that man isn't making mistakes, drawing him as potentially making mistakes.
>
> A cartoon is really a reflection [of] what that character does in public life, and what he does for you and me and everybody else. But I've got to make the point: you can't slash and trash just for the hell of it. It has to depend on the performance the politician does (CKRK-FM interview, November 22, 1993).

My own guideline parallels what Jeff MacNelly (1972), formerly of the *Richmond News Leader*, called "settling for little truths here and there."

But the ethical question expands when we realize that the cartoonist builds a following and a body of opposition with no cartoonist of its own to show the other side of the question in the same newspaper. Is that fair? The cartoonist answers, "Yes, because *I* am on the side of truth and fair play as *I* know it, and *I* have pierced the humbug of Whatever." In the end, what is left unspoken is, "If you don't like it, go buy another paper and find your own cartoonist."

It is possible to theoretically extend ridicule and analogy to the extremes of depicting murder, obscenity, cruelty and downright misrepresentation. Here, ethical questions are paramount.

The finest editorial cartoonists use their wit to reveal hypocrisy with telling lines of ink. As we will see, there are definite limits of public tolerance for their acidic brushes.

THE VIEW FROM WITHIN

> On the face of it, one would not say the attitude of political caricaturists was one of admiration or even goodwill. The traditional terms of their expressions are perhaps better adapted to censure than to praise. Admiration is for the poets. A satirist perverted to hero worship becomes pathetic and sickening. His approval can best be expressed by leaving its object alone—David Low (1957)

Is everything fair game? Is nothing sacred? The answers lie in the question: Who can mock the king with impunity if not the court jester? The court jester of yesterday is the editorial cartoonist of today. While other editorial-page players represent sober responsibility, the cartoonist comes from a wilder family tree, a tradition which includes Goya, Daumier, Hogarth, Low, Mauldin, and that nineteenth-century caricaturist who transformed King Louis-Phillipe into a pear (*poire* being the contemporary slang for dullard) and was taken to court for libel (and no doubt lèse-majesté) and acquitted.

Editorial cartoonists' totemic heroes have struck to the heart of complacency. Goya showed the cruel horrors of war during the Peninsula Campaign; Hogarth described the underbelly of London poverty; Bill Mauldin's cartoons for *Stars and Stripes* infuriated the brass by showing what life was really like in the foxholes (see page 156).

One of the saints in the cartoonists' heavenly host is Thomas Nast (see page 157). In the late nineteenth century, Nast destroyed the New York City boss system of Tammany Hall, created what would become the symbols for the Republican and Democratic parties and designed the Santa Claus figure we know today—all in the salad days of yellow journalism when "ethics" was just a Greek word for something or other to do with "character."

It was during this era that the dailies began to expropriate the political cartoon from weekly illustrated magazines such as *Puck* and *Judge*, and transformed them into "editorial" cartoons by putting them on the editorial pages. Some papers, such as the *Milwaukee Journal* and *Chicago Tribune*, put them right under the paper's banner on the front page. One of the few perks when I worked in the New York office of the *Chicago Tribune* ("The World's Greatest Newspaper") was to be the first each day to see John McCutcheon's exquisite work in colour (no matter how ultra-right he was).

Today's slick magazines, such as the *New Yorker*, *Changing Times*, *Esquire* and *Ladies' Home Journal*, continue the tradition of commenting on the conditions and mores of our times with panel cartoons, much in the tradition of the old illustrateds. Although their cartoons are

"Fresh, spirited American troops, flushed with victory, are bringing in thousands of hungry, ragged, battle-weary prisoners. . . ." (News item)

Bill Mauldin, "Up Front"; *Stars and Stripes,* United Features Syndicate.

subtler and more sophisticated than the dailies', and their artwork capable of more refinement, the magazine cartoons lack the daily cartoons' spontaneity, savagery and on-the-ground local interest. From the cartoonist's point of view, they're just printed on better paper.

There is no better way to understand the guidelines of political cartooning than to listen to cartoonists describe themselves and their work:

> **Ross Thomson** (*Punch*): All political cartoons are critical; they attack, that is their nature. They never qualify, or say "on the other hand," or pull punches. They amuse,

"The Tammany Tiger loose— what are you going to do about it?"

"Thomas Nast takes on Tammany Hall"; *Harper's Weekly,* November 11, 1871.

they infuriate, they reinforce a reader's prejudice. The most effective cartoonists are those who are natural cynics and whose view of the political scene is essentially a wary one (Thomson and Hewison 1985).

Osbert Lancaster: The cartoonist must remain fundamentally bloody-minded, hold no cows sacred, and be capable of thoughts in the worst possible taste (Nelson 1975).

Aislin: Sacred cows make the best hamburger (interview, September 4, 1993).

Bill Mauldin (*St. Louis Post-Dispatch*): Opposition is where cartoonists do their best. They are not so good at defending convention or pure moral rectitude (Richardson 1977).

Herb Block (*Washington Post*): Cartoons don't make up into lace valentines very well. I could do pictures every day of the week showing Uncle Sam resting his hand on someone's shoulder and saying, "Well done, Insertname," and I think we'd all get pretty sick of them (Block 1952).

David Rosen (editor, *Target: The Political Cartoon Quarterly*): This is not to imply that cartoonists thrive on the trials and tribulations of the masses (as weapons contactors do, for example). They simply try to make sense of it all, to poke holes in the windbags and point ink-stained fingers at the perpetrators (Stahl 1984).

CHARLES RODRIGUES

"Hey, man, would you hold my sign while I go for a sandwich?"

Charles Rodrigues, "The Art in Cartooning."

Nicholas Stahl (editor, *Best Canadian Political Cartoons*): Joey Smallwood, late premier of Newfoundland, once remarked that political cartoons, friendly or unfriendly, are so good that he hated to see them wasted on his opponents. Mr. Smallwood likely realized what political cartoonists are quick to argue—that they cause no more harm to politicians than the politicians cause harm to themselves (Mosher 1975).

Andy Donato (*Toronto Sun*): Drawing political cartoons [is] my passion. I take particular joy in hearing politicians say things which give their press secretaries migraines, allow the opposition to heap scorn upon them and send the general public into a fury (1993).

THE ART

> Are the details nicely composed so that the eye slides easily to the full meaning? Has the drawing the appropriate blend of fantasy and realism to insinuate the satire? Does the wit of its caricature suggest sound judgement of essentials? Do the portraits of the people suggest insight into character? Does the performance fit the intention—not too labored to defeat the spontaneity, not too facile as to be insignificant? Is it, in short, a good cartoon, or just another plate of hash?—David Low (1957)

THE IDEA

There are many, many ways to get the idea across. Here's one way Aislin does the trick:

> I often hang around in coffee shops and cafeterias to hear what people are talking about. And on a slow day, if there are two or three conversations going on about the same subject, then that's what I'll draw for the following day, as opposed to wage and price controls in Panama that the editorialists might deal with. It's important to me to deal with subjects that people are talking about or thinking about (CKRK-FM radio interview, November 22, 1993).

That may be the best of all possible ways to reflect the day's opinions in the next cartoon. Some cartoonists read up to three papers a day just to follow the trail of public opinion, political pickles or emerging scandals. Then there are those who follow in the footsteps of lawyers and detectives: they follow the money, asking the traditional when, where, who, why, and what happened?

Many of my ideas stem from my other job as host of a talk-radio phone-in show in my community of Kahnawake, population seven thousand. I talk to the shakers and movers, I listen to the phone-in public, I learn. The one thing that separates me from other community editorial cartoonists is that any negative Native pronouncements coming from federal, provincial and local municipal politicians are grist for my mill, a unique situation not available to others in my perverse trade.

THE DEVELOPMENT

Once you have the argument, the next step is to find a suitable analogy, an instantly understandable vehicle in which to express the satire and ridiculousness of the person or situation. The cartoonist calls on the resources from his or her ragtag recollection of fables, fairy tales, historical events, characters, proverbs, clichés, song titles, advertising slogans, puns and, more recently, popular movie, TV and stage titles.

Once argument and vehicle are mated, it remains for the cartoonist to place the action in a setting recognizable to the paper's clientele. Len Norris of the *Vancouver Sun* plays on the eccentricities of the Vancouver-Victoria citizenry; Aislin and the amazing hyperbole-inclined francophone artists glean the fertile fields of Montreal and Quebec lifestyles, proving that, after all, Canada is no more than a collection of communities.

THE CARICATURE

To appreciate the high and dastardly art of caricature, as Roy Nelson calls it, one must imagine the cartoonist as part of a wolf pack coming upon the prey, stalking the doomed creature in ever-decreasing circles. The prey is taken when its persona is devoured in caricature and the publicly perceived character re-emerges as living self-parody.

Unfortunately, the victim had no choice about looks and the wolf pack knows this. The close-set, shifty eyes—surely there must be some deceit. The mouth—is it too tight, too ungenerous? The nose—it must be gargantuan or so small as to be ridiculous. There is no escape, no middle ground. A small waist—lean and mean-minded. If the girth is too generous—a hint of self-indulgence? God help the victim who is an eccentric dresser, given to odd habits, who has bad hair days or wears glasses. Some cartoonists twist and morph their victim's face with their Mac graphics until it fits their characteristic style.

As Aislin puts it:

> There's a momentum to political cartooning. A politician has to put himself or herself in a position where they really deserve it. There's a momentum as the politician's reputation evolves and their personality comes out—then their caricature grows, as it did with Mulroney. And as it had with Trudeau and Levesque, and any number of people.
>
> You have these facial characteristics you can take advantage of in terms of suggesting cartoons. But a good caricature, to a good cartoonist, goes deeper than that. It suggests other things. You can use that, but . . . if you can only draw Mulroney's chin, but you can't suggest him. . . . It goes further than just the business of physiognomy and the facial characteristics of somebody.

It all seems so unfair. Yet invariably, within hours of the paper hitting the streets, the battered object of the wolf pack will call the cartoonist and ask for the original drawing to hang in his or her office.

INTERNAL ETHICS

In some ways, the internal ethics of the guild are more powerful than overt public ethics. There is a bond among editorial cartoonists, even though they may bicker among themselves about such things as imitative styles and plagiarism. After all, how many times can a country be shown as a train engine being fueled by dollar bills, or the ship of state sinking from debt? A favourite ploy is to parody an existing comic strip to fit an ongoing real-world situation. Although the cartoonist is quick to add "apologies to" the creator of the original strip somewhere near his or her own signature, some are not happy. Charles Schultz, creator of "Peanuts," certainly isn't; he worries that the public may think the editorial cartoon was *his* idea.

Cartoon styles are changing. The passing of the last generation of artists who executed somber-messaged masterpieces, opened the door to the humour of the younger cartoonists. Don Wright (1971) laments that many young cartoonists lock themselves into this light, humorous style and can't do the heavy dramatic cartoon when an issue calls for it.

However, Jeff MacNelly (1972), who won the Pulitzer Prize after only two years in the trade, thinks:

> you can get the reader's attention and hold it better through humor than with a hatchet. This is not to say that I avoid the serious issues and the serious approach to many issues. . . . I'm not a big dogmatic, doctrinaire type. . . . People get turned off by that kind of thing.

MacNelly now creates the comic strip "Shoe" which is set in an editorial office in the trees, not far from Washington, in Virginia. It is named for 1938 Pultitzer Prize–winning cartoonist Vaughn Shoemaker of the *Chicago Daily News*.

Ed Valtman of the *Hartford Times* lets "the characters in my cartoon say that something is bad or that something should be done, rather than . . . preaching to the reader in the form of my own words in a caption" (Nelson 1975).

CHANGING ATTITUDES

> The colored people are good subjects for action pictures; they are natural-born humorists and will often assume ridiculous attitudes or say sidesplitting things with no apparent intention of being funny. The cartoonist usually plays on the colored man's love of loud clothes, watermelon, chicken, crap-shooting, fear of ghosts, etc.—E.C. Mathews (1920).

In recent times, newspapers and their columnists and cartoonists have had to deal with the sensitivities and concerns of minorities. In the United States the change began as early as 1948 with the desegregation of its armed forces, gained strength through federal school and busing laws and culminated in the peace marches of the early 1950s.

There were no effective limits on racial stereotyping before this time. Stereotyping built on a tradition which arose from the Reconstruction era, abetted by accepted stereotypes from Vaudeville and minstrel stages. The illustrated magazines poked fun at thick-headed Irishmen, bickering Jews, superstitious and ignorant blacks and pigtailed Chinese coolies. America's Native population was so low in the food chain they weren't even worth considered stereotyping, until the advent of afternoon movie matinees.

The quotation which heads this section is from the early twentieth-century book *How To Draw Funny Pictures* written by E.C. Mathews (1920) and illustrated by a famous cartoonist of the time. Mathews warns:

> The Jewish people are given to expressing themselves by hand. Be careful not to offend the Jewish people in your cartoons, or you may be unable to get them published.

" Ah don't see how dat lazy niggah lives widout no missible means ob suppo't."
" Well, Ah reckon, Mr. Thompson, dey mus' be somethin' wrong wid yoah eyesight."

Otto Lang, *Caricature*; Leslie-Judge Co.; H.T. Rockwell.

Mindsets changed in mid-century. Dave Breger (1966), creator of "G.I. Joe," "Pvt. Breger" and "Mr. Breger," said:

> It's fine when you make your usual cartoon character look funny, but I found it was something else again when your cartoon characters are Negroes. I knew it wouldn't come off as intended. So, as the lesser of evils, I had no choice but to avoid the subject altogether. This was shying away from the problem, of course—not solving it.

Judging from today's crop of cartoons, it seems the problem has yet to be resolved, either in political cartoons or comic strips. The age of "political correctness" dawned with publisher McGraw-Hill's distribution of an eleven-page set of guidelines in 1978. Since that time there has been a growing awareness of sensitivity in almost every area of communications except in the fields of stand-up comedy and editorial cartoons.

"I'm curious about this political correctness," Aislin said in a 1993 radio interview.

> Who are these people? Who are these people who invent what we're supposed to say? I don't actually meet any of them. I've got a strange feeling it all comes out of a computer somewhere. Suddenly there's a dictum that this can't be mentioned, or that can't be mentioned anymore. I try to ignore it myself, but it's a curious business. I think a lot of it comes from failed Lefts who got themselves into the university syndrome, because a lot of it seems to come from there" (CKRK-FM radio interview, November 22, 1993).

Sports cartoonist John Richardson says that, with rare exceptions, the best editorial cartoonists have been liberals but, although they are in a position to mould public opinion, the changes they effect are glacial. There are current examples of editorial cartoons which show black and Native people, but they are not given the "big nose and tiny eyes" treatment. The Black Panthers were depicted as muscular giants. Cartoonists invariably make Native people impossibly good-looking. Are these the results of guilt-trip jet lag? The pendulum has swung so that only white Anglo-Saxon Protestants can now be safely caricatured, or so it seems.

CONSTRAINTS

I would say I have 99.9 percent control—Don Wright (1971)

Editorial cartoonists say that the line in the sand is drawn at taste and/or choice of analogy. Some of the new cartoonists push the envelope wider, a little at a time, sometimes setting precedents. Aislin stands tall among those who pioneered the envelope game. His ridiculing of the royal family, the Pope playing the accordion and the Quebec provincial police as pit bulls brought blizzards of letters to the editor of the beleaguered *Gazette*, but no retraction or apology.

LIBEL

Although there are general rules of libel, specific laws vary from province to province and from state to state. Libel is a rock on which a journalist can founder, yet it is not *the* big threat facing editorial cartoonists. While writers agonize over making their statements accurate, not repeating someone else's libel and scrupulously avoiding malicious reporting, the India-ink throwers blithely picture heads of government (and states) in the most embarrassing and compromising poses.

Politicians may slur and libel other politicians in the heat of debate but journalists cannot. Does that mean editorial cartoonists work under the same bubble of protection as politicians? No, even if it appears so. Their defence is "fair comment," as opposed to the "absolute privilege" sometimes given participants in an official proceeding. "Fair comment" is an opinion, useful only when criticizing official and public figures (those who don't have rights of privacy), generally speaking. Therefore the cartoonist can attack, charge, ridicule and caricature any official or public figure with impunity unless the cartoonist states an untruth in the process. The cartoon is seen as a satirical personal comment. Besides, how can an "important figure" sue a cartoonist without bringing some degree of ridicule upon themselves? Look at what happened to U.S. Vice President Dan Quayle when he heaped scorn on Murphy Brown's morals.

Through process of elimination, the cartoonist's limitations lie somewhere short of graphic depiction of murder, cruelty, pornography, obscenity, racism or treason. Yet one cartoon showed British Columbia Premier Vander Zalm pulling a fly apart. Vander Zalm sued and lost; the cartoonist was not prohibited from showing the act of dismemberment. Even if there were a list of taboos, not every cartoonist would play at the edge; each has their own individual ethic and style.

CORPORATE CONSTRAINTS

In the realm of bounds, political leanings can have a profound effect. Newspapers often passively constrain what they consider problematic comments or issues. During the 1952 elections the *Washington Post* backed Eisenhower. Its cartoonist, Herblock (Herb Block), a Stevenson liberal, excused himself until the election blew over by going on vacation while the paper brought in a replacement.

Every so often a cartoon lands on the op-ed side when the day's editorial runs counter to its message. Lynn Johnston's popular Canadian strip, "For Better Or For Worse," was dropped by some conservative American papers during the run of a "gay" sequence. And Gary Trudeau's "Doonesbury" is regularly placed on op-ed pages instead of comic pages because of its politics, not to mention its references to sex and drugs.

Foreign editorial cartoonists work under a different set of ethics. Stereotypes of Arabs, Jews, Africans and Asians are exaggerated more than in North America where political

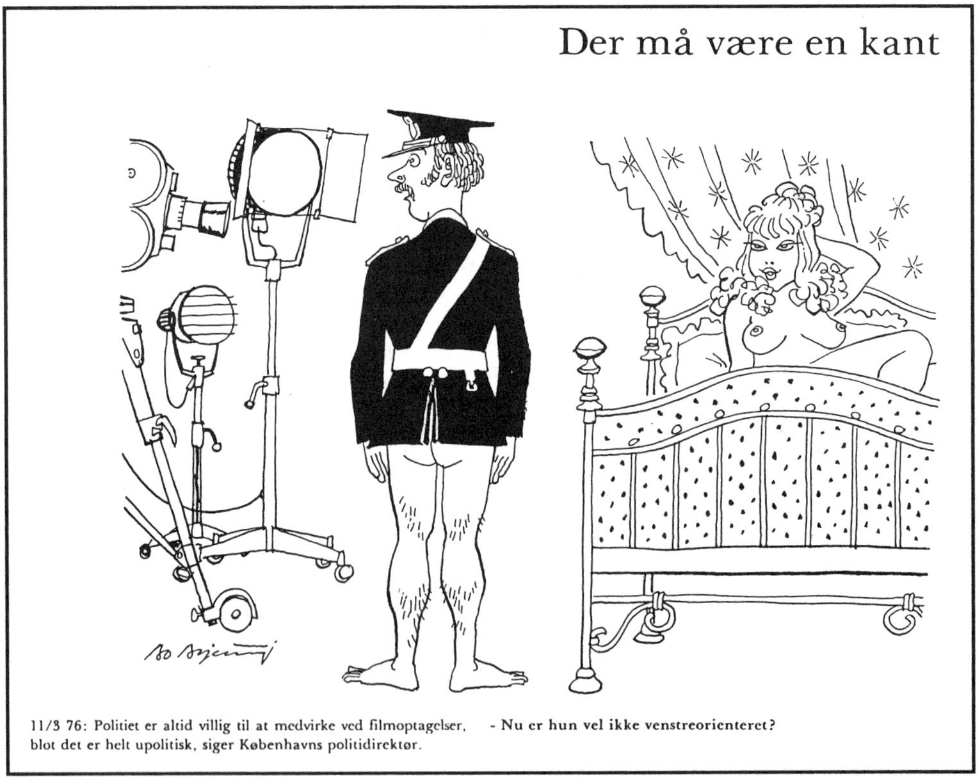

BoBojesen, *Politikens*; *Forlag*, Copenhagen, Denmark; 1976.

Title: You have to draw the line somewhere
Caption: Are you sure she isn't left-wing?
The Event: 11/3/76: Police are willing to cooperate with film producers as long as they're not political, says Copenhagen's police director.

correctness may be just a local phenomenon. An interesting feature of global cultural diversity can be seen in mainline cartoons in Scandinavia and Germany where Protestant ethics allow something unknown on this side: nudity.

"OUR TOWN IS NICE"

That's the unwritten subtext in small market newspapers, and it's a problem for political cartoonists whose fodder is usually corruption and wrongdoing. When I first signed on with the *Eastern Door*, our community paper, I was told that poking at certain internal problems was taboo; otherwise, I had a free hand. Although that one restriction was onerous, I was aware that there were volatile factions here which could pose problems for my family and me if they were taunted or ridiculed. And it would appear the paper itself was under the same unspoken restraint. But whereas a paper is a faceless monolith, a cartoonist (or columnist) is a high-profile individual target. Yet not to speak out on taboo subjects is tantamount to disguising reality, and hiding the dirty laundry is no excuse.

That was a dilemma I thought existed only for me. Then I came upon two pieces, one by cartoonist and journalism professor Roy Nelson, the other by *London Free Press* writer Sandra Coulson. I was not alone. Roy Nelson (1975):

> "Afghanistanism" is a disease in American journalism that allows cartoonists to speak out forcefully on evils back in Washington or in some other part of the world, but paralyzes them when it comes to attacking local cupidity. You tend to be more circumspect with an official when you live within walking distance, and he might appear at the local coffee shop.
>
> This may explain why my editorial cartoons, freelanced over a twelve-year period to the *Eugene Register-Guard*, were not quite the blunt instruments one would hope for. Certainly I cannot blame the *Guard* itself, which is admirably free of the disease. I became what a colleague refers to as a "knee-jerk middle of the roader." That a blandness had crept into my work was never more apparent to me than when I received from one of my readers a contribution labeled "Typical Roy Paul Cartoon." Two persons, indifferently drawn, were shown talking. One was saying, "I think Eugene is nice." The other was saying, "I think everything is nice."

Sandra Coulson (1993):

> They are the court jesters of small towns. But instead of playing before royalty, editorial cartoonists for some of Southwestern Ontario's weekly newspapers perform in the court of public opinion.

Unlike cartoonists for much larger newspapers, these small-town cartoonists can't hide behind the anonymity of big-city life. Their targets are also their neighbours. And yet they can't dodge the issues. The soul of editorial cartooning at weekly papers is local news.

THE DOUBLE-TAKE

Unfortunately, those two examples don't explain how small-town cartoonists operate under stifling circumstances. My personal solution is a "double-speak" message, which I use in certain situations and which can be read both ways. In the Christos Sirros cartoon, I was ostensibly criticizing the Quebec government's characterization of our council's decision to oust specific non-Native residents from the reserve. However, some Native residents, including myself, disapproved of the council's method, comparing it with the infamous "ethnic cleansing" programs. The flip side of the cartoon's message is that the council's methodology was no better than Quebec's restrictive language and education laws.

The same technique was employed in the Oka citizens demonstration for justice cartoon. The Kanehsatake council is shown complaining about a token non-Native roadblock, just as the Oka town council complained about the Kanehsatake roadblock in the summer of 1990—a case of what's inane for the goose is inane for the gander.

Being all things to all people verges on being ethically reprehensible, as if the *Eastern Door* and I (and many community paper editorialists) practiced muted, double-talking, cautious hypocrisy, as Tom Wicker (*Boston Globe*, n.d.) called it. The question revolves around the constraints of community standards as uniquely applied to this particular community and perhaps to other small towns as well. Let's just say I have "99.9 percent control."

My only saving grace in working within the "Afghanistani" parameters in this manner is that I can continue to voice my opinions but it takes twice as long to chip away at the cube of truth to find the analogy. My day job as host of a phone-in radio talk show has certainly shown how volatile a public can be. But unlike print journalism, what I can do or say over the public airwaves is restricted by the Broadcast Act and the CRTC.

Conway Jocks [1], *Eastern Door*; Kahnawake, Quebec.

Conway Jocks, *Eastern Door*; Kahnawake, Quebec.

THE AISLIN CONVERSATIONS

The *Gazette* is located in a newer building in Montreal's old financial district. I called on Terry Mosher there on Saturday, September 4, 1993; he had just returned from vacation. His studio is located on a utility floor, and getting to it requires passing through a storage area for back issues and rooms set aside for janitorial supplies. It's a comfortable room. The walls are lined with originals from other cartoonists, pictures, working guides, memos and a rackful of baseball caps. Several desks are put together to form an island in the centre, and the ubiquitous Mac computer is placed near his drawing board. Terry works on contract and rents space from the paper to avoid being an employee and hence subject to editorial control. And, oh yes, his is the only office in the building where smoking is not only allowed but encouraged.

As I left the studio following the interview, I said he would have the right to approve the transcript. He brushed this aside with a genteel "I don't give a shit what you do with it." In a later conversation, I said the transcript would be worth its weight in gold to students of editorial cartooning. He responded with a harumph.

Terry is one of the most erudite, forthright and interesting people in the business. Like all lifestyle commentators (critics, talk-show hosts, deejays) he has a grab-bag memory of esoteric facts, figures, names and literary allusions, plus a knack for lateral thinking. In other words, he is the very model of a modern editorial cartoonist. In the context of this study, his ethics and the ethics of those who have gone before him stand in sharp contrast with the ethics of text journalism. Here is Aislin:

On the Mulroney cartoon:

I got denounced in the House of Commons. It was my red-letter day for the year. Just to give you a bit of background, it was a slow day and often what I do is sit in the cafeteria and listen to what people are talking about as opposed to editorial meetings. It seemed for a few days everybody was talking about Mulroney's new house. I started to draw something about Mulroney's new house and I thought about him out for a walk. But Trudeau's always out for a walk too. Well, Trudeau's tripping him up in the snow. So I drew a Trudeau, sort of walking away in the distance with a cape, and everybody would know this—that's only Trudeau with a hat and cape, whistling and walking away with a walking stick. And Mulroney, the buffoon that he is, all tripped up. There's a

Terry Mosher, Aislin; *Montreal Gazette.*

beautiful contrast between the two men too. Overall, we love the arrogance of Trudeau and we hate the arrogance of Mulroney. So it became a cartoon for Montrealers, who would understand it. I wasn't even going to syndicate it.

But then Barbara MacDougall happened to be in town the morning it appeared and misread the cartoon. She thought it was somebody with a walking stick having just shot Mulroney, in front of his house. So she began comparing this to the U of M, and that sort of thing. And then I said, "What's going on here?" And then faxes began coming in, all with 613 Ottawa area codes. So obviously Babs had flown back and said, "Let's get the . . ." and then faxes from Lowell Murray and that sort. By afternoon they denounced me in the House of Commons—but misread the cartoon.

It was one of the beautiful situations where they just played into our hands and people began to pay attention and realized . . . and then we got letters and faxes of support. It was just one of those marvelous things that happen where something was just misunderstood and they began a campaign.

On risks:

There are other times I know there's going to be a reaction. For example, during Oka, when I drew the cop as a pitbull, I knew. And as a result they beat up a couple of Quebec reporters—*Gazette* reporters. Sometimes it's deliberate [the intent], and other times it comes out of nowhere—you don't expect it at all. They [the cops] were going over the edge. Somebody had to say something. And it's easier to do it in a cartoon where you're allowed to be . . . let's say in a cartoon or in satire . . . where there's a suggestion of smoke, you're allowed to draw the fire. You exaggerate. When you smell something then you can go a little further with it. I think that's probably an important part of satire.

On responsibility:

Certainly there are parameters that you have to work in. For some oddball reason of history, cartooning—political cartooning—is a vault of the editorial page that drives part of the paper, perhaps for a little comic relief. But if you talk to a number of cartoonists, you'll find they're almost diametrically opposed to the editorial writers, who are perhaps the most responsible people in the paper. The cartoonists, almost by definition, have to be the most irresponsible.

Do writers have limits?

Yes, they do. Far more than we do. But humourists and cartoonists are allowed to go further. A stand-up comic, for example, will give you a conversation that doesn't take place. The same with a cartoon. So therefore you're really on the cutting edge of what's allowed and what isn't. But then again, you can't take what applies to us and apply it to regular journalism because then regular journalism would become irresponsible. Because it's satire, it's a whole different kettle of fish.

The editorial hand:

It's not invisible. It's quite visible. It applies in cartooning too. As opposed to being political, occasionally the *Gazette* will say, "Well, you've gone too far." It's a

Terry Mosher, *Montreal Gazette*.

question of taste. I submit one cartoon [rather than a choice] and they don't see a rough. I feel that my role is kind of like that of a columnist. I'm exercising my own opinion. Some cartoonists submit several. Sort of a result of the bad old days when I think cartoonists were deliberately sort of told, or it was indicated that, "Look, you're just some sort of appendage to the responsible editorial page."

Then we have to look at surveys and realize 80 percent of the people are looking at our cartoons and only 40 percent are reading the editorial, but 50 percent of those 40 percent are lying. I think probably for the last twenty to thirty years there's been a tendency among editors, the good ones anyway, to just say, "Look, leave the cartoonists alone. They'll screw up sometimes, but occasionally they do come in with good things."

People tend to loathe cartoons with mourning black faces or big hands—the easiest thing to do. But editors like them. They're full of easily understood symbolisms. But when you do a real clever dig that you're happy with, that you know that perhaps only a dozen other people will understand the parameters of the situation, then sometimes the editors will say, "What are you doing? You're getting too complicated." And perhaps you are. But that's really sort of satisfying stuff.

On litigation:

They've tried it with cartoons. They've always been thrown out. Libel. In "The Hecklers," there's the whole story about the famous suit against the cartoonist in B.C. by Vander Zalm, and he lost. And again the judgment was a very good one, in terms of satire. The fact that I can draw somebody in a hilarious way—a prime minister shooting somebody. But people know it is meant in a funny way in a sort of Gilbert and Sullivan kind—humouresque, if you will.

You can't do it any other way. You're allowed to exaggerate, you're allowed to put words in people's mouths—for the better good, to suggest that this may be bad—and to poke fun.

On satire and humour:

You're best at doing what you know. Satire is always at its best when you do what you know. And you test. He's [a Native cartoonist] testing the ability of Natives in certain situations to laugh at themselves, and if they can't, it means they're collectively insecure. There's a collective insecurity that exists, and if you find it, then people are going to react.

Gerald Pelletier, years ago, once said to somebody, "I love Aislin's cartoons, except when he draws me." That's part of your role, to sort of dig and scrape the nerves a little bit.

We live in interesting times, and to draw satire in this day and age, again, trying to make people a little uncomfortable and question themselves, because nobody's perfect. I mean, if we had perfection, we wouldn't have humour. I don't think that you can really include satire within some sort of ethical standard you set up within journalism because satire has to run against the grain. Good satire does, by nature. Whatever is prevalent, then you want to sort of question it, question it, question it. I remember I did a cartoon when a *so* politically correct politician in Toronto (it's *so* Toronto and *so* p.c.) . . . said something about a cartoon that a colleague had done, about how it's demeaning and hurtful. And I did a cartoon about it in response, saying, "Thank God. All cartoons should be demeaning and hurtful." You can't fall within that group (the p.c.).

Humourists run with the hare, satirists run with the hounds. So much of satire is humour, and not necessarily ha-ha humour. If you can't define humour and what's going to make people laugh and what isn't, then you've got yourself in a very murky area. I think it's only after reflection that you define it, what becomes popular and what isn't. Humour is often a result of things we're terribly insecure about. It's so difficult to pull in the reins and say this is allowed and this isn't, when you can't even define what humour is.

On ethics:

What is ethical? I mean this is fascinating. We live in a strange world where we're taught that certain things are important. Then as we grow up and we mature, we realize they're not that important at all. If Quebec were to separate, it really wouldn't matter worth a shit, but if people stopped paying their Visa bills, the marines would move in within three months. Money determines everything at the border now. Money determines everything. When I'm not sure in a cartoon, I say, "Where's the money? Where's the money?" If you look for the money, that's usually where the problem is.

On reaction:

A lot of politicians claim to like cartoonists. I've had executive assistants write me notes asking me when I'm going to draw their boss. You write back and say, "Have them do something interesting." Because there are only a limited number of people you can draw on the editorial page who'll be recognized. Not every cabinet minister is well known, only the top five, six, seven or eight, perhaps. Barbara MacDougall said in her letter, "I used to love Aislin, but obviously I don't love him anymore." When did she ever love me? That worries me. You're not in the business to satisfy politicians. I don't even have to deal with them, which is nice. Those poor reporters who have to sort of talk to them, I don't envy them.

We sit in our studios and we perceive the way people in the cafeteria perceive. And if you try to get any higher than that, you're in trouble. I'm drawing for the people. It's very much a populist art form. The point you really have to make in this is to define what humour is; and therefore it's very difficult to sort of come up with a list of ten rules that have to apply to cartoonists. You can't do it.

16. Talk of the Town: Radio Talk Shows

Conway Jocks

The radio talk show is now the most popular AM radio format in the United States and is on a strong upswing in Canada. Two things gave rise to this format: the quality of AM radio sound and the information explosion.

When mainstream music abandoned AM radio for stereo FM some thirty years ago, AM stations were largely left with talk radio: news, sports, weather and traffic reports. Talk/variety shows had risen to prominence in the late 1940s beginning with the Garry Moore show in the United States, followed by the Arthur Godfrey show, and then revived on TV by Steve Allen and Jack Paar. It was a short leap to open-line radio where the audience is given a chance to participate.

In recent years, radio talk shows have spawned the immensely popular TV talk shows such as Oprah Winfrey which attracts an average audience of 19 million viewers per show. These shows now outdraw the afternoon soap operas. Of course, many AM stations still carry music but a careful listen reveals they are usually playing pre-stereophonic golden oldies or country music where (not to put too fine a point on it) the listener is not overly fastidious about sound quality. Generally speaking, these program formats wallow at the bottom of the ratings within competitive urban markets.

There are two types of talk radio: chatty talk shows proper (objective) and phone-in shows (subjective). Talk shows usually chew over prearranged topics with invited guests and phone-ins are usually extemporaneous.

A burgeoning population, the problems of our time, the leveling off of class distinctions and the veering towards political populism has made everyman (and woman) an expert who wants his or her voice heard. Enter talk radio. There are more radio sets today than during all the years of radio's "golden age" combined. Phone-in programs may focus on current events or on basic advice on matters such as sports, auto repair, health, outré psychic information or candid sex advice, usually given by in-studio guest experts.

In the United States, frank language is de rigueur—in fact, the more de rigueur, the more popular the show. Some shows are "zoo" radio—crazy, inane, rude and unpopular with more mature listeners. Phone-in radio has become the people's dais.

Thanks to the Canadian Radio-Television and Telecommunications Commission (CRTC) and the Broadcast Act, Canadians draw the line at much of what makes the American programs hot. But that doesn't prevent eavesdropping Canadian listeners from tuning in to Boston, Buffalo, Detroit or Seattle to hear the likes of Rush Limbaugh or Howard Stern. Larry King's CNN show from Washington, D.C., is so influential that sitting presidents, wannabe presidents and prime ministers welcome the chance to visit him, publicize their good side and schmooze with America. Frequently, the show offers genuine news items or at least reveals another aspect of the VIP's personality.

By contrast, Canada's most influential talk show is on radio: "Morningside," hosted by Peter Gzowski. The national phone-in show, "Cross Country Check-up," is also on CBC.

Community radio, a genre in which Canada is a world leader, has talk radio too. Talk radio forges the communication links in ethnic neighbourhoods, small towns and aboriginal communities from the farthest Arctic coasts to the outskirts of major Canadian cities, sending hundreds of languages through the air. Phone-in shows are lively, extended family affairs where listeners play their favourite game: trying to identify the caller.

In more remote regions, AM is not a player. FM, easier and cheaper to build, is king, followed by trail radio, sometimes called "moccasin telegraph." Some time ago I was part of such a round-table talk show produced by the Conseil Attikamek Montagnais. The phone-in program is the only personal interface between corporate-community radio stations and the listening public and, because of its freewheeling and potentially volatile nature, it has its ethical and regulatory problems.

ETHICAL CONSIDERATIONS

The Canadian government, through the Broadcast Act and the CRTC, has laid down regulations concerning phone-in broadcasting, as have individual radio stations. All these agencies recognize phone-in radio as a vital part of radio's public service. Anticipating the potential dangers of open lines, there are, within these regulations, rules regarding polling public opinion, mechanical overrides, slander and discussions of objectivity, balance and takeover. The agencies don't explain or ameliorate the basic faults of most talk radio or their unseen consequences.

A GOOD THING

Talk radio supplies what the individual wants to know about what concerns him or her, whether it might be how to do spring planting or where our country is headed. It personalizes government and diffuses knowledge about familiar and arcane subjects. Phone-in shows attract a very broad segment of the public. Stations receive calls from night watchmen, householders and even executives calling in on their cellular phones while stalled in downtown traffic. Depending on the format, the listener can call to get specific information or just sit and listen to a political deposition, hear various viewpoints and even vicariously participate in some aspect of a gripping human-interest story. Phone-ins let the listener blow off steam, albeit within strongly defined bounds, all in the time-honored spirit of the newspaper's letters to the editor. The difference is: in radio there's a response.

BUT IS IT AN HONEST MEDIUM?

Phone-in radio is a show with a permanent cast of two: the host and the caller. The backstage crew consists of the producer, the assignment editor, researchers and the screener. The occasional guest is the hypothetical volunteer taken from the audience. Each member has an equally important role to play.

Producers pay close attention to the media, tracking current trends, controversies and politics, searching for the topic of the day, looking for all the world like pack journalists. Everything is fair game: some politician's audacious scheme, a scandal with a fresh twist, even a turn in the weather. The main problem with daily phone-in shows is that there are about 260 programs per year, and that generally means at least 260 on-air hours to fill, topics to find and guests to track down and then cajole into donating their time. So the producer often resorts to feeding on pop culture, psychology and mores, as well as the sensational and, of course, trivia. What this does—if the host is deemed to be responsible and respected—is to blur in the listener's mind the frontier between major problems and inanity. The participating public's sense of values could be on unsteady ground.

The program also implies that the guest or the caller can contribute to the solution of the problem of the day, but there are no solutions forthcoming because the problem has only been posed to scratch off one day on the 260-program line-up.

The program has no one to account to because there is no follow-up. One factor that makes discussion of a serious issue futile on these shows is the on-air conduct of the callers and/or the invited guest. Since they both have an extremely short time to get their point across, they will invariably talk *at* each other rather than *to* each other. Rarely does a guest or caller really listen to what the other is saying. In the meantime, the listener in his car or home is enjoying the "interplay," rooting and cheering for whoever espouses her or his own point of view. In truth, any chance of transferring intellectual ideas or information is doomed. The sham is that the show is improv entertainment rather than an intellectual exchange, putting it on the same level as the worst of the daytime TV talk shows.

Phone-in shows attract their share of troubled people who sometimes have a grudge to air no matter what the subject of the day is. If these people are known to have given the producer trouble before, they are put on a 'banned' list and the screener has instructions to keep them off the air. If enough of these troubled souls manage to get through, the general direction of the day's program will be skewed because these callers do not represent the majority.

It must be said that the foregoing relates to Canadian corporate broadcasting of "serious" talk radio. Canadian regulations constrain the broadcasting of U.S.-style "gonzo" radio. However, a little-recognized fact is that micro-market community radio operates talk radio from another, more personal perspective, as participatory organizations whose support and staff come directly from the community. Community phone-in radio instinctively fosters political expecations rather than entertainment. Its protocol is more basic; whether intentional or not, it pursues a subject guided by cultural uniqueness. Station CINQ-FM in Montreal is an outstanding example of cultural diversity—more than a dozen languages might be heard during the course of a day.

First Nations stations regularly broadcast in their own languages as a matter of course. In those communities where language is threatened, Native-language programs become the star attraction to their listeners. Native phone-in producers have difficulty in applying Canadian regulations to their operations because of their cultural mores. So the ethic here is the reverse of the corporate coin: operate the unit *in spite* of government dictum. If a wrong or slight occurs over the air, it can usually be resolved through traditional compromise and reasoning.

Regulations

Among the federal regulations governing talk radio, a few concern the ethics of dealing with the public. However, the CBC policy book has a great deal to say about the hazards of slander, which says a lot about corporate concerns. Slander is saying something false or defamatory which could damage someone's reputation. The strongest defence against a charge of slander, apart from not making the statement in the first place, is the use of a mechanical device, usually an electronic time delay, which can give the host or engineer about six seconds maximum to decide whether or not to mute out the naughty bits.

The cost of a time delay begins at around one thousand dollars, something not every community radio station can afford, especially because these devices are prone to spend a lot of time in the repair shop. Another device required by the CRTC is a log—a special tape recorder that logs every minute of the broadcast day. That's another few thousand dollars for another device that will also spend some time in the shop. Like many others, my own radio station resorts to running VCRS at extra slow speed with extra long tapes. All tapes are kept for thirty days and are subject to audit by the CRTC.

The perils of slander usually come from call-ins and, in the case of a successful litigation, the licensee must pay the piper, according to the CRTC. A few of the more common complaints the commission has received from the public include:

- abusive comments about race, religion, sex and disabilities;
- failures to maintain a balance between differing opinions;
- failures to prevent personal attacks; and
- carelessness in dealing with controversial issues.

Although the commission requires the host to challenge callers and guests on their views, the host is forbidden to badger or ridicule them. In fact, most stations restrict the host's options much more than they do those of the callers and guests.

PROGRAMMING

As a phone-in host, I once chatted with two people who had what I thought were radically inclined political viewpoints. My intention was to reserve the last twenty minutes for call-ins, although I expected a ho-hum response at that hour of the evening because of the topic's obscure nature. Before long the phone lights were beginning to look like a Christmas tree. From my point of view, it was a very good session because there were so many calls with interesting comments, with lots of give and take. As the guests left the studio smiling, I overheard one say to the other that not one of their "plants" had been able to get through—the calls had all been spontaneous.

Although I have never resorted to plants, I have been asked once or twice to call someone else's phone-in show as "just another interested caller." It's a curious fact that no matter who you are, when you're on an open line, you become the "caller." Plants are a common expediency to kick-start what might be a non-starter topic. And it all begins with the story conference.

TRIVIAL PURSUITS

The process usually begins with a meeting of the show's crew after the following week's line-up has been set. The challenge is to fill up all the empty boxes on the big white calendar hanging on the wall. Recent news clippings and off-air news clips abound. Once a particular topic and/or guest is selected, the researchers go to work writing up background information for the host's use. Many radio phone-in programs ease their scheduling problems by pencilling in recurring topics and guests. These are very popular with the listeners because they can prepare their questions on anything from garden care to financial investments.

If the story session hits a stone wall or if a guest doesn't materialize, there's a scramble for the standby: trivia. That's the sort of show where rolodexed people like myself are invited in as plants.

Recently I heard a reputable radio station ask listeners to call in and tell them what dangerous pastimes they indulge in, and the grammatical mistakes that really bug them. One listener called in to ask why they were discussing subjects like this when the country and the world were going to hell in a handcart. The grammar program was followed the next day by a discussion of Canada's immigration policy with a parliamentarian as guest, and the phone-in debate was heated and emotional. Once again, the faithful listeners' emotions were spun around after listening to the perils of the split infinitive one day to angry outbursts on whether or not to admit non-whites to Canada the next. Nothing was served except for the general frustration among all participants. As this is being written, there is an ongoing interview with

Gary Trudeau, *Doonesbury*; Universal Press Syndicate, Kansas City.

a representative from Fodor's travel guides, talking about the newest wrinkle in guide books. It all allows the producer to subtract one more number from the 260.

No one is exempt. Recently I ran two consecutive programs about our water and sewer systems with a man I eventually dubbed "Ed Norton." The last time he was on the air, I completely ignored him in favour of our community's safety inspector who shared the bill.

Programs featuring travel-guide representatives bring up the ethical quandary of whether to invite commercial spokespeople. The challenge then is to prevent the product plug because the audience is hip to advertising hype of any sort. Toning down blatant boosterism, whether of a political party, product or community, is just another problem to overcome.

THE HOST

Sitting near the talk show host on the upscale shows is a computer monitor that provides him or her with electronic cue cards. More likely, the host is also in headphone talk-back contact with the engineer and producer. The host is now the instant expert. Like a good lawyer, he's not going to ask his guest any question for which he doesn't already know the answer. This paraphernalia goes a long way towards establishing the host as credible. However, through the process of thousands of interviews and parries with callers, the host has developed an instinct for shaping questions in a way that elicits more than a simple yes or no.

If time permits, the host will meet the guest and allow him or her to get comfortable before they go on air. Maybe the host will go over the guest's C.V. and clear up any uncertain points, or the guest might tell the host what he doesn't want to talk about, which could be self-defeating. Montreal media types still remember the TV talk show host who nodded sympathetically when a guest in the green room asked her not to bring up his rumoured prostate trouble. Once on the air, her first question to the man was to ask how his prostate was coming along—he walked off the set.

Every once in a while the host will interview authors who are plugging their latest book. Just one hour prior to such a show, I was given a thin book to scan before I met the author and his publicist. The young author was suffering from full-blown AIDS and I wanted to know how he felt about this and what advice he could give to his generation. During the course of the interview, I became aware that he was diverting the conversation to the political and industrial high-rollers he had relations with and at one point he actually named them. It was obvious the book was part of some sort of personal vendetta. Luckily the program was being prerecorded and could be edited, but I put my guard up for the rest of the program and the interview may have suffered for that.

Once on air, some hosts undergo a transformation. Gone is the agreeable, easy-going conversationalist and enters the cynical, outrageous hardball player who will challenge the guest and callers, looking for a ratings boost to confirm his reputation. It's a type that's fading away since Webster hung up his headset.

The public doesn't realize the host is being tightly controlled by the backstage crew, station policy, the Broadcast Act and the CRTC. But the host gives the impression of being a wide-ranging, no-holds-barred expert on everything from travel guides to Canada's immigration policy. Eventually, if mature and sufficiently respected, the host might even be invited to run for public office on the basis of his or her public image. But we know he or she is only an instant expert.

ON AIR

Certain radio stations attract certain types of listeners, as radio demographers will tell you. The deciding factors include lifestyle, age, income and education. Since an AM station will generally broadcast news and sports rather than classical music, it will tend to attract a younger and brasher male clientele. Phone-in shows on FM and TV are generally more sedate, have a larger number of female listeners and lack a reputation for outrageousness. The ethical consideration here is the choice of topic or the question posed by the program.

Depending on the program's demographics (or "psychographics," the coming buzzword), the tenor of response will be directed by the prevalent male or female concerns of the listeners. Polling the yeas and nays coming out of the program is now forbidden by the rules but, at one time the CBC's "Cross Country Check-up" national phone-in show recapped the day's pro and con respondents.

Another precaution laid down by the CRTC compels stations to beware of takeovers by special interest or pressure groups. If, for example, the question of the day concerns a controversial subject such as abortion, the producer and screener must ensure that both sides of the argument are represented and balanced. Balance can sometimes be a problem when the question revolves around the concerns of a specific visible minority. The out for the station is that balance can be achieved over a period of time. One wonders if the CRTC expects stations to have a specific staff employee on hand to maintain a "special interest" balance account.

FREE SPEECH

That opens the larger question of free speech. It's easy to pick out controversial subjects for public discussion—smoking, taxes—but if, for example, the question of immigration is posed, will the callers, in the spirit of freewheeling debate, be allowed to say things like Asians and East Europeans don't assimmilate or Latinos don't try to learn English? Could there be suggestions that Orientals tend to form gangs? As mentioned previously, there is a CRTC caution concerning abusive racial comments, yet the response, however wrong it might be, could be an individual's honest reaction in a forum of free speech.

Does that make the caller guilty of abusive racial comment? The producer or the host has to answer that question on the spot. They can either quickly shuffle off the caller or they can hear him out and hope for someone to rebut the statement. If that caller's position is rejected, is the station taking on a political position of its own? But if the station takes a passive stand, could it be seen as a de facto outlet for validating prejudice and hate?

We have to assume that the station management has a freedom of speech policy for the crew of the phone-in show, perhaps based on legal precedents. But the host is the station's front line, and it is he or she who must make the immediate decision whether or not to mute a problematic statement. If their decision is wrong, it is the licensee who must take the eventual legal blame. The whole exercise is a severe tax on the host's focus and self-control.

ACTIVISTS

Part of the phone-in cast is the audience. Only a fraction of this group will ever call in, generally on a regular basis. Most of the audience are passive listeners. They are a fascinating group because their habit is unique. One wonders what sort of life they lead. Do they carry the day's radio topics into their own conversations? Do they *have* conversations of their own?

Then there are the dial chasers who tune in one phone-in program because they like one host's aggressiveness, then jump to another station because the host there has a sympathetic personality. In a small town, it's not uncommon for listeners to call the host at home to continue the argument or advise her that she should have said this or that.

Phone-in shows are public platforms to some people who claim it is their legal right to be a participant. These are the same people who will call the station demanding that the speaker on-air be cut off. Pressure or activist groups continually bombard radio talk shows with faxed press releases and an eager willingness to appear anytime on the show as often as the producer wants. Activists are also dial chasers. Those who monitor stations can recognize individuals who jump from one phone-in show to another when the topic can be seen to be anywhere near abetting their cause.

During the summer crisis of 1990, CKRK-FM in blockaded Kahnawake was the sole connection with the outside and as such was an important link between the communities. During that time, CKRK's phone-in show was put in an unwelcome adversarial position with a Montreal francophone talk-show host. One day a bilingual anglophone listener called to tell us that this host had just urged his listeners to do some sort of action against CKRK. Shortly thereafter, all three of our studio lines were blocked by rotating incoming calls. Whatever comments the callers might have made were competely wasted on our unilingual anglophone screeners.

LOADED LANGUAGE

Phone-in and talk radio hosts can be either males or females whose politics are often linked to their gender, experience and age. For example, liberal-minded hosts of either gender can be identified by code words, such as *inclusive*, *bias*, *sensitivity* and *cross*-whatever. They are uncomfortable with unreconstructed guests or callers. If callers want to arouse such a host's ire and consternation, they should select the host's protected pets and pounce on them. For example, it wouldn't take much to stir two current nationally broadcast talk-show hosts. Both are fervent feminists, but one is female, the other male.

Right-wing hosts such as Rush Limbaugh can likewise be quickly put off by liberal callers but, in this instance, if one were to try anything funny, they'd get the old heave-ho, unlike the liberal host's reaction where no doubt there would be some attempt at conciliation. Unfortunately, both types of programs are preaching to the converted. For this reason, callers tend to favour certain programs because their unspoken politics tend to agree with them.

Key phrases, words or attitudes flag callers who are biased in one direction or the other. A host can almost predict where the conversation will head as soon as he or she becomes aware of what is going on. There are pets on both sides of the mike.

The victory of survey demographics over sexual equality is nowhere more evident than in program host assignments. Female hosts are generally assigned afternoon time slots for the same obvious demographic reasons that sports hosts are usually male and given over to evening or late nighttime slots. Here's how sexual demographics works. My station has a weekly psychic talk/phone-in program. The psychic host has a bullet-proof attraction: call her if her prediction doesn't come true, she wants to know what happened. It's a three-hour show and there isn't one phone line that isn't busy when she announces the lines are open. In the many years the show has been on the air there have been an average of only five male callers per year, although her guest experts have invariably been males. The psychic's language is clearly attractive to female listeners.

Phone-in sports programmers are refreshingly free of covert bias. Jock shows are blatantly aggressive as if the show itself were a game in which the host is the opponent captain and invariably the most arrogant of the participants. He'll tell the world at the top of the show which team or which player is his favourite and he will challenge any caller who dares to say he is wrong. This is one show that welcomes "groupies," callers whose personal name or handle and sports favourites are known to the host. Needless to say, there are very few female callers.

SOME ETHICAL PROPOSITIONS

A PREMISE

The open-line show appears to be an insightful medium for polling current opinion when in reality it is presumptuous theatre, daily driving towards a dead-end denouement while operating within stifling perimeters. Although open-line radio might exist on the outer fringes of traditional journalism, like journalism it also deals with politics, human interest, sports and industry. However, unlike traditional journalism, open-line radio's ethical guidelines come from rigid station policy handbooks based on the requirements of the Broadcast Act and the CRTC.

As the nation's public network, the CBC offers several meaningful political-interview radio programs, discussions and national weekly overviews. The public understands the nature of these programs and expects the network's interviewers to play hardball with politicians and public figures. That is the nature of those genres and, because they are virtual-news programs, journalistic codes come into play. Consequently they are not part of this discussion.

Putting aside open-line programs that bring in guest experts to advise on gardening, cooking, auto repair, astrology, health, sports, life skills and hobbies, let's look at how the ethics of public forum (open-line) radio can be reshaped to more accurately reflect the public's perceptions or tastes.

DEAD ENDS

Perhaps open-line radio's biggest inherent weakness is that by giving air time to listeners to call in with their opinions on an issue, a possible solution is inferred as if they were voting in an ad hoc referendum. If "Cross Country Check-up" held a national call-in on the question "Should Quebec separate from Canada?" with Jacques Parizeau and Mel Hurtig as in-studio guests, you can be assured there would be emotional and heartfelt call-ins from both those in favour and those opposed. Tempers would probably flare and, no doubt, insults would fly back and forth. When the program was over and the dust had settled, we could well find that not only has not one mind been changed but that no one has learned anything new in the exchange. The debate may have reinforced the prejudice in both camps. It's a frustration to all, nothing more than a moot forum of no pragmatic significance despite its undoubted appeal.

OPEN ROADS

On issues regarding the national or regional conditions, it would be helpful if there could be an accounting to listeners. Stations could establish an ombudsperson who would regularly report back to listeners the trend of opinions for prior programs and investigate problems or find answers to questions arising from the discourses. This solution would require a change in the CRTC ruling that bans the polling of listeners' opinions which was no doubt intended to discourage the swamping of lines by pressure groups.

REGULATIONS AND FREE SPEECH

There is a background clutter that affects the operation of talk shows: the regulations and policies that govern program conduct according to someone's perception of Canadian society. Regulations in Canada and the United States are based on the premise that the airwaves are public property and therefore federal governments are bound to control them for the good of the whole, the amount of force varying in the two countries.

Open-line hosts and producers have a problem as to where to draw the line at free speech when it comes to obscenity or loaded language. Certain objectionable statements are easy to spot, having been previously ruled on by the courts of Canada and covered by high-profile media reports. Balance, fairness and objectivity are other problems that have to be faced on the run and which sometimes work in awkward ways. If the rules that sanitize public airwaves were modified, these factors could be looked at from the perspective of the editorial cartoon where conventional journalistic ethics are few and far between.

Some program hosts across Canada are advocates of one personal persuasion or another. In Quebec, at least three major francophone hosts are nationalists and support the concept of separation and because of this they have good numbers of like-thinking listeners. The reason, I think, is that these hosts come closer to the American "gonzo" style of free-association hosting.

One of the many entertaining anglophone open-line hosts in Canada is Lowell Green of CFRA ("Newstalk") from Ottawa. His operation is funny, witty and provocative, yet he exudes a sense of invincible arrogance that attracts a neverending stream of daring callers. All the gonzo paraphernalia is there: the staged "I know better" voice, the irritating gimmicky comebacks and the instant sound effects or "stingers." He represents the Canadianized version of over-the-top American hosts.

The American Federal Communications Commission's (FCC) rules are strongly against obscenity and the promotion of hatred but these laws have been found to be difficult to enforce, as recent U.S. court cases demonstrate.

The background behind the ongoing feud between the AM stations and the FCC is interesting. The FCC is given authority to enforce laws (Section 1464 of the Criminal Code) in the area of obscenity and profanity "by means of radio communications." Radio in this sense also includes television. A landmark case began when, in 1973, George Carlin presented a program called "The Seven Words You Can't Say on Radio and Television" on a Baltimore radio station. During the ensuing court case, Carlin said speaking the people's language was not threatening or obscene. The FCC put the station on probation, saying the words were patently offensive by contemporary community standards. The station appealed and, in 1978 the U.S. Supreme Court finally ruled that: (1) the government has the right to forbid such words; (2) broadcasting has the most limited protection under the First Amendment (free speech); and (3) the FCC restriction rested on a nuisance rationale. "Shock Jocks" were later given a tolerance for indecency after 10:00 p.m. but that was cut back in 1987 to between midnight and 6:00 a.m. Finally, in 1988, Congress removed that right altogether.

Open-line hosts and deejays who have a reputation of continuing to bend the bounds are

Patrick Corrigan, *Larry King Live*, The Toronto Star Syndicate, Toronto.

the ones who now pull down the big dollars in American radio because they draw the listeners. In the political arena, the big three of open-line hosts—Rush Limbaugh, Howard Stern and Larry King—all have their detractors and yet they draw, being the men people love to hate.

My own open-line show has a reputation for being on the conservative side, yet I once gained an all-too-brief notoriety, and that by accident. My guest and I were listening to a caller speaking in the Mohawk language, and he proceeded to tell a dirty joke to emphasize a point. Although I had broken a CRTC rule, my guest and I, and the whole community, broke up at the punchline. It seems I was too fascinated by the story to bleep him out. I think I would do it again.

University radio leads the way towards more open radio programming in Canada. Niche listeners can tune in programs hosted by and for segments of the public of various racial, political and sexual stripes. Or they can tune out. But though university radio defends free speech and the right to be obscene, there are instances when various university societal advocates suppress public discourses they perceive to be contrary to their dogma, and that is odd.

One lawsuit currently making its way through the legal corridors would allow abusive language (in the sense of incorrectness) in the university milieu; this is rather like a counterattack on the extreme right of politically correct imperialism. In a way the litigant is asking for the right to be wrong. Likewise, depending on the format, abusive or critical language should be permitted in mainstream radio; it should be more controlled than on the American open lines but looser than the present regulations—similar to the way sports program hosts operate, to their fans' delight.

How far can abusive comments go? There are no constitutional bars against being wrong, only legal precedents and comments in the Broadcast Act and the CRTC policy papers which are, after all, subject to change. But there are limits. Hosts should be able to defend their personal persuasions, however unpopular or controversial. Constitutionally, they even have a right to be rude. But the overall monitoring of slander, invasion of privacy, racism, sexism, religious bias, abusive comments about the disabled or minorities, and activist takeovers should remain in place.

Balance and objectivity

Surely, if the open-line host is unabashedly pro this political party or the other, or supports Quebec separation, he or she is going to get like-minded callers, partly to reinforce their own existing biases. Already this host is coming close to overstepping the rules about maintaining objectivity. And if the majority of calls support the host's position, the balance provision in the CRTC policy will also be violated. However, if there was another program in the line-up that promoted the opposite view, then a balance could be achieved. That would make for more lively radio, especially if the pros and cons called their opposite numbers' host.

Programming

Although the weekly story conference might come up with a provocative question of the day, the listeners will determine the direction of the conversation in the end. The problem is to maintain the program's consistency. Will it be playing trivial pursuit or soberly debating the day's genuine moral dilemma? Will the discussion be about the dangers of the split infinitive or the concept of judicial information bans? Once a program decides what it will be, then listeners are in a better position to adapt themselves when they tune in rather than be wrenched about from day to day. In the interest of listenership loyalty, this change in policy plus a regular "ombudsman's accounting" would be very habit-forming and profitable. I have no doubt there are enough topics or questions to address to fill the relentless 260 shows a year.

Such tactics as planting friendly callers in the audience and banning unwanted callers might be called justifiable subterfuge. In the first place, the audience is usually unaware of these devices; second, the program operates more smoothly because of these practices. Within my admittedly small circle of acquaintances, I know at least three people who are banned by major Montreal radio open-line programs. This knowledge was accidentally gained in casual conversation with other open-line hosts—a tiny, nervous segment of the public. As a result of something said on my own phone-in show, one listener was banned for a full quarter-year, the first such ban in the station's history.

SUMMARY

To recap changes in the ethical parameters of open-line radio, I suggest the following revisions to the Broadcast Act, and relevant CRTC policy and station policy guides:

- an accounting to listeners of the opinion trends on subjects discussed in prior programs;
- answers to questions arising from prior programs;
- an easing of the balance and objectivity rules to allow more interesting interplay between hosts and audience; and
- formalization of a program's format, whether it be geared towards public service, trivia or intellectual discovery.

17. More than a Game: The Business and Ethics of Sports Journalism

William Law

The Age of Innocence

There was a time when sports was a very comfortable place for journalists. The stories came easily, along with the perks: free tickets, free meals, access to the heroes of the day. Not a complex job, perhaps, but not as simple as it looked either. You had to know the sport and communicate its intricacies, excitement and energy in language the ordinary fan could appreciate and enjoy. It was not a job that called for much hard analysis about the business or politics of the game off the field, nor one that caused sports reporters to lose much sleep over ethical issues.

There was an "innocents abroad" quality to sports and sports reporting, a never-never land of sweet and pure escape. The athletes and the owners made money but not, in hindsight, a lot of money. And then television discovered sports and utterly transformed it. The athletes became cultural icons, the owners multimedia barons, the advertisers, sponsors and administrators creators of sporting "events" that defy description.

And what about the journalists? Too many of us behave as if sports coverage is caught in a 1960s time warp. Back then, it was a place where the heroes were the hometown guys and the villains were the other team. It was an uncomplicated place where players knew their position in the scheme of things, and the owners were benign and occasionally cantankerous father figures to the players, the media and the fans (on those rare occasions when fans displayed an interest in the owners).

The fans wanted the scores, the stats, the colour article on their favourite players. They demanded little of the journalists. So did their editors. Not much got spiked or scrubbed, so there wasn't much encouragement to do stories that got under the scores, or the skins, of the athletes. The good writers, people like Trent Frayne, did it anyway, recognizing that sports is a wonderful territory for the writer to explore.

The explorers were few and far between. Reporters usually stayed close to home. The worst sin was to dump on the hometown team—"your team"—when it was winning. This was okay during a prolonged losing streak, though, because it reflected, legitimized and magnified the fans' own anxieties. When the journalistic pack had its back up and was baying for the head of a manager or coach, the fans felt vindicated. When the manager was dumped, it was as if the entire community were cleansed of some unspeakable evil in a great exorcistic ritual. That much hasn't changed.

Professional sports was a male domain—the audience and the athletes. Organized amateur and recreational team sports such as football, baseball and hockey reflected the same values. Women and girls were tolerated, even accepted, as fans, so long as they accepted the limits of their gender, the definition of their role as cheerleaders, supporters, coordinators, fundraisers, drivers to and from the rinks or ball fields, but not real participants.

Underlying all this was the apparently innocuous assumption that sports was good for society, that a community prospered from an active sports life. Serious cities had professional sports franchises which were an effective measure of a community's stature. Sports, practised by the male of the species, were good for everyone.

Into that comfortable world of assumptions came the journalist who loved sports, had played high school ball and was still the kid at heart, secretly excited to be talking to the hero right there in the dressing room with the sweaty equipment piled on the floor. He was there for the jocular whoops and backslaps when the team won and the gloomy silence when it didn't. A journalist could feel right at home, reliving and recreating over and over again his boyhood fantasies and reporting back to the other kids on the block, so they too could live the fantasy.

It was an easier age when the Olympics really was for amateurs. Fat endorsement contracts were not even a gleam in the eye of some streetwise New York ad agency executive. Western Canadian communities got together to create and own professional football teams and build facilities for them. It all seems so long ago. Yet, go to the sports pages of your daily newspaper, sit in on a sports press conference, flick on your television set and it is all still there. The old values are still very much in the foreground, as if television hadn't fundamentally altered the rules of the game.

This state of affairs might be acceptable if the enterprise of sport had remained stuck in the time warp. Sports as a business, fuelled by television, has taken off into the stratosphere and left sport journalism sitting in the starting blocks, behaving as if the revolution hadn't happened. Revolution or not, the only real change is the emergence of women as equals on the field of play, but only in certain elite sports. And how many women, I ask myself, are sports journalists? And of those, how many have suffered harassment men have never experienced, let alone been forced to tolerate?

Put aside those troubling thoughts. It's time warp 1961. The Montreal Canadiens are the best team in hockey. Some of my friends are talking about the New York Giants but I'm not interested. I love the Canadian Football League's Ottawa Rough Riders and their Canadian quarterback Russ Jackson. If I think about baseball at all, I think about the Detroit Tigers. Don't ask me why, I probably just like the name. I'm a ten-year-old kid and, after I get through the comics, I head for the sports page. In the fall, I listen to football games on the radio when my team is out of town and sneak into games when the team is at home. I live and die as they win and lose. In the winter I watch "Hockey Night in Canada" with Foster Hewitt, Danny Gallivan and Ward Cornell. I'm a rink rat and the goalie for our local PeeWee team. In the spring I play street hockey, and in the summer I just goof off, waiting for the football season to come around again. Sports defines me as I grow up. Growing older, I still look for that comfortable place where sports always seems to be: free of complexities but full of wonderful, pure, raw emotion. The media are my mirror.

The Business of Sports

Fast-forward to October 1993. Michael Jordan, the world's greatest basketball player according to those who follow the game, abruptly announces he is retiring from the Chicago Bulls. At his internationally televised press conference, he expresses contempt for sports journalists. He says he is giving up a job that paid him $4 million a season, on the court, because he has done everything, attained every goal he set. Off the court, Michael Jordan earned another $36 million in endorsements—in one season.

A few days later, in an internal investigation, the National Basketball Association clears Jordan of any wrongdoing connected to his personal gambling habits. The league states emphatically that Jordan's retirement and the investigation which exonerated him are not connected. And we will just have to take the NBA's word for it. As in every other professional sports enterprise, investigations are conducted internally. In an extraordinary acknowledgment of his impact, *Newsweek* releases a special edition dedicated to the life and times of Michael Jordan, American hero. Sixteen months later, after a bizarre stint playing minor league baseball, Jordan rejoins the team and resumes his lucrative career.

Rewind the video to the winter of 1992. Bruce McNall, then owner of the National Hockey League's Los Angeles Kings of Prime Ticket (a Los Angeles TV sports outlet), and chair of the board of the NHL, runs into Disney empire CEO Michael Eisner at a glitzy Hollywood affair. Eisner tells McNall he loves hockey and, by the way, as he drives to work every day he notices an arena going up. The city of Anaheim has thoughtfully built it, at a cost of $103 million. Wouldn't it be swell to put a hockey team in there?

McNall moves very quickly. Among other things, he slashes his territorial fee from $50 million to $25 million. (The fee was originally intended to discourage other franchises from encroaching on the territory of an established team; in a market as big as L.A., it is just another way to make a lot of money easily.) McNall dangles the world's greatest entertainment corporation before the dazzled eyes of the other owners. He even brings in another entertainment magnate and hockey fan, Floridian Wayne Huizenga, owner of the giant garbage disposal company, Waste Management Inc. and Blockbuster Entertainment Corporation. He also owns a major league baseball team and, early in 1994, will complete the sports-franchise hat trick by purchasing the National Football League's Miami Dolphins. As Huizenga recalls, McNall

> said if I were serious about wanting a team in South Florida, something would probably be happening at the next owners' meeting. He said Disney was in (in fact it wasn't yet). It all happened so quickly—in five weeks—there wasn't time to put a partnership together.[1]

And so are born the Mighty Ducks of Anaheim (the name being taken from a Disney film) and the somewhat more pedestrianly named Florida Panthers (operating, as Huizenga's two other franchises do, out of Miami.)

Both teams commence play in the fall of 1993, just about the time one of the world's most prestigious and respected newspapers, the *Times* of London, owned by media mega-baron Rupert Murdoch, launches its very own professional sports championship in, of all things, chess. Earlier in the year the *Times* had secured the championship by adroitly manoeuvring the world's two best players, Garry Kasparov and Nigel Short, out of the existing international chess body, FIDE—with most of the moves finessed by *Times* chess correspondent Raymond Keene.

A shell organization, the Professional Chess Association, is created and consists of two players: Kasparov and Short. Bids are entertained.[2] The *Times*, submitting a lower bid than another consortium, wins. They call their match "The Times World Chess Championship."

The event is lavishly and, needless to say, very positively covered by a phalanx of *Times* journalists. In addition, Raymond Keene provides TV "colour" commentary, does the voice-over for a beer commercial and flogs his books on chess and Garry Kasparov.

Fast-forward again. In December 1993 the ubiquitous Rupert Murdoch announces a U.S. $1.58 billion deal that secures for him the television rights to National Football League games for four years, outbidding a rival network, CBS, by $130 million.[3] Just when the NFL thought it might have to take a beating in television rights fees because cash-strapped networks like CBS can't afford the freight, along comes a ruthless press magnate with the right stuff.

In the proliferating world of satellite TV, money is no barrier. Murdoch needs prestige sports programming to pull his American-based Fox TV network into the big time. The NFL deal will also provide programming for his British satellite channel, Sky Sports, at a time when he is aggressively selling his fifteen-channel BSkyB satellite pay network in the U.K. A couple of months later, Murdoch becomes co-owner, with the NFL, of the World League of American Football. Most entrepreneurs would be happy with one, two or (in the case of Wayne Huizenga) three sports franchises. Through Fox TV, Rupert Murdoch buys a whole league.

Murdoch is building what he likes to call "the new superhighways of communication,"[4] tapping into satellite and cellular phone technology. He has sent two really fast vehicles hurtling down his electronic highways: movies (he also controls Twentieth Century Fox) and sports.

How big is Murdoch? His News Corporation has annual revenues in excess of U.S. $4 billion. In the world of broadcast sport, television executives say

> if Murdoch's BSkyB can now outbid the terrestial organizations for major sporting events such as Premier League live football (the top tier of British professional soccer), its financial firepower by the turn of the century will mean that—short of government intervention—it will be able to mop up anything with more viewer appeal than snail racing.[5]

In other words, broadcast rights to virtually all major and specialty sports in the U.K., professional or amateur, will be in the hands of Rupert Murdoch. It is no surprise that Murdoch regards sports as essential to his goal of doubling the number of U.K. satellite dishes from 3.5 million to 7 million before the year 2000. As part of his strategy, he manoeuvres the BBC into a joint deal to secure broadcast rights to Premier League soccer matches—Sky gets the games and the BBC gets the highlights. It is an intriguing example of how a private sector corporation uses a public broadcaster and public funds in a gambit to shut its private sector rivals out of key sports programming. With the BBC on board, Murdoch is able to deflect criticism that he is removing a British sports tradition from so-called free television by putting it on his pay network.

Murdoch also plans to import American football and other sports into Asia via his Hong Kong-based Star TV. Simultaneously, he is downgrading news and filling more and more air time with movies. Neither sports nor movies run the independent news service's risk of government censure or intervention from countries such as China. Besides, they are a lot cheaper.

In North America, Fox shelled out $155 million in a five-year deal for the broadcast rights to National Hockey League games. And in Australia, Murdoch created a rugby "super" league simply by offering top clubs $1.46 million apiece.

Murdoch is not alone in observing the power and potential of linking sports with another broadcast product. In March 1994, BBC Radio launched Radio 5 Live, a news and sports network. The new network, which costs the BBC £30.2 million a year, had a simple mission: to attract a younger, less metropolitan, more downmarket audience and help shore up the BBC's declining numbers. No doubt the BBC's decision was influenced by the fact that the fastest growing radio stations in the United States are all-sports stations.

Meanwhile, shed no tears for CBS. The network surprised observers by bidding a record U.S. $375 million for the broadcast rights to the 1998 winter Olympics. ABC held the previous record of U.S. $309 million for the 1988 Calgary Olympics. Flick the video switch again: in January 1994, International *Amateur* Athletic Federation (IAAF) president Primo Nebiolo tells the Italian newspaper *La Stampa* that an athlete under his jurisdiction will receive a $40,000 Mercedes for a win and a smaller car for a second or third place finish at an upcoming international meet in Germany.

For years, athletes have been receiving appearance payments and "prize money" held in loosely administered athletic trust funds. And why not? Advertisers, networks and the chief executives of sports-governing bodies all make vast amounts of money. The athletes deserve their cut. In succumbing to demands for bigger prizes, Nebiolo noted—without a trace of irony—a disturbing trend: "Demands of athletes are growing and I believe this problem will also involve organizers of the 1996 Olympic Games."[6]

THE NEXT FRONTIER

One more video shot: witness Silvio Berlusconi, the media magnate who roars out of the political wilderness to win the biggest upset in Italian political history on the back of his broadcast, publishing and sports conglomerate. Berlusconi's three TV networks, his network of five million AC Milan soccer club supporters, and his newspapers and magazines delivered a powerful image of a hero who would rescue his nation from the abyss of corruption into which it had sunk. Not a modest hero either—after his stunning election win, he philosophized:

> In my life, I have already accomplished three miracles: as a builder, creating one of the most beautiful suburbs in Northern Italy with cycle tracks and green space; as a sportsman, making my soccer club AC Milan champions of Italy, then Europe and now the world; and as an editor creating a multi-media group that has no rivals in Europe and has broken the monopoly of state TV. Now, all pulling together as a team, we have to create a new Italian miracle.[7]

Knute Rockne couldn't have said it better. However, unlike Rockne, Berlusconi's political empire soon crashed around him, the new Italian miracle mired in scandal and corruption. Still, he had his moment riding to glory on the cheap and easy metaphors of sports.

Big money, big media, big sports and—as Berlusconi so adroitly and fleetingly illustrated—big politics are increasingly entwined. From a business perspective, sports seems the perfect product. It has massive consumer appeal and is apparently recession-proof. It sells products like nothing else and is an advertiser's dream. If one sports hero goes down, the victim of aging, injury or a doping scandal, another pops up to replace the fallen gladiator. The stories, the heroes and the fabulous money figures proliferate.

Sports journalists are ill-equipped to cover the stories from fresh angles. Complex business deals, conflicts of interest, protection of the public good, and political and social issues have all become relevant to the coverage of sports. Berlusconi doesn't just see a soccer team in AC Milan, he sees the future:

> Milan is my laboratory. We have to reach an audience beyond the stadium. That means television, the theatre of the global village. . . . Our mentality is not parochial, it is universal.[8]

To which the sports journalist responds (without, I'm sorry to report, even a hint of mockery): "Many have wondered what kept the Italians for so long, through so many short-lived parliaments, from turning to a man of football to run their country." But politics, like football, is a cruel business. Prime ministers can be dumped as abruptly as football managers, as Silvio Berlusconi discovered less than a year into his "managership" of Italy.

Sports, we are told, is entertainment, a business, popular culture (or as BBC has taken to calling it, "recreational culture"). *Globe and Mail* sports columnist Stephen Brunt and others call it "a secular religion, a belief system." Brunt says the journalist must deal with myth and image, "with the position of sport in this universe" (Law 1993c). It's a tall order for young reporters taught in journalism school that sports journalism is an oxymoron. It's an even tougher proposition for older journalists whose craft has revolved around careful cultivation of players and insightful and often encyclopaedic understanding of the nuances of sports. Furthermore, editors, owners, players and fans would probably prefer not to have the in-depth investigative treatment given to business in recent decades or the scrutiny politics and politicians have always faced in societies where an unfettered press is allowed to do its job.

Yet consistent, tough investigative journalism is what sports coverage urgently needs, if only because the financial figures are truly staggering. By the end of the 1980s, *annual* sport expenditures in the U.S. and Canada exceeded U.S. $88 billion with corporate sponsorship accounting for roughly two percent (U.S. $1.7 billion).[9]

In some ways, journalists who want to tap into the rich story vein are like those on other "beats." What's different is the attitude. Sports journalism, to steal an old cliché, has an attitude problem. Although sports has overflowed its traditional boundaries and flooded into virtually every aspect of contemporary life, it is treated as if it were still just a game, as if all those old intrinsic values of my time warp '61 were immutable.

WHAT'S A JOURNALIST TO DO?

Some values remain: the pure joy of winning in sports, the sweet agony of losing, the simplicity (win, lose or draw, there is always a conclusion). Other values are altered forever. The age of innocence, if it ever truly existed, is long dead. So why do we pretend that it isn't? And why is it that journalists who attempt to shatter the myth are frequently the target of abuse from players, owners, fans and other journalists?

It may be that sports is still regarded as the last unsullied territory in an otherwise corrupt landscape, an illusion fans don't want wrecked. There's more than enough shit going around, thanks very much, so just leave sports out of it. All I want to do is turn on the TV, crack a beer, sit down and enjoy the game. The trouble is: this attitude gives owners, media moguls, TV networks, advertisers, sponsors and players carte blanche. And it leaves sports journalists caught between a rock and a hard place.

The pressure to maintain the status quo is enormous. Challenge it and you're out in the cold. Nowhere is the pressure more intense than on beat reporters. In sports, beat journalists cover the games, interview the players and provide informed commentary and analysis. In the old days the beat reporter was just one of the guys. *Toronto Star* writer Dave Perkins (1993) tells of a baseball writer who was invited up to Babe Ruth's hotel suite for a drink and a chat. After a half-hour of this and that, he suddenly realized Ruth had a woman in the other room. The reporter was a tad unnerved and asked Babe why he'd invited him up. To which Ruth replied, "I wanted you to come up. I thought I'd need a rest."

Times have changed. Only a foolish athlete would use a writer that way today. Yet, in many ways, sports figures still expect beat reporters to do no more than polish their superhero finishes and are enraged when reporters veer off the adulation road. Through their public relations departments, the owners and the leagues work hard to get the reporter onside, ensure that *he* is still just "one of the guys" or, to put it another way, an *ex officio* member of the team.

The treatment has a powerful emotional appeal; most of us still harbour secret sports fantasies (that wasn't Jacques Plante playing goal for the Montreal Canadiens, that was me). The reporter slips into a comfortable role, losing any objective distance. Since sports is really just a game, you don't need to get hard-nosed.

And then there are the giveaways, the ubiquitous "freebies." Anywhere else, it would be called bribery. Any journalist who has covered sporting events will tell you about the free booze, meals, team paraphernalia, the free tickets and easy access to players. The more sophisticated the hard sell, the bigger the giveaways. At the Super Bowl, every accredited reporter (there are thousands) gets a piece of luggage. Over the years, you could put together a very handsome set. Sports departments such as those at the *Globe and Mail* and the CBC have firm policies about non-acceptance of major "freebies." The *Globe* auctions off less valuable gifts and donates the money to charity. CBC personnel may not accept gifts, travel or accommodations.

Time and deadline constraints mean journalists often have no alternative but to accept a free meal, although the age of the free meal may be finally passing into history. The Montreal Expos and several other major league baseball clubs have started to charge reporters for meals but other giveaways remain commonplace. *Hockey News* editor Steve Dryden says such presents are unlikely to affect the way a good sports journalist covers a story. Nevertheless,

> it starts with this whole idea of, for instance, the meal for the media. I don't know that on Parliament Hill before question period they say "Come on guys, come on in here, we are going to give you lunch."... When you go to [sports] events they give you things. Why? I don't understand that whole philosophy. Everyone says the same thing "You can't be bought off with a bag." Well, you are not bought off, but it engenders a different kind of atmosphere and I think that it is less adversarial than you might expect (Law 1993d).

He says the role of the beat reporter in sports is special. Reporters covering politics or business can keep their distance. The lines of battle, or communication, are far more clearly demarcated in political coverage than in sports, where

> the beat reporters live with these guys. They go to practice with them. They travel on the road with them. They see them everywhere. It is a different sort of thing. It is not like you are going in there and lobbing your grenades over the pack and into the politicians and then making your getaway (Law 1993d).

The reporter must get the sound bite, the quote. If he or she gets a player's back up, or the whole team's back up, then no quote, no story.

Dave Perkins (1993) argues that electronic media, especially television, have redefined the way baseball reporters get their quotes and the nature of the quotes themselves:

> For decades, the writers—the game's widely accepted euphemism for . . . all media except for former players—have slipped silently backward on baseball's ecology scale. It is to the point where they barely have developed appendages to hear most players describe them. . . . These days the baseball writer is in competition with the electronic media. . . . To glean any inside information, the writer needs to get the player alone and get him talking, before someone shows up and sticks a microphone into the conversation. . . . TV never has difficulty landing a player for an interview. Some TV reporters slip a player $50 for a few minutes of his time—it's amazing how much players making $3 million value this pittance. . . . Most players also know the TV questions will be along the lines of "Why are you so great?"

Given the pressures of live electronic interviews or tight print deadlines (most dailies are now morning papers, most sports events are at night), the temptation, the strategic move, is to play it safe. You ask the easy question or, better yet, incorporate the answer you want into the question. It makes for very predictable and sometimes dreadful coverage. More to the point, it perpetuates within journalism the image of sports as a Mickey Mouse form of reporting. The alternative is a journalistic Siberia—out in the cold with no quote and an angry editor to face.

The players are well aware of the power they wield and how much the contest is tilted in their favour. Dave Perkins' remarks about baseball apply equally to all professional sports:

> The ballplayers began to resent the presence of the media. Lines were drawn and they are reinforced every day. As salaries between the two groups (journalists and players) began to widen—even before the gigantic proportions of today—the players began to feel they were the special ones, the young, strong, rich and favored. The reporters, often none of the above, no longer were respected except by a few select players (Perkins 1993).

The reporter cultivates certain players. They develop friendships and loyalties. Thus, the reporter is assured of a good clip and occasionally a scoop. It is just what any good beat reporter does, whether in politics, entertainment, business, the city desk or sports. Difficulties arise because athletes demand a loyalty that politicians and businesspeople long ago stopped expecting from good journalists.

TARNISHED HEROES

Beat reporters "live with" the athletes. They have access to privileged, and sometimes personal, information. What do you do when you discover an athlete has a serious drug, alcohol, gambling or marital problem? Most reporters will say that only if the problem affects the athlete's performance is it the wider public's business. Having crossed that bridge, who breaks the story? At the height of his stardom with the Edmonton Oilers, goaltender Grant Fuhr was a heavy cocaine user. It was common knowledge in the locker room, among players and reporters.

When the story finally broke in the *Edmonton Journal*, it was not a sports reporter who handled it, but city-desk journalists who interviewed Fuhr's ex-wife. Fearing reprisal from the organization and loss of carefully nurtured links with players, sports journalists let others break the story so they would be distanced from it. Once it was broken, the sportswriters jumped back in. Some journalists think the story should not have surfaced at all. Stephen Brunt says it's an inappropriate airing of dirty family laundry in public.

> On things like drugs or sex or marriages breaking up, I think that stuff is out of bounds for me. I try to treat it the way I treat my own life. On what are you passing judgment? If a guy gets busted for doing it, then it is a story. Other than that, it isn't. If I had run into the story, I would have passed on it.

It is a judgment call. I happen to think that the extent to which athletes abuse alcohol and drugs, to say nothing of spouses, is not nearly as out in the open as it needs to be (Law 1993c). Grant Fuhr was a very likeable guy. He was treated gently, his TV image that of a modest, diffident, even shy superstar. That's the myth that grew up around him, the myth the media nurtured, cultivated and presented to the public. Because the cocaine habit didn't fit the image, it was ignored for a long time.

THE MYTH-MAKING MACHINE

Sports figures are wrapped in a mantle of myth: the myth of the indestructible, iron man, the heroic and brilliant leader, the courageous underdog, the swaggering overachiever, the transcendent superman, the modest genius. The beat system helps to perpetrate the myths. Heroes sell copy, fill air time and "move" products.

Reporters only give consumers of the sport mythology (the fans) what they want : an uncluttered image far removed from reality. Let's be honest here. We *need* a place to play out the myth of superior beings, unencumbered by the complexities and little tragedies of ordinary life. People hunger for gods and heroes. Religion, politics, science, arts and even commerce used to supply the goods and sports heroes were part of the mix.

Gradually at first, and then with ever-increasing momentum, sports heroes began to displace the other gods. In part it's because sports can leap so easily over boundaries of language, culture, creed and politics—an enduring strength, I think, and one the world would be a poorer place without. Nowhere is the creation of heroes less complicated than in sports. No movie star, politician or rock star commands a higher ground than a Michael Jordan. There is an undeniable, almost frightening legitimacy to this myth machine.

What happens, though, when you marry this most primal and powerful of needs with the power of television, especially television as it creates itself now—as a transnational, instant electronic transporter of an artificial value system worshipped by millions and controlled by a tiny elite? Perfect heroes are churned from the perfect hero machine, night and day, every day. The darker the rest of our world becomes, the more we want to celebrate the pure, sweet simplicity of breathtakingly skillful, enchanting, intriguing or antagonistic young gods and goddesses. But at some point the celebration has to stop, the mythology must be questioned, if by no one else than those who report it.

It is a tough call for any journalist, this business of when celebration ends and thoughtful and provocative examination begins. As Stephen Brunt says:

> I don't think our role is to go out, necessarily, and puncture the fantasy. . . . It's a little dance you have to do sometimes. For myself, there are times when I have to write very much like a fan, very emotionally about something. When the Blue Jays win the World Series, people want to celebrate that event in an emotional way. . . . Sometimes my job is to go with that, sometimes it's to go the other way, to get into the business and politics of sport. It is a very strange split and I don't know if I could tell you exactly where that line is drawn sometimes. A lot of people draw it just by not doing the business part of it, especially the older generation of guys. They just don't deal with it at all or don't deal with it very well. Their general take is, "Isn't this a shame it gets in the way of the game" (Law 1993c).

Older sportswriters are far less likely to take risks and treat sport in new and provocative ways. The old guard is still dominant. I caught a classic example in the pages of the British newspaper, The *Independent*, where a senior soccer commentator criticized a superb television documentary about the tortuous demise of English soccer coach Graham Taylor. Taylor was filmed and miked through all of the qualifying games for the 1994 World Cup. When England failed to make it, he was sacked. The hundreds of film hours were edited down to a single hour—a remarkable portrait of the agony of one man watching and reacting with rage as his lifelong dream slips away. The *Independent* correspondent wrote:

> "Graham Taylor—The Impossible Job" unquestionably was rivetting television, but it raised an issue that the sporting authorities, especially the Football Association, would do well to address. Providing a suitable base for media prying ought not to be the primary objective of co-operation in sport, nor is it necessarily an indispensable one. In other words, I believe for the greater good there are areas that should remain strictly off limits. You may think this is an elitist point of view, but no matter.[10]

So there. If you think this a peculiarily British response from a particular class, you are right. If you dismiss it for being just that, you are mistaken. Sports reporting remains a conservative bastion which puts up obstacles for those who deviate from the path and ask tough questions. With so much emphasis placed on camaraderie and well-oiled contacts, independent analysis and investigative questioning are not welcomed, not just by athletes and owners but the sports journalist fraternity. (My use of "fraternity" is deliberate. The number of female sports journalists is depressingly small, particularly when compared to other media sectors in which women have been able to achieve significant breakthroughs.)

Now, more than ever, the "don't rock the boat" ethos needs shaking up. The superheroes, their images tied to global marketing strategies of mega-corporations, need to be looked at in a different light, *before* they fall from grace or slip into obscurity.

While some carry the mantle of superhero with apparent ease, others stumble and, like sprinter Ben Johnson, fall very far, very fast. We record the fall with even more relish than the rise. This is only to be expected. As Brunt explains:

> The . . . rise and fall story is . . . deeply imbedded in the culture. It goes with hubris. It is a big tale no matter where we are telling it. There is always that sense of people flying too high and then crashing. . . . The human interest stories, the on-the-way up, on-the-way down stories are always the best. There is a dynamic to them (Law 1993c).

I'll grant the dynamic and my own passionate interest in the stories. The difficulty is in separating out the part of the myth-making machine—which puts bums on the seats and money in the owners' and players' (and agents') pockets—from the legitimate task of fulfilling society's need for heroes. Somewhere along the way, the two got tangled up to the enormous benefit of business. And business begins to take it for granted that the purpose of media is to serve it. All too often, journalists go along with that assumption.

A CASE IN POINT: BEN JOHNSON

Why was Ben Johnson a media hero one day and the nation's shame the next? The sprinter ran for Canada in the Seoul Olympics in the summer of 1988, won gold in record time and was promptly disqualified and disgraced for using performance-enhancing steroids. You hear often in the sports world, "everyone knew Ben was on steroids, all you had to do was look at him." If everyone knew, why wasn't a journalist investigating the story? Johnson was an emerging sports hero, the man who would carry the flag of Canada when he won a gold medal.

Ben Johnson was a naive, poorly educated young man who needed to parlay his major asset into a big financial payoff. He was a willing victim, but a victim nonetheless. All this was evident before Seoul. But in the run-up to the Olympics, a story on Ben Johnson as steroid abuser would have wrecked a lot of agendas, not the least that of the media which had long since determined, to the delight of Johnson's corporate sponsors, that this poor black immigrant kid would be the next Canadian hero. In the sports world's strange and seductive way, Ben Johnson became an icon for all that was thought good about this country. The myth goes something like this: "We took him to our bosom, this talented and impoverished child from the third world, nurtured him and helped him hone his marvelous physical ability. In return, with the whole world watching, he will carry our flag around that track in Seoul and, in ten seconds or less, make us (if only fleetingly) a great nation in the eyes of the universe."

Johnson, or rather, the media image built around him, was poised to validate a myth about Canadian society. In the aftermath of his expulsion in Seoul when the full story of his drug abuse finally broke, it brought forth a torrent of rage from sports reporters. Ben Johnson had betrayed the country. Worse yet, he had disappointed the youth for whom he was role model.

A great deal of arrogant nonsense and holier-than-thou posturing took the place of tough analysis in the days and weeks that followed Johnson's fall from grace. It made sensational copy but was it good sports journalism? It can be argued that sports journalism simply filtered and refined the icon the public wanted, and even needed, to have. When the hero proved fatally flawed, his inadequacies revealed by a doping test in the harsh glare of a suddenly hostile world, journalists led the pack in the trampling of the statue of Ben Johnson, sports icon. Conveniently, they forgot that that statue had been created by the media.

A journalist with the temerity to seek out the real Ben Johnson story before Seoul might have been ransacked by an enraged public. The fact remains: there was a story to be done and it wasn't done. One has to wonder whether it would ever have been done had Johnson not been caught.

Buying into the Business Agenda

I raise the Ben Johnson story in part because it says a great deal about how media cover sports events, in part because it was my own little Rubicon in the Olympics. It was not simply that Ben Johnson was poised to reap millions from a so-called "amateur" event; or that the games were staged in a repressive and violently anti-democratic society; or that tawdry, flag-waving nationalism replaced any thoughtful examination of what a country was supposed to be. It was that, with rare and isolated exceptions, the media bought, totally and uncritically, the chimera of the Olympics and then, with smug and savage complacency, walked away from Ben Johnson and its own role in turning him into a Canadian superhero. It wasn't just the Canadian media that played the game. The juggernaut of U.S. television also decreed that the race between Johnson and American sprinter Carl Lewis to see who would emerge as "the world's fastest man" would be the major event of the Seoul Olympics.

The agendas of the International Olympic Committee, international television, advertisers and mega-corporations dominated the buildup to the race. It was an elaborate hype and it turned tawdry so quickly. In hindsight, even the slogan has an air of carnival hucksterism. Most mainsteam media not only didn't learn from the Johnson debacle, they never stopped to analyze or even contemplate how effectively they were co-opted into the elaborate sports circus.

When the next big Canadian Olympic story came around—Toronto's bid for the 1996 Olympics—journalists (with noble exceptions such as Stephen Brunt) were not asking serious questions. There was no tough, consistent investigative journalism. Once again, the media jumped right on the Olympic bandwagon. Those who challenged the bid or questioned big-money Olympics were deemed unpatriotic or worse.

Canada is obviously not alone. The city of Manchester spent tens of millions of pounds in a bid for the 2000 summer Olympics, in the midst of the grimmest recession the city and Great Britain had experienced since the end of the Second World War. As happens whenever a city contests an Olympic bid, statistics were trotted out to support the argument that the games would boost an ailing local economy. The theory that the Olympics delivers an "economic shot in the arm" has been questioned by some journalists and many economists, most notably Robert Baade.

More to the point was the question of whether Manchester, Berlin or Istanbul had any chance of winning the games against the leading bids from Beijing and Sydney. The answer was apparent well in advance: the odds of Manchester's winning were remote to nil. Beijing had the support of Kodak and Coca-Cola, two of the games' largest corporate sponsors. They and Beijing would have won if not for the western media's spirited attack on China's human-rights track record (this same media had blithely ignored the lamentable record of South Korea).

There was also suspicion (so far, unsubtantiated) that the Chinese were doping female athletes in track events. Beijing's loss by one vote to Sydney was hailed as a triumph for democracy and the integrity of the Olympics. How anyone at this late stage in the decay of the games could speak of integrity, let alone democracy, is beyond me, but many commentators did.

Manchester received thirteen votes out of a possible ninety. Like Berlin and Istanbul, Manchester was merely cannon fodder for a site-selection process that has reached unparalleled heights of corruption. During the bidding, IOC members are wined and dined from city to city, at enormous public expense. And they are not the only ones. A Canadian journalist I know was offered an all-expenses-paid trip to the U.K. by a consular official on the off-chance he might write favourably about Manchester's bid and influence the Canadian delegation. He turned down the offer.

At one point, ten cities were in the running for the 2002 Winter Games including, pathetically, locations in bankrupt countries such as Russia, Slovakia and Kazakhstan. The IOC is considering changes to the process, not because of the taint of corruption and allegations of bribery, but because of the logistics of junketing all those members and their entourages to so many cities.

The real story about the Manchester bid was not told in the mainstream British press. The city now aims to host the Commonwealth Games in 2002. The bid includes a stadium that will cost £187 million. After the games, the facility will be available to professional soccer clubs such as the hugely successful Manchester United. Coincidentally, the Football Association (FA) has a contract with London's Wembley Stadium that ends in 2002—a state-of-the-art stadium in a football hotbed like Manchester looks very tempting indeed. At the least, it will be a powerful bargaining chip in the FA's negotiations with Wembley. In what amounted to an endorsement of the Manchester Commonwealth bid, a BBC sportscaster said fans supported the bid because "sport, especially athletics and football, desperately need a new stadium in the north of England"[11]—but at taxpayers' expense, in an economy where health and education services are deteriorating?

The Commonwealth Games demonstrate the power of sports. As a political, social and economic institution, the Commonwealth is virtually extinct. The games, once almost incidental, are now centrestage. Like all other international sports ventures, they meet media and advertiser needs by generating hundreds of hours of low-cost, high-audience programming for an international market. When the games are over, the predators move on, leaving communities with facilities that are either junked or require vast amounts of public money to maintain. In 1978, Edmonton built a massive stadium for the Commonwealth Games; used a dozen times a year (at less than half capacity) by the Edmonton Eskimos football club and once for the 1982 World Student games, the 62,000-seat stadium now sits empty most of the time.

Meantime, owners of sports teams in North America play a ruthless game of pinball stadium politics. Peter Pocklington, the owner of the Edmonton Oilers, threatened to move the team unless he got what he wanted from the city and Northlands Coliseum. In the end, to keep the Oilers in town, the politicians and administrators caved in to virtually all of Pocklington's demands. The same thing is happening south of the border. National Football League and Major League Baseball teams demand state-of-the-art facilities and a virtual monopoly on lucrative stadia concessions revenues. They couple their demands with the threat to move. It is a very real threat. True, there is an element of bluff, but not much. The owners know no politician wants to be seen as the one who let a professional sports team slip away—down that path lies political oblivion. So the owners play off one municipality against another, in what amounts to a bidding war conducted out of the taxpayer's pocketbook and at vast expense.

Marketing the Role Models

How and why does it happen over and over again, this incorporation of media into the agendas of multinational corporations and sports organizatons? In part, it is the power television must bring to the games, having invested so much to secure them; it is also in part what Brunt calls "the sports machine," the companies that use superstars and sporting events to sell products. Sports is the perfect vehicle. The myth-making machine constantly churns out heroes for the corporations to choose from, as role models to sell their products.

I have never bought the line that athletes are role models, but many people have. While media sustain the illusion, they aren't the cause. So Stephen Brunt says:

> I don't think we do it. . . . Nike does, Reebok does. [Companies] have far more power in creating the image beyond the game than we do. . . . The sports machine which includes television . . . is incredibly powerful. The advertising machine that has grown up, especially in the last few years, is even more powerful. . . . Those are the people who are really paying the bills now in international sports (Law 1993c).

How does a journalist avoid getting sucked into that agenda? Stephen Brunt again:

> It's tough. What you try to do is to decode things as much as you can. You've got to deal with . . . myth and image . . . figure out why people care. . . . I think if you start getting at that, that's maybe where we can do something . . . try to decode the symbol. . . . Michael Jordan . . . is a classic example. You weren't just dealing with the fact a guy retired, you were dealing with the whole notion of who this guy was . . . way beyond [a man] from North Carolina who plays basketball. It's like he's floating in air forever, in Kenya, in India, in China. And that is a whole other thing. It is iconography. . . . Our job then is to step back and say, "Look, what is happening here, what does Michael Jordan mean in this world at this time?" (Law 1993c).

The journalist who does step back faces a hard reality. At a time when the media are engaged in cutthroat competition, only a rare editor or organization will foot the bill for investigative work which is by nature expensive, time-consuming and potentially litigious, especially if the consumer prefers sports reporting straight up and simple.

Is Rupert Murdoch interested in the sleazy underside of British professional soccer when the event anchors his satellite sports channel? Does CBC want to explore the extent of alcohol abuse in the NHL when the corporation has sold the show title to a brewery ("Molson's Hockey Night in Canada")? Which begs another question: the propriety of a public broadcaster's selling not only a title, but time, to a private sector company. If disaster strikes during a "Hockey Night in Canada" broadcast, the terms of the contract require CBC to seek Molson's permission to break into the game! Even if such obstacles are overcome, does the fan give a damn? The short answer is no.

THE FAN

I can think of no other sector of society that consumers so willingly subsidize. Fans continue to accept inferior products sold at escalating prices. Fans—and I'm one of them—put up with the antics of wealthy individuals with the emotional maturity of twelve-year olds. They support losing teams for years. They cheerfully allow expenditure of millions of public dollars for "state of the art" sport palaces that age in a decade. They satisfy owners' demands for more concessions and better facilities while watching transportation and school systems decay and health care crumble.

Their passivity dry-gulches the best intentions of crusading journalists. Yet, sheep become wolves when their heroes are maligned. Jennifer McGuire produced CBC Radio's "The Inside Track," the only investigative sports show in Canadian broadcasting. She commissioned a piece on baseball's Toronto Blue Jays.

> We did a commentary in 1992 when the Blue Jays won their first World Series, by John Allemang at the *Globe and Mail*, a beautiful commentary. The spark for me was the way the media had built the Blue Jays up to be these gods. They were this, they were that, "Dave Winfield for Prime Minister," that kind of thing. At their homecoming, I was watching the speeches and they were a bunch of boors, talking about "Well I'm gonna' go home and thank my wife."... It seemed to me that there was an imbalance there in how they were being portrayed and it was the wrong place and . . . time to be talking about what they do in their bedrooms. So we did this commentary which was, I think, not overly critical. The tone was "Well, they are baseball players, don't have unrealistic expectations of them, but, on the other hand, hey guys, this isn't a frat house." That pretty much sums up the commentary.... The reaction [from listeners] was "Don't touch them. They just won." The commentary was stepping on the aura. We had crossed a line (Law 1993b).

That line, that fantasy, is the mystical power of sports. It cannot be denied. A whole community is ignited and united by a single sporting event.

I was in Toronto in 1993 when the Blue Jays were wrapping up their second consecutive World Series. Leaving a friend's house on my way downtown, I saw two old men ahead of me, one Italian, the other Japanese. They spoke very little English, but there they were on a brisk November morning, on a street corner north of Bloor and Spadina, talking about the Blue Jays. And I thought, "That's the magic of it, that is the fantasy become real and meaningful."

But there's another side to the fantasy. That side, or its manipulation, has become the engine that drives the sports business. It is the skill with which business is able to conjure the fantasy, the ease with which massive audiences are mesmerized, that makes it so damn tough to do investigative, challenging sports journalism.

When Richard Pound, chair of the IOC television negotiating committee, announced the successful CBS bid for the 1998 winter Olympics, he said,

> The IOC depends on television broadcasters to bring the Olympic Games to the world and in CBS we have the absolute best for our Winter Games. The Winter Olympics is an event of incomparable stature. It takes imagination and talent to translate the magic of these Games and CBS will be our magician.[12]

In England, where for several years, shellshocked soccer fans have watched their athletes' humiliation with genuine anguish, the issue of who will coach the national team out of the wilderness has taken on enormous importance. The leading candidate was Terry Venables, a fan favourite, first as a player for the Tottenham Hotspur in the 1960s and 1970s, and then as a manager. In 1993, Venables was accused of irregularities in the transfer, or sale, of players. The allegations emerged during a nasty fight with Alan Sugar, majority owner of the Spurs. Sugar also chairs Amstrad, the company that manufactures satellite dishes that beam Rupert Murdoch's Sky TV products into British homes—products like Premier League football where the Spurs are still legendary, if troubled.

Venables, the former Spurs star, had a minority share in the club. His tangled financial dealings were the subject of a television documentary and of close analysis in the press. Even the *Financial Times* of London, which rarely explores sports, got into the act. Meanwhile there was enormous popular pressure to install Venables as the English manager, despite the cloud of suspicion above his head.

Some "quality" papers took the line that the appointment was inappropriate. David McKie argued in the *Guardian* that, "This is a front-line national job, where the hopes of thousands hang on you, where you represent the nation and the sense it has of itself."[13] The tabloid *Daily Mirror* was less restrained: "To a fanfare of trumpets, Venables will be paraded before the public who have waited so long to acclaim him."[14] Religious overtones aside, investigative journalism did its job and the public couldn't care less. They wanted Venables, and they have him. They don't care about financial irregularities or the business side of sports, they want Terry Venables to make England great again. It may be a fool's dream, but there it is.

It is easy to be cynical of British soccer fans, and cynicism is the leavening of investigative journalism. But it's damnably hard, and often journalistically unrewarding, to be a cynic when it comes to sports. The eternal fan in us will always want to deny reality when it intrudes on our fantasy zone.

INVESTIGATING SPORTS

The ethos of investigative journalism has yet to take hold in sports reporting. Because investigative sports reporting remains rare, journalists run higher risks than those who expose corruption in politics or business. So it is a lonely and sometimes dangerous road. The road could not have been any lonelier than for Cliff Temple.

British sportswriter Cliff Temple was the Sunday *Times* athletic correspondent. His suicide in early 1994 stunned the British track world. For some time, he had been depressed about his marriage breakup and financial difficulties. He was also extremely depressed about allegations that he had sexually harassed female athletes.

The unsubtantiated allegations came from Andy Norman, promotions officer for the British Athletic Federation (BAF). Many people considered Norman, an ex-police sergeant, the most powerful man in British sports—in addition to assembling and promoting athletic events, Norman is an agent. His clients included track world champions Linford Christie and Colin Jackson. Under his guidance, Britain held more international meets per year than any other country, which meant TV exposure for promising athletes and the opportunity to showcase established stars like Christie and Jackson.

It meant money flowing into the pockets of the BAF, the athletes and their agents, not only from TV. The BAF takes in roughly £4 million a year from corporate sponsors. It's a two-way street: sponsors buy television exposure for their products and networks sell advertising time. Sitting in the middle, catching the money coming both ways, are the sports organizations, elite athletes and agents.

Who contributes to the BAF? In 1993 the U.K. automotive giant Vauxhall contributed £275,000; Pearl Assurance £450,000; Panasonic £360,000; and Lucozade (a fruit drink for athletes sold to the youth market) £200,000.

Norman was the chief architect of this corporate-sponsorship bonanza. His dual role as meet promoter and agent did not escape media scrutiny. He was the subject of a critical 1992 BBC TV documentary, "Norman's Conquests." A journalist who researched material for the documentary was also a target of charges of sexual impropriety—made by Norman. Two *Times* journalists who wrote a critical story in 1987 say they were similarly attacked.

The allegations against Cliff Temple began around the time he was putting the finishing touches on an investigative piece on Andy Norman. Norman launched a whisper campaign against Temple, then insulted and embarrassed him publicly at meets. Implying the falseness of the charges, the BAF secured an assurance from Norman in September 1993 that "such activities would cease forthwith." However, the assurance was never made public, let alone conveyed to Cliff Temple or the Sunday *Times*.

It took Temple's suicide to bring the story of his harassment by a powerful sports administrator into the open. For years, Norman had expressed his contempt for sports journalists, addressing them as "you arseholes." No politician would dare show such contempt for the press. It derives not only from the intoxication of power but from a baser attitude that sports journalists can be fed the line, sold the goods, coddled by giveaways. Journalists are merely conduits of product. If they are passive and uncritical, i.e., if they do not do a journalistic job, they are rewarded. If they ask questions, the sports machine plays hardball.

CONFLICTS ABOUT CONFLICT OF INTEREST: MATE AND CHECKMATE

Besides writing about track, Cliff Temple coached at the international level, one thing that made the whisper campaign so devastating. Far more than their Canadian counterparts, British media see no difficulty in hiring correspondents who are still actively involved in the sports about which they write.

Earlier, I mentioned Raymond Keene, the *Times* chess correspondent. Keene is an international grandmaster of the game. In the professional chess world, everyone knows everyone else very well, and most of them write for the dailies. So it isn't all that surprising to see him in his self-styled role as the "Don King of international chess." What is surprising is that virtually no one in the media perceived any conflict whatsoever in what Keene was doing.

Rival correspondents do speak disparagingly and question Keene's integrity off the record. One told me he didn't want to say too much because "Keene is particularily litigious."[15] Keene was pleased as punch that he was the *éminence grise* behind the *Times'* gambit to secure the services of Kasparov and Short. In the same breath, he told me chess was helping to sell not only newspapers but beer.

Remember the beer commercial he voiced? It featured Nigel Short, the British challenger to Kasparov's title. I don't know how much of that particular brand of brew was sold on the strength of the match. The *Times*' newsstand sales increased dramatically the week its chess championship commenced. I suspect that a drastic slash in the price, from 45 to 30 pence, played a bigger part than the blanket coverage of Kasparov methodically crushing the hopelessly out-manoeuvred Short.

The Murdoch Gambit

To fully understand the story behind the *Times* World Chess Championship, we must remember that Rupert Murdoch owns the *Times*. He was unhappy that the paper was steadily losing ground in the perpetual circulation wars that swirl though Fleet Street and was determined to turn the *Times* around. He brought in Peter Stothard as editor in 1992. Stothard is young and upwardly mobile, with a well-deserved reputation for ruthlessness. Shortly after he arrived at the Wapping plant (scene of the historic 1987 battle in which Murdoch broke the backs of the print unions), Stothard sacked some thirty journalists to underline his message that the *Times* needed to lose its elitist image.

Chess, too, has an elitist image. Stothard gambled that taking chess downmarket and making it populist in the pages of the *Times* was a smart way to go. By any measure, the *Times* coverage was extraordinary. Every positive aspect was covered, in mind-numbing detail. We were told what Garry Kasparov eats before the big match and learned the name of Nigel Short's head masseuse. An editorial on the day of the match gushed:

> There is a big idea behind this match: it is freedom from Cold War bureaucracy, freedom for individuals to compete for proper rewards, the democratic freedom that comes from maximizing the advantages of modern communications to popularize the game.[16]

Not to be outdone, a columnist wrote,

> There has never been anything quite like the match between Kasparov and Short. It has been the launching pad for the game's biggest media explosion, on a global scale comparable only to the greatest events in the international sporting calendar.[17]

So ubiquitous was the chess match in the *Times*, that a rumour went the rounds of Fleet Street that all the journalists writing for the paper had been instructed to work chess into their copy at every opportunity. It was big-event journalism at its worst.

While most of the *Times*' media rivals flailed away at the match itself or attempted to bury it, few looked at the larger issues at stake. One of the few was Raymond Snoddy, media correspondent for the *Financial Times* of London. He called the *Times* editorial "total self-serving nonsense"

> to justify what I see as a rather tacky commercial opportunity which they have pushed remorselessly. It is entirely proper and reasonable for a newspaper to sponsor a sporting event. It is reasonable to have advertisements advertising that event in their columns. What I think is not reasonable is when the two things become completely mixed up—the promotion and the puffery involved in the commercial event migrating into the news columns and the coverage. . . . And there is one other

> important point . . . the extent to which the *Times* connived in and possibly even encouraged the breakaway from the international chess federation. . . . When you do have your chess correspondent involved in enticing a breakaway movement, backing it with your money and then giving it uncritical coverage, the *Times* is not in a position to say this match is boring. . . . All of that is worrying. There are papers who would do that and you wouldn't care very much, but for heaven's sake this is the *Times* (Law 1993a).

In blatantly flogging a sporting event it had fully financed and largely created, the *Times* certainly lost its elitist image, as well as a fair chunk of the editorial and journalistic integrity that had buttressed that image. Never mind, sales soared. But perhaps more ominous, the independence of *Times* journalists was eroded. Whether or not the Fleet Street rumours were correct (and Stothard denies them), the content of the paper, both before the championship and for the two months it lasted, was significantly affected by an agenda set by senior management. The agenda was clear: an event with which the *Times* was intimately associated would receive only favourable coverage. Therefore, there was never any doubt that the *Times* would avoid one of the bigger stories: the match was a flop at the box office. Ticket prices were slashed before it even opened and were even given away. As it ground on to its inevitable end, fewer and fewer paying customers showed. I was present near the end, at what could have been the deciding game. The theatre was perhaps a quarter full.

Thus a sporting event became both a weapon in a circulation war and an illustration of the power of management to curb the editorial independence of its journalists. It may be the first time that sports has been so used. I don't expect it will be the last.

CLAIMING THE HIGHER GROUND

Earlier, I wrote that sports is a rich territory for investigative journalists to mine. I argued that, given its massive corporate nature and high levels of corruption, and the growing power of sports and media mega-barons, it is essential that sports be covered as business, in a consistent and ongoing way. Having said that, I would be the first to say that the traditional reportage of sports still has, and will always have, an important role to play. But it can no longer be the single, dominant role. Perhaps the biggest step towards achieving the necessary balance is the rotation of beat reporters, not just into other sports but other departments. The sports ghetto must be dismantled. Some media outlets are doing it. Reporters who have experienced rotation say it has been enormously beneficial to them. It also sends a signal to the teams not to take reporters for granted. Professional sports (and I include the Olympics under that umbrella) will be unable to cultivate an individual and will have to come to terms with a profession. Skeptical reportage of sports and the challenging of "gee whiz" coverage will make sports organizations more responsible and responsive in their handling of the media.

It has to do with respect. Politicians and business leaders have learned to respect, or at least be wary of, the journalists who cover them. It will mean a more adversarial approach. And I'm not talking about angry managers throwing chairs and bottles of booze about when asked dumb questions. I'm talking of a more serious engagement that will challenge some of the underlying assumptions of sports. It is an engagement that requires the full support of editors and media organizations. Will they give it?

I hope the answer, in the long run, will be yes. There are so many good stories to tell about faulty assumptions and phony images, about greed and corruption. Will the fans buy it? In the short run, no. They'll howl and snipe. So will some of the old-line sports journalists. Never mind. There will be energetic debate, debate that for once will be led by sports journalists.

One way to move towards balance is to cultivate women journalists. The old boys club desperately needs breaking up. Women bring fresh perspectives and fresh insights to sports. They challenge old attitudes about the role of sports in society. Women also happen to be a rapidly growing sports market, as both viewers and participants. Smart media management will sense this trend and bring women into sports journalism in a major way. It can't happen too soon.

And there has to be some way to crack the monolithic television coverage, particularily in North America. It is beginning to happen in England—this business of first-rate documentarists seizing on the huge opportunities sports provide to exercise their talents. The same thing needs to occur in the heartland of the TV sports empire, North America.

Canada is particularly fortunate to have a public broadcaster (CBC) with a large viewing audience and a tradition of investigative documentaries. All of the conditions are there for a serious, ongoing exploration of sports. It takes a certain confidence and, dare I say, courage that may be lacking right now, but somebody has to get the ball rolling.

Curing the attitude problem in sports will require serious revamping and rethinking at journalism schools. Such an initiative calls for a degree of forward thinking that universities may feel unable to provide. Fine, let the students who will be good journalists and who care about issues (and may indeed not have a sporting bone in their bodies) demand the change, so that never again will students be told that covering sports is a throwaway of talent.

A basic code of conduct for sports coverage—no free meals, no free rides, no free tickets—would go a long way towards liberating the media from the pernicious shackles of being inside the sports club. In organizations such as the *Globe* and CBC where journalistic policy books exist, the rules have been very useful to journalists if only as a means of deflecting unwanted and unsolicited gifts. Journalists in organizations without these guidelines would do well to sit down with management and create them. Freelance or staff, journalists ought to have the financial support of their companies, so they need never take free tickets, rides or accommodations. That should be the cornerstone of any policy book.

I can hear the wails of business managers already. How can they ever afford to absorb those costs? Come on! This is the technological age, and it ought to send sports pack journalism the way of the dinosaurs. Does the profession really need *all* of those reporters and commentators, thousands of them, at the Super Bowl or the Olympics? I say, watch it on TV and do the traditional reportage that way. The money you save can be put to good use digging into the background stories, getting the critical distance every good journalist needs.

As a fan, I would hate to see sports simply as a battleground. I don't want to lose the fantasy. As a journalist, I want more and expect more from myself and my colleagues. Contentious, tough, hard-hitting journalism doesn't necessarily pose a threat to the magic element of sports. The fantasy is there, it will always be there. It needs to be covered, given its due. And it will be, of that I have no doubt. But it is time to explore that other world of sports, time to attack hidebound assumptions and ancient attitudes.

The game has changed. It doesn't run the way it used to. It never will again. Sports is a major new reality in contemporary life. The way it is covered, analyzed and reported will have profound implications for everyone. If journalists don't do the job the way it needs doing, sports will continue to reshape and redefine our lives, but not for the better.

I don't want to sound like a prophet of doom. Let me conclude by saying that the radical shaking down that sports journalism urgently needs will not diminish the fantasy but restore and perhaps even ennoble it.

18. Reviewing the Arts: Better than Suicide?

Valerie Alia

> Reviewing has one advantage over suicide. In suicide you take it out [on] yourself; in reviewing you take it out [on] other people —George Bernard Shaw (Bentley 1956).

> With the exception of Wodehouse's *Oh Lady, Lady!,* where she deemed it politic to lay praise on thick, she proceeded to [stick] the rest with a poison stiletto. Since it is always more fun to revile than extol . . . she made it her modus operandi (Meade 1988).

The points about Dorothy Parker are familiar to arts journalists. In reviewing a bouquet of five musical comedies, Parker was uniquely kind to the work of P.G. Wodehouse, her predecessor as *Vanity Fair* drama critic and a member of the magazine's "family." Most of the time she was free to revile and skewer artists at will. Although she had a clear preference for the negative, Parker's personality and incisive and witty evaluation made her a bestselling critic. Despite the intensity of today's focus on consumer- and personality-driven media, it is not new to entertain readers or use the personalities of journalists to sell magazines and newspapers. In a column on the landmark U.S. case in which an author sued for libel over a book review, Rick Salutin separates criticism into two categories: the "tough-love division" in which reviews are "a form of support for the arts," and the "exercises in cultural sadism" (Salutin 1994)

In all the literature on journalistic ethics, little has been said about the arts. Yet newspaper, radio and television give substantial space to arts and entertainment coverage. This chapter and the next are intended to bring the dialogue into the ethics arena.

Who Are the Critics and How Did They Get That Way?

On the eve of my departure from a small Michigan town to the intimidating vastness of Boston, a kindly mentor warned, "You'll never get to be a critic—there simply aren't any jobs. Unless, of course, you're willing to sleep with an editor."

I swear he said it. This isn't the place to recount my amorous adventures, but I want you to know I have never slept with an editor, not even for fun. The mentor was making two points. First, there were no jobs for critics (something Shaw said a long time ago). Second, if you were a woman, there were always mitigating circumstances.

So, I didn't lure an editor into bed (my bed was usually covered with manuscripts-in-progress anyway). What really happened is, like many other journalists, I became an instant expert. A reporter generally accepts that the ever-changing news demands constant relearning. A critic, however, *knows* things. I knew things. They weren't always the things I was asked to cover. As a child, I scribbled critical notes on concert and theatre programs and grew up on my father's book reviews and treasured volumes of James Gibbon Huneker. From these,

I absorbed the prespecialist tradition of an earlier age, a time when a (well-educated) critic might cover opera and painting at the same time.

I didn't choose journalism, it chose me. In university and unable to afford tickets, I learned you could get the best seats in the house, five dollars and a byline merely for giving your opinion in print. I don't think I hurt anyone, and some early judgments proved accurate. (A couple of my summer-theatre reviews hailed the promise of a wonky and precocious eighteen-year old actor named William Hurt.)

Reviewing was so much fun, I abandoned plans to become an academic and set off to seek my journalistic fortune. The *Boston Phoenix* was a wonderful place to learn the community and the ropes. I wrote on music and theatre, subjects I knew fairly well, having had training in both. Then I went to the *Boston Herald-Traveller* arts desk and asked Sam Hirsch if I could review theatre or music. No, but he needed a dance critic, immediately. I had taken modern dance classes and had bought a ballet book at age five. Did that count?

Apparently it did. They sent me to cover a major ballet company. I wrote possibly the most embarrassing review of my life, underwent the horror of seeing it in print and then went crawling home to do my homework. I took class, watched rehearsals and attended Selma Jeanne Cohen's wonderful critics' training ground at the American Dance Festival. Pretty soon, I really did know something about dance. I was lucky, I had a chance to learn, especially from colleagues.

I had no idea how lucky we were or how radically things would change. On any given night, half a dozen reviewers would show up representing three dailies, two or three weeklies, monthlies, radio and television. We could compare observations and test perceptions; if one of us missed a detail, another would catch it. No one person can ever recapture an entire event. "It's partly the *Rashomon* thing," says novelist and playwright Timothy Findley, returning us to the Rashomon principle. "Three people seeing the same event and they remember three separate versions" (Black 1993).

Audiences and artists had many sources of information. None of us saw the brave new world of narrowing coverage that lay just ahead. Today, the typical city has a daily, perhaps a weekly and the occasional radio or television review covering a smattering of events, often by generalists who must serve as both reporter and reviewer. It's a far cry from the time-honoured ideal of the historian-critic who evaluates, serves and preserves art and audience.

That was the image of "critic" in my mind when I landed my first job. There was an opening, I was female, I got hired. I soon learned that lots of women got hired to cover dance. Years later I was offered the music critic's job as well. Suddenly, there were grumblings. What right did a young woman (I was faulted on both grounds) have to cover music? Dance was the stepchild of the arts—underfunded, even in relation to other underfunded arts. "Serious" music was another matter.

According to John E. Booth (1990), things haven't changed all that much. "Nearly two-thirds of U.S. newspaper critics are male, the overwhelming majority are white, and their median age is around 40." The field remains stacked and unrepresentative. Toronto critic William Littler bent over backwards to grant credibility to a Toronto Symphony Orchestra guest conductor, noting awards for excellence and a gender-barrier-breaking career path. The trouble is, he had never written an equivalent story about a male conductor, he had simply reviewed the performance. This review is full of special, and patronizing, appreciation. Catherine Comet "belonged" on the podium "by virtue of sheer musicianship, rather than in response to a legitimate call for affirmative action" (Littler 1989). It starts with a cute story about Comet's five-year-old daughter. The day I read a comparable description of Seiji Ozawa's children, I will cease to protest. As a lapsed critic, I felt distanced enough and incensed enough to respond in a letter to the editor.

> [The] review of Catherine Comet's . . . Toronto Symphony concert is all too familiar. The reviewer flaunts his tolerance, while treating Comet unequally from the start. His lead isn't about music at all—it's a mommy-daughter story. . . . The performance isn't mentioned until the seventh of thirteen paragraphs. [The review] serves neither music nor affirmative action. It segregates Comet and compares her only to other (female) maestre (Alia 1989).

When in doubt, try the "test of parallels": if you report John's shirt in the same way as Jane's dress, it's fair. If you substitute "Michael Tilson-Thomas" for "Catherine Comet," you see immediately that a story about a five-year-old daughter is no way to review a conductor. Such treatment is unethical because it is founded on a different premise from a "normal" review, pretends to be a review of a concert and is not.

Principles and Problems

Responsible reviewing is driven by respect for the arts and artists. I cannot imagine covering music if, left to your own devices, you would not spend time in concert halls. When actor and director Charlie Tomlinson (1992 and 1994) visited my arts criticism seminar, he told startled critics-to-be that they are the enemy. Robert Brustein (1992) agrees that critics and artists are adversaries:

> For more years than I care to count, the critic and the artist have circled each other warily, staring into each other's eyes with coldness and suspicion, in a manner usually associated with the mongoose and the snake.

Searching for commonalities between "two warring factions," Brustein convened a symposium. At one extreme is the *tabula-rasa* critic who claims no biases or agendas, at the other are those such as George Jean Nathan who insist "there can be no such being as an impersonal critic until there is an impersonal person" (Brustein 1992). For Nathan, responsible criticism is the record of the critic's personal experience among masterpieces. Benedict Nightingale and others worry about critics "parading" their "moral, social, or political bias" (Brustein 1992) and thus imply that art and criticism are apolitical, white-noise-neutral. This position is full of inconsistencies. Critics who rail against the political agendas of contemporary playwrights but not those of Molière or Shakespeare suggest the argument is more about posterity than politics.

> In most cases objective criticism means that someone whom you have slammed wishes that you hadn't slammed them and says John [Simon] should be more objective. . . . The only thing that can be objective is a machine, and we know now that even computers can't be objective (Brustein 1992).

Some critics pretend there is such a thing as apolitical art. Art has sometimes represented the status quo, but it has never been apolitical. For Timothy Findley, art must be courageous and challenging:

> A book *should* be dangerous. . . . If a book isn't dangerous, it's worthless. Art must menace. It can be gentle menace, but it must make you feel quite uncomfortable (Black 1993).

Under repressive regimes, courageous artists are often the first to be imprisoned or killed (for example, the musician-poet Victor Jara in Chile). Perhaps because of the very freedom North American journalists enjoy, we ignore this chilling reminder of the link between politics and art and maintain separate premises for criticism and reportage. As film critic Jay Scott (1991) put it, "the difference between criticism and straight reporting is that reporting *lies* about the *person who's writing*, and criticism doesn't." Even in third or second person, the reviewer's persona is present. The reporter is a non-person, objectified by the third-person neutral and the stance of non-involvement, while the critic is a purveyor of opinion, by definition involved.

Too much has been made of the differences between "reviewers" and "critics." Some journalists separate the daily-deadline "reviewer" from the longer-deadline "critic." Others insist only a scholar can be a "critic." Because there are so many ambiguities, I tend to use the terms interchangeably. The scholar-critic, seldom a journalist, is usually confined to small journals, magazines or books. All responsible criticism is careful, thoughtful, educated—within the restrictions of time and space. It's a matter of style, medium and degree (and I don't mean third- or academic). I think the fuss over distinctions is a snob thing, more about class than function.

More important than how we label the evaluators is the extent to which their perspectives are made available to the public. As a critic in the 1970s, I covered premieres in remote places. When there was more than one important event, we had "stringers" (second-string reviewers). Today, newspapers pool coverage, cover only some events and lump reviews and reportage together. When I arrived in London, Ontario, in 1989, the *London Free Press* published many reviews of local performances. Today, most arts and entertainment coverage comes from wire services, too often with little bearing on art in the community. Tactics such as the *Globe and Mail's* "Arts +" section (really "Arts minus") substitute mini-reviews and rating codes for the depth we used to expect. Even where arts pages are substantial, there are double standards.

Jazz has long been relegated to small columns and back pages. No theatre critic would cover only one of a play's three acts. No music critic would hear two movements of a concerto and run across town to catch the third movement of another. The critic covers the artist's shaping of a performance, not just a musical moment. Yet in Toronto and other large cities, jazz critics habitually cover fragments of two or three performances a night. I have heard the solo of the century in a third set, only to read in the next day's review that the player was bland (by implication, all evening).

POWERFUL? WHO, ME?

> Drama critics tend to regard playwrights, actors, directors and designers as thin-skinned egotists who respond only to ecstatic and unqualified praise, while theater people tend to think critics lack any understanding of their process, preferring to treat them as sacrificial animals. . . . Artists are so alienated from the critical process that they profess not to read reviews [and] . . . deny that criticism ever played any part in the development of their art.[15]

John E. Booth says the *New York Times* has enormous power in the arts world. Although James Duff's play, "Home Front," won universal raves in London, it was doomed in New York. The first paragraph of the *Times* review "was O.K," according to Booth. Then he read the second paragraph,

> and I said, "Well, sorry guys. . . . It doesn't look like we'll be able to do it. . . ." Everybody understood that. . . . The *New York Times* goes against you, and you don't run (Booth 1990).

Some critics play a "little old me" game of posing as average citizens whose ephemeral (re)views evaporate in the morning air. I think that is an irresponsible and groundless game. If I confront my power, I have the honesty to acknowledge whether my headaches or hangups affect appreciation of a work. I place myself in the audience, not to abandon critical judgment but to consider its effect on others. I place myself onstage, to avoid gratuitous cleverness at the performer's expense. I avoid becoming the story.

In 1993, Toronto art critic Kate Taylor inadvertently abandoned that last principle. Reviewing an exhibition by a young artist, she found the treatment of the intentionally shocking subject matter (children and adults in sexual play) "self-conscious" and "juvenile," the gallery's euphemistic commentary offensive, but the artist's technical abilities considerable. She wrote, "Langer is young and he can paint marvellously well. Maybe when he grows up he'll be an artist" (Taylor 1993b). What followed was a drama which still continues. Merely by covering the show, Taylor called attention to its existence. The day after the review was published,

> two people who had read it complained to Toronto police. The morality bureau visited the show the same day, seized work the following day . . . laid charges against Langer . . . [and] charged art gallery director Sharon Brooks with possession of child pornography and displaying obscene material (Taylor 1993a).

The critic's impact was unambiguous and irrefutable. Until her review, the show had gone unnoticed for three weeks.

> Had I not written about it, I believe it would have wrapped up quietly this week as scheduled. Instead, Langer is the first artist to be charged under new child pornography provisions added to the Criminal Code last summer (Taylor 1993a).

The story does not end there. Taylor was vilified at a press conference sponsored by free-speech activists, criticized for having ignored the history of "sexual material in art" and misquoted as having said the paintings, rather than the acts they depicted, were illegal. In fact, she did not judge the work pornographic. She defended her position with eloquence and passion.

> Although I reviewed it very negatively . . . it could be argued that I made a much stronger statement about its artistic merit than those Toronto media who chose not to review it at all. I am . . . one of only two critics who wrote about the show. . . . I believe it is the Mercer Union's right and responsibility to show art, Eli Langer's to make it and mine to write about it—without any of us being stifled by the police, the courts or the tyranny of public opinion. I believe in free speech for Eli Langer . . . and for Kate Taylor (Taylor 1993a).

The now prominent case is not just about free speech or definitions of pornography. Taylor made two choices which led directly to the artist's arrest: she decided to review the show (for a major newspaper) and she described the content of the work (such description being a typical component of a review). She believes that, "If I had not revealed the explicitness of the work, in all likelihood Langer would not have been charged" (Taylor 1993a) Whether Taylor performed a public service or a disservice, her small review for a large newspaper has had enormous impact on media consumers (the "public"), artists, gallery directors and other players in the continuing drama. So much for the "critics-have-no-power" school of thought.

It must be pointed out that although critics have real power, they are not all-powerful. As Brian Brennan points out in the next chapter, many shows survive, and even triumph over, bad reviews.

CONFLICTS OF INTEREST

Many people are worried about the growing tendency to hire generalists.

> On most newspapers . . . critics are required to double as art news reporters and interviewers. (Or is it that reporters and interviewers double as critics?) The arrangement can breed conflicts of interest, for the purposes of each are quite separate (Booth 1990).

When I became a critic in the United States in the 1970s, it was a time of specialization. My Boston and New York state newspapers were concerned about projecting an image of expertise. They never asked about my arts training but did ask me not to write about anything else, saying it would harm my (read, the newspaper's) credibility to have a byline associated with another field (or worse, with general reporting). To keep the byline pure and indulge other interests, I wrote on politics and other issues under different names. I never saw it as conflict of interest because nobody criticized the quality of my reviews and the work was unrelated to the events I covered.

Globe and Mail arts and books editor Katherine Ashenburg prefers to assign one person to interview an artist and another to review the work. She cites film critic Pauline Kael's avoidance of industry press kits, directors' lunches and social events. For Kael, the responsible critic sits in dark houses, watching movies:

> In general, we aim to minimize the possibility that a critic will be charmed (or antagonized or distracted) by the artist rather than the art. . . . When the dance critic has listened at length to the choreographer explaining the meaning of his new ballet, it's tough to see the piece uncoloured by its creator's account of it (Ashenburg 1993).

Staff cutbacks and other institutional constraints make it increasingly hard for news organizations to follow such principles. It used to be a given that audiences and artists could access a range of reviews and local events were reviewed locally. Late in 1993, Canada's major newspaper chain, Southam, announced it would pool cultural coverage.

> The policy delights book publicists [but] alarms journalists. . . . Running the same review in more than one newspaper will amplify the effect of a rave or a pan; there will be fewer voices to take a contrary position (Ross 1993).

I define "conflict of interest" rather broadly, referring not just to unethical financial gain but to conflicts of *loyalty*. Too often, ethical principles are founded on ahistorical fictions. Although today's increasing consolidation of arts coverage creates what some call conflict of interest, it is not the first time accepted roles and practices have shifted. In the early days of newspapers, multiple roles were not only accepted but were the norm. People worked part-time as journalists and part-time as artists or politicians with little worry about overlapping loyalties. Rules and mores keep changing. In hard times, part-time and freelance journalism is again on the rise.

If all critics get the same services—theatre tickets, a press kit, excellent seats, parking privileges—it could be argued that the dilemma disappears, that it is fair and such "gifts" have no effect on quality, quantity or content of coverage. That was the policy in my early years as a critic. It is not the argument currently in fashion. In my experience, all of us could confess to moral imperfection. Some things have changed and others have not. News organizations now prefer to purchase reviewers' tickets and refuse "press comps." Press conferences drive news and reviews too often. Press kits remain powerful marketing and lobbying tools. Although meant to influence us, they are unlikely to bias a review. In the best instances, they not only hype artists or entertainers but are educational tools that expand the critic's (and therefore, the public's) knowledge. The outstanding example in my own experience is the work of New York City Ballet publicist Virginia Donaldson. She was not a "flak" but a colleague whose wonderful press kits contained meticulously researched documents that enriched many a review.

CONFESSIONS OF MORAL IMPERFECTION

- Journalists, including arts journalists, still moonlight. Whether full- or part-time, staff or freelance, most journalists I know have worked "on the side" as speech writers, publicists or trainers (coaching people they sometimes cover on how to use the media).
- During a hungry period, I worked as an editor for a weekly with double standards for employees who were, or were not, friends of the publishers. I had to choose between publishing incoherent, ungrammatical copy so bad it would fail a school exam or

"editing" to the extent of virtually ghost-writing the columns of some of the bylined critics.

- When I worked for a major newspaper, the arts staff took turns covering an annual society charity event. It was an inside joke and we all learned the rules: we were to "review" the amateur performers "seriously," yet avoid damaging their egos, their cause or their reputations. The blessing was that no one had to review it two years in a row. When my turn came, I did not uphold morality and risk my job, I took the assignment.
- On another paper, a spouse of a highly placed employee gave occasional concerts, distinguished by a striking and consistent lack of musicality or pitch. Again the arts staff were expected to rotate the reviewing duty. If I recall correctly, I wriggled out of *my* ethical dilemma by passing the assignment off on a colleague.

As a rule, we should not apply different standards in different places. I am no more, or less, a tourist in Iqaluit than in Ottawa. If I can't accept a gift in Toronto, neither can I accept an airline ticket and a free "Northern adventure." A moral absolute? Yet, suppose there is a story of global importance, the fare is astronomical (as Northern fares are) and my publisher won't foot the bill? For John Hulteng (1981),

> the ethical rights and wrongs in this area are particularly difficult to sort out. Journalists cannot be expected to lead antiseptic lives . . . a kind of double standard sometimes seems to be in effect. In small towns, particularly, the editor or reporter may indeed hold office on the city council.

In some communities, there is nothing left to review and no one left to do the reviewing unless you allow conflicts of interest or hire visitors. As an outsider wintering in Whitehorse, I was asked to review Yukon artists. A year later, I knew most of the artists and some were friends. Artists need reviews for professional credibility, funding and feedback, and the public is also entitled to this service. In the Yukon, artists kept asking to be reviewed but complained about bias when they were, a Catch-22 much lamented by *Whitehorse Star* editor Jim Butler (Alia 1992d). The unanswered question is: How do you review in a community in which there is no conflict-free beat for anyone?

The public's view of a region, an art or an entertainer may be dictated by a single junket sponsored by a company promoting its own interests. The American Society of Professional Journalists (1992) takes the position that

> any kinds of gifts, favours, free travel, special treatment or privileges can compromise the integrity of journalists and their employers. . . . Nothing of value should be accepted.

Applied to remote communities, this means covering even less than we do now. If I'm the only reviewer in town and the performer is a friend, do I refuse to cover the performance? If I occasionally perform, am I disqualified from reviewing in the same field? Do the rules change if I perform *frequently*? Is it ethical to set the same standards for an amateur company as for a company of professionals? Is it ethical to set *different* standards? What principles apply if I write under different names?[1]

Framing the Issues

After several years as a critic, I began to reflect on my experiences (Alia 1980). When I attended dance critics' conferences, I was struck by the realization that most critics were in or near New York City and writing for "serious" publications—magazines, weekly news or arts papers. That these publications seldom paid may explain a further division among dance critics: labour-of-love critics with day jobs, and independently wealthy critics with the freedom to pursue their passion.

Listening to senior critics, I was both inspired by their expertise and love of dance and frustrated by their biases. They spoke of the elusiveness of dance and the critic's obligation to history (a dance performance is not a book or a recording, its survival is assured only by those who film, broadcast or write about it). It is an awesome responsibility which the daily journalist must often put aside. It is a joy to write at length. Occasionally, the newspaper critic has this opportunity. More often, her writing happens in the shadow of the journalist's chamber of professional horrors. There is always the fear of having a corner cut, a crucial word misprinted or omitted. How frustrating to describe an essential element of a performance, only to see it replaced by a plug for a car wash or steak house!

There is the additional delight of late-night deadlines where you can commit spontaneous (and perhaps overly hasty) responses to irrevocable print. And the delight of seeing the editor's superior knowledge at work. I once referred to Margot Fonteyn's "Aurora" (the protagonist in "The Sleeping Beauty") and read it the next morning as "her aura." Evidently, the editor had confused New Age mystery with dance history!

Because they consider dance specialized and remote, some editors get angry. I have endured complaints about "all those foreign words" and questions about why "dancers have such strange names" or "pick such outlandish titles" as if I had brought in all this weirdness out of spite. I have phoned in a review on deadline from Saratoga Springs, where horse racing competes with the New York City Ballet and Philadelphia Orchestra each summer, only to hear an irate editor yell, "Call back later; we're waiting for the racing results." In a contest between horses and dancers, the horses always win.

It isn't fair to complain about the difficulties of being a daily critic without also acknowledging the pleasures. If you are less the historian, you are more dynamically involved with the instant communication of an experience. You can affect, to some degree, an audience, a community, an institution. While I was still a daily critic, I wrote:

> I love the immediacy of daily journalism, with all of its disgusting flaws. I delight in the swiftness, the instant gratification, the here and now of it. I like having a chance to share what happens tonight with readers of tomorrow morning's paper. I like having a chance to make readers aware of events they might otherwise ignore, to stimulate controversy or reflection. The overwhelming scariness of making an instant commitment to an opinion is offset by the chance to rephrase, restate, or recant at a later date.[30]

The critic experiences a performance in illness or health, joy or depression, comfort or discomfort. She is open or closed to an artist because of these physical or mental states, the ambience of setting, the season, company, mystique of place and time. I try to see a performance more than once. Sometimes I change my mind, as in the case of Paul Taylor's

"Runes." When I first saw it, in its pre–New York City debut at Lake Placid, it seemed pretentious and cultish. When I returned, I saw texture and depth and was profoundly moved, and wrote a very different review. It is important to share that experience with audiences to remind them of the validity of their own experience, the fallibility and changeability of one's own. It is inaccurate and irresponsible to pretend that I can evaluate "the piece" from a single performance.

We must beware of making class or cultural distinctions in the guise of evaluating quality. I have tried to give "classical," "popular," "folk," and other art equal credibility. I don't think folk dance or music is inherently less important, less serious, less skillfully performed than so-called "high" art. It's not enough to look for the folk roots in classical performances (folk themes in Tchaikowsky or Beethoven, folk dances in Petipa). In North America, critics too often call Danish or Russian ballet "classical," but then they label classical Indian or Cambodian dance "ethnic" along with the true folk arts of those countries. It confuses and angers me to hear someone say a folk dance with no "story" is always dull and ought to be confined to someone's backyard while at the same time accepting a storyless George Balanchine ballet. If Balanchine can make lovable dances about "just" dancing, why can't a farmer make lovable dances about "just" dancing?

The dilemmas are endless. The best we can do is acknowledge and address them, struggle with temporary solutions and search for codes and continuities. Some issues are clear and unarguable. I remember my shock, years ago, on reading a colleague's review of an entire performance after having seen him leave at intermission. And who among us would not blush with shame at Frances Somerville's (1991) recollection:

> From 1939 until 1942 I was often engaged as a recitalist on CBC Radio. On one occasion my programme had to be cancelled at the last moment because I was ill. But it had been advertised earlier with a list of the songs to be included. One was a Bach aria, "My Heart Ever Faithful"; it would have been my first time to sing Bach on the air. Imagine my surprise when Hector Charlesworth, then *Saturday Night*'s music critic, acclaimed me as "an accomplished Bach interpreter." This would have thrilled me if I had sung the recital. As it was, it left me with considerable skepticism about newspaper reviews of concerts or plays.

I think we can agree that here is a moral absolute: no one should review a performance he or she has not attended!

Beyond such extreme examples of unconscionable behaviour, we must attend to our inadequacies without excessive beating of breasts. While we sometimes let ourselves off hooks we should stay caught on, we also overdo the self-flagellation. In Brustein's Harvard symposium, critics and artists alike skewered the critical profession. John Simon caught them at it:

> You may have noticed that two critics in the last couple of days have come in for the most praise . . . Bernard Shaw and Kenneth Tynan. If you ask yourself what do these two critics have in common, the obvious thing is that they're both dead, which is why, perhaps, I should . . . possibly soon join their ranks. . . . Bernard Shaw was a much hated person in his day. All kinds of venomous and vituperative things were

> written and said about him and this was simply because he was sharp and a tough critic.[2]

Still-living critics should be able to write and broadcast responsibly and incisively. Respect for the work of artists is our foundation, adulation is not.

Actor Alisa Palmer (1994) told journalism students that "good critics are like family—they give you unconditional love and also criticism." I agree. I also think that it isn't entirely reciprocal, that the critic's job is to be always a little unloved. Maybe that is the job of all good journalists.

19. Confessions of an Unlettered Arts Critic

Brian Brennan

There are two kinds of critics," said the American humour writer Evan Esar (1968), echoing familiar refrain, "those who write what they don't know about, and those who don't know what they write about." The majority opinion on critics, as indicated by Esar's acerbic remark, is generally negative. Look in the criticism section of any collection of quotations, and you will find pages of evidence corroborating what every critic already knows: there is a venerable tradition of critic resentment dating back to the late seventeenth century. For about as long as there has been published criticism, there has been resentment of it. Much of the indignation has to do with the fact that critics are popularly believed not to know whereof they speak.

There may be some justification for the indignation. During the early 1960s, Charles Marowitz, an American stage director, took time off from his theatre work to write drama reviews for London newspapers and magazines. He collected them in book form under the title, *Confessions of a Counterfeit Critic* (1973). Why counterfeit? Because Marowitz felt his theatrical credits were insufficient to qualify him as a "real" critic, whatever that might be. The same goes for me. Because I never trained for the job of arts critic, I felt like a pretender to the throne when I started writing theatrical and music criticism for the *Calgary Herald* in the mid-1970s.

I wasn't the only accidental tourist on the reviewers' airplane. During the 1970s, arts criticism at many Canadian newspapers was practised by persons without specific training as critics, engaged in the business of conducting their education in public. If these undertrained novices ever needed to defend their ignorance, they could look to "Advice to a Young Critic," from one of the heroes of the profession, George Bernard Shaw.

> There is no way of becoming a dramatic critic. It happens by accident. But when the accident happens, it happens to a journalist. It is to men who are already in the profession, and known as men who can write, and who know the ways of papers, that editors turn when a vacancy occurs (Shaw 1932).

If the neophytes needed further bolstering, they could turn to such other giants of the critical arts as George Jean Nathan, Harold Clurman, Stanley Kauffmann and John Simon. They were all on record as saying that the only qualifications a critic needed were intelligence, curiosity, some general arts education and an ability to write accurately and engagingly.

Such reassurances from the giants of the critical profession may have been encouraging to those Canadian journalists like myself who moved from general reporting to arts criticism. But could they resolve the ethical dilemmas which must inevitably arise when critics who are learning on the job purport to offer informed commentary on the contributions of those who dedicate their lives to artistic expression? Hardly. Could these rookie Canadian critics ever hope to add to the understanding of their readers when their own understanding was so limited? Sadly, no. Could the homework assignment of producing analytical or critical writing for the liberal arts classroom adequately prepare a budding critic for the task of reviewing under a tight deadline? Not in my experience.

When I started reviewing for the *Calgary Herald* in 1975, I could claim some advantage over other neophytes because I had dabbled in the arts. I could offer a little learning because I had earned a teaching diploma from the London College of Music in my teens, played piano professionally from age 14 onward, read theatre at University College Dublin and acted on the semi-professional stage in Ireland and Canada. I could claim a certain limited experience with practical criticism, having written some hastily researched, carefully worded and somewhat superficial theatre reviews for a student newspaper when I studied journalism at Vancouver City College in 1968. I had also later done some theatre and concert reviewing for the daily *Citizen* in Prince George, B.C.

For all my dabbling, however, I could not in all honesty say I had what it took to be a competent critic when I wrote my first theatre reviews for the *Herald*. Later on, I could point to the training I received at the National Critics Institute in Connecticut and to workshops at conferences of the International Association of Theatre Critics as formative experiences that deepened my work as an arts commentator. But when I started, I had little more than my gut to rely on. My kind of criticism could have been practised by almost anyone who had read a few plays and seen a few productions. It consisted of allowing the waves of a performance to wash over me, then analyzing the markings in the sand like some amateur fortuneteller reading the tea leaves.

The methodology was primitive, the tools for analysis of a stone age variety. I had only limited knowledge of what was involved in writing, producing and acting in the theatre. I might have been able to talk about plays I had seen in Dublin, London and New York, but that was hardly sufficient to qualify as expertise in the field. In any other specialty branch of journalism, such as sports or business, if I had tried to pass myself off as competent with a corresponding lack of qualifications, I would have been denounced as a fraud.

I make these confessions now not to reveal a great scandal but to describe a situation typical in Canadian journalism at that time. The fact that I had no problem landing the theatre critic's job at the *Herald* says a lot about the way arts coverage was viewed by some Canadian newspapers. If I had applied for a job in the sports department, I would have been expected to know something about hockey and baseball. If I had applied for a position as financial writer, I would have been expected to know how to read a balance sheet and analyze a company's fiscal performance. Yet anyone who had ever seen a play could become a theatre reviewer.

Newspaper editors didn't go to the theatre much, so they didn't really care how well it was covered. This would change during the 1980s when newspapers began to develop higher standards for all aspects of their journalistic coverage. But in the early 1970s the standard for arts coverage in most Canadian newspapers was as low as it had been in the 1950s when Robert Fulford started contributing art reviews to the *Toronto Star*. Music and theatre coverage, to the editors of the 1970s, was still what Fulford (1988) terms a suburb of journalism. The city centre was political, business and crime reporting.

Lack of knowledge was a failing I knew I had to remedy once I decided to specialize in arts journalism and criticism. Unlike others in the field, I never saw ignorance as a justification for irresponsibility. By irresponsibility, I mean resorting to the dubious tactic of wearing one's lack of credentials on one's sleeve and using them as a pretext for identification with the mythical newspaper reader politicians like to refer to as the "ordinary Canadian." Once I became the *Herald*'s theatre critic, I determined not to let my ignorance stand in the way of doing the best job I could. I acquired a library card from the University of Calgary, bought several reference books and began to study the essays of Shaw, Dryden, Matthew Arnold, Kenneth Tynan, Lionel Trilling and Northrop Frye.

Such scholarship helped make me an informed critic but it didn't make me an ethical critic. I know this now because I remember that some of my early reviews had more to do with creating displays of verbal brilliance than with giving readers the kind of basic information they needed before they could decide whether or not to spend precious coin on a show.

As I think back, I know that it was hardly ethical to get into criticism thinking it might be a good way to get show-off prose and collegiate wisecracks into the newspaper. But over time, conscience and a sense of ethical responsibility did prevail. Over time, I learned to develop compassion, independence of mind and the confidence to say that something was good (or bad) when my colleagues were saying the opposite.

It was easy to say something was good when my opinion was part of the consensus. If Frank Rich of the *New York Times* said August Wilson was the most important black playwright in America, it wasn't any risk for me to say the same thing. But it took a certain stubborn faith for me to say that a Calgary playwright, Sharon Pollock, had the potential to be successful internationally when the same Frank Rich was warning his readers to beware of Canadian plays.

After I left the *Herald*'s theatre beat in 1988, I was gratified to be told by people in the theatre that they thought I had done some useful work as a critic. But I suspect I may also have done harm with my early reviews, squelching promising talents while trying to impress readers with my wit, intelligence and the fruits of my reading list that week. Because criticism often has a direct and immediate effect on a theatrical production, I fear some actors, directors and playwrights may have had their careers damaged by my early reviews.

I once mentioned this to the playwright John Murrell, whose works were produced across Europe and throughout the United States, after I singularly failed to see the promise in such early plays of his as "Waiting for the Parade" and "A Great Noise, A Great Light." His response was characteristically generous. "Perhaps we weren't very good," he said. "Remember, we were learning our craft too."

Though we learned our craft as amateurs, I like to believe we eventually acquired professional standards. I like to think a sense of higher purpose began to prevail as theatre in Canada moved towards a point where an actor would not be asked: "Yes, and what else do you do?"[1] The previous generation of theatre people had been of the little-theatre or community-theatre kind. They worked at other jobs during the day and did theatre in their spare time for the sheer enjoyment of the art form. For them, the reach of their favourite pastime extended no further than the nearest high school gym or the annual attempt to get a showing at the amateur Dominion Drama Festival. The arts reporters who followed their endeavours contributed to the cause by taking on the spirit of home-team boosterism. For them, "Little Mary Sunshine" was as good as anything by Shakespeare.[2]

My generation also became involved with theatre for the sheer enjoyment. But we had our eyes on the stars. The actors wanted to make a living on the stage without having to subsidize their craft by waiting on tables. The playwrights wanted to see their works performed on Broadway. And the critics wanted to show they knew more about theatre than the sports guys knew about hockey.

If ignorance posed the first ethical dilemma for me as a theatre critic, it was a quandary I was determined to resolve by reading and learning. I believe it was the same for many of my fellow neophytes (aside from the ignorance-is-bliss types I mentioned earlier). If they lacked the necessary training, they took crash courses in specialization. Ego would not have allowed them to do otherwise. As self-appointed specialists, they had to know more than the people they were writing for. And the newspapers contributed to this general upgrading of critical standards by first hiring writers grounded in the fundamentals of arts disciplines and then sending them off to seminars and workshops for further improvement. In my own case, one of my most valuable learning experiences took place during the two months I spent at the National Critics Institute affiliated with the Eugene O'Neill Theatre Centre in Connecticut. With such senior colleagues as Dan Sullivan of the *Los Angeles Times* looking over my shoulder while I composed my reviews, I became my own most demanding editor. No disgruntled arts practitioner could have been more censorious. I questioned and challenged every idea, every word, as I put them to paper.

Today, I fear, things are different. Editors no longer prize specialization or the quest to attain higher standards in criticism. The cult of philistinism claims converts everywhere. Yet even today, I still believe that, as a matter of pride, if nothing else, critics will make a point of knowing something about their subject before they write. I believe this to be true even for critics who work in radio and television where—I have learned from doing theatre reviews for CBC Radio—the ability of critics to create arresting images for listeners and viewers is considered more important than their ability to substantiate their opinions. At least, these electronic reviewers have some basis for comparison, having seen more than most of their listeners and viewers.

TOOLS FOR DESTRUCTION

A second ethical dilemma for arts critics, after that of ignorance, arises when the critics have knowledge, perspective and the ability to write useful and instructive reviews. Sometimes, for whatever reason—personal vendetta, malice aforethought, rampant egotism, the need to score points at the expense of others—they may choose to use their talents in ways that are hurtful and destructive. I must hasten to add here that I have never consciously indulged in such mean-spirited criticism myself, my previous admissions of early show-off reviewing notwithstanding. But I can recall some instances, most recently in the case of a Frank Sinatra concert I reviewed (I said his singing at 75 was inferior to his voice at 40) where my remarks might have been viewed as cruel and insulting. In such instances, my defence would have been that accuracy in reporting is the relevant issue here, not the words used in the process of reporting. Waffling in a review, as Frank Rich (1994) of the *New York Times* says, only deceives readers:

> If I did that, I'd become the boy who cried wolf. Those same readers would not believe me when I praised the really good play that came along.

Besides, "cruel" and "insulting" are irrelevant and meaningless terms when applied to criticism. Sometimes the truth can be cruel. Sometimes we need to hurl insults (I prefer to think of them as clever ripostes) to make our points effectively. Criticism does not abide by the rules of good manners, as normally applied to behaviour in social settings. If it did, Swift, Voltaire, Nietzsche and Shaw would be housed in the same section of the library as Emily Post. To suggest that criticism should be couched in the language of the drawing room is to confuse the art of reviewing with the art of making polite cocktail party chatter.

Criticism that censures is usually a form of retaliation for a performance a critic found offensive. The words used to describe that performance must be appropriate and cogent. When the performance is particularly offensive, the critic is sometimes pushed beyond patience to retaliate in less than genteel fashion. If the truth hurts, then so should the words serving that truth.

John Simon, the theatre critic for *New York* magazine, maintains that cruelty is inevitable. Even when critics are scrupulously even-handed, they will inevitably cause hurt when they pass judgment on an actor's physical appearance. Such criticism, he adds, is unavoidable when the play calls for beauty and the performer does not possess it. "For historical, psychological or aesthetic reasons, an actor must look the part he is playing" (Simon 1980).

An ability to transcend physical limitations is possible but it is comparatively rare. Most performers are not endowed with histrionic gifts able to overshadow all else. Spiritual beauty may be a much finer thing, but it is a slow worker and, after two hours, it might barely begin to make its presence felt. Physical beauty, as if aware of its transience, wastes no time in casting its spell.

I part company with Simon when he says an actor's appearance is fair game for a critic. I think that Simon's kind of personal criticism is often inhuman, bound to create embarrassment and serves no real critical function. What possible purpose can be served when an actor is put down for being too fat, too short or having a big nose? Better to criticize the casting director or the producer for making an inappropriate choice. But I do think there are times when personal appearance has to be taken into account. For example, if an actress playing Piaf looks more like Kate Smith than the famed Little Sparrow, I think it's legitimate to point out that certain expectations have not been met.

Stanley Kauffmann, the former theatre critic of *Saturday Review*, calls such evaluation of personal attributes one of the "necessary injustices of theatre criticism." The unjustness must continue "because it's ingrained in the circumstances of the theatre." A critic cannot be expected to know why an actor is unsuitably cast, and

> thus there's injustice. The actor is blamed or praised for choices that may not have been freely made, and for performances that may not be of his own design, and may even be contrary to his taste. And nothing can be done about the injustice (Kauffman 1982).

Arts criticism is perhaps unique in journalism in this regard. Notwithstanding Joan Didion's (1968) comment that writers are always selling somebody out, the fact remains that only in arts criticism can a writer indulge in the kinds of ad hominem attacks that likely would not be tolerated elsewhere.[3] If a city-hall columnist criticizes the appearance or personal style of the mayor, the laws of libel and slander are invoked. If a business columnist dares to comment on the personal attributes of a CEO, retractions and public apologies are the order of the day. But a critic can take shots at a performer, using language that would be considered rude and discourteous in any other public context (except perhaps in sports commentary of the kind practised by the Canadian TV hockey analyst Don Cherry) and rarely have to worry about retribution.[4]

If Simon and Kauffmann are right about injustice being inevitable, they offer an easy out for critics whose natural tendency is to hurt. So what recourse is left for the victims of such injustice? One commonly heard suggestion is that they should ask critics to adhere to a code of ethics similar to that devised in the 1980s by the Canadian Theatre Critics Association (CTCA), a fifty-member national organization of print and broadcast reviewers of which I was a founding director.

The CTCA code was the brainchild of Herbert Whittaker, chief theatre critic of the *Globe and Mail* from 1949 until his retirement in 1975. He based his code on the premise that theatre artists deserve respect, and criticism "offers no licence to insult, ridicule or denigrate artists who are serious about their work."[5] His code urged proper preparation before reviewing, objectivity and balance in commentary, all framed within a presumption of respect for the contributions of "artists and technicians who have worked long and hard on their presentation."[6]

Although the Whittaker code was adopted by the English-speaking members of the Canadian Theatre Critics Association in 1991, it turned out to be of no practical use in preventing injustice. It contained no enforcement provisions and was never sanctioned by any of the media organizations that publish and broadcast arts criticism in Canada despite its wide circulation among them. And it could never change the mindset of critics like the *Toronto Star* reviewer who once told me gleefully that "my column is the only place in the paper where I can call a person a fascist and get away with it."

The Association québécoise des critiques de théâtre didn't help matters when, without elaboration, it dismissed the code developed by its English-speaking affiliate as trite ("Mickey-Mouse" was the actual word used, as I recall) and unworkable, and undertook to develop its own code. To date, I have not seen a copy of this Quebec code.

Without a workable and widely accepted ethics code, what recourse exists for victims of critical injustice? It seems to me that aside from mandatory empathy training—obviously an impossible goal—the only real protection against injustice is artistic merit. In the long run, unjust attacks will surely backfire on the attacker because true artistic talent is something the most unethical review cannot eradicate.

> The man who spits at Praxiteles' Venus is really spitting in his own face. The beauty and nobility of the statue, which does not spit back, remain unimpugned (Simon 1975).

COMPROMISING CIRCUMSTANCES

For victims of injustice, ethics in criticism is a consummation devoutly to be wished. For the practitioners of criticism, the achievement of ethical behaviour may also be desirable but it can also be compromised or made difficult by circumstances such as the following:

1. *The policy of the media organization for which the critic works.* If an editor insists that a critic only write favourable reviews of a particular dinner theatre in town because such reviews will result in a lucrative advertising contract for the newspaper, how should the critic

respond? My response is that the critic should risk firing, claim the independence from interference granted to others at the newspaper who express their opinions in print and respond with an emphatic "No!"

> This is the sacred duty of the critic, to become indispensable, and then independent of interference from above, so they can neither fire us nor tell us what to do or what not to do (Simon 1980).

2. *The promotional role played by newspapers and broadcast outlets in publicizing the arts.* Feature stories on the arts are usually rooted in hype. The subtext is: See this show, watch this performer, buy this CD. This, despite the fact that, in most instances, the writer has yet to see or hear the subject of the feature story. The hype becomes particularly noticeable when the news organization happens to be a sponsor of the event. The critic-journalist, as a dutiful employee of the sponsor, is expected to fall in line and assume the role of publicist. What should this critic do? My feeling is that this critic should balk and refuse to become an extension of the public relations arm of an arts organization. If an advance feature story is called for, and the critic must do it, it should be clear to the readers that the story is in no way a validation of something the critic hasn't seen yet.

In fact, the critic can often provide useful information to the consumer by pointing out that the visiting play ran on Broadway for only four nights, that the performer's last recording failed to make the charts or that the long-awaited prime ministerial memoirs were rehashed from old television program transcripts. This is the kind of information that I, as a paying customer, would want to receive before I had to decide whether or not to spend my money.

At the *Globe and Mail*, critics are often exempted from writing advance publicity and thus are not put in the position of having to endorse what they have yet to encounter. At most other Canadian papers, however, the arts writers wear two hats. On Friday night, they review the show. On Monday morning, they interview the director for a feature on the upcoming production. How do they prevent the feature story from turning into something resembling an act of homage to an unseen show? Simply, I believe, by treating the director's puffery with the same healthy skepticism they would apply to the promises of a politician.

3. *The difficulties associated with overnight reviewing.* Because of early deadlines and the consequent move to next-day reviews, overnight reviewing has become less of a concern for critics now than in the past. Even with early deadlines, though, some editors still insist that critics review the first half of a concert "just to get something into the paper." Other editors want their reviewers to hit several nightspots in the same evening and give a sampling of what's out there. This results in a formulaic type of reviewing where the opinions expressed may be valid up to a point but the manner of expression leaves a lot to be desired. As the American drama critic George Jean Nathan (1928) wrote,

> Writing takes thought, and quiet, and time. The finest examples of critical writing that have come down to us from the past were not written between eleven o'clock and twelve of a night. They were written leisurely. Even a cannon, best to discharge its projectile, has to be carefully and scrupulously oiled and polished.

Frank Rich (1994) of the *New York Times* notes that the old opening-night system of reviewing was

> deplored by many critics, who often had to miss the end of a show to make a deadline, and felt it unfair to review an artist's work as if it were a fire or a sporting event. Covering the opening night of "A Streetcar Named Desire" in 1947, Brooks Atkinson had to miss the last scene, which meant that he reviewed the play without having heard "the kindness of strangers."

Because of such problems, the standard practice for Broadway reviewing from the 1960s onward was for the critic to attend a final preview and write at a somewhat more leisurely (and more thoughtful) pace. Using this precedent for support, along with Nathan's and Rich's aforementioned comments, my inclination would be to tell an editor today that there is nothing particularly heroic or admirable about putting a hastily written review of half a concert into the following day's paper. I would also point out that one reason the reviews of Shaw, Tynan, Simon, Nathan, Kauffmann, Robert Brustein, Sheridan Morley and James Fenton are important—aside from the fact they were written by critics of wit, intelligence, knowledge and humanity—is that they were not written against time.

Reviews are not news. Partial reviews amount to a form of professional dishonesty. If reviews are to serve any useful function for the reader beyond the rudimentary business of saying whether or not the critic liked the show, they should be suffused with intelligence, wit, metaphor, clarity, concision, illumination, instruction and the quality to delight. Such writing, as Nathan says, is rarely achieved while the last of the applause is still ringing in the critic's ear.

4. *Having to reduce a review to a certain number of stars (* * * 1/2) or a report-card grading (C+).* I hate these myself, but time-challenged consumers in the 1990s seem to demand them, along with instant food, instant gratification and instant slogans for T-shirts and bumper stickers. "Phantom is Phantastic!"—how can critics persuade editors to avoid using such shorthand? The short answer is they can't. Instant ratings are everywhere: throughout the *TV Guide*, on Siskel and Ebert's thumbs, in the out-of-context quotes in movie ads and on theatre marquees. Critics can, however, make the case that such capsule comments are no replacement for a detailed articulation of subtle shades of opinion. A tasting of a critic's writing can never be a satisfactory substitute for the whole meal. "I know the critic gave it four stars," the consumer will say, "but why? What's it about anyhow?" As long as such questions are being asked, the critic has a responsibility to ensure that reviewing is never reduced to computer-generated star ratings.

THE DEMAND FOR CRITICISM

Criticism persists, along with other forms of journalistic commentary and reportage because the public wants to read it. Even in an age of instant gratification, the reading public wants more than a collection of headlines. The proliferation on the newsstands of specialty magazines for everyone from computer buffs to dance lovers to cigar smokers suggests to me that readers want as much information as possible about the subjects that interest them. They may not read every section of a general-interest newspaper but they demand comprehensive coverage of their favourite topics.

Newspapers have responded to this demand in recent years by offering phone-in services similar to the "Talking Yellow Pages," supplying every kind of information from stock quotations to the current weather conditions in Sydney, Australia. New magazines have appeared to satisfy an increased public demand for stories about movies, television and the entertainment business. Even with all the information now available from the print media, satellite TV channels and computer bulletin boards, the public wants even more and better coverage. And that includes more coverage of the arts: review coverage as well as reportage. In the midst of such demand, the responsible and ethical arts critic plays a more important role than ever before.

CONCLUSION

Arts criticism is under siege. Like consumer-complaint and labour-strife reporting, it is heartily disliked by those organizations who advertise in the media and then expect the media to respond by writing nice things about them. What they perceive as "negative coverage" has never been easy for these organizations to accept. But their complaints have invariably died a quick death in the past because newspapers and television stations were flush with advertising revenue. Today, the story is different. If Joe Moneybags, president of Big Bucks Corp., warns the publisher he will withdraw his advertising if the newspaper keeps publishing the writings of a business columnist with declared pro-labour prejudices, the publisher now sits up and takes notice.

Similarly with arts criticism: in the past, it didn't seem to matter if a dinner theatre or movie house threatened to pull its advertising in a dispute over negative reviews. At the *Calgary Herald*, for example, I remember the satisfaction I felt during the 1970s when a representative of Famous Players told the editor of the paper, William F. Gold, that it would move its advertising to the *Albertan* if the *Herald* continued to run weekly capsule versions of negative reviews. Double jeopardy, charged the movie distributor. Gold was unmoved. "You remove your advertising," he told Famous Players, "and we will decide whether or not we ever want to let it back into the paper again."

Today, the loss of any revenue is a major concern for editors and publishers under constant pressure from shareholders to increase the return on their investment. Rather than force an independent-minded critic to toe the line and write more sympathetically, the publisher is more likely to replace the critic with a kinder, gentler soul who better understands the profit-making ideals of the publishing organization.

Such commercial pressures must inevitably lead to bad criticism and, ultimately, to unethical criticism. If the critic always downplays the negative and reports that everything is essentially good, the consumer has no real basis for deciding what is worth seeing and what is not. In the final analysis, such criticism serves nobody.

Should we be concerned? As a superannuated newspaper critic who still goes to the theatre and now increasingly finds himself reliant on the opinions of others, I firmly believe so. The "softness" that has crept into criticism because of latter-day pressures from media advertisers is of no use to me when I am deciding how to spend my entertainment dollars tonight.

The tougher brand of criticism I practised for twenty years functioned like strong medicine. Sometimes it was hard to swallow but ultimately, I hope, it was good for all concerned. Occasionally it may have brought hostility from artists and the public. But I always considered such hostility as something that came with the territory, something that was part of the job description, not a crown of thorns for me to be whining about. It may have caused me a few sleepless nights but, on balance, I feel it was a worthy cross to bear and that, in the long run, I served even those I annoyed.

Notes

Introduction: Valerie Alia, Barry Hoffmaster and Brian Brennan

1. "Jimmy's World" was the Pulitzer Prize-winning *Washington Post* series by Janet Cooke. Found to be a fabrication based on a composite portrait rather than a single boy, it sparked an outpouring of journalistic self-criticism, collective guilt and ethical inquiry which included texts, workshops, conferences and seminars (including those at the Gannett Center and the Poynter Institute for Media Studies). No texts on journalism ethics were produced in Canada during this period, except for Dallas Smythe's (1981) structural analysis in *Dependency Road*; and few were published in other parts of the world. As anyone with a sense of journalism history knows, "Jimmy's World" was not the beginning of ethical or critical writing but merely the beginning of a renewed wave of questioning.

Chapter 1: Pierre Mignault

1. All quotations are from the (1992) CBC documentary "Eva the Evergreen Lady."

Chapter 2: Earl Winkler

1. This sketch of the instrumental conception of social morality is derived from Philips (1993).
2. For a more complete account of justification in actual moral reasoning, see Winkler (1993).
3. Journalism may not meet all of the standard sociological criteria that are claimed to constitute a profession strictly speaking. Nevertheless, the journalistic enterprise as we know it concentrates enormous power in the hands of a few and includes licensing procedures and certain legal protections, such as the freedom of the press, the right to protect sources and so on. All of this, and particularly the concentration of power over the processing and distribution of information, legitimizes the inclusion of journalism within the class of professions, at least for my purposes.
4. Quoted from the documentary film "Manufacturing Consent: Noam Chomsky and the Media," Part Two, National Film Board of Canada, ISBN 0-7720-464-0.
5. I want to thank my colleague Peter Remnant for helpful suggestions and editorial assistance in the preparation of this paper.

Chapter 4: Nicholas Russell

1. For discussion and definitions of objectivity, accuracy and fairness, see, for instance, Merrill and Odell (1983: 174–76); for the Canadian context, see Miller (1990: 14–45) and Desbarats (1990: 16–19, 115–23).
2. Good journalism goes far beyond "reporting." To report is simply to document—a stenographic role. The journalist who merely reports (fairly and accurately) the words of a white supremacist is being used as a mouthpiece for hate propaganda. The newsroom must expand the definition to include the public good: What does the public need to know? Should hate-mongers be ignored or should other views be sought to debunk them?
3. Some of these situations are explored later. Deceitful news-gathering is typified by a journalist passing himself or herself off as an "ordinary citizen" to gather information. Deliberate lies are less common; an example would be a police request to report a fictional arrest to increase the credibility of an undercover drug-enforcement officer whose contacts suspect him of being a "narc."
4. Bok (1978) says truthtelling is mandatory unless a jury of disinterested peers can accept the necessity of the lie.

5. Curtis MacDougall (1940) documented the rise of newspapering April Fool's jokes in his classic study *Hoaxes*. For a more recent discussion of hoaxes in the media, see Johnston (1984).
6. *Vancouver Province*, date lost.
7. The seriousness with which such infractions are regarded is evidenced by the Associated Press's firing of an employee for putting a vulgarism in a story as an inside joke. An AP spokesperson said staff "well understand" it is a firing offence to put anything into the computer "that can't go out on the wire." (Anonymous 1985b)
8. Many books on journalism ethics discuss the Mirage case (e.g., Goodwin 1983: 135–44). The way it was contrived is admirably described by the two reporters, Zay N. Smith and Pamela Zekman in *The Mirage* (1979). See also Tony Case's description of British reporters who dressed as a priest, an undertaker and an x-ray technician to try to interview an injured jockey in a Florida hospital (Case 1992: 14).
9. Nancy Doyle Palmer (1987) discusses the issues effectively in "Going After the Truth—In Disguise," and Paul Braun (1988) adds some useful scenarios. Harvey Schachter (1983: 7) infers that while two budget-leak stories may have been legal, "to the public the leaks symbolized the brazen immorality and arrogance of journalists. . . . If we employ measures the public considers unethical to carry out our investigations, we will lose public support. If we look like we're gleefully out for a scoop (and the supposed profits that accrue to our bosses from such scoops) rather than out to serve the public interest, we will lose public support. And if we lose public support, we will give our bosses one more reason not to underwrite our investigations."
10. Credibility surveys tend to give journalists poor ratings. For instance, a major survey conducted for the American Society of Newspapers Editors in 1985 found news consumers rated editors and reporters seventh and eighth in terms of ethics on a list of ten professions; police were rated third (after clergy and doctors) (see McGrath and Gaziano 1986: 59). Braman (1988: 77) finds the public believes errors and distortions in the media are deliberate.
11. Radio regulations of the Canadian Radio-Television and Telecommunications Commission (CRTC) specify that permission must be acquired from sources before interviews are broadcast (CRTC 1986, s.3e).
12. For example, in the Bud Smith incident in British Columbia, a non-journalist systematically monitored the attorney general's somewhat indiscreet conversations on a radio-phone in the spring of 1990 and then passed tapes on to members of the provincial press gallery.
13. *Sports Illustrated* documented such techniques in a eulogistic profile of Ozzie Sweet, a veteran sports photographer of the 1950s and 1960s. For instance, a shot of pitcher Luis Aparicio in 1962 shows the ball a few feet from his hand. "Actually he never threw that ball—it's suspended by fishing line," ingenuously relates the cutline (Anonymous 1991).
14. Despite this admonition, Overbury shows no compunction about passing himself off as somebody else to get information. See, for instance, Overbury (1985), "Finding Missing People," Chapter 2.
15. Of course, this can backfire even more if the original story was a lie. Recalls one *Calgary Herald* reporter, "A *Herald* reporter lifted some quotes from the *Sun* when he couldn't reach the mayor on a story, only to suffer embarrassment later when it transpired the *Sun* had fabricated the quotes" (Brian Brennan, personal communication, June 11, 1993).

Chapter 5: Robert A. Hackett

1. The code is expected in Griffin et al. (1991), citing the society's 1986 ethics report.

Chapter 6: Robert A. Hackett and Yuezhi Zhao

1. For comments on earlier drafts, the authors are indebted to Michael Yeo and to members of the journalism ethics project, especially Barry Hoffmaster, Frank Howard, Nick Russell, Pierre

Mignault, Rita Deverell and Brian Brennan. The themes of this chapter are further developed by the co-authors in a book in progress for Garamond Press, entitled *Regimes in Crisis: New Objectivity and Sustainable Democracy.*

2. A parallel venture, Project Censored Canada, was co-initiated by Simon Fraser University's School of Communication and the Canadian Association of Journalists in 1993–94.
3. It should go without saying that we are not arguing in favour of unethical behaviour; nor are we suggesting that journalism's current ethics are inevitably reactionary or counterproductive.
4. For expressions of this libertarian view, see Udell (1979) and Crown (1979).
5. We are indebted to Barry Hoffmaster for pointing out that the possibility of objectivity as such is not necessarily undermined by the intrusion of values; for instance, one could argue (as presumably would many religious believers) that some values are objectively given and are more universally valid than others. Such a question is mercifully beyond the scope of this chapter, which is concerned with a historically and occupationally specific ethic of objectivity.
6. For an incisive critique of the relativist attack on news objectivity, see Lichtenberg (1991). For a broader critique of relativism, see Lovell (1983).

Chapter 8: Lorna Roth

1. Within the Canadian media system, the term "ethnic" is used to refer to those broadcasting undertakings which are neither French, English nor aboriginal in origin. Unfortunately, the assumptions underlying the use of this term imply a blind spot. *We are all ethnic.* Ideally, the term "ethnic" should not be restricted in this manner.
2. In the summer of 1990 the Mohawk community of Kanehsatake (40 kilometres west of Montreal) blockaded a tertiary access road to their commons land on which is located a sacred burial ground and a lacrosse arena. They were protesting the adjacent community of Oka's municipal council's decision to extend a local golf course onto what the Mohawks believe to be their territory. The Sûreté du Québec (Quebec's provincial police) were called in to control the initial conflict and the rest of the summer was spent in an armed confrontation among the Mohawks of Kanehsatake and Kahnawake (a community on the south shore of Montreal) and the governments of Oka, Quebec and Canada. The period, which lasted seventy-eight days, came to be known in Canada as its "Indian Summer."
3. The 1976 modification refers to the change in name and mandate of the CRTC, Canada's broadcasting regulatory agency, from Canadian Radio and Television Commission to Canadian Radio-television and Telecommunications Commission.
4. Louis Edmond Hamelin, a well-known Canadian geographer, defines the North as the lands and waters above the 60th latitude line. He divides the North into three zones: the "Middle North," the northern areas of the ten provinces, Labrador and much of the Yukon where road access is possible; the "far North"; and the "Extreme North" which takes in the Arctic archipelago, much of the Northwest Territories and northern Quebec (Shields: 168–70 1991).
5. See Appendix I for details.
6. See Appendix III for case-study materials.

Chapter 9: Bud White Eye

1. Paul Harvey News, July 1994, WJR Radio, Detroit. In 1994 the well-known American athlete was accused of brutally murdering his ex-wife and her friend.
2. See, for example, Canadian Press (1994). The message about reporting is clear: in the ninth of ten paragraphs, there is a very brief paraphrase of a comment by Vincent Tookenay, "a spokesman for Native Physicians of Canada." The story does not say "so and so from Indian Health has complained for years about this same thing," although most Band offices and Native organizations have had health representatives for years, and recommendations, portfolios, etc.

3. See, for example: Canadian Press (1993), a story about First Nations hunting and fishing rights which quotes and cites only non-First Nations "experts"—members of the House of Commons, the federal fisheries department and a university faculty; Power (1993), a story about Caldwell Nation deer hunting—Power goes all the way around it without saying it—he quotes representatives of the Ontario Federation of Anglers and Hunters and other interest groups and organizations, government representatives and others, but offers no First Nations view of the hunt from any interviews with First Nations people. The same story is treated the same way Van Brenk (1993); several people are interviewed here, but none of them are First Nations people!

Chapter 10: Valerie Alia

1. The title comes from the 1950 film, "Rashomon," by Japanese filmmaker Akira Kurosawa. A story is told several times by several characters. Each time the viewer sees "truth" through the character's camera-eye, and each "truth" is entirely different from the others. In the end, we don't know which version is the "real" one.
2. The material that follows is from a discussion between William Law and Valerie Alia at the Briars, Jackson's Point, Ontario, October 1993; and from William Law's radio documentary, "There Is No Death Here," CBC Ideas, June 1990.

Chapter 11: Brian Brennan

1. A copy of "The Custom of the Brothers of the Coast, or the Pirates' Creed of Ethics," 1960, can be found in the library of the Poynter Institute for Media Studies in St. Petersburg, Florida. It contains fourteen commandments, including the stark warning that "if ya introduce on board a woman in disguise, ye shall be punished by death."
2. Although called the Canadian Association of Journalists, the organization does not limit membership to journalists. An unspecified minority are journalism students, journalism educators and others involved with journalism, though not necessarily as practitioners.
3. A typical anticode response was articulated by CAJ board member Don McGillivray (1990). McGillivray argues that journalism in a democracy is not a profession like law or medicine, and therefore shouldn't be regulated like a profession.
4. A *Los Angeles Times* newspaper poll conducted in January 1993 found only 17 percent of those surveyed classified the media as doing a "very good" job. This figure was down from 30 percent in 1985. Nearly 70 percent agreed with the statement: "The news media give more coverage to stories that support their own point of view than to those that don't." The poll concluded generally that public confidence in the news media has eroded because of the perception that reporters are "insensitive elitists out of touch with the common people" (Associated Press, January 4, 1993). These findings parallel the results of an unpublished March 1993 survey conducted by the Times Mirror Center for the People and the Press, showing that the "believability" ratings for several major U.S. news organizations and news media celebrities dropped steadily between February 1993 and June 1985.
5. In the Bernardo-Homolka case, involving the murders of two young women, two Toronto newspapers battled with their chequebooks to obtain graduation photographs of defendant Bernardo. Ontario Court Justice Francis Kovacs subsequently imposed a Canadian publication ban on the facts of the case. In the Simpson case, where a well-known U.S. sports figure was charged with murder and immediately made front-page news around the world, the CBS network invited viewers to phone in votes on the guilt or innocence of the accused. A New York *Daily News* columnist commented, "Isn't anyone supervising this pack?" ("O.J. Just Fodder on Prime-time TV," New York *Daily News*, June 25, 1994).
6. Benjamin Harris, 1690, *Public occurrences both foreign and domestick*, September 25 (Phoenix: International Newspaper Collector's Club, facsimile). Harris's newspaper is referred to in F.L.

Mott's *American Journalism: A History: 1690–1960* (New York: Macmillan, 1962), 9.

7. "Red light ethics" is an expression used by the Poynter Institute to characterize restraint in ethical decision-making. Joann Byrd, executive director of the *Herald* in Everett, Washington, describes red light ethics as "the old lady with the pursed lips constantly saying 'don't.'"
8. Politicians have yet to call for ethical regulation of Canada's newspapers and broadcast outlets, but a Quebec Court judge, Guy Guerin, has recommended that the media in his province be given a code of ethics and that law-enforcement officials be limited in what they tell reporters (Canadian Press story, dateline Montreal, January 23, 1992).
9. Good examples of ethical decision-making models can be found in Dominick (1983: 411–15), Goodwin (1987: 24–25) and Gert (1988).
10. For an American reflection on the issue of ethics vis à vis First Amendment freedoms, see Christians (1985–86).
11. The question of enforcement has been a focal point of disagreement among Society of Professional Journalists' members since they copied their first code, in 1926, from a code adopted by the American Society of Newspaper Editors in 1923. Hence the various revisions of the Society of Professional Journalists code; in its current form, the code exhorts society members to "by programs of education and other means, encourage individual journalists to adhere to these tenets."
12. Journalists often joke that taking from one source is plagiarism, but taking from many sources is research.
13. Associated Press 1993 report of *Los Angeles Times* poll, as mentioned in footnote 4 above.

Chapter 14: Frederick J. Fletcher

1. This chapter could not have been written without the assistance of Theresa Kiefer, or the financial support of York University. I am also grateful to Elly Alboim for his insightful advice and to the many journalists and politicos who have shared insights and experience with me and my researchers over the past two decades of election campaign research. Errors of fact and interpretation or other acts of folly remain my responsibility. It should be noted that this essay deals primarily with the English media. Although many of the points made here apply to the French media, it must be kept in mind that French-language journalists operate in a distinctive cultural milieu (see Gilsdorf and Bernier 1991).
2. Many of these points were suggested by Elly Alboim during an interview by Fletcher (1994b).
3. See Rutherford (1986) for discussion of the party press and the period when journalists were closely tied to parties and government.
4. Charlotte Gray, quoted in a case study submitted to the journalism ethics project from which this book was created. Thanks are due to Ivor Shapiro for soliciting and collecting cases.
5. Gray, case study.
6. For a discussion of these trends in the United States, see Patterson (1993 and 1994: 8–9); and with respect to Canada, see Fletcher and Everett (1991: 374–83 and 471–80).

Chapter 15: Conway Jocks

1. My cartoons are signed "Tsiti," a pen name. The Mohawk pronunciation of those letters comes out "CJ"—my initials. I thought it would stay a big secret, but it didn't take long for everyone in the community to figure it out.

Chapter 17: William Law

1. *Sports Illustrated*, October 11, 1993.
2. William Law, 1993, documentary for "The Inside Track," CBC Radio, September 25.
3. William Law, 1994, documentary for "Sports America," BBC Radio 5 Live, March 31. For a good

account of Keene's wheeling and dealing, see Smith (1993).
4. *New Scientist*, September 11, 1993.
5. *The Guardian*, January 20, 1994.
6. *The Guardian*, January 4, 1994.
7. *The Observer*, May 1, 1994.
8. *The Times*, April 5, 1994.
9. *Marketing*, May 18, 1992.
10. *The Independent*, January 22, 1994.
11. BBC Radio 4, February 2, 1994.
12. The Guardian, January 12, 1994.
13. Ibid.
14. *The Daily Mirror*, January 18, 1994.
15. William Law, 1993, documentary for "Sports America."
16. *Times*, September 7, 1993.
17. Ibid.

Chapter 18: Valerie Alia

1. Before 1982, for example, I wrote under the names Valerie Restivo, Valerie Graber and (in Vermont) Carla Dor.
2. Brian Brennan reminds me that the Toronto theatre community burned Nathan Cohen in effigy, then when he died (at only 47), hailed him "as the only real theatre critic Canada ever produced."

Chapter 19: Brian Brennan

1. The perception still exists in parts of Canada that actors can only survive if they moonlight as waiters or pizza deliverers. Being a critic, however, is now regarded as a legitimate full-time occupation.
2. One of the most prominent "cheerleaders" of this type was Herbert Whittaker, theatre critic of the *Montreal Gazette* from 1945 to 1949, and chief theatre critic of the Toronto *Globe and Mail* from 1949 to 1975. For an evaluation of Whittaker's "sports columnist" style, see Ronald Bryden's introduction to *Whittaker's Theatre*, 1985 (University Press).
3. Janet Malcolm discovered this the hard way, after accusing fellow journalists of betraying their subjects "without remorse," when she was hit with a $10 million libel suit for allegedly faking quotes and making maverick psychoanalyst Jeffrey Masson appear, in the words of documents filed with the U.S. Supreme Court, as "unscholarly, irresponsible, vain" and lacking honesty and integrity.
4. One notable exception to this was the case of the hapless critic Robert Brasillach, judicially executed at Montrogue, France, in 1945 for criticizing resistance actors such as Georges Mandel and expressing a virulent hatred of Jewish performers in his magazine *Je suis partout*.
5. "Code of Ethics of the Canadian Theatre Critics Association," circulated to all print media and broadcasting outlets in Canada in February 1991.
6. Ibid.

Bibliography

Compiled by Sophia Harris, Christopher Irwin, Nancy Mucklow and the Authors and Editors

Abel, Elie. 1981. *What's News: The Media in American Society*. San Francisco: Institute for Contemporary Studies.

Adam, G. Stuart. 1976. "The Journalistic Imagination." In G.S. Adam (ed.), *Journalism, Communication and the Law*. Scarborough, Ont.: Prentice-Hall, 3–22.

Adbusters (magazine), Vancouver.

Albens, R.R. 1993. "When Is News Not News?" *presstime*, April 1993, 52–55.

Alia, Valerie. 1995. *Nunavut: Where Names Never Die*. "Ideas," CBC Radio, February 13 and 20.

———. 1994. *Names, Numbers and Northern Policy: Inuit, Project Surname and the Politics of Identity*. Halifax: Fernwood.

———. 1992a. "Aboriginal People and Campaign Coverage in the North." In R. Milen (ed.), *Aboriginal Peoples and Electoral Reform in Canada*. Toronto: Dundurn, 105–46.

———. 1992b. "Northern News: Canada's Communication Cutbacks." In M. Dufour and F. Thérien (eds.), *Regard sur l'avenir/Looking to the Future*. Ste. Foy, P.Q.: Association Inuksiutiit Katimajiit: *Études/Inuit Studies* special issue, 37–45.

———. 1992c. "Seeing racism from the inside." *Globe and Mail*, March 24, A18.

———. 1992d. Conversation with Jim Butler. Whitehorse, Yukon.

———. 1991a. "Ethics in Journalism." *Westminster Affairs* 4 (2): 7–8.

———. 1991b. "The powwow is more than just a carnival of color." *London Free Press*, July 16, A7.

———. 1990a. "Aboriginal People and News Media in Canada." In P. Desbarats (ed.), *Encounter 91: Media and Development in the Post (Cold) War Era*. London, Ont.: Graduate School of Journalism.

———. 1990b. "Fact, Fiction or Fantasy: Journalism Ethics in Canada." Videotape. London, Ontario: Graduate School of Journalism, University of Western Ontario.

———. 1989. "Female conductor unequally reviewed." *Toronto Star*, January 18, editorial page.

———. "Media and Social Change: Notes on a Politics of Journalism." *Theaterwork* 1(4): 8–9.

——— and Bud White Eye. 1992. "Brief on First Nations Communications and Journalism." Ottawa: Royal Commission on Aboriginal Peoples, October 21.

———. 1980. "Out of the Mainstream: Dance and Dancers Outside the American Center." Unpublished manuscript.

Allman, T.D. 1993. "Serbia's Blood War," *Vanity Fair*, March: 114.

Altheide, David L. and R.P. Snow. 1979. *Media Logic*. Beverly Hills: Sage.

Altschull, J. Herbert. 1984. *Agents of Power*. N.Y.: Longman.

American Society of Professional Journalists. 1992. "Code of Ethics." 38.

Anderson, David and P. Benjaminson. 1976. *Investigative Reporting*. Bloomington: Indiana University Press.

Anderson, Walter Truett. 1990. *Reality Isn't What It Used to Be*. San Francisco: Harper & Row.

Anonymous. 1994. "Obit exaggerated." *Calgary Herald*, May 8.

———. 1993. "Posing as patient's son is an unfair reporter trick." *Editor & Publisher*, March 27, 10.

———. 1991. "Sweet memories." *Sports Illustrated* (Fall 1991): 38–46.

———. 1989. "Spy Tape Verdict: ABC Blew It." *Washington Journalism Review*, September, 15.

———. 1985. *Policy Manual*. Toronto: *The Toronto Star*.

———. 1985b. "AP employee fired for frivolous use of the wire." *Editor & Publisher*, October 5.
Arant, Morgan David Jr. 1991. "Press Identification of Victims of Sexual Assault." *Journalism Quarterly* 68(1/2): 238–52.
Argyris, Chris. 1974. *Behind the Front Page*. San Francisco: Jossey-Bass.
Arnold, Tom. 1990. "Gallery ethics debate continues." *Content* (Nov./Dec.): 24–25.
Aronof, Craig, ed. 1979. *Business and the Media*. Santa Monica: Goodyear.
Ashenburg, Katherine. 1993. "Paper Making." *Globe and Mail*, August 28.
Ashley, Lynda. 1988. "Ethics and marketing: An analysis; so what price glory now?" *Marketing* 93(41): 1–3.
———. 1986. "Ethics and Journalism: Discussion at the Banff conference." *Broadcaster* 45(8).
Audi, Robert. 1990. "The Function of the Press in a Free and Democratic Society." *Public Affairs Quarterly* 4(3): 203–15.
Austin, Edie. 1989. "Scrum 89: Integrity on the Travel Pages." *Bulletin*, Center for Investigative Journalism 39: 34.
Babb, Laura L. 1974. *Of the Press, By the Press, For the Press (and others, too)*. Washington: Washington Post.
Bagdikian, Ben. 1992. *The Media Monopoly*. Fourth edition. Boston: Beacon.
———. 1972. *The Effete Conspiracy and Other Crimes by the Press*. New York: Harper & Row.
———. 1971. *The Information Machines*. New York: Harper & Row.
Baldwin, Donald, ed. 1983. *The Adversary Press*. St. Petersburg: Modern Media Institute.
Balkan, Donna. 1984. "Podium: Journalists are also citizens." *Content* (Sept./Oct.).
Barron, Jerome. 1973. *Freedom of the Press for Whom?: The Rise of Access to Mass Media*. Bloomington: University of Indiana Press.
Bauer, Traci. 1991. "Privacy and the Press: When to Name Names." *Quill* 79(8): 21–23.
Bay, Christian. 1970. *The Structure of Freedom*. Stanford: Stanford University Press.
Bennett, W. Lance. 1988. *News: The Politics of Illusion*. Second edition. New York: Longman.
Bentley, Eric. 1956. *Shaw on Music*. Garden City, N.J.: Doubleday, Anchor.
Bernstein, Carl, and Bob Woodward. 1974. *All the President's Men*. New York: Simon & Schuster.
Black, Jay. 1992. "Taking the pulse of the nation's news media." *Quill* 80(9).
——— and R. Steele. 1991. "An ethics audit of the professoriate." *Journalism Educator* 46(3): 3–17.
Black, Patricia. 1993. "Writer Timothy Findley." *Scene*, March 25–April 7, 3.
Blanchard, Robert, ed. 1974. Congress and the News Media. New York: Hastings House.
Block, Herbert. 1952. The Herblock Book. Boston: Beacon Press.
Blumer, Herbert. 1969. Symbolic Interactionism: Perspective and Method. Englewood Cliffs, N.J.: Prentice-Hall.
Boisvert, Yves. 1990. "Conseil de presse: Un problème d'immunodéficience." *Le 30* 14(10): 9–10.
Bok, Sissela. 1983. *Secrets: On the Ethics of Concealment and Revelation*. New York: Pantheon.
———. 1978. *Lying: Moral Choices in Public and Private Life*. New York: Pantheon.
Boorstin, Daniel J. 1980. *The Image: A Guide to Pseudo-Events in America*. New York: Atheneum.
Booth, John E. 1990. "A Universe of Anxiety." *Gannett Center Journal* (Winter): 42.
Boston Globe. *Paul Szep [cartoons]*.
Boudreau, Philippe. 1990. "Ottawa Press Gallery." *Le 30* 14(7): 10.
Boyce, William and L. Jensen. 1978. *Moral Reasoning*. Lincoln: University of Nebraska Press.
Boyd, William. 1992. Presentation to a media ethics examiner, Poynter Institute, St. Petersburg, Florida.
Braman, S. 1988. "Public Expectations of Media." *Journalism Quarterly* 65(1): 71–84.
Braun, P. 1988. "Deception in Journalism." *Journal of Mass Media Ethics* 3(1): 77–83.
Breger, Dave. 1966. *How to Draw and Sell Cartoons*. New York: G.P. Putnam's Sons.
Brenner, Steven N. and Earl A. Molander. 1977. "Is the Ethics of Business Changing?" *Harvard Business Review* 55: 62.
Brustein, Robert. 1992. "Critics and the Arts." *Nieman Reports*, Fall. Cambridge, Mass.

Bukro, Casey. 1985. "The SPJ code's double-edged sword: Accountability, credibility." *Journal of Mass Media Ethics* 1(1): 10–13.
Bulletin of the American Society of Newspaper Editors (ASNE).
Byrnes, Gene. 1953. *The Complete Guide to Cartooning*. New York: Grosset & Dunlap.
Cahn, Edmond. 1956. *The Moral Decision*. Bloomington: Indiana University Press.
Cameron, Stevie. 1995. "A troublesome deal: Concern is growing about a CBC partnership." *Maclean's* 108(9): 64.
———. 1993. Presentation to "Ethics in Journalism Class" (V. Alia, professor), University of Western Ontario, Graduate School of Journalism, London, Ontario.
Campbell, Robert M. and Leslie A. Pal. 1994. *The Real World of Canadian Politics: Cases in Process and Policy*. Third edition. Peterborough: Broadview Press.
Canada. 1991a. Broadcasting Act. June 4.
———. 1991b. Royal Commission on Electoral Reform and Party Financing (RCERPF). *Reforming Electoral Democracy*. Ottawa: Supply and Services.
———. 1986. *Report of the Task Force on Broadcasting Policy* (Caplan-Sauvageau Report). Ottawa: Supply and Services.
———. 1981. Royal [Kent] Commission on Newspapers. Report. Ottawa: Supply and Services.
———. 1968. Broadcasting Act. March 7, 16 & 17 Eliz. 2, c. 25.
Canadian Broadcasting Corporation. 1993. *Journalistic Standards and Practices*. Toronto: CBC.
———. 1992. "Eva the Evergreen Lady." January 30. Montreal: CBC.
———. 1982. *Journalistic Policy*. Toronto: CBC.
Canadian Multiculturalism Council. 1988. *Reflections from the Electronic Mirror: Report on the National Forum of Multiculturalism in Broadcasting/Les Médias électroniques, Miroir de la Société? Rapport du forum national sur le multiculturalisme et la radiodiffusion*. Toronto: May 13, 14.
Canadian Press. 1994. "Native health, conditions intolerable: CMA." *Brantford Expositor*. Week of August 13.
———. 1993. "Indians favored, angry fishermen say." *Toronto Star*. March.
Canadian Radio-Television and Telecommunications Commission (CRTC). 1992. *Policies for Community and Campus Radio*. Public notice 1992–38, May 29.
———. 1990. *Native Broadcasting Policy*. Public notice 1990–89. Ottawa.
———. 1986. *Regulations Respecting Radio Broadcasting*. Ottawa.
———. 1985. *A Broadcasting Policy Reflecting Canada's Linguistic and Cultural Diversity*. Public notice 1985–139. Ottawa, July 4.
———. 1983. *The Northern Broadcasting Policy*. News Release, March 10.
Canadian Theatre Critics Association. 1991. "Code of Ethics of the Canadian Theatre Critics Association."
Cannon, Lou. 1977. *Inside Reporting*. Sacramento, Ca.: California Journal Press.
Caplan, Gerald, Michael Kirby and Hugh Segal. 1989. *Election: The Issues, the Strategies, the Aftermath*. Scarborough: Prentice-Hall Canada.
Case, T. 1992. "In Disguise." *Editor & Publisher* 14(November): 14.
Chancellor, John and W. Mears. 1983. *The News Business*. New York: Harper & Row.
Charron, Jean. 1991. "Relations between political parties and the media in Quebec election campaigns." In Frederick J. Fletcher (ed.), *Reporting the Campaign: Election Coverage in Canada*. Toronto: Dundurn.
Chávez, Ramón. 1995. "Ethnic Stereotypes: The Mexican Americans." In P. Lester (ed.), *Images that Injure: Pictorial Stereotypes in the Media*. New York: Greenwood.
Chittick, William. 1970. *State Department, Press and Press Groups*. New York: Wiley-Interscience.
Christians, Clifford, J. Ferré and P. M. Fackler. 1993. *Good News: Social Ethics and The Press*. New York: Oxford.

———. 1985. "Enforcing Media Codes." *Journal of Mass Media Ethics* 1(1): 4–24.

———, K. Rotzoll and M. Fackler. 1983. *Media Ethics, Cases and Moral Reasoning*. New York: Longman.

Cirino, Robert. 1974. *Power to Persuade: Mass Media and the News*. New York: Bantam.

Cleghorn, Reese. 1992. "Bimbonic Plagues and ethics: What next?" *Washington Journalism Review* 14(2): 4.

Clifford, James. 1987. "On Ethnographic Authority." *Representations* 1(2): 118.

Cohen, Jeff and Norman Solomon. 1995. *Through the Media Looking Glass*. Monroe, Me: Common Courage Press.

Cohen, Stanley and Jock Young, eds. 1973. *The Manufacture of News: A Reader*. Beverly Hills: Sage.

Cohn, Martin. 1989. "Press Conference Payoffs a Fact of Life in Jakarta." *Bulletin, Centre for Investigative Journalism* 39(fall): 21–22.

Coles, Robert. 1989. *The Call of Stories: Teaching and the Moral Imagination*. Boston: Houghton Mifflin.

Collins, Randall. 1985. *Three Sociological Traditions*. New York: Oxford University Press.

Columbia Journalism Review, Columbia University, New York.

Comber, Mary Anne and Robert S. Mayne. 1986. *The Newsmongers: How the Media Distort the Political News*. Toronto: McClelland and Stewart.

Commission on Freedom of the Press (Hutchins Commission). 1947. *A Free and Responsible Press*. Chicago: University of Chicago Press.

Connell, Ian. 1980. "Television News and the Social Contract." In Stuart Hall, D. Hobson, A. Lowe and P. Willis (eds.), *Culture, Media, Language: Working Papers in Cultural Studies, 1972–79*. London: Hutchison, 138–56.

Cook, Peter G. and Myles A. Ruggles. 1992. "Balance and Freedom of Speech: Challenge for Canadian Broadcasting." *Canadian Journal of Communication* 17(1): 37–59.

Cooper, Thomas W. 1992. "Review Essay: Lorraine Code's *Epistemic Responsibility*, Journalism, and the Charles Stuart Case". *Business and Professional Ethics Journal* 12(3).

Coulson, Sandra. 1993. *London Free Press*, November.

Cox, Kevin. 1990. "Asleep at the Wheel: For years, media turned blind eye to Mount Cashel." *Content* (Sept./Oct.): 20–21.

Crawford, Nelson. 1924. *The Ethics of Journalism*. New York: Alfred A. Knopf.

Crean, Susan. 1985. *Newsworthy: The Lives of Media Women*. Toronto: Stoddart.

Creswell, Deme. 1985. "Dead mouse in the dog biscuits stuns shopper." *Edmonton Journal*, September 10.

Crouse, Timothy. 1972. *The Boys on the Bus*. New York: Ballantine.

Crown, John A. 1979. "Manufacturing Newspapers." In Craig E. Aronoff (ed.), *Business and the Media*. Santa Monica, Ca. Goodyear, 227–36.

Cumming, Carman. 1988. "Ethics: No easy answers." *Content* (May/June).

Curran, James. 1991. "Mass Media and Democracy: A Reappraisal." In James Curran and Michael Gurevitch (eds.), *Mass Media and Society*. London: Edward Arnold, 82–117.

Curry, Don. 1995. *Fact or Fantasy? Diversity and Employment Equity Handbook for Journalism Schools*. North Bay, Ont.: Canadian Centre for Social Justice.

———. 1995. *Using the Newspaper as an Anti-racism Resource*. North Bay, Ont.: Canadian Centre for Social Justice.

Daley, Patrick and Dan O'Neill. 1991. "Sad is too mild a word: press coverage of the Exxon Valdez oil spill." *Journal of Communication* 41(4): 42.

Dalla Costa, John. 1990. "Reflections on the power of advertising" (Montreal Massacre). *Marketing* 95(12): 4.

Demers, François. 1989. "Journalistic ethics: The rise of the 'good employee's model'—a threat for professionalism?" *Canadian Journal of Communication* 14 (2): 15–27.

Dempson, Peter. 1968. *Assignment Ottawa: Seventeen Years in the Press Gallery*. Toronto: General Publishing.

Deneen, Sally. 1992. "A prostitute's clients: Fair Game?" *Washington Journalism Review* 14(1): 13–14.

Dennis, Everette and William Rivers. 1974. *Other Voices: The New Journalism in America*. San Francisco: Canfield Press.

Desbarats, Peter. 1990. *Guide to Canadian News Media*. Toronto: Harcourt Brace Jovanovich.

Dexter, Lewis A. 1970. *Elite and Specialized Interviewing*. Evanston, Ill.: Northwestern University Press.

Diamond, Edwin. 1982. *Sign Off: the Last Days of Television*. Cambridge, Mass.: MIT Press.

———. 1975. *The Tin Kazoo: Television, Politics, and the News*. Cambridge, Mass.: MIT Press.

Didion, Joan. 1968. *Slouching Towards Bethlehem*. New York: Dell.

Doan, Daniel. 1993. Telephone interview with Dan David. August 28.

Dobson, Cathy. 1993. "Natives say they're being 'set up' over helicopter shooting." Sarnia *Observer*, August 26, 1.

Dominick, J. 1987. *The Dynamics of Mass Communication*. New York: Random House.

Donato, Andy. 1993. *The Neverending Tory*. Toronto: Key Porter.

Donsbach, Wilfgang and Bettina Klett. 1993. "Subjective objectivity: How journalists in four countries define a key term of their profession." *Gazette* 51(1): 53–83.

Dorman, William A. and Mansour Farhang. 1987. *The U.S. Press and Iran: Foreign Policy and the Journalism of Deference*. Berkeley: University of California Press.

Downie, Leonard. 1976. *The New Muckrakers*. Washington, D.C.: New Republic.

Dunn, Delmer D. 1969. *Public Officials and the Press*. Reading, Mass.: Addison-Wesley.

Dussault, Jean. 1987. "Presse Financière: scepticisme face à un code d'éthique." *Le 30* 11(5).

Edelman, Murray. 1988. *Constructing the Political Spectacle*. Chicago: University of Chicago Press.

Editor & Publisher.

Elliott, Deni. 1991. "Moral Development Theories . . . Teaching Ethics." *Journalism Educator* 46(3): 18–24.

———. 1990. "The Problem Is the Writing." *FineLine* 1(10): 8.

Epstein, Edward J. 1975. *Between Fact and Fiction: The Problem of Journalism*. New York: Vintage Books.

———. 1973. *News from Nowhere*. New York: Random House.

Ericson, Richard V., Patricia M. Baranek and Janet B.L. Chan. 1991. *Representing Order: Crime, Law and Justice in the News Media*. Toronto: University of Toronto Press.

———. 1989. *Negotiating Control: A Study of News Sources*. Toronto: University of Toronto Press.

———. 1987. *Visualizing Deviance: A Study of News Organizations*. Toronto: University of Toronto Press.

Esar, Evan. 1968. *20,000 Quips & Quotes*. New York: Doubleday.

Evans, M. 1989. "An open question: 'Emphatically accurate photos.'" *News Photographer* (November): 26–28.

Fallaci, Oriana. 1976. (Translated by J. Shepley.) *Interview with History*. Boston: Houghton Mifflin.

Ferré, John P. 1989. "Contemporary Approaches to Journalistic Ethics." In Anthony Serafini (ed.), *Ethics and Social Concern*. New York: Paragon, 488–95.

FineLine. 1990–91. Louisville, Kentucky.

Fisher, Paul L. and Ralph Lowenstein, eds. 1967. *Race and the News Media*. New York: Anti-Defamation League of B'nai B'rith.

Fishman, Mark. 1980. *Manufacturing the News*. London and Austin: University of Texas Press.

Fletcher, Frederick J. 1994a. "Media, Elections and Democracy." *Canadian Journal of Communication* 19: 131–50.

———. 1994b. Interview of Elly Alboim. Ottawa, July 11.

——— and Robert Everett. 1991a. "The Mass Media and Elections in Canada: An Overview." In Frederick J. Fletcher (ed.), *Media, Elections and Democracy*. Ottawa: Dundurn.

——— and Robert Everett. 1991b. "Television and the 1988 Campaign: Did It Make a Difference?" In Paul W. Fox and Graham White (eds.), *Politics: Canada*. Seventh edition. Toronto: McGraw-Hill Ryerson.

———. 1987. "Mass Media and Parliamentary Elections in Canada." *Legislative Studies Quarterly* 12: 341–72.

———. 1981. "Playing the Game: The Mass Media and the 1979 Campaign." In Howard R. Penniman (ed.), *Canada at the Polls, 1979 and 1980: A Study of the General Elections*. Washington, D.C.: American Enterprise Institute for Public Policy Research.

———. 1975. "The Mass Media in the 1974 Canadian Election." In Howard R. Penniman (ed.), *Canada at the Polls: The General Election of 1974*. Washington, D.C.: AEI.

Flint, Leon N. 1925. *The Conscience of the Newspaper*. New York: D. Appleton & Co.

Friedan, Betty. 1960. *The Feminine Mystique*. New York: Dell.

Friendly, Fred W. 1967. *Due to Circumstances Beyond Our Control*. New York: Random House.

Friesen, D. 1993. "Don't Read This Story." *This Magazine* (June/July): 9–10.

Frizzel, Alan and Anthony Westell. 1989. "The Media and the Campaign." In Alan Frizzel, Jon H. Pammett and Anthony Westell (eds.), *The Canadian General Election of 1988*.

Fulford, Robert. 1994. "Journalism ethics often mean just saying no." *Globe and Mail*, June 22.

———. 1988. *Best Seat in the House*. Toronto: Collins.

Funnell, Catherine. 1991. "Maning names." Letter to the editor. *Maclean's*, May 20.

Gagnon, Martha. 1989. "Devoiler l'identité d'un suspect?" *Le 30* 13(4): 10–11.

Gans, Herbert J. 1980. *Deciding What's News*. New York: Vintage.

Garfinkel, Harold. 19647. *Studies in Ethnomethadology*. Englewood Cliffs, NC: Prentice-Hall.

Garnham, Nicholas. 1990. *Capitalism and Communication: Global Culture and the Economics of Information*. London: Sage.

Garneau, George. 1991. "Ethics debate reprised: junket journalism charges again raised as journalists are offered free visit to Disney bash." *Editor & Publisher* 124(42): 14–15.

———. 1986. "Ethics or simply bad journalism: bias in the Canadian media." *Media Magazine* 5(3).

Gauthier, Gilles. 1993. "In defence of a supposedly outdated notion: The range of application in journalistic objectivity." *Canadian Journal of Communication* 18(4).

———. 1991. "La mise en cause de l'objectivité journalistique." *Communication Information* 12(2): 86–15.

———. 1990. "L'éthique de la Communication Publique: Une approche analytique." *Communication Information* 11(2): 121–52.

Gerald, J. Edward. 1963. *The Social Responsibility of the Press*. Minneapolis: University of Minnesota Press.

Gerbner, George and Nancy Signorielli. 1978. "The world of television news." In William Adams and Fay Schreibman (eds.), *Television Network News: Issues in Content Research*. Washington, D.C.: School of Public and International Affairs, George Washington University, 189–96.

Gersh, Debra. 1991. "Doctors, Patients and the Press: How much information on VIPS should be made public?" *Editor & Publisher* 124(3): 14–15.

———. 1991. "No-name justice is just not good enough." *Marketing* 95(37): 2–74.

Gert, B. 1988. *Morality: A New Justification for the Moral Rules*. Oxford University Press.

Ghiglione, Loren, ed. 1973. *Evaluating the Press: The New England Daily Newspaper Survey*. Southbridge, Mass.: Loren F. Ghiglione.

Gilsdorf, William O. and Robert Bernier. 1991. "Journalistic Practice in Covering Federal Election Campaigns in Canada." In Frederick J. Fletcher (ed.), *Reporting the Campaign: Election Coverage in Canada*. Toronto: Dundurn.

———. 1987. Interview with Carol Goar. Ottawa, July 28.

———. 1981. "Getting the message across: Media strategies and political campaigns." In Liora Salter (ed.), *Communication Studies in Canada*. Toronto: Butterworths, 52–67.
Gitlin, Todd. 1980. *The Whole World is Watching*. Berkeley: University of California Press.
Gladney, George A. 1991. "Technologizing of the World: . . . Ethical Understanding." *Journal of Mass Media Ethics* 6(2): 93–105.
Glasser, T.L. 1985. "On the Morality of Taped Interviews." *Nieman Reports* (spring): 17–20.
Glessing, Robert. 1970. *The Underground Press in America*. Bloomington: Indiana University Press.
Glover, Jonathan. 1977. *Causing Death and Saving Lives*. New York: Penguin.
Goffman, Erving. 1959. *The Presentation of Self in Everyday Life*. Garden City, N.Y.: Anchor.
Golding, Peter and Philip Elliott. 1979. *Making the News*. London: Longman.
Goodwin, H. Eugene. 1983. *Groping for Ethics in Journalism*. Ames: Iowa State University Press.
Gordon, David. 1979. "Chicago journalists and ethical principles." *Mass Communications Review* 6.
Graber, Doris. 1980. "Mass Media and Modern Politics." Congressional Quarterly. Washington, D.C.
Graham, Barbara Florio. 1988. "Ethical traps for the freelancer, Part 1." *Content* (March/April).
Greenfield, Jeff. 1982. *The Real Campaign: The Media and the Battle for the White House*. New York: Summit Books.
Griffin, Robert J., D. Molen, C. Schoenfeld and J. Scotton. 1991. *Interpreting Public Issues*. Ames: Iowa State University Press.
Griffith, Thomas. 1974. *How True: A Skeptic's Guide to Believing the News*. Boston: Atlantic-Little, Brown.
Grindal, B.T. and R. Rhodes. (date lost). "Journalism and Anthropology Share Several Similarities," *Journalism Educator* 41(19): 11–13.
Guay, Jacques. 1990a. "Conseil de Presse: Les prêtres ont droit a leur vie privée. Le 30 14(3): 16.
———. 1990b. "Conseil de Presse: Qu'enseigne la jurisprudence?" Le 30 14(2): 6–17.
———. 1988. "Conseil de Presse: Les journalistes ne sont pas des devins." Le 30 12(8): 21.
Hackett, Robert A. 1991. *News and Dissent: The Press and the Politics of Peace in Canada*. Norwood, N.J.: Ablex.
———. 1984. "Decline of a paradigm? Bias and objectivity in news media studies." *Critical Studies in Mass Media Communication* 1(3): 229–59.
———. 1983. "The depiction of labour and business on national television news." *Canadian Journal of Communication* 10(1): 5–50.
———, William O. Gilsdorf and Philip Savage. 1992. "New balance rhetoric: The Fraser Institute's political appropriation of content analysis." *Canadian Journal of Communication* 17(1): 15–36.
Hall, Edward T. 1991. *The Silent Language*. New York: Anchor.
———. 1983. *The Dance of Life: The Other Dimension of Time*. New York: Doubleday.
———. 1966. *The Hidden Dimension*. New York: Doubleday.
Hall, Stuart, C. Critcher, T. Jefferson, J. Clarke and B. Roberts. 1978. *Policing the Crisis: Mugging, the State, and Law and Order*. London: Macmillan.
Hallin, Daniel C. 1992. "The passing of the 'high modernism' of American journalism." *Journal of Communication* 42(3): 14–25.
———. 1986. *The Uncensored War: The Media and Vietnam*. Berkeley: University of California Press.
Hammill, J. 1993. "The *Star* Set the Trap, then Stepped in It." *Ryerson Review of Journalism* (spring): 20–23.
Hanno, Hardt. 1979. *Social Theories of the Press*. Beverly Hills and London: Sage.
Harris, M. 1990. *Unholy Orders*. Toronto: Penguin.
Harrison, John and Harry Stein. 1973. *Muckraking: Past, Present, and Future*. University Park: Pennsylvania State University Press.
Hartley, John. 1980. *Understanding News*. London: Methuen.
Hartford Courant. 1973. November 12, 6–7.
Hartman, Barrie. 1987. "Does Your Newspaper Have a Code of Ethics?" ASNE *Bulletin* (December).

Hartz, Louis. 1955. *The Liberal Tradition in America*. New York: Harcourt Brace.
Haselden, Kyle. 1968. *Morality and the Mass Media*. Nashville: Broadman Press.
Hayes, D. 1992. *Power and Influence*. Toronto: Key Porter.
Hernandez, Debra Gersh. 1995. "J-school faculties get F in diversity." *Editor & Publisher*, September 9, 17, 37.
Hersch, Seymour. 1992. "Nixon's Last Cover-up: The Tapes He Wants No Archives to Suppress," *The New Yorker*, December 14: 82–84.
Hertsgaard, Mark. 1989. *On Bended Knee: The Press and the Reagan Presidency*. New York: Schocken.
Hillerman, Tony. 1971. *The Fly on the Wall*. New York: Harper.
Hocking, William. 1947. *Freedom of the Press*. Chicago: University of Chicago Press.
Hodges, Louis, ed. 1978. *Social Responsibility: Journalism, Law, Medicine*. Lexington, Va.: Washington and Lee University.
Hoffmaster, Barry. 1992. "Can Ethnography Save the Life of Medical Ethics?" *Journal of Social Science and Medicine* 35(12): 14–25.
Hoggart, Richard. 1972. *On Culture and Communication*. Cambridge: Oxford University Press.
Hohenberg, John. 1983. *The Professional Journalist*. New York: Holt, Rinehart and Winston.
———. 1974. *The Pulitzer Prizes*. New York: Columbia University Press.
Howard, Frank. 1990a. "Gallery urged to clean up." *Ottawa Citizen*, June 15, A4.
———. 1990b. "Ethics probe on back burner because of Meech crisis." *Ottawa Citizen*, June 8, A6.
———. 1990c. "Letter writer hits back." *Ottawa Citizen*, April 20, A4.
———. 1990d. "Old Tories graduate to ranks of lobbyists." *Ottawa Citizen*, April 19, A4.
———. 1990e. "Press divided over what are unethical acts." *Ottawa Citizen*, April 16.
———. 1990f. "Newsmen worked for government." *Ottawa Citizen*, April 12, A4.
Hughes, Mike. 1992. "Ethics: déjà vu all over again? Plagiarism persists..." ASNE bulletin 783: 14–18.
Hulteng, John. 1985. *The Messenger's Motives: Ethical Problems of the News Media*. Second edition. Englewood Cliffs, N.J.: Prentice-Hall.
———. 1981. *Playing it Straight: A Practical Discussion of the Ethical Principles of the American Society of Newspaper Editors*. Chester, Conn.: American Society of Newspaper Editors, Globe Pequot Press, 29–31.
——— and R. Nelson. 1971. *The Fourth Estate*. New York: Harper & Row.
Hynds, Ernest C. 1980. *American Newspapers in the 1980s*. New York: Hastings House.
Innis, Harold A. 1951. *The Bias of Communication*. Toronto: University of Toronto Press.
Jameson, Frederic. 1981. *The Political Unconscious: Narrative as a Socially Symbolic Act*. Ithaca, N.Y.: Cornell University Press.
Jensen, Carl. 1993. *Censored: The News That Didn't Make the News—and Why*. Chapel Hill: Shelburne Press.
Johnson, J.T. 1994. "The private I, you, they." Special Issue: Privacy II, *Journal of Mass Media Ethics* 9(4): 223.
Johnson, William. 1993. "Hatchet on Campbell profile shows media at its worst." *Vancouver Sun*, May 19, A4.
Johnston, D. 1984. "The Wrong Stuff." *Washington Journalism Review* (June): 24–28.
Johnstone, John, E. Slawski and W. Bowman. 1976. *The News People*. Urbana: University of Illinois Press.
Journal of Mass Media Ethics.
Journalism Educator.
Journalism History.
Journalism Quarterly.
Journalism Studies Review.
Kauffmann, Stanley. 19482. "Letter to an Actor." *TheatreCommunications* (March): 22–24.
Keifer, Theresa. 1994a. Interview with Martin Mittelstaedt. Toronto, June 7.

———. 1994b. Interview with Pamela Wallin. Toronto, June 22.

———. 1994c. Interview with John Dawe. Toronto, July 7.

Kenney, K. 1991. "Ethical Attitudes." News Photographer, November 12–14.

Kent, Chris. 1991. "Most of Press Declines to "out" DOD Officials." *Washington Journalism Review* 13(8): 13–14.

Kinard, J. D., Spencer, D. Elliott et al. 1991. "Cases and commentaries: Confidentiality and promise keeping." *Journal of Mass Media Ethics* 6(4): 245–56.

Klein, Herbert. 1980. *Making It Perfectly Clear*. New York: Doubleday.

Kramarae, Cheris. 1988. *Technology and Women's Voices*. New York: Routledge and Kegan Paul.

——— and Jana Kramer. 1995. "Net gains, Net losses." *Women's Review of Books* 12(5): 33–5.

Kramer, Satci D. 1991. "Alternatives to an enforceable code of ethics and news council." *Quill* 79(9): 20.

Krieghbaum, Hillier. 972. *Pressures on the Press*. New York: Crowell.

Krishna, S. 193. "No experience necessary." *Ryerson Review of Journalism* (spring): 5–6.

Kruuse, Helle Nissen. 1991. *Etik i Journalistik*. Århus, Denmark: Forlaget Ajour.

Lacroix, Liliane. 1992. "Guy Bourgeault, Conseil de Press: L'ethique ne se limite pas." *Le 30* 16(1): 10–11.

Ladd, John, ed. 1973. *Ethical Relativism*. Ca.: Wadsworth.

Lambeth, Edmund B. 1986. *Committed Journalism*. Bloomington: Indiana University Press.

Lasch, Christopher. 1979. *The Culture of Narcissism*. New York: W.W. Norton.

Law, William. 1993a. Interview with Raymond Snoddy. September 21.

———. 1993b. Interview with Jennifer McGuire. October 13.

———. 1993c. Interview with Stephen Brunt. October 14.

———. 1993d. Interview with Steve Dryden. October 14.

Leclerc, Jean-Claude. 1991. "Éthique journalistique et crise constitutionelle." *Le 30* 15(5): 11.

Lee, Martin A. and N. Solomon. 1991. *Unreliable Sources: A Guide to Detecting Bias in News Media*. New York: Lyle Stuart.

Lees, N. 1985. "Riel rebellion changed the West." *Edmonton Journal*, winter.

LeRoy, David and C. Sterling. 1973. *Mass News: Practices, Controversies, and Alternatives*. Englewood Cliffs, N.J.: Prentice-Hall.

Lester, Paul. 1991. *Photojournalism: An Ethical Approach*. Hillsdale, N.J.: Lawrence Erlbaum.

Levine, Allan. 1993. *Scrum Wars: The Prime Ministers and the Media*. Toronto: Dundurn.

Levy, H. 1993. "The ethics of sleuthing for information." *CIJ Bulletin* (March/April): 16–17.

Leyne, Les. 1990. "Media Ethics: The Complicated Case of Bud Smith." *Bulletin, Canadian Association of Journalists* 41: 17–18.

Lichona, T., ed. 1976. *Moral Development and Behavior: Theory, Research, and Social Issues*. New York: Holt, Rinehart & Winston.

Lichtenberg, Judith. 1991. "In defense of objectivity." In James Curren and Michael Gurevitch (eds.), *Mass Media and Society*. London: Edward Arnold.

———. 1990. "Introduction." In Judith Lichtenberg (ed.), *Democracy and the Mass Media: A Collection of Essays*. Cambridge: Cambridge University Press.

Liebling, A.J. 1964. *The Press*. New York: Ballantine.

Lind, Loren. 1990. "The Death of Objectivity." *Globe and Mail*, March 3, C18.

Lindstrom, Carl. 1960. *The Fading American Newspaper*. Garden City, N.Y.: Doubleday.

Linn, Travis. 1991. "Staging in TV News." *Journal of Mass Media Ethics* 6(1): 47–54.

Lippmann, Walter. 1965. *Public Opinion*. New York: Macmillan.

———. 1929. *A Preface to Morals*. New York: Macmillan.

Littler, William. 1989. "Conductor knows her business." *Toronto Star*, December 14, C6.

Lloyd, Scott. 1991. "A criticism of social responsibility theory: An ethical perspective." *Journal of Mass Media Ethics* 6(4): 199–209.

Lont, Cynthia M. 1995. *Women and Media: Content/Careers/Criticism.* Belmont, Ca.: Wadsworth.
Lovell, Terry. 1983. *Pictures of Reality: Aesthetics, Politics and Pleasure.* London: British Film Institute.
Low, David. 1957. *Low's Autobiography.* New York: Simon & Schuster.
Lowi, Theodore. 1969. *The End of Liberalism.* New York: W.W. Norton.
Luedtke, Kurt. 1981. *Absence of Malice.* New York: Ballantine. Film: Columbia Pictures, produced and directed by Sydney Pollack.
Lurie, Ranan. 1975. *Pardon Me, Mr. President.* New York: Quadrangle.
Lyons, Louis, ed. 1965. *Reporting the News.* Cambridge: Harvard University Press.
Macdougall, A. Kent, ed. 1972. *The Press.* Princeton: Dow Jones.
MacDougall, Curtis. 1977. *Interpretative Reporting.* New York: Macmillan.
———. 1971. *News Pictures Fit to Print . . . Or Are They?* Stillwater, Okla.: Journalistic Services.
———. 1940. *Hoaxes.* New York: Macmillan.
MacNelly, Jeff. 1972. *MacNelly, the Pulitzer Prize Winning Cartoonist.* Richmond: Westover.
Malcolm, Janet. 1990. *The Journalist and the Murderer.* New York: Vintage.
Martin, Edwin. 1991. "On Photographic Manipulation." *Journal of Mass Media Ethics* 6(3): 156–63.
Marowitz, Charles. 1973. *Confessions of Counterfeit Critic.* London: Eyre Methuen.
Mass Communications Review.
Massecar, Bob. 1993. "Thief picked wrong car." *London Free Press,* April, B3.
Matheson, George. 1993. "Police seeking evidence after helicopter hit." Sarnia *Observer,* August 25, 1.
Matthews, E.C. 1920. *How to Draw Funny Pictures.* Frederick J. Drake & Co.
McClaren, Steve. 1989. "Broadcasters set up own press council." *Content* (July/August): 14–15.
McCormick, Chris. 1995. *Constructing Danger: The mis/representation of crime in the news.* Halifax: Fernwood.
McCulloch, Frank, ed. 1984. *Drawing the Line.* Washington, D.C.: American Society of Newspaper Editors.
McGillivray, Don. 1990. The Impossibility of a Media Ethics Code. *Bulletin, Canadian Association of Journalists,* no. 41: 29–30.
McGinnis, Joe. 1969. *The Selling of the President, 1968.* New York: Trident Press.
McGrath, K. and C. Gaziano. 1986. "Dimensions of Media Credibility: Highlights of the 1985 ASNE Survey." *Newspaper Research Journal* 7(2): 55–67.
McIntosh, Andrew. 1989. "The Case of Ken Adachi (suicide over book critic plagiarism)." *Bulletin, Center for Investigative Journalism,* no. 38: 5–6.
McLuhan, Marshall. 1964. *Understanding Media: The Extensions of Man.* New York: McGraw-Hill.
McQuail, Denis. 1992. *Media Performance: Mass Communication and the Public Interest.* London: Sage.
Meade, Marion. 1988. *Dorothy Parker: What Fresh Hell Is This?* London: Heineman, 44–45.
Media Ethics (magazine/journal). Two issues a year. Department of Mass Communication, Emerson College, 100 Beacon Street, Boston, MA 02116.
Medina, A. 1988. "Fuddy Duddy Journalism." The James M. Minitie Lecture, University of Regina, March 7.
Mencher, Melvin. 1981. *News Reporting and Writing.* Dubuque, Ia.: William C. Brown.
Merrill, John C. 1984. *Existential Journalism.* New York: Hastings House.
———. 1981–82. "A semantic analysis of the SPJ, SDX code of ethics." *Mass Communications Review* (winter).
———. 1974. *The Imperative of Freedom: A Philosophy of Journalistic Autonomy.* New York: Hastings House.
——— and Ralph Barney, eds. 1975. *Ethics and the Press: Readings in Mass Media Morality.* New York: Hastings House.

——— and S. Jack Odell. 1983. *Philosophy and Journalism*. New York: Longman.
Metzler, Ken. 1977. *Creative Interviewing*. Englewood Cliffs, N.J.: Prentice-Hall.
Meyer, Philip. 1987. *Ethical Journalism*. New York: Longman.
———. 1983. *Editors, Publishers and Newspaper Ethics*. Washington, D.C.: American Society of Newspaper Editors.
———. 1973. *Precision Journalism*. Bloomington: Indiana University Press.
Mignault, Pierre. 1994a. Interview with Jean-Michel Leprince, Radio-Canada correspondent, Washington, D.C.
———. 1994b. Interview with Neil MacDonald, CBC journalist, "Prime Time News." Montreal.
———. 1994c. Interview with Normand Rhéaume, TVA parliamentary correspondent, Ottawa. September 30.
Miliband, Ralph. 1973. *The State in Capitalist Society*. London: Quartet Books.
Miller, J. 1990. "Rethinking Old Methods." *Content* (Sept./Oct.): 23–25.
Mills, Rilla Dean. 1982. "Newspaper Journalists' Perceptions of Ethical Decisions." Paper presented to the Association for Education in Journalism, Athens, Ohio. Cited in Robert J. Griffin, D. Molen, C. Schoenfeld and J. Scotton, *Interpreting Public Issues*. Ames: Iowa State University Press.
Miraldi, Robert. 1990. *Muckraking and Objectivity: Journalism's Colliding Traditions*. New York: Greenwood.
Molander, Earl A. 1987. "A paradigm for design, promulgation and enforcement of ethical codes." *Journal of Business Ethics* 6.
Mollenhoff, Clark. 1981. *Investigative Reporting*. New York: Macmillan.
———. 1976. *Game Plan for Disaster*. New York: W.W. Norton.
Morgan, C., ed. 1989. *Editorial Department Policy Manual. Windsor Star*, Windsor, Ont.
Morgan, Michael, Justin Lewis and Sut Jhally. 1992. "More viewing, less knowledge." In Hamid Mowlana, George Gerbner and Herbert Schiller (eds.), *Triumph of the Image: The Media's War in the Persian Gulf—A Global Perspective*. Boulder: Westview Press, 216–33.
Morissette, Rodolphe. 1986. Éthique du journalisme au-delà des codes. *Le 30* 10(4), April.
———. 1985. "Nommer ou ne pas Nommer?" *Le 30* 9(10), December.
Mosher, Terry. 1975. "The Hecklers" (film). Directed by Ian McLaren. Ottawa: National Film Board of Canada.
Muggeridge, Malcolm. nd. *Chronicles of Wasted Time*, Volume 2.
Nash, Knowlton. 1988. "This Imperfect Necessity." *Content* (January/February).
Nathan, George Jean. 1928. "The Question of Reviewing." *American Mercury* 15(58), October.
Natt, Ted M. 1991. "Ethics: red light ethics vs. green light ethics." *ASNE Bulletin*, no. 731(April): 14–15.
Nelson, Joyce. 1989. *Sultans of Sleaze: Public Relations and the Media*. Toronto: Between the Lines.
———. 1988. *The Colonized Eye: Rethinking the Grierson Legend*. Toronto: Between the Lines.
Nelson, Roy Paul. 1975. *Cartooning*. Don Mills: Fitzhenry & Whiteside.
Nesbitt, Kiri. 1994. "Abortion and karma: A Japanese perspective." *Globe and Mail*, January 25, A22.
Obe, Don. 1982. "Media: Not for Publication." *Toronto Life*, July.
O'Brien, David M. 1981. *The Public's Right to Know*. New York: Praeger.
O'Brien, Sue. 1991. "As We Stoop to Conquer, We Obliterate (Outing Gays)." *Quill* 79(9): 9–14.
Oliveira, J. and Bernard Beguin. 1983. *L'Ethique professionelle des journalistes*. Fribourg, Switzerland: Éditions universitaires.
O'Sullivan, Tim, J. Hartley, D. Saunders and J. Fiske. 1983. *Key Concepts in Communication*. London: Methuen.
Ouston, Rick. 1991. "Unnamed sources." *Vancouver Sun*, May 30.
Overbury, S. 1985. *Finding Canadian Facts Fast*. Toronto: Methuen.
Overduin, Henry. 1986. "News Judgment and the Community." *Communication* 9(2).
Paletz, David L. and R. M. Entman. 1981. *Media Power Politics*. New York and London: Free Press.
Palmer, Alisa. 1994. Discussion with Brooke Johnson and Charlie Tomlinson, Valerie Alia's arts

criticism seminar. Graduate School of Journalism, University of Western Ontario, London, Ontario.

Palmer, N.D. 1987. "Going After the Truth—In Disguise." *Washington Journalism Review* (November): 20–22.

Patterson, Philip and Lee Wilkins. 1994. *Media Ethics: Issues and Cases*. Second edition. Madison, Wis.: Brown & Benchmark.

Patterson, Thomas E. 1994. "A puzzle, and an answer." *Political Communicaton Report* 5(1).

———. 1993. *Out of Order: How the decline of the political parties and the growing power of the news media undermine the American way of electing presidents*. New York: Alfred A. Knopf.

Pelchat, Martin. 1989. "Flics et Journalistes: Une relation compromettante?" Le 30 13(4): 14–15.

Perigoe, R. 1990. "Shades of Grey." Content (May/June): 18–19.

Perkins, Dave. 1993. *Toronto Star*. April 10.

Philips, Michael. 1993. "How to Think Systematically about Business Ethics." In E. Winkler and J. Coombs (eds.), *Applied Ethics: A Reader*. Oxford: Blackwell, 185–200.

Phillips, E. Barbara. 1977. "Approaches to objectivity: Journalistic versus social science perspectives." In Paul M. Hirsch, Peter V. Miller and F. Gerald Kline (eds.), *Strategies for Communication Research*. Beverly Hills, Ca.: Sage.

Porteous, Sandra. 1991. "Discrimination ruled out at women-only magazine." *Marketing* 97(13): 4.

Portis, L. 1988. "On the rise and decline of totalitarian liberalism: Schlesinger, Bell, Larouche." *Canadian Journal of Political and Social Theory* 12(3): 20–36.

Postman, Neil. 1984. *Amusing Ourselves to Death*. New York: Penguin.

Power, John. 1993. "Rondeau deer a repugnant plan." *Toronto Star*. November 10, A6.

Poynter Institute. 1991. *The Poynter Report*. St. Petersburg, Fla.: Poynter Institute for Media Studies.

Pritchard, David and Madelyn Peroni Morgan. 1987. "Impact of ethics codes on judgments by journalists: A natural experiment." *Journalism Quarterly* (summer).

Quill.

Quindlen, Anna. 1994. "Talking About The Media Circus." *New York Times Magazine*, June 26, 26–62.

Racovali, John. 1985. "Publication Ban Depends Now on Judge." *Content* (March/April).

Rawls, John. 1971. *A Theory of Justice*. (See especially Chapter 9). Cambridge: Harvard University Press.

Repo, Satu. 1986. "Journalistic Objectivity, the Discourse on Democracy, and the Birth of the Popular Press." Unpublished Ph.D. dissertation, University of Toronto.

Rich, Frank. 1994. "Exit the Critic." *New York Times Magazine*, February 13, 32–79.

Richardson, John Adkins. 1977. *The Complete Book of Cartooning*. Englewood Cliffs, N.J.: Prentice-Hall.

Rivers, William L. 1982. *The Other Government: Power & the Washington Media*. New York: Universe Books.

———. 1965. *The Opinionmakers: The Washington Press Corps*. Boston: Beacon Press.

——— and Cleve Mathews. 1988. *Ethics for the Media*. Englewood Cliffs, N.J.: Prentice-Hall.

———, Wilbur Schramm and C. Christians. 1980. *Responsibility in Mass Communication*. Third edition. New York: Harper & Row.

——— et al. 1972. *Backtalk: Press Councils in America*. San Francisco: Canfield Press.

Roberts, Anne. 1993. "All the news we can manage." *New Directions* (October): 30.

Robinson, David C. 1993. "Taking 'freedom of the press' seriously: Critical media sociology and the challenge of democracy." *Alternate Routes* 10: 57–83.

Rogers, E. 1989. "Now you see it, now you don't." *News Photographer* (August): 16-19.

Roshco, Bernard. 1975. *Newsmaking*. Chicago: University of Chicago Press

Ross, Ishbel. 1936. *Ladies of the Press*. New York and London: Harper.

Ross, Val. 1993. "Southam to pool cultural coverage." *Globe and Mail*, December 7, C1.

Roth, Lorna. 1993a. "Mohawk Airwaves and Cultural Challenges: Some Reflections on the Politics of Recognition and Cultural Appropriation after the Summer of 1990." *Canadian Journal of Communication* 18(3).

———. 1993b. Personal correspondence with Joe Aguiar, CRTC Radio Directorate representative. August 20.

———. 1992. "Media and the Commodification of Crisis." In M. Raboy and B. Dagenais, *Media, Crisis and Democracy*. London: Sage, 144–65.

———. 1983. "The Role of Communication Projects and Inuit Participation in the Formation of a Communication Policy for the North." M.A. thesis. Montreal: McGill University.

——— and Gail Guthrie Valaskakis. 1989. "Aboriginal Broadcasting in Canada: A Case Study in Democratization." In M. Raboy and P. Bruck (eds.), *Communication: For and Against Democracy*. Montreal: Black Rose.

Rowland, W. 1979. *Making Connections*. Toronto: Gage.

Rowse, Arthur E. 1957. *Slanted News*. Boston: Beacon Press.

Ruane, M. 1987. Series in *Philadelphia Inquirer*. May 27–Sept. 16, 1987.

Rubin, B. ed. 1978. *Questioning Media Ethics*. New York: Praeger.

Russell, Nick. 1994. *Morals and the Media: Ethics in Canadian Journalism*. Vancouver: UBC Press.

Rutherford, Paul. 1986. *The Making of the Canadian Media*. Toronto: McGraw-Hill Ryerson.

Saint-Jean, Armande. 1993. *L'Évolution de l'éthique journalistique au Québec de 1960 à 1990*. Ph.D. thesis, Department of Communications, McGill University.

———. 1991. "Women in the Media—The Real Picture." In Toronto Women in Film and Television (eds.), *Changing Focus: The Future for Women in the Canadian Film and Television Industry*. Toronto: Toronto Women in Film and Television.

Salter, Liora. 1980. "Two Directions on a One-Way Street: Old and New Approaches in Media Analysis in Two Decades." *Studies in Communications* 1: 85–117.

Salutin, Rick. 1994. "Suing and reviewing: A critical issue." *Globe and Mail*, July 28.

———. 1993. "Profiles have two sides—good and bad." *Globe and Mail*, April 2.

Sanit, T. 1992. "The New Unreality." *Columbia Journalism Review* (May/June): 17–18.

———. 1992. "Stand and Deliver." *Columbia Journalism Review* (July/August): 15–16.

Saunders, Eileen. 1991. "Mass Media and the Reproduction of Marginalization." In Frederick J. Fletcher (ed.), *Reporting the Campaign: Election Coverage in Canada*. Ottawa: Dundurn.

Sauvageau, Florian. 1988. "La Solution Corporatiste." *Le 30* 12(10): 32–33.

Schachter, I.L. 1983. "Garbage Journalism." *C.I.J. Bulletin* (Summer): 708.

Schiller, Dan. 1981. *Objectivity and the News: The Public and the Rise of Commercial Journalism*. Philadelphia: University of Pennsylvania Press.

Schlesinger, Philip. 1978. *Putting "Reality" Together: BBCNews*. London: Constable.

Schramm, Wilbur and W. Porter. 1982. *Men, Women, Messages and Media: Understanding Human Communication*. New York: Harper & Row.

Schudson, Michael. 1978. *Discovering the News: A Social History of American Newspapers*. New York: Basic Books.

Schulte, Henry H. 1981. *Reporting Public Affairs*. New York: Macmillan.

Scott, Jay. 1991. Discussion with Valerie Alia and students. Arts criticism seminar, Graduate School of Journalism, University of Western Ontario, London, Ontario.

Sears, Val. 1988. *Hello Sweetheart . . . Get Me Rewrite*. Toronto: Key Porter.

Seldes, George. 1935. *Freedom of the Press*. Indianapolis: Bobbs-Merrill.

Serafini, Anthony. 1989. *Ethics and Social Concern*. New York: Paragon.

Shapiro, Ivor. 1989. "No Comment: the subject of newsroom ethics." *Saturday Night* 104(3): 27–29.

Shaw, George Bernard. 1932. *Our Theatres in the Nineties*. London: Constable.

Shaw, Gillian. 1990. "Disclosure without malice? BC Scandal focuses on media ethics." *Content* (Sept./Oct.): 15–16.

Sherefkin, R. 1984. "Rood Joke." *Washington Journalism Review* (June): 13.
Shields, Rob. 1991. "The True North Strong and Free." *Places on the Margin: Alternative Geographies of Modernity*. London: Routledge.
Siebert, Fred, T. Peterson and W. Schramm. 1956. *Four Theories of the Press*. Urbana: University of Illinois Press.
Siegel, A. 1983. *Politics and the Media in Canada.* Toronto: McGraw-Hill Ryerson.
Sigal, Leon V. 1973. *Reporters and Officials*. Lexington, Mass.: D.C. Heath.
Silburt, David. 1986. "Newfoundland's scab affair: murky questions about ethics." *Content* (July/August).
Simon, John. 1980. Address to the Canadian Theatre Critics Association. Toronto, Essex Park Hotel, November 15.
———. 1975. Singularities: *Essays on the Theater, 1964–1974*. New York: Random House.
Sinclair, Upton. 1920. *The Brass Check: A Study of American Journalism.* Pasadena, Ca.: Published by the author.
Singer-Ferris, Vivian. 1986. "Theatre of Hate: Zundel . . . and the weakness of the press." *Ryerson Review of Journalism*, winter.
Skaggs, Albert C. 1985. "Today's Codes Mirror Credo of Benjamin Harris." *Journal of Mass Media Ethics* 5(1): 37–42.
Skerrit-Cramer, Cecile. 1988. "Front Page Justice." *Ryerson Review of Journalism*, spring.
Small, William J. 1972. *Political Power and the Press*. New York: W.W. Norton.
Smith, Anthony. 1991. *The Age of Behemoths: Globalization of Mass Media Firms*. New York: Priority Press.
Smith, Geraint. 1993. "The Strange Story of the Penguin, the Chess Master and a Midnight Meeting at the Chelsea Hotel." *London Evening Standard*, May 10.
Smith, Zay N., and Pamela Zekman. 1979. *The Mirage*. New York: Random House.
Smythe, Dallas W. 1981. *Dependency Road: Communications, Capitalism, Consciousness and Canada*. Norwood, N.J.: Ablex.
Sobel, L., ed. 1981. *Media Controversies*. New York: Facts on File.
Society of Professional Journalists. 1992. "Code of Ethics." Adopted 1926; revised 1973, 1984 and 1987. Reprinted in *Quill* (November/December): 38.
Somerville, Frances. 1991. "A Reader's Thoughts." *Saturday Night* (May): 9.
Sontag, Susan. 1977. *On Photography*. New York: Ferrar, Straus and Giroux.
Spradley, James R. 1980. *Participant Observation*. New York: Holt, Rinehart and Winston.
Stahl, Nicholas, ed. 1984. *Best Canadian Political Cartoons*. Toronto: McClelland and Stewart.
———. 1983. *Best Canadian Political Cartoons*. Toronto: McClelland and Stewart.
Stein, M.L. 1994. "No Joke: No Snakes." *Editor & Publisher*, March 12, 9.
———. 1991. "Advocacy Journalsim and Activist Lives." *Editor & Publisher* 124(36): 16–35.
———. 1986. "Hoax sheet has town up in arms." *Editor & Publisher*, March 15, 17, 34.
Stein, Robert. 1972. *Media Power: Who is Shaping Your Picture of the World?* Boston: Houghton Mifflin.
Stewart, Walter. 1980. *Canadian Newspapers: The Inside Story*. Edmonton: Hurtig.
Stone, I.F. 1970. *Polemics and Prophecies: 1967–1970*. Boston: Little Brown.
Strauss, Marina. 1990. "Buying 'News': Advertorials invade editorial departments." *Content* (Sept./Oct.): 17–18.
Strothers, W.G. 1989. "Troubles with re-creating news." *News Photographer* (November): 25.
Sundar, S. Shyam. 1991. "Techno-Ethics: as a Matter of Fax." *Journal of Mass Media Ethics* 6(1): 24–34.
Sutherland, Frank. 1987. "Journalist groups arguing over need for strong ethics codes." *ASNE Bulletin*, December.
Swain, Bruce M. 1978. *Reporters' Ethics*. Ames: Iowa State University Press.

Swedish Press Council. 1991. "Mass Media Codes of Ethics and Councils: A Comparative International Study on Professional Standards." Presented at the Stockholm Symposium on Press Councils and Press Ethics, June 11–14.

Sylvester, Cam. 1988. "Ethical journalism isn't accidental." *Content* (March/April).

Taras, David. 1993. "A Question of Character: Political Reporting in Canada and the United States." In David Thomas (ed.), *Canada and the United States: Differences that Count*. Peterborough, Ont.: Broadview.

———. 1990a. *The Newsmakers: The Media's Influence on Canadian Politics*. Scarborough, Ont.: Nelson Canada.

———. 1990b. "Davids and Goliaths: Critical journalism and Canadian politics." *Content* (May/June): 20–21.

———. 1989. "Television and Public Policy: The CBC's Coverage of the Meech Lake Accord." *Canadian Public Policy* 15(3): 322–34.

Taylor, Kate. 1993a. "Don't shoot the messenger . . . or arrest the artist." *Globe and Mail*, December 24, C5.

———. 1993b. "Show breaks sex taboo; Review: Eli Langer, paintings and pencil drawings at the Mercer Union." *Globe and Mail*, December 20.

Teague, Bob. 1982. *Live and Off-Color: News Biz*. New York: A&W.

Television Northern Canada (TVNC). 1993. *CRTC Intervention—Structural Cable Hearings*. Ottawa, March 1.

Theberge, Leonard. 1982. *TV Coverage of the Oil Crises: How Well Was the Public Served?* Vols. I–III. Washington, D.C.: Media Institute.

Thiroux, Jacques P. 1980. *Ethics, Theory and Practice*. Encino, Ca.: Glencoe.

Thomson, Ross and Hewison. 1985. *How to Draw and Sell Cartoons*. London: Quatro.

Times. 1989. "Responsible free speech." Editorial. London, November 28.

Tombs, George. 1991. "Éthique journalistique: une question de credibilité." *Le 30* 14(4): 23.

———. 1989. "La Presse Dans le Monde (Press Ethics in France, United Kingdom, Canada)." *Le 30* 13(9): 6–13.

Tomlinson, Charlie. 1992 and 1994. Discussions with Valerie Alia and students. Arts criticism seminar. Graduate School of Journalism, University of Western Ontario, London, Ontario.

Tomlinson, Don E. 1991. Where Morality and Law Diverge. *Journal of Mass Media Ethics* 6(2): 69–82.

Toulmin, Stephen. 1970. *The Place of Reason in Ethics*. New York and London: Cambridge University Press.

Tuchman, Gaye. 1978. *Making News: A Study in the Construction of Reality*. New York: Free Press.

———. 1971/72. "Objectivity as strategic ritual: An examination of newsmen's notions of objectivity." *American Journal of Sociology* 77: 660–79.

Udell, Jon G. 1979. "Economics and freedom of the press." In Craig E. Aronoff (ed.), *Business and the Media*. Santa Monica, Ca.: Goodyear, 207–15.

Van Brenk, Debora. 1993. "Deer cull proceeds despite protest." *London Free Press*. November 2.

Van Zoonen, Liesbet. 1994. *Feminist Media Studies*. London: Sage.

Villedieu, Yanick. 1991. "Mass Media Ethics in the Information Age: A Conference Report." *Journal of Mass Media Ethics* 6(1): 5–23.

———. 1989. "Les Médias et le Sida: le Non-Lieu pour les Journalistes?" Le 30 13(6): 22–27.

Walker, R.B.J. 1988. *One World, Many Worlds: Struggle for a Just World Peace*. Boulder: Lynne Rienner/London: Zed Books.

Wallace, Clement and Ralph Miliband. 1975. *The Canadian Corporate Elite: An Analysis of Economic Power*. Toronto: McClelland and Stewart.

Washington Journalism Review, Washington, D.C.

Weaver, Mary Ann. 1992. "Hunting with the Sheiks." *The New Yorker*. December 14, 60–61.

Weinberg, Steve. 1981. *Trade Secrets of Washington Journalists*. Washington, D.C.: Acropolis.

Westell, Anthony. 1980. "The press: Adversary or channel of communication?" In H.D. Clarke, C. Campbell, F.Q. Quo and A. Goddard (eds.), *Parliament, Policy and Representation*. Toronto: Methuen.

White Eye, Bud. 1991. "Indigenous Peoples Conference: Lack of awareness of issues frustrates native leaders." *London Free Press*, May 11.

Will, George F. 1972. *Press, Politics and Popular Government*. Washington, D.C.: American Enterprise Institute for Public Policy Research.

Williamson, Linda. 1988. "Spotlight Turned onto Winnipeg Jury Members." *Investigative Journalism Bulletin* (36): 11.

Winkler, Earl. 1993. "From Kantianism to Contextualism: The Rise and Fall of the Paradigm Theory in Bioethics." In E. Winkler and J. Coumbs (eds.), *Applied Ethics: A Reader*. Oxford: Blackwell, 343–65.

Winship, Judith. 1987. *Inside Women's Magazines*. London and New York: Pandora.

Wise, David. 1973. *The Politics of Lying: Government Deception, Secrecy, and Power*. New York: Vintage.

Wolfe, Tom. 1973. *The New Journalism*. New York: Harper & Row.

Wright, Don. 1971. *Wright On! A Collection of Political Cartoons*. New York: Simon & Schuster.

York, Geoffrey. 1992. "Canadian troops reach Somali town." *Globe and Mail*, December 16, A14.

Young, Iris Marion. 1990. *Justice and the Politics of Difference*. Princeton: Princeton University Press.

Yu, Frederick T.C. 1968. *Behavioral Sciences and the Mass Media*. New York: Russell Sage Foundation.

Ziesenis, Elizabeth B. 1991. "Suicide Coverage in Newspapers." *Journal of Mass Media Ethics* 6(4): 234–44.

Biographies of the Authors and Editors

Valerie Alia is an award-winning journalist, poet, photographer and social scientist with a Ph.D. in Social and Political Thought from York University. She is a professor at the University of Western Ontario Graduate School of Journalism and the author of *Names, Numbers and Northern Policy*, the CBC "Ideas" documentary "Nunavut: Where Names Never Die" and books on the politics of naming and northern communications. She was a consultant to the Royal Commission on Electoral Reform and Party Financing and twice won the McCracken journalism research prize. A 1995 Tilden National Literary Awards finalist in poetry, she is listed in *Canadian Who's Who* and *Who's Who of Canadian Women*.

Brian Brennan is an award-winning Calgary jounalist, musician and broadcaster. He writes a daily column for the *Calgary Herald* and does arts commentaries for CBC Radio. He is past president of both the Canadian Association of Journalists (Calgary chapter) and the Canadian Theatre Critics Association, and has served as a national board member chairing the CAJ ethics committee.

Rita Shelton Deverell has a Ph.D. in Educational Theory from the University of Toronto, an M.A. in History of Religions and a B.A. in Philosophy. She won the Canadian Black Achievement Award for Media, honoured by Toronto Women in Film and Television, won a Gemini Canada Award, was named to the *Maclean's* Honor Roll of outstanding Canadians and received the Dodi Robb Award from Media Watch. She was one of *Chatelaine*'s Women to Watch and served as Acting Director of the University of Regina School of Journalism. A founding producer for VISION TV, she serves on the board of the Ontario Film Development Corporation.

Fred Fletcher is a professor of Political Science in Environment Studies and Coordinator of Mass Communication Studies at York University. He covered federal elections for Southam News, advised the *Globe and Mail* and other news organizations, authored or co-authored *Media, Elections and Democracy*, three editions of *Canada at the Polls* and other studies. As research coordinator, media and elections, for the Royal Commission on Electoral Reform and Party Financing, he edited five volumes of research studies and organized symposia on media and elections and political ethics. He is a past president of the Canadian Communication Association and member of the Canadian Journalism Foundation research committee and the advisory council of the Graduate School of Journalism at the University of Western Ontario.

Robert A. Hackett teaches communication at Simon Fraser University and co-directs Project Censored Canada which researches blind spots in the national news agenda. His various publications on media and politics include *News and Dissent: The Press and the Politics of Peace in Canada*, book chapters and articles for scholarly journals, newspapers and magazines.

C. Barry Hoffmaster is the Director of the Westminster Institute for Ethics and Human Values in London, Ontario, and is a professor in the departments of Philosophy and Family Medicine at the University of Western Ontario. In 1994–95 he served as president of the Canadian Bioethics Society. He writes and teaches in the areas of health care ethics, philosophy of law and moral philosophy. His current research projects examine the contributions of the social sciences to health care ethics, cross-cultural approaches to health care ethics and the nature of legal ethics and legal professionalism.

Frank Howard has covered federal and provincial governments for the *Globe and Mail* and the *Ottawa Citizen*. In the early 1970s he held director-level jobs in the government of Canada. Returning to journalism in 1974, he wrote a daily column on government in the *Citizen* for the next nineteen years. He was a member of the Parliamentary Press Gallery until early 1995. He now runs internet.POST, a news and research service reporting on news and opinions found on the Internet.

Conway Jocks founded CKRK-FM at Kahnawake, Quebec, in 1979 and ran the station until 1992. Retired, he writes and broadcasts daily three-minute Iroquois historical documentaries, deejays a weekly program and occasionally hosts the phone-in show for CKRK-FM. He won the Native American Journalists Association 1993 award for the best political cartoon and draws editorial cartoons for the Kahnawake newspaper, the *Eastern Door*. He is currently working on a novel centred around the founding of the Iroquois Confederacy and "We Are the Iroquois," a radio series of historical episodes on the Iroquois people.

William Law is a freelance journalist living in London, England. He worked for several years with the Canadian Broadcasting Corporation in Edmonton as a features producer and documentary maker for "Sunday Arts and Entertainment," "Ideas," "Sunday Morning" and other programs. His documentaries have appeared on public radio in the United States and Europe, and he is a regular contributor to radio sports programs for the CBC and the BBC.

Pierre Mignault is a journalist with Current Affairs, French CBC TV, Montreal. During the first fifteen years of his career, he worked as a news reporter for the French network national news covering social issues, Native affairs and politics. For the last three years he has been involved in investigative documentary production with the CBC in Montreal. He is a member of the Quebec press council's honour tribunal which hears citizens complaints against the press.

Lorna Roth is a professor in the Communication Studies Department at Concordia University. She has been involved in broadcasting policy analysis and consulting with first peoples and multicultural and multiracial groups since the late 1970s and is completing a book on the development of first peoples' television broadcasting in the Canadian North. She holds a Ph.D. in Communications from Concordia.

Nicholas Russell is a professor in the School of Journalism and Communications at the University of Regina where he has taught since 1983. He has been a reporter, copy editor, news editor, editorial writer and radio producer in media ranging from the BBC World Service and Canadian Press to the *Whitehorse Star* and CFCF-TV. He holds a British Certificate of Journalism, a B.A. in English from McGill, M.A. in Middle English from London and a Ph.D. in Journalism from Wales. He has conducted workshops on writing, editing and ethics from coast to coast, and is the author of *Morals and the Media: Journalism Ethics in Canada* (1994).

Armande Saint-Jean pursued a twenty-five-year career as a journalist and broadcaster, at Radio-Canada and a number of other outlets, and then turned to teaching in the mid-1980s. She acted as co-head of the Journalism program at l'Université du Québec à Montréal from 1985 to 1994. In 1994 she joined the Faculty of Social Sciences at l'Université de Sherbrooke. Her research interests are journalistic ethics, feminist theory and research methodology, and the representation and presence of women in the media. She holds a Ph.D. in Communications from McGill.

Bud White Eye is a graduate of the Program in Journalism for Native People at the University of Western Ontario and the founder and first president of Native News Network of Canada (NNNC). He was a producer for CBC "Morningside"; and has freelanced for CBC, *Nativebeat,* the *London Free Press, London Magazine* and other media, served as arena coordinator and flag bearer for the Walpole Island powwow, anti-racism coordinator and policy analyst for the Association of Iroquois and Allied Indians, and adjunct professor at the Graduate School of Journalism at the University of Western Ontario. A member of the Moraviantown Delaware First Nation, he lives in Sarnia, Ontario.

Earl Winkler is a professor and head of the Philosophy Department at the University of British Columbia, and Senior Research Fellow at the Centre for Applied Ethics, UBC. He is co-editor of *Ethics and Aging* (1989) and *Applied Ethics: A Reader* (1993), as well as author of numerous articles in philosophical journals, particularly in ethical theory and applied ethics. He is a member of the Advisory Council on Ethical Issues in Health Care for the British Columbia provincial government.

Yuezhi Zhao holds a Ph.D. from and is an instructor at the School of Communication at Simon Fraser University, and has written on theories of ideology and news discourse in academic journals. With Robert Hackett, she is co-author of *Regimes in Crisis: News Objectivity and Sustainable Democracy*, forthcoming from Garamond Press.

Index

Related titles from Fernwood Publishing

Outsider Blues

A Voice from the Shadows

Clifton Ruggles with Olivia Robinescu

"The articles that appear in this book originate in the shadows—those marginal spaces that Black people have been forced to inhabit ever since the first slaves reached the shores of North America ..."

"I experienced what I call the 'shadowlands' while working in the back rooms of restaurants and hotels and on the trains, when people looked through me but didn't see me."

"The Black male in North America is forever treated as suspect. Border guards suspect us, police suspect us, store owners suspect us, school officials suspect us. In this society Black males become visible only when we become suspects. The rest of the time, we are 'invisible.' "

Ruggles tells us that "Black is more than just a racial category, it's a way of viewing the world." It is out of this set of eyes that Clifton Ruggles writes a column in the Montreal Gazette. This book is a collection of those columns and of Ruggles' photographs, which visually illustrate the "Black" experience. He tells stories of Black people everyday lives, provides non-stereotypical role models, details their contributions to culture, politics and so on—stories which are often either ignored or underplayed. Among the photographs are two photo essays, one autobiographical and one entitled *Shadowlands*. The book also includes an article by Olivia Robinescu entitled "Deconstructing Racism."

256 pages Photos Paper ISBN 1 895686 65 2 $19.95
Publication Date: April 1996

More Perishable than Lettuce or Tomatoes

Labour Law Reform and Toronto's Newspapers

Edward T. Silva (Toronto)

How fairly do Canadian newspapers cover labour issues? This book presents an in-depth analysis of "unbalanced" treatment by the four largest Toronto dailies, using the Ontario NDP's 1992 proposed labour reform law (Bill 40) as an example. The book closes with suggestions for what might be done to prevent such bias in the future.

100pp Paper ISBN 1 895686 50 4 $12.95

Constructing Danger

The Mis/representation of Crime in the News

Chris McCormick

Crime news focuses on the sensational and the unusual, quite often reinforcing biases and stereotypes. In misrepresenting and exaggerating events, a fear of crime is created which is out of proportion to the actual risk of victimization. Law reform bills are proposed by politicians to get tough on crime and yet the underlying conditions which cause it are left unaddressed. This book examines different criminal topics through looking at actual news articles and analyzes how subtle distortions creep into crime coverage. The underlying perspective is that the news not only reports crime but socially constructs it, reproducing crime myths in the process. This book is sure to change the way you think about crime in the news.

Contents: Section One: Gender and the Media—A String of Sexual Assaults • Women who Work as Prostitutes • Domestic Terrorism • Section Two: Distortion in the Media—The Mount Cashel Orphanage Inquiry • Aids Fiends and High-Risk Groups • The Halifax Race Riot • Section Three: The Law and the Media—Crime Rates and Crime Fear • Crime Stoppers and the Police • Lawyers and Serial Killers • The Westray Mine Explosion

234 pages Paper ISBN 1 895686 45 8 $19.95

Thunder in My Soul

A Mohawk Woman Speaks

Patricia Monture-Angus (Saskatchewan)

> *This is a prayer for my people and for all First Nations. It is shared with you in the spirit of gift giving. It is, in part, a reflection on my own journey down the healing road. It is also a reflection on my own struggle to shed the colonized shackles which bind my mind, my spirit and my heart.*

This book contains the reflections of one Mohawk woman and her struggles to find a good place to be in Canadian society. The essays, written in enjoyable and accessible language, document the struggles against oppression that Aboriginal people face, as well as the success and change that have come to Aboriginal communities. It is written from a woman's place. A possible text in a variety of disciplines—women's studies, Native studies, sociology, education, politics and law—it is an excellent book for anyone who wishes to better understand Aboriginal experience. It speaks to both the mind and the heart.

273 pages Paper ISBN 1 895686 46 $19.95

Becoming an Ally

Breaking the Cycle of Oppression

Anne Bishop (Henson/Dalhousie)

This book is a delight to read, its language simple and clear, its examples vivid, and its message profoundly useful. It's changed the way I look at my own oppression and the way the way I do social change work. I recommend it highly."—*Diana Ralph, Social Work, Carleton University*

"The result is a book that never flinches from the hard truths of our behaviours, socially and individually, yet provides a paradigm for change."
—*Patricia Whitney, Herizons*

This book is a dialogue—by a white, lesbian feminist who co-leads with a Black colleague a workshop on racism—about the answers to questions on the nature of oppression: where does it come from, has it always been with us, what can we do to change it, what does individual healing have to do with struggles for social justice, why do members of the same oppressed group fight each other, why do some who experience oppression develop a life-long commitment to fighting oppression, while others turn around and become oppressors themselves?

137 pages Paper ISBN 1 895686 39 3 $14.95

Stifling Debate

Canadian Newspapers and Nuclear Power

Michael Clow (St. Thomas)

This study of nuclear coverage in four dailies in Ontario and New Brunswick finds that it is the promoters, not the opponents, of nuclear energy that over-whelmingly dominate news coverage.

123pp Paper ISBN 1895686 15 6 $12.95